The Art of the Weaver

Cover illustration: Shaft-loom coverlets. Plate III from *Keep Me
Warm One Night: Early Handweaving in Eastern Canada* by
Harold B. Burnham and Dorothy K. Burnham. Courtesy,
Royal Ontario Museum, Toronto, Canada.

ANTIQUES Magazine Library

AMERICAN AND BRITISH PEWTER
An Historical Survey
Edited by John Carl Thomas

THE ART OF THE POTTER
Redware and Stoneware
Edited by Diana and J. Garrison Stradling

CHINESE EXPORT PORCELAIN
An Historical Survey
Edited by Elinor Gordon

LIGHTING IN AMERICA
From Colonial Rushlights to Victorian Chandeliers
Edited by Lawrence S. Cooke

NEEDLEWORK
An Historical Survey
Edited by Betty Ring

PHILADELPHIA FURNITURE & ITS MAKERS
Edited by John J. Snyder, Jr.

PILGRIM CENTURY FURNITURE
An Historical Survey
Edited by Robert Trent

PORTRAIT PAINTING IN AMERICA
The Nineteenth Century
Edited by Ellen Miles

ANTIQUE METALWARE
Brass, Bronze, Copper, Tin, Wrought & Cast Iron
Edited by James R. Mitchell

A SHAKER READER
Edited by Milton C. and Emily Mason Rose

The Art of the Weaver

Edited by Anita Schorsch

A Main Street Press Book

Universe Books   New York

Articles included in this volume are printed as they appeared in the following issues of *The Magazine* ANTIQUES:

Part I: James Alexander, Weaver, April, 1956; Some Rare Spinning Wheels, October, 1929; Old-Time Methods of Spinning and Weaving, August, 1951; Mrs. Mifflin's Fringe Loom, October, 1945.

Part II: Cloth of Colonial America, January, 1941; Upholstery Fabrics for Antique Furniture, July, 1949; Slipcovers of Past Centuries, October, 1951; Fabrics in Early America, July, 1949; A Glossary of French Silks, December, 1959; Woolen Window Curtains, December, 1964; Jefferson's Curtains at Monticello, October, 1947; The Textile Furnishings (Colonial Williamsburg), January, 1969; Room Furnishings As Seen In British Prints From The Lewis Walpole Library; Part II: Window Curtains, Upholstery, and Slip Covers, March, 1974.

Part III: The Textiles (Farmers' Museum), February, 1959; Connecticut Homespun, September, 1954; The Collections: Textiles and Costumes (Old Sturbridge Village), September, 1955; Tennessee Textiles, September, 1971; What Was Dimity in 1790?, July, 1940; Colonial Dimities, Checked and Diapered, September, 1940; Calamanco, April, 1941; Masterpieces of Western Textiles, February, 1969; European Tapestry, December, 1969; The Wealth of Boucher Tapestries in American Museums, August, 1972; Moreen—A Forgotten Fabric, December, 1940; Flat-Woven Rugs of the Middle East, September, 1969.

Part IV: Quilts and Coverlets from New York and Long Island, May, 1938; Kentucky's Coverlets, April, 1974; The Bed Rug in Colonial America, January, 1964; A Southern Bed Rugg, June, 1974; Two Hand-Woven Tufted Rugs, January, 1929; Eighteenth-Century Brocade Costumes; Some French and English Costumes in the Elizabeth Day McCormick Collection, May, 1945; A Pattern-Woven "Flamestitch" Fabric, November, 1961; The Returning Popularity of Many-Figured Carpets, October, 1932; Washington's American Carpet at Mount Vernon, February, 1947; Oriental Carpets in Seventeenth and Eighteenth-Century America, January, 1976; The Turkey Carpet in Early America, March, 1954; Rugs of Turkestan, January, 1966; Some Peasant and Nomad Oriental Rugs, May, 1962; Early Influences in Turkish Rugs, June, 1969; Rugs of the Caucasus, March, 1969; The Islamic Tradition in Spanish Rug Weaving: Twelfth Through Seventeenth Centuries, March, 1974.

Part V: Some Hand-Woven Coverlets, February, 1925; Ohio Coverlets, January, 1946; Hand-Woven Coverlets in the Art Institute of Chicago, May, 1970; Five Related Coverlets, October, 1972; The Tyler Coverlets, March, 1928; Weavers of New York's Historical Coverlets, July, 1930.

First Edition

Library of Congress Catalog Card Number 77–91925

ISBN 0-87663-982-1, paper
ISBN 0-87663-297-5, cloth

Published by Universe Books
381 Park Avenue South
New York City 10016

Produced by The Main Street Press
42 Main Street
Clinton, New Jersey 08809

Contents

GENERAL INTRODUCTION

I   THE WEAVER AND HIS TOOLS

James Alexander, Weaver, *Virginia D. Parslow*   17
Some Rare Spinning Wheels, *Serge Daniloff*   21
Old-Time Methods of Spinning and Weaving,
   L. M. A. Roy   25
Mrs. Mifflin's Fringe Loom, *Elizabeth Haynes*   28

II   TASTEFUL HOUSEHOLD "FURNITURES"

Cloth of Colonial America, *Cedric Larson*   32
Upholstery Fabrics for Antique Furniture,
   Ruth Bradbury Davidson   35
Slipcovers of Past Centuries, *Marion Day Iverson*   39
Fabrics in Early America, *Franco Scalamandre*   41
A Glossary of French Silks, *Ruth Davidson*   42
Woolen Window Curtains, *Anna Brightman*   48
Jefferson's Curtains at Monticello,
   Fiske and Marie Kimball   54
The Textile Furnishings (Colonial Williamsburg),
   Mildred B. Lanier   57
Room Furnishings as seen in British Prints from the Lewis
   Walpole Library, Part II: Window Curtains, Upholstery,
   and Slip Covers, *Florence M. Montgomery*   64

III   SIMPLE "STUFFS"—FROM FIBER TO FABRIC, PLAIN TO FANCY

The Textiles (Farmers' Museum), *Virginia D. Parslow*   76
Connecticut Homespun, *Abbott Lowell Cummings*   79
The Collections: Textiles and Costumes (Old Sturbridge Village),
   Catherine Fennelly   83
Tennessee Textiles, *Richard H. Hulan*   87
Colonial Dimities, Checked and Diapered,
   Hazel E. Cummin   94
Calamanco, *Hazel E. Cummin*   96
Masterpieces of Western Textiles, *Christa C. Mayer*   99
European Tapestry, *Ruth Davidson*   105
The Wealth of Boucher Tapestries in American Museums,
   Madeleine Jarry   111
Moreen—A Forgotten Fabric, *Hazel E. Cummin*   121
Flat-Woven Rugs of the Middle East, *W. R. Pickering and
   Anthony N. Landreau*   123

IV   THE MORE COMPLICATED CONSTRUCTION—
      SUPPLEMENTARY SETS IN COSTUME, COVERLET, AND CARPET

Quilts and Coverlets from New York and Long Island,
    Florence Peto   132
Kentucky's Coverlets, *Lou Tate*   135
The Bed Rug in Colonial America, *Marion Day Iverson*   140
A Southern Bed Rugg, *Sandra Shaffer Tinkham*   143
Two Hand-Woven Tufted Rugs, *Louise Karr*   145
Eighteenth-Century Brocade Costumes, Some French and Eng-
    lish Costumes in the Elizabeth Day McCormick Collection,
    Gertrude Townsend   147
A Pattern-Woven "Flamestitch" Fabric,
    Florence M. Montgomery   150
The Returning Popularity of Many-Figured Carpets,
    Homer Eaton Keyes   153
Washington's American Carpet at Mount Vernon,
    Marian Sadtler Carson   155
Oriental Carpets in Seventeenth- and Eighteenth-Century
    America, *Sarah B. Sherrill*   157
The Turkey Carpet in Early America,
    Joseph V. McMullan   183
Rugs of Turkestan, *Christopher Dunham Reed*   187
Some Peasant and Nomad Oriental Rugs,
    Maurice S. Dimand   192
Early Influences in Turkish Rugs, *H. McCoy Jones*   198
Rugs of the Caucasus, *Harold M. Keshishian*   203
The Islamic Tradition is Spanish Rug Weaving: Twelfth Through
    Seventeenth Centuries, *Sarah B. Sherrill*   209

V   DOUBLE CLOTHS—COMPLEMENTARY SET

Some Hand-Woven Coverlets, *Catharine R. Miller*   229
Ohio Coverlets, *Irma Pilling Anderson*   233
Hand-Woven Coverlets in the Art Institute of Chicago,
    Mildred Davison   235
Five Related Coverlets, *Mildred Davison*   243
The Tyler Coverlets, *Etta Tyler Chapman*   246
Weavers of New York's Historical Coverlets,
    Jessie Farrall Peck   250

Index   254

General Introduction

No more boundless or exciting spectacle stood before the American technological horizon in 1800 than the weaving manufactory:

> [The] ponderous wheel that communicates life and activity to the whole establishment; the multitude of bands and cogs, which connect the machinery. . . ; the carding engines, which seem like things of life, toiling with steadfast energy; the whirring cylinders, the twirling spindles, the clanking looms—the whole spectacle seeming to present a magic scene in which wood and iron are endowed with the dexterity of the human hand—and where complicated machinery seems to be gifted with intelligence—is surely one of the marvels of the world.[1]

Religious thinkers of the age saw the American weaving manufactory variously as the great balance between commerce and agriculture, a symbol of man's beneficence to man innocently imposed on his wilderness, an improvement on man's material world that would also improve his moral condition. For the contemporary historian, however, the weaver, his tools, and his textiles reflect some of the first great changes coming from the inquisitive age of science and from the pursuit of American perfectionism.

Like other arts and trades identified by Diderot and the Encyclopedists in the eighteenth century, weaving had become a knowledge-producing activity worthy of study. It supported economic independence and national assurance, and provided one alternative to the poverty and depression that had crept up on America after the Revolution. The prosperity that was encountered by the turn-of-the-century weaving manufactories was treated "like fame accruing to the man of merit, something that comes unlooked for, if it comes at all."[2]

Judge Joseph Story of Harvard, and later Henry Ward Beecher, gave the craftsman and his machine a dignity in work once reserved for intellectual pursuits, an honor as well as profit in plying his trade.[3]

A survey of weaving—both of that produced in the colonies and also that imported from abroad after the first years of the 1770s—is the main focus of this compilation of articles drawn from *The Magazine* ANTIQUES. The largest body of documented "stuffs" appears after this period. The term *weaving* implies a particular activity, a distinct product, and a craftsman's point of view. The articles, which have been grouped to emphasize three basic fabric structures, might also suggest an alliance between weavers of a certain class, sex, nationality, and the structures they tend to produce.[4]

Americans have had their share of weavers almost from the beginning. But theirs was a craft limited in the early days by a lack of materials, a preoccupation with survival, and the restriction of English mercantile policy. Who were the weavers in the American colonies? They were nonconformist freemen, sometimes indentured servants, traditionally skilled professionals as the trade had demanded since medieval days. They came early in the seventeenth century from the English clothmaking centers of Gloucester, Somerset, Bristol, and London, and settled on the American coast from New England to Virginia. Extreme hardships in the English clothmaking trades of the seventeenth century had forced weavers, worsted combers, feltmakers, and tailors to head for the American wilderness.[5] And tradesmen, like yeomen, looked forward to the prospect of becoming landholders. In the eighteenth century they were joined by a large influx of Scotch, Irish, Dutch, German, and some French clothworking classes.

The weaver, like the spinner and the fuller both in England and in America, was dependent on the entrepreneur class of clothier-merchants—that is, the men who "caused cloth to be made."[6] The merchant's first beginnings in America initiated a kind of proprietorship over the local spinners and weavers. By the 1790s the merchant-manufacturer became centralized, living in the port cities where he could merchandise the "dry goods," divide the labor, and provide the patterns that were popular abroad. He consulted the latest print cloths and upholsterers' guides. Such manuals of taste as Thomas Sheraton's *Cabinet-Maker and Upholsterer's Drawing-Book* (1791)) recommended, among other things, the color green, the fiber silk, the fabric chintz, the motif foliate to schematize furniture designs. English designer Thomas Chippendale and architect Robert Adam had their own preferences in carpet weaves and weavers: Chippendale's was for the Axminsters made by Thomas Whittey; Adam's was for the knotted carpets of Thomas Moore.[7] The pattern books and family diaries of weavers themselves, brought over among their personal belongings, also supplied the American weaver with design sources.

Taste in household furnitures, whether based on taste manuals or pattern books, was formed by European preferences.

The dyer historically was a man of considerable prestige above that of the spinner, weaver, or fuller; but in the famous *Domestic Manufacturer's Assistant* (1817), the art of manufacture was divided equally between weavers and dyers. The vitality of the European printer's trade influenced, but remained outside, the realm of American structural weave patterning. Until the printer was more firmly established in America, the printed fabric served the interests of European commerce and craftsmen competing with, as well as inspiring, some of the woven designs of American manufacture.

Like the merchants, some professional weavers lived in the cities and worked together under the same roof. Some weavers worked singly at home. It was the manner in which they were paid, and not the location of their jobs, that first determined the boundaries of a manufactory system or the judgment of professional status. Between 1789 and 1830 when the rhythm of the marketplace took over the economic beat of the household, payment by the hour or by the day was the mark of the professional, the master-craftsman, the male American.[8] Piecework done at home, paid for by the task and yet connected to the manufactory, was a remnant of the older agricultural/artisan economy in the new machine age.[9]

Some women in America, like women in England—single women of the lower classes—did work in the mills splicing rolls, knotting Axminsters, sewing list strips, and being paid on a time basis.[10] However, the large body of women, married and of the middle class in rural towns and cities, wove as nonprofessionals, serving the family and fulfilling a mission. The emergence of the domestic female weaver was a result of geography, wealth, and marital status. "Domestic avocations," as this trade and others were called in 1802, were their own rewards, moral stepping stones to Heaven for the pure and the pious.[11] Since all women in the New England and middle states were expected to display an industrious nature, even the upper-class lady of "leisure" often took up the tape loom or worked on the lace pillow.[12] Expectations of Southern women in a cavalier-like society were less geared to the virtues of a large middle class.[13]

Although spinning had always been closely associated with women's work, the professional spinner by 1786 was as often a man as a woman. Professional weaving by this date, however, was almost entirely the work of men. Of the 287 tradespeople associated with weaving who advertised in the newspapers of Philadelphia, Maryland, and South Carolina between 1786 and 1800, only ten were women. Of the 287, 182 were listed specifically as weavers and of these only one was a woman, and she was a stocking weaver. Four of the eight people listed as professional spinners were women; one woman made fringe and lace; three were silk dyers; one woman was a wool carder. Of the ten women, five had the title "widow" following their surnames which signified, as it had since the fourteenth century, an inherited trade.[14]

There were, as well, itinerant weavers in America. Although not part of the manufactory system, they were nonetheless professional apprentice-trained craftsmen paid on a time basis. They traveled from place to place finishing the linen sheeting women in the home could not find time to complete and drumming up trade for their town or village looms already set to produce one or two favorite overshot or double-cloth coverlets or carpets. The literary world has turned itinerant weavers into romantic, semimystical heroes who are still remembered in the twentieth century. Richardson Wright in *Hawkers & Walkers in Early America,* for example, describes the joys of ornithologist-weaver Alexander Wilson of Philadelphia County as he combined the pursuit of birds with that of customers while traveling from house to house.[15]

Within the present anthology Jessie Farrall Peck in "Weavers of New York's Historical Coverlets" (pp. 249–252) continues in this idealistic mode by describing naturalist-weaver Ira Hadsell who "spent hours tramping through the woods, learning the shape of leaf and flower and vine, and their ways of winding and clustering" to enhance his woven garden designs with nature's divine inspiration.

The title of this survey suggests that weaving is an art, but in most cases the techniques involved in drafting, warping, threading or drawing-in, wrapping, and treadling are more mathematical and mechanical than the classical or Renaissance definition of art implies. In the structural patterning of French and Flemish pictorial tapestries, however, the nonutility and rarity of their design makes them part of the classical definition of art.[16] But for the more repetitive designs, the beauty of weaving rests entirely in the qualities of handling the tool that creates sheds and interconnects threads and is more properly, and with dignity, called a machine. As late as 1857 when the power loom was admittedly in production, manufacturers in Philadelphia still employed 1500 hand-loom carpet weavers with only one mill using a few power looms. As long as the man was still part of his loom and the winders, spoolers, warpers, and dyers were still part of the trade, weaving remained handwork on a machine.

Just as mechanized work—which implies precision, regularity, and production—was regarded by the eighteenth century as enlightened, moral, and patriotic, the nineteenth-century Arts and Crafts movement of John Ruskin and William Morris saw it as a form of slave labor and a work empty of pleasure and human satisfaction. Many of the early writings in *The Magazine* ANTIQUES reflect the aesthetic of this movement and these men. Purposeful in its support of creative man, the 1870 movement was less concerned with the freedom of Americans from the sinful luxury of European taste than with the freedom of Americans from the mechanical world. While the effect of social concern for the sweat of each man and an understanding of his imperfections was valuable, it robbed the weaver—indirectly and unintentionally—of recognition for his craftsmanlike behavior. His orderly and mechanical translation of drafts into dimension was not unique and beautifully imperfect, but precise and qualified hard work. The emphasis on "hand" and "home" crafts elevated and glorified by the Arts and Crafts movement carried with it a sense of the amateur, leading to the generalization of "hand"-weaving as folk art. One must remember, however, that education, fashion, and popular taste had affected the products of the American textile market—covers or coverlets, carpets, and cloth. Because of these complex factors —and with the exception of a few nomadic Oriental rugs, Navaho and other American Indian rugs, fabric in some rural household furniture, and French Acadian costume—most cloth made in or imported to early America was, in form, construction, and use, subject to its contemporary society and not governed by a traditional, nonpopular, geographically-narrow culture exhibited in those objects termed "folk."[17]

In reading the articles in this survey some identification of textiles is necessary. But such identification is complicated by the historical mutilation over time of the names of fabrics. Some materials have taken their names from surface patterning—printing, stamping, watering, calendering, glazing, embroidering, appliquéing. Some derive their names from association with ports of distribution or with the town of the weaver— e.g., osnaburg, also spelled oznabrigg, and techlenburg cloths named for German cities; calico from Calicut, India; pullicate from the Madras coast. Unfortunately, this kind of identification changes the fabric name (or, if not, its connotation) when the ports or mercantile conditions change. When fulling mills were first invented in England during the Middle Ages and weavers moved out of the cities, the same cloth that was once called fine Lincoln and Beverly, after the towns, became fine Cotswolds and Castlecombes, after the new wool areas. When the French Huguenot silk weavers fled from France into England after the revocation of the Edict of Nantes in 1685, the silk of Lyons became part of the silk of Spitalfields. The "Transylvania" carpet, on the other hand, took

its name from the location where it was found—in Transylvania, Hungary—rather than from the place where it was probably made—Bergama, Turkey. Turkey-work carpets were neither from Turkey nor necessarily woven, and carpets "Turkey Fatchion" were often merely painted cloth. Samuel Rowland Fisher reported to Philadelphians in 1767 that he saw Scotch, Wilton, and Turkey carpets being made in Kidderminster, England, and William Peter Sprague manufactured Axminsters and ingrains in Philadelphia. The movement of people and patterns—seventeenth-century weavers from Scotland and Germany to New York and Pennsylvania, and later eighteenth-century weavers from Pennsylvania to Canada—gives a universality to designs and a certain confusion when attributions are made of local or national origin. That "one cannot describe floor coverings by their place of manufacture" remains an axiom in the identification of all woven fabrics.[18]

Identifying cloth and carpets according to their use also has its problems since use and words to denote use change without warning. One wants to say "rug" or "carpet" when one means a floor cloth, but it is now generally known that until the early eighteenth century "rug" was meant to refer to beds. "Bed rug," though usually suggesting a surface-embroidered pattern, was still used as a general term for any heavy pattern-woven or surface-patterned rug laid on the bed. In the 1730s, "carpet" was defined in Nathan Bailey's *Universal Etymological Dictionary* as "a Covering for the Table." And in 1769 Wilton carpet, ordered for James Beekman of New York, was used as upholstery to cover seven chair bottoms. Carpets, in the Near Eastern decorative style, were used as coverings for tables, beds, cupboards, and windows and had been since at least the fifteenth century. The cover when it is called a "coverlet" often conjures an image of quilts—patched, pieced, or appliquéd, such designs developing from accessory techniques lying on the surface, and not from patterns formed with the fabric.

Visual or surface patterning has its own romantic history in America. Users' names were sometimes associated with fabrics like "Mariners Shirtings" and "Negro Plaids." But more usual was the naming by sentimental association after flowers, feelings, and events. As many as fifteen different references for the same pattern have been recorded with as many structural possibilities as there are fabric names. Technically, "Bonaparte's March," also called "Lily of the Valley" and "Rose in the Wilderness," is contructed with an extra shot or set of wefts called, because of it, supplementary set construction.

Such early catalogues as *American Hand-Woven Coverlets in the Newark Museum* as well as the oft-quoted book by Mary Meigs Atwater, *The Shuttle Craft Book of American Hand-Weaving*, string out an array of charming names.[19] Even fifty years ago, Mrs. Atwater was aware that "the matter of names has proved extremely puzzling. . . the same pattern is sometimes known under many names, and . . . a name was often used in different places for patterns not in the least similar." One can only enjoy Mrs. Atwater's own inclination toward didactic prose when she lovingly talks about weaving:

> It is like running a race, with victory always at the end. Victory is good for the soul, and in this race one may always win, for the adversary is one's own sloth and carelessness—an adversary that "takes beating" to be sure so that victory tastes very sweet.

A look at twentieth-century textile catalogues reveals classification systems that may have been useful to textile scholars, but equally confusing to the general reader. Where the Newark Museum catalogue is simply divided into "Overshot," "Double," and "Jacquard," the Art Institute of Chicago uses the terms "Overshot," "Summer and Winter," "Multiple Shaft," "Double Cloth," and "Biederwand" among others. The authors of *Keep Me Warm One Night* create divisions by objects, fabric names, and structure, employing such terms as "costume," "carpets," "blankets," "linens," "coverlets," and "two-shaft," "overshot," "summer and winter," "multiple-shaft," "twill diaper," "double-cloth," and "jacquard types."[20] The *America Underfoot* catalogue is divided into such fabric names and historical classifications as "Floorcloths," "Oriental Rugs," "Turkey Work and the Axminster Carpet," "Folk Rugs," "The Great American Carpet Industry (Ingrains, Brussels, Wiltons, and Other Commercial Carpets)," "The Second Revolution: The Tufted Carpet and Other Modern Innovations."[21] The multiplicity of terms here so enshrouds the craft of weaving with mystery that in the interest of precision and directness the editor returns gladly to "the primary structures of fabrics," a felicitous phrase and the title of a most useful book by Irene Emery.[22]

Following Irene Emery, the present anthology begins with the simple "stuffs" both plain and fancy. Though "plain" and "fancy" are not structural terms and have been alternately used to describe both embroidery and popular art, they suggest to many weavers the difference between diagonal and vertical patterning. The meaningful use of other interlacing terminology—plain, twill or satin, kilim, tapestry, and tabby—does not change the fact that *simple construction has only one set of warps and one set of wefts.* Irene Emery warns that "tabby," like "fancy," though not a structural term, is widely used by hand-weavers. Often a synonym for plain weave or ground shot as opposed to other simple weaves or pattern shots,

"tabby" has also been associated with the fiber silk and the technique of watering. It suggests more than a plain weave and should be avoided.

The second primary structure is the supplementary set, or *the addition of one extra set of either warps or wefts.* Included here are the overshot and "summer-winter" weaves; the knotted, looped, and pile cloth and carpets. It is a surprise to some that Scotch carpets and ingrains are the same weave as double-cloth; that Wilton and Brussels are the same weave as warp velvet; that corduroy and fustian are both weft pile fabrics. The extra float in overshot or "summer-winter" weaves lies flat instead of being looped or knotted to affect the pattern. The phrase "summer and winter" weave is descriptive of the light and dark faces of a coverlet, but "neither the basic weave structure itself nor the particular way of using it to pattern [can] be attributed to any specific time or place or either origin or exclusive use." Irene Emery's words unseat the myth repeated in the Atwater book assigning this pattern wholly to American invention.

The most complicated structure, the complementary set, becomes the third category. This structure has *two sets each of wefts and warps* so equal that they develop two complete cloths at the same time that interconnect or interchange with each other. The term "Jacquard" refers to a mechanism and its maker, not to a specific weave. Jacquard fabrics can be made using any of the three basic structures. They are, however, classified here with double-cloth because both span the most complex weave construction.

The articles in this anthology, then are divided into three basic web structures and are preceded by a short section on the decorative habits of American society, and another on tools. The language of construction necessarily involves some familiarity with the wheel, the reel, the swift, the carder, the spool, and the loom with all its parts—the reed, beam, shuttle, pulley, heddle, treadle, batten or beater, crossrods, raddle, and bobbin as a sampling. Allied trades in Philadelphia alone between 1791 and 1799 included nine reed makers and nineteen card makers. Late eighteenth-century Philadelphia wheelwrights were deluged with orders for spinning wheels. Weavers understood the language of processed natural fibers of hair, wool, flax, cotton, silk, jute, and hemp; the finished spun fibers of tow, tare, linen, cotton, "woolen and worsted yarnes"; the allied units of labor, twist, wind, ply, reel warp, sley, knot, loop, and weave; and any number of words to mean cloth, rug, carpet, fabric, material, stuffs, and cover.[23] Textile curators and craftsmen still use these terms to identify fabric down to the twist of the fiber in order to evaluate workmanship and relate the run of a cloth to its maker and to his loom. A fine example in the use of such structural information is shown in *The Copp Family Textiles* by Grace Rogers Cooper, curator of textiles at the National Museum of History and Technology.[24]

Minute structural information can reinforce or revise points of view already based on newspapers, historical records, or family account books. Under the scrutiny of construction, for example, the carpet from The Mount Vernon Ladies Association of the Union, which had been thought to be the same carpet that sat in the dining room of Washington's Philadelphia residence and was made by William Peter Sprague of the same city, was discovered, through structural identification, to have been misattributed to Sprague. According to his advertisements, Sprague's manufactory was for Axminster or ingrain construction, both of which were worked on a large loom. An examination of the carpet in question revealed it to be woven in strips, indicating that it had been woven on a narrow Wilton-type loom.[25] Recent scholarship has uncovered Sprague correspondence in Baltimore that suggests that Sprague might have used a Wilton-type loom; however, the identification of this carpet with the Philadelphia manufactory still remains in doubt.[26] Whether Sprague did or did not make the Washington carpet, the story reveals how a careful analysis of construction helps to identify the kind of loom, type of weave, place of manufacture, and maker responsible for the woven covering.

This survey is a compilation of articles about weaving, about tools, about home decoration. It is intended as an invitation to enter the larger world of ideas and books as they relate to the work of the weaver and his place in the economy of the new nation. Every effort has been made in arranging the material to reveal the artistic judgment of the craftsman, the nature and level of the workmanship, and the structural or woven quality of the textile.

For assistance at various places along the thorny path to compiling this anthology, the editor gratefully acknowledges the cooperation and inspiration of Charles F. Hummel, Florence M. Montgomery, D. W. Robertson, Jr., John Mulder, Natalie Rothstein, Lee Clawson, Doris Dinger, and Irvin Schorsch.

Notes

1. Perry Miller, *The Life of the Mind in America from the Revolution to the Civil War* (New York: Harcourt Brace Jovanovich, Inc., 1970), p. 300.

2. James Dean, quoted in Ibid., p. 288. Dean was a disciple of the Enlightenment who offered apologias for the social utility of philosophic and scientific investigation.

3. Ibid., p. 292.

4. See the research of John Heisey in Andrews, Heisey, and Walters, *Checklist of American Coverlet Weavers* (Williamsburg, Virginia: Colonial Williamsburg for Abby Aldrich Rockefeller Folk Art Center, 1978).

5. Mildred Campbell, "Social Origins of Some Early Americans," in James M. Smith, *17th-Century America* (Chapel Hill: The University of North Carolina Press, published for The Institute of Early American History and Culture at Williamsburg, Virginia, 1959), p. 85.

6. E. Carus-Wilson, *Medieval Merchant Ventures* (London: Methuen & Co., Ltd., 1954), p. 235.

7. Mildred B. Lanier, *English and Oriental Carpets at Williamsburg* (Williamsburg: The Colonial Williamsburg Foundation, 1974), p. 24.

8. T. Freedley, *Philadelphia and Its Manufactures* (Philadelphia: Edward Young, 1858), p. 241.

9. E. P. Thompson, *Past and Present*, quoted in Nancy Cott, *The Bonds of Womanhood* (New Haven: Yale University Press, 1977), p. 58.

10. Ibid., p. 38; Rodris Roth, *Floor Coverings in 18th-Century America* (Washington, D.C.: Smithsonian Institution Press, 1976), p. 46. For an interesting article on "the factory girls," see George Sargent, "The Beginning of the House Organ," *Antiques* 7 (May, 1925): 160–162.

11. Cott, pp. 26, 44.

12. See Elizabeth Haynes, "Mrs. Mifflin's Fringe Loom," pp. 28–29 of the present volume. Though lace relates more to knitting and knotting than to woven fabric construction, men who made lace and fringe advertised themselves in the third quarter of the eighteenth century as weavers. Even then, lace weavers distinguished themselves from weavers in general.

13. William R. Taylor, *Cavalier and Yankee,* quoted in Cott, p. 11.

14. Carus-Wilson, p. 235.

15. Richardson Wright, *Hawkers & Walkers in Early America* (Philadelphia: J. B. Lippincott Co., 1927), p. 106.

16. For a thorough explanation of the differences between artistic invention and craft tradition, see George Kubler, *The Shape of Time* (New Haven: Yale University Press, 1962), pp. 14–16.

17. For a definition of folk materials, see Henry Glassie, *Pattern in the Material Folk Culture of the Eastern United States* (Philadelphia: University of Pennsylvania Press, 1968); see also Kenneth Ames, *Beyond Necessity: Art in the Folk Tradition* (Winterthur, Delaware: The Henry Francis du Pont Winterthur Museum, 1977).

18. Charles Hummel, "Floor Coverings Used in 18th-Century America," *Irene Emery Roundtable on Museum*

Textiles 1975 Proceedings, Patricia L. Fiske, ed. (Washington, D.C.: The Textile Museum, 1975), p. 67.

19. Margaret E. White, comp., *American Hand-Woven Coverlets in the Newark Museum* (Newark, New Jersey: The Newark Museum, 1947); Mary Meigs Atwater, *The Shuttle-Craft Book of American Hand-Weaving* (New York: The Macmillan Co,, 1928).

20. Dorothy K. and Harold B. Burnham, *Keep Me Warm One Night* (Toronto: University of Toronto Press & Royal Ontario Museum, 1972).

21. Anthony N. Landreau, *America Underfoot* (Washington, D.C.: Smithsonian Institution Press, 1976).

22. Irene Emery, *The Primary Structures of Fabrics* (Washington, D.C.: The Textile Museum, 1966).

23. For a list of popular eighteenth-century dictionaries, see the glossary in Abbott Lowell Cummings, *Rural Household Inventories* (Boston: The Society for the Preservation of New England Antiquities, 1964).

24. Grace Rogers Cooper, *The Capp Family Textiles* (Washington, D.C.: The Smithsonian Institution Press, 1971).

25. Roth, p. 43.

26. Hummel, p. 78.

The Art of the Weaver

I The Weaver and His Tools

The terminology of weaving found in early advertisements, inventories, diaries, and drafts can reconstruct in thought, if not in fact, many materials which have never actually been found. When a domestic weaver in 1775 described how she "beamed on a piece" and "drawed it through the harness," she was focusing her language on loom parts. Governor Printz of New Sweden, when he requested "different sorts of stuffs" in 1644, was asking for woven textiles, possibly only woolens. Connecticut weavers spoke of weft threads as "underfilling," suggesting the dimension under and over a warp. New York weaver James Alexander's advertisement for "Float Coverlids" informed the customer that he was probably buying an overshot coverlet, a piece of cloth made with an extra set of threads which usually provided more complicated patterns and additional weight. Evidence gathered from written sources also provides the skeletal form on which a weaver's shop can be reconstructed, since dated tools, like the loom at the Ephrata Cloister and a few flax wheels, are by themselves insufficient documentation for the crafts historian.

Manasseh Minor, an Englishman who emigrated to America, was one of several seventeenth-century professional weavers who left diaries for posterity. In Minor's diary, the New London, Connecticut, weaver enumerated the textiles he wove—"Blankuts, Cloath, Coverlids, Drugit [a coarse, durable protective cloth], Rugs, and Lining [linen] and Coten Cloth." The list suggests the type of loom Minor would have used, an English four-post loom like the one pictured on p. 77. A German loom would have had only two high posts, the other two being waist-high. The drawing on p. 26 illustrates such low posts. The angled supports shown in the accompanying photographs, the reed teeth, as well as the metal heddles—which in the original would

have been string—are probably not contemporary to the loom.

A major contribution to the study of weavers comes from the account book of James Alexander, a Scotch-Irishman from Orange County, New York. It has provided Virginia Parslow, in "James Alexander, Weaver," with a fascinating document on a "typical" country farmer-weaver who turns out to be not so typical after all. Because of the "flowert" and full-width "coverlids" listed in his records, one can assume that he wove jacquard-type coverlets before the Jacquard mechanism was brought to America in the 1820s. To accomplish this task, he would have used a draw-loom—a rarity in America. That he kept two weavers in his employ after 1806 is not unreasonable, since a draw-loom needed a draw-boy and a fly-shuttle or two weavers for the type of ninety-inch fabric and full-width coverlet that Alexander advertised in the 1818 *Political Index*.

The Parslow article reproduces a page in Alexander's ledger in which "diaper" cloth and "double snow ball" coverlet drafts appear. Drafts, like musical scores, are weaving directions for the trade. A close look at the two photographs (p. 20) showing a "diaper" tablecloth and a "block" coverlet reveals the difference between pattern and weave, design and structure. Though both patterns are formed in the weave and look alike, the structural elements, the number of sets of threads are different. The simple structure of the "diaper" cloth has one set of warps and one of wefts, and the double structure of the "block" cloth has two sets of each. The manipulation of the sets, the interlacing change of direction, spaces, and lengths of floats, create variety within the structure which is labeled "plain," "twill," "satin," and "gauze." Similar patterns do not necessarily mean similar structures any more than "flowert" coverlets necessarily mean a Jacquard mechanism.

If the loom is the most important tool of the trade, the wheel has second priority. The design and texture of any web construction depends on the quality of the spun yarn—its thinness, tightness, evenness, and softness. The warp yarns when spun are tight and strong; the weft yarns, loose and soft. A knowledge of Z twists and S twists is necessary for plying and for an analysis and identification of any fabric.

In the eighteenth century two, three, or four spinning wheels used in a single rural New England household would in no way have been unusual. Much less often were "loombs and tacklin" found, only four in almost fifty inventories between 1675 and 1775. (See Abbott Lowell Cummings, *Rural Household Inventories 1675—1775.*) A typical practice was to spin the yarns at home and take them to be woven at the weaver's shop. One rural inventory listed "yarne" that was still at the weavers. Manasseh Minor's diary reveals that he allowed his loom to be used by other people, including one of his own customers.

Like flax and wool, cotton was also spun, but fine cotton cloths such as dimity were often imported from India or England because of the higher quality of the spinning. The weaver Alexander must have found a satisfactory source for good cotton yarn, for he wove his own dimity at home in America. Silk was reeled rather than spun and was never very successfully raised in America.

Other tools are pictured in Serge Daniloff's "Some Rare Spinning Wheels" and in L. M. A. Roy's "Old-Time Methods of Spinning and Weaving— carders, a clock reel, a niddy noddy, a shuttle, and a temple. Missing from the illustrations are a few tools necessary to the history of the working weaver—the drop spindle, warping board, swift, and quill winder. In addition, hatchells, cards, and combs are listed in almost every inventory mentioning wheels. A picture of elegant taste in tools appears on p. 23 of the Daniloff article—an English spinning wheel of mahogany banded with satinwood inlay and obviously meant for the main bed chamber or parlor.

Perhaps the most intriguing and unexplored tool of the trade is the tape loom pictured in the portrait of Thomas Mifflin and his wife by John Singleton Copley. Mrs. Mifflin is pictured making fringe on a loom meant for decorative tapes. Until Elizabeth Haynes's article on Mrs. Mifflin's loom, one of the only references to such "woven" fringe was in Alice Morse Earle's *Home Life in Colonial Days* (1898). Mrs. Earle called it "merely an industrial amusement" for girls. Further illustrations of tape looms, not included in this anthology, can be found in Mrs. Irving S. Sammis, "Using the Tape Loom" *Antiques* 10 (July,

1926): 47, and in Edith Miniter, "When Woman's Work Was Never Done" *Antiques* 10 (September, 1926): 205—208.

Fringe—like lace, ribbons, gartering, and tapes— was a luxurious adornment for costume, window curtains, and furniture. These elegancies were associated with luxurious European imports even though tapes had practical use as hangers, binders, and ties. The presence of eighteenth- century professional lace and fringe makers in Philadelphia, and of fringe-making ladies like Mrs. Mifflin, demonstrate the interest and activity of Americans in the production of more costly materials. A sense of patriotism in the Revolutionary and post-Revolutionary period as well as an inheritance of Calvinist-Reformed spirit in the ladies of all classes encouraged women to work some of their own fabric and, if buying, to purchase it from local manufactories. John Hill Morgan, quoted in the Haynes article, suggests that Copley himself provided such props as the tape-loom which he felt were appropriate to the character of his sitter. In this case he was providing Mrs. Mifflin with the trappings of a gracious industrious nature that Horace Bushnell, the Connecticut clergyman, would have considered a sign of benevolence towards men and piety towards the Divine Being.

Suggested Reading

Androsko, Rita J., "18th-Century American Weavers, Their Looms and Their Products." In *Irene Emery Roundtable on Museum Textiles 1975 Proceedings,* edited by Patricia L. Fiske. Washington, D.C.: The Textile Museum, 1975.

Cummings, Abbott Lowell. *Rural Household Inventories 1675—1775.* Boston: The Society for the Preservation of New England Antiquities, 1964.

Earle, Alice Morse. *Home Life in Colonial Days.* New York: The Macmillan Company, 1898.

White, Margaret E. "The Pattern Books of Weavers," *Antiques* 53 (February, 1948): 134—135.

James Alexander, weaver

BY VIRGINIA D. PARSLOW

JOSEPH
YOUNGS
SEPT. 4
1822

IT IS A RARE TREAT INDEED to have the opportunity of studying a manuscript as interesting to a modern-day handweaver as the account book kept by James Alexander, weaver of fancy linens. This manuscript, in the collection of the New York State Historical Association at Cooperstown, New York, starts with an entry for February 5, 1798, and runs to 1831, listing receipts and expenditures in goods, services, and cash.

According to the *Portrait and Biographical Record of Orange County* (1895), James Alexander was born of Scottish parentage in Belfast, County Antrim, Ireland, on November 2, 1770. He emigrated to the United States in 1798 and settled on a farm near Little Britain, Orange County, New York. There he engaged in farming and in weaving. He married Catharine Bullard in 1800. Thirteen children had been born to them by 1827. Alexander died

Advertisement in the *Political Index*,
Newburgh, New York, May 9, 1820.

FANCY WEAVING.

THE subscribers respectfully inform their friends and the public in general that they carry on the WEAVING BUSINESS, in its various branches, to wit—

Diaper and Damask Diaper, of the compleatest European patterns, from 1 to 2 1-2 yds. wide, Flowered Carpets, Carpet Coverlids, full breadth or half, as suit the owners, Counterpanes, of any pattern or size, together with all kinds of Fancy Weaving.

Likewise—All kinds of Float Coverlids, Carpets, single and double, and all kinds of plain work such as linen and woolen.

N. B. The above business is carried on by a complete workman, lately from Europe, and a man who professes nothing but what he performs.

Any person wishing to leave their work shall have it attended to with punctuality and done in a workmanlike manner, by applying to the subscribers, near the Little Britain meeting-house.

JAMES ALEXANDER.
JOHN GIBB.

New-Windsor, June 1, 1813.

---

at Newburgh, September 8, 1870, having lived ninety-nine years, ten months, and six days. Supplementing this bare statement of facts, his gravestone in St. George's Cemetery in Newburgh is lettered *Aged 100 years*.

Many other Scottish and Scots-Irish weavers were to follow Alexander to America in the next thirty or forty years, men trained in the rigorous tradition of the weavers' guilds of England and Scotland which required seven years of apprenticeship followed by another seven years of work as a journeyman before a weaver could be admitted to the guild as a master. It may well have been at this point in his life that James Alexander came to New York State.

A trained weaver was capable of producing intricate fabrics well beyond the skill of the farm wife on her simple four-harness loom. Weaving is a time-consuming, laborious process, and the advent of a professional weaver must have been most welcome to the housewives within traveling distance. Not only would he weave plain goods for those who could afford to hire this done, but he could turn out real show pieces for the linen closet and dower chest. Many of these products are familiar to us all, but since there is still much confusion

over some of the fancy weaves, a little explanation of the terms used by Alexander may be helpful.

Under the heading *diaper* he includes all small-figured linens, but especially the linen fabrics used for tablecloths and towels which have patterns composed of square and oblong forms—blocks of warp-face twill contrasting with blocks of weft-face twill. *Damask diaper* has the same type of geometric pattern, but the basic weave is a broken twill or satin of five or more harnesses. This weave gives a fuller, richer effect than diaper. *Damask* is really a glorified form of damask diaper: the pattern, instead of being composed of large geometric blocks, is a naturalistic one of floral or other designs made up of thousands of small blocks in a warp-face satin on a ground of weft-face satin.

The traditional draw loom, used for damask, could be adapted for making double-weave carpets and coverlets. New York State weavers in the 1830's wove damask linen tablecloths in the identical patterns that they used for their double-weave coverlets of cotton and wool.

Alexander's first weaving entries are in 1800 and are mostly for plain linen and woolen cloth, but by 1805 fancy linens and complete coverlets appear. He did much weaving from 1816 to 1824, and it is during this period that the most complicated types of fabrics are mentioned.

Perhaps the most important fact revealed by the account book of James Alexander is that he was weaving figured coverlets and carpets in the United States at an earlier period than any other known weaver. All other coverlets of this type that I have seen have been dated in the early 1830's and later, but James Alexander seems to have specialized in double-weave, or "flowert," coverlets in the early 1820's. They first appear by name in

Part of a page of Alexander's ledger showing list of flowered coverlets for 1822, including one for Joseph Youngs.

Except as otherwise noted, photographs are by courtesy of the New York State Historical Association. Miss Parslow is crafts expert of the Farmers' Museum of the Association.

Part of a page of Alexander's ledger showing names to be put on coverlets, including Joseph Youngs'.

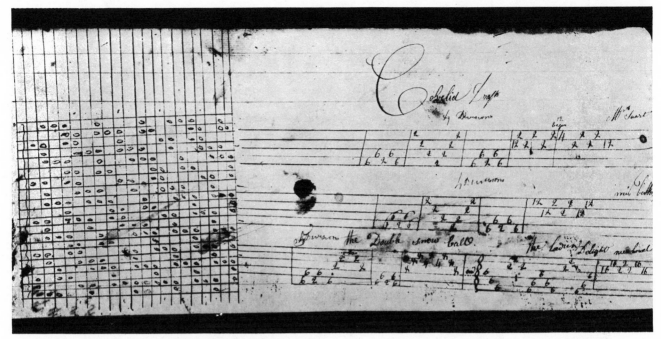

Page of Alexander's ledger showing drafts for diaper and "covelids," including "the Double snow ball" and "the Ladies Delight."

1820, and he lists orders for 274 of them with the names of the persons who brought in the orders and the "names to be put in the corners."

The earliest example I have seen was shown me by the Misses Corwin, who occupy a house near the Newburgh-Little Britain road where, according to local tradition, Alexander's son Harvey was born in 1816. This "flowert" coverlet was woven by James Alexander for Mary Waugh, great-grandmother of the Misses Corwin, and carries, beside her name, the date *Feb. 14, 1821.* I have seen other examples dated 1822, 1823, and 1824.

These flowered, double-weave coverlets are often called Jacquard weaving, on the assumption that they were produced on looms activated by punched pasteboard cards which selected the cords to form the pattern. Joseph Marie Jacquard produced his first model of this apparatus in 1800, and it was presently put into use in France, Scotland, and England. The first recorded instance of its introduction into the United States, however, was in 1825, when William H. Horstmann of Philadelphia imported a Jacquard attachment to be used in the manufacture of coach lace. John Murphy, writing his *Art of Weaving* in Glasgow in 1827 (2nd ed.), describes it but does not connect it with carpet or coverlet weaving; apparently it was very new to Scotland.

It seems extremely unlikely, if not impossible, that Alexander used a Jacquard machine. Whether he used a full draw loom, or a patent carpet loom of a type invented about 1814 but still requiring a draw boy, we will probably never discover, as all trace of his shop and tools has disappeared.

From his advertisement in the *Political Index,* which ran at intervals from June 1818 to May 1820, it appears that Alexander was weaving full-width coverlets as early as 1818, as well as linen ninety inches wide. This would have required a loom twice as wide as the regular one and either a fly-shuttle or two weavers sitting at the loom to throw the shuttle between them. No examples

of his wide coverlets or linen, or of his double-weave carpets, have come to light in my search.

Inserted at random in Alexander's ledger are drafts (weaving plans) for all kinds of weaving including fancy linens of up to thirty harnesses or "leaves." The only missing patterns are the ones for damask and his "flowert coverlids." Many of his patterns for "block" coverlets are exactly the drafts published in the early nineteenth-century Scottish weaving book by Murphy. It would be interesting to know whether Alexander owned a copy of this book or others of the period.

Interesting items in the accounts are the listing of the weaving of dimity in 1807, rag carpet in 1810, "gingham" in 1813, and "cotton stript" in 1814. Cheesecloth was often woven at the end of a warp. Most, if not all, of these fabrics were custom woven—that is, the customer brought in the warp and weft yarns and ordered certain pieces. Sometimes cotton yarn supplied by the weaver was mixed with the homespun linen. According to advertisements of the period, a cotton mill at Hampton, near Goshen, was producing yarns for hand weaving as early at 1806. Alexander's accounts show that he purchased both cotton warp and filling yarns in quantity from Cornwall Company in 1819. He wove linen as plain, striped or "streeket," twill, handkerchiefs, plain and twill ticking, plain woven linsey and twilled "toe," as well as diaper and damask diaper. Cotton was woven into dimity and "gingham." Woolen was designated simply as "cloth" or as "wide cloth," flannel, and blankets. He wove coverlets in varieties of "float," "block," "carpet," and "flowert." His carpets were "rag," "striped," "double," and "flowert."

Though there was a demand for Alexander's work, one wonders how he managed to feed all his family and one or two assistant weavers on the proceeds recorded in his account book. Entries are usually in sterling, the later ones sometimes in dollars. Many simple items were woven at one shilling (twelve and one-half cents) per yard:

plain linen, bed ticking, linsey, "toe" cloth, rag carpet, plain woolen, blanket, and flannel. Twilled fabrics and simple plaids, as in handkerchiefs and blankets, were woven for eighteen and one-half cents a yard. Fancy linens including diaper and damask diaper were from twenty-five to seventy-five cents a yard, depending on width and complexity. Coverlets were from two dollars to five dollars and fifty cents. The slightly lower price in each case was given if two or more were ordered of the same pattern. One must bear in mind that these are only the costs of labor and do not include the yarns used. A summary of weaving done in 1815 shows 1379 yards, totaling one hundred and twenty pounds and eighteen shillings.

Alexander occasionally employed others to weave for him and by 1805 he had a man weaving every month in the year. In 1806 at least two weavers were constantly employed. One was James Robinson, who worked for Alexander at various periods for many years. James Aikens wove from July 1817 until March 1818, John Gibbs from 1818 to 1820.

During his early years in Orange County and before his weaving trade had been built up, Alexander did many other jobs to earn a living. There are items in the account book (the spelling is his) which show that he received cash or credit for: driving team, clearing summer fallow, cutting hemp, crackling and dressing flax, picking stone, making fences, ditching, moing, reping, thrashing, planting and hoing corn, loding dung, cutting hooppols, picking apples, husking corn, planting and digging potatoes, makin rop, digging a drain and a millrace, working on the roads, cutting logs, and scoring ship timber. He

seems to have been in great demand for laying stone as there are many items such as "working at wall," "building fence," and "stoning the wall." The children were sent out to work at an early age. John was driving team in 1812, when he was only eleven, and Thomas and Joseph were working out in 1813, when they were eleven and nine.

Rarely did Alexander receive cash for his labor, either at the loom or at these many other tasks. According to the custom of the day he gave credit to his employers for receipts of butter, "flower," "candels," "vail," "motton," beef, spirits, "rie," 1 barrel of pork, buckwheat flower, bushels of corn, "pettos" and apples, clams, coffee, tea, "chees," heads of "cabig," shad, barrels of "sider," 1 pig, 1 sheep, barrel of "sop," flaxseed, 1 sickle, 1 pine board, side of sole leather, killing hogs, making shoes, mending boots, and pasture for 2 cows. One interesting account seems to prove that all was not labor, as it lists the use of a team or a horse from Gilbert Totten during the winter of 1804-1805. Items include: "1 horse to Newburg, 1 horse to Bethlehem" and, most revealing, "pleasuring to Neelitown" and "pleasuring 1 day to Little Britain."

James Alexander's record, and the investigation to which it has led me, have revealed much about the manner of living and working of a man who may be taken as a typical country weaver in early nineteenth-century America. Moreover, his entries of weaving done for local families indicate the kinds of fabrics produced at the time, and also show that figured carpets and coverlets were being woven in the United States considerably earlier than has been known.

"Diaper" tablecloth.
Unbleached linen on a cotton warp.

"Block" coverlet by a professional weaver.
Double weave, red wool and white cotton.

Some Rare Spinning Wheels *

Serge Daniloff

WE have become so accustomed to the more usual types of spinning wheels that altogether too little attention is given to the study and history of various other and far rarer kinds. Today the spinning wheel is viewed almost as a piece of furniture. This, however, was not the object which our forefathers had in mind when they invented, and then improved, an apparatus the sole function of which was actually to spin yarn.

The history of the spinning wheel is, in itself, a very fascinating tale, but it does not form the subject of these few notes. Let us simply observe that the "flyer"— that little wooden, horseshoe-shaped, revolving device, by means of which the fibrous material is twisted and wound on the bobbin — was, according to some authorities, invented by Leonardo da Vinci, artist, engineer, soldier, and scientist, as far back as 1519.

A late eighteenth-century descendant of Leonardo's wheel, the more common type of flax wheel, is shown in Figure 1. Its operation is doubtless fairly well understood by the reader. Sitting in front of the wheel, the "spinster," with her left hand, drew off a rather heavy strand of the fibrous material in the distaff, while the motion of her foot was transmitted, through a treadle, to the wheel, and thence to the flyer. With her right hand, she fed the strand to the eyelet of the flyer and down one arm of the latter to the bobbin mounted within the flyer. The combined rotation of flyer and bobbin, driven from the wheel, produced the twisting and the winding, while the varied motion of the spinner's hands drew the originally heavy strand into a finer one, prior to feeding it to the flyer.

The reader will readily see that the evenness and fineness of the yarn depended entirely on the skill of the spinner.

Fig. 1 — Common Flax Wheel (*late eighteenth century*)
From the Nutting Collection, Wadsworth Atheneum, Hartford, Connecticut

It may also interest him to know that all the elements entering into the spinning of yarn on a spinning wheel — namely, *drawing*, *twisting*, and *winding* — form the basis of the highly developed spinning machinery of today.

An interesting example of an unusual spinning wheel is shown in Figure 2. It is very old, having been brought to the Colonies, it is believed, during the early period of their settlement, or made here shortly after. We may, perhaps, place the date at 1700, or thereabouts. Its workmanship is simple, but some interesting painted decorations appear on the wheel supports, and on top of the base. The distaff is most primitive. Spinning wheels of the second half of the eighteenth century, and later, such as that shown in Figure 1, usually had a distaff carefully built up to form a cage adapted to carrying the fibrous material to be spun. The distaff on this wheel is a plain branch, the natural form of which has been utilized to approximate the cage construction desired.

Another noteworthy and very unusual feature is that the wheels are solid. These wheels point definitely to the early origin of the machine; for, obviously, it is considerably easier to make a solid wheel than one with spokes. Incidentally, the greater weight of the solid wheels made it easier to keep them running at a continuous speed, so essential to good and uniform spinning. We shall also mention, in passing, the double treadle, to facilitate the work of the spinner; the screw adjustment for keeping the driving band tight; and the countershaft drive, making it possible for the spinner to obtain the necessary speed of the flyer without unduly rapid motion of the feet — all interesting features of this specimen.

The wheel shown in Figure 3, we may place about 1750. Apparently this type of wheel is not known in Europe, although several examples have been recorded in the United States. Thus Figure 4 shows, from a good angle, a wheel embodying the same features as that of Figure 3, except, perhaps, for the somewhat simpler workmanship

* *Note.* — The writer of this paper wishes to thank the Essex Institute of Salem, Massachusetts, the Wadsworth Atheneum of Hartford, Connecticut, the Old Dartmouth Historical Society of New Bedford, Massachusetts, and the Victoria and Albert Museum of London, for permission to picture and describe some of their wheels. Above all, he would express his gratitude to Henry W. Belknap, Secretary of the Essex Institute, for much invaluable assistance. — *S. D.*

Fig. 2 — Rare Flax Wheel (*c. 1700*)
For more than six generations in the Sherman family of Connecticut.
Owned by Mayor Ralph S. Bauer of Lynn, Massachusetts

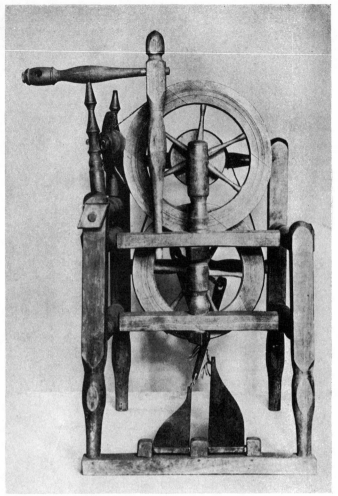

Fig. 3 — "Chair Frame" Spinning Wheel (*c. 1750*)
A type peculiar to the American colonies.
From the John Ward House, Essex Institute, Salem, Massachusetts

of the former. The striking thing about this type of wheel is the general shape, strongly resembling that of an ordinary chair frame. It has two spoked wheels. Here, again, we find a double-treadle motion, countershaft drive, and provision for tightening the driving band.

The reason for the chair form of the two latter specimens is not clear. One may venture to suggest that, in early days, old chair frames were, at times, actually employed by the first settlers as skeletons for their wheels. Later, perhaps, the unusual shape caught the eye of a following generation, and the original chair-frame wheel was duly imitated. On the other hand, an opinion has been voiced in England to the effect that this type of wheel is really nothing more than a "sport" — which, of course, is quite possible.

Figure 5 shows a tall, triangular specimen, three turned legs supporting the wheel at the top, and a single treadle at the bottom. The flyer is located below the wheel, and may be moved up and down to obtain the necessary tension of the driving band. The spokes of the wheel are turned in orthodox fashion, and the wheel itself has a heavy rim. Its date is probably the second half of the eighteenth century. It is said to have come from a mill in Pennsylvania, where a great many other wheels were

used for spinning.

A late eighteenth-century English spinning wheel of exquisite workmanship is pictured in Figure 6. It is the work of one John Planta, of Fulneck, near Leeds, England. The cabinetwork, of mahogany with inlays, is worth noting. A drawer is provided, apparently for the convenience of the spinner. Where the braces cross, at the bottom of the frame, is placed an urn-shaped knob, and the same design terminates the distaff, most carefully built up into a pear shape, which is quite unusual.

The whole affair is three feet high, the ordinary height of a table. A single treadle is used, the connecting link being unusually long. The flyer is very carefully built, and has two eyes for the guiding of the strand, instead of the usual hooks used on most flax wheels. Apparently, provision has been made to have the bobbin slide to and fro on the spindle, insuring a uniform winding of the yarn. The mechanism for this purpose — rarely found on a wheel of this period — is located on the top of the table.

Thus, in producing this wheel, the maker combined a number of interesting mechanical features with perfectly delightful workmanship. Obviously this wheel was not meant merely to spin yarn, but also to add to the beauty of the home in which it might be used.

Fig. 4 — "Chair Frame" Wheel (c. 1750)
From the Nutting Collection, Wadsworth Atheneum

Fig. 5 — Tripod Spinning Wheel (second half, eighteenth century)
From the Nutting Collection, Wadsworth Atheneum

The spinning wheels thus far described belong in the same general category, characterized by the use of a flyer and a treadle motion. They were ordinarily used for the spinning of flax, from which they take their name of "flax wheels."

There is, however, another type of wheel, generally known as the "wool wheel," and to this variety a few closing remarks will be devoted. In order better to show the difference in size and construction between a flax and a wool spinning wheel, common specimens of these two types are pictured side by side in Figure 7. As its name implies, the wool wheel was used primarily for the spinning of wool. The driving wheel is considerably larger than that of a flax wheel — ordinarily about 50 inches in diameter. No treadle motion is used: the large wheel is rotated by hand, and the motion is transmitted, by a

Fig. 6 — English Spinning Wheel (late eighteenth century)
Of mahogany, banded with satinwood. Signed Made by John Planta at Fulneck, near Leeds.
From the Victoria and Albert Museum, London

band, to a small countershaft at the opposite end of the machine, and thence to the spindle proper. The relative sizes of the wheel and pulley are so arranged that a high spindle speed is readily obtained.

The construction of the wool spindle is entirely different from that of the spindle of a flax wheel. It is a small, metallic shaft without any flyer whatever. Its rotation is made either to twist the yarn or to wind it, depending on the position, with respect to the spindle, in which the strand of wool is held by one hand of the spinner, while the other hand rotates the driving wheel — either forward for twisting, or backward for winding.

From the above description it will be clear that, while, in the flax wheel, twisting and winding are going on simultaneously — thanks to the flyer — in the wool wheel they are

Fig. 7 — Flax and Wool Wheels (*eighteenth century*)
Common examples showing the relative sizes of the two types and the special construction of each.
From the Essex Institute

carried out consecutively by means of a plain spindle. In other words, on the flax wheel the spinning process is carried out continuously, while on the wool wheel it is intermittent. This is the fundamental difference between the two types, which accounts for their difference in appearance and construction.

Historically, the wool wheel probably came into existence first, being directly related in principle to the oldest method of spinning known to humanity — the spindle and distaff, employed by the ancient Greeks, and still in use, today, by the natives of some of the less civilized countries of the world.

The development of both types of wheel was parallel, but fewer unusual examples of the wool wheel are found than of the flax wheel. However, one exceptional wheel,

Fig. 8 — Unusual Wool Wheel (*c. 1800*)
Made by Thomas Howland. Adjustable to varying heights.
From the Old Dartmouth Historical Society, New Bedford, Massachusetts

dating about 1800, is depicted in Figure 8. It is small, made of oak, simple in design, but of good workmanship, and is accredited to a Thomas Howland. Its use for the spinning of wool is indicated by the spindle construction and the hand drive. The more common form of wool wheel, with its large driving wheel several feet in diameter, has been described above. It is usually both bulky and cumbersome. Perhaps it was the intention of Thomas Howland to design and build a wheel of more comfortable dimensions, although, by reducing the size of the wheels, he lost something of spindle speed. In this apparatus the beam supporting the wheels may be raised or lowered, and fastened in any desired position, doubtless to enable the spinner to adjust it at the most convenient height.

OLD-TIME METHODS OF SPINNING AND WEAVING

By L. M. A. ROY

Mr. Roy performs a valuable service by seeking out craftsmen who still remember the old-time methods and recording these techniques with his camera. Spinning is demonstrated here by Mrs. Stevens of Deering, New Hampshire, while the weaving is done by Mr. Roy's mother, who has appeared in some of his other pictorial demonstrations.

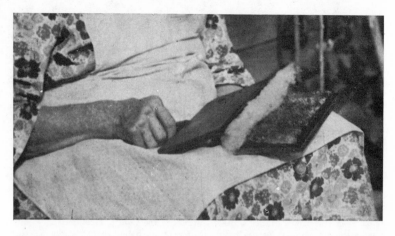

CARDING. Raw wool must be carded in order to line the fibers up in one direction and produce a roll which may be spun into yarn. Now done by machinery, carding was once done by hand, by means of two flat, rectangular boards covered with leather, into which fine hooked wires were embedded, all pointing towards the handle. By pulling in opposite directions, the fibers were combed out straight, and then the carders were turned, as shown here, to make a roll.

SPINNING. Both the small flax wheel and the large wool wheel were used to spin yarn. In the latter, shown here, the spindle was turned by means of a long cord wound around the large wheel and fastened to the head by pulleys. As the spindle turned, the roll of carded wool attached to it was twisted into yarn. The large wheel was rotated by striking it with a wooden pin. The spinner held the roll of wool taut with her left hand while it spun into yarn, and drew it away from the spindle.

WINDING THE YARN. When the spindle was full, the yarn had to be removed and wound into skeins. This might be done by means of a niddy-noddy, or hand reel, as seen at right, with two curved arms at right angles to each other (the bottom "head" is so much foreshortened in the photograph that it is hardly visible). Another device was the clock reel, shown above, which consisted of spokes terminating in round bars about 5 inches long. As the wheel turns, the yarn is wound into a skein. In both cases, 40 turns were marked by a knot, and 7 knots made a skein.

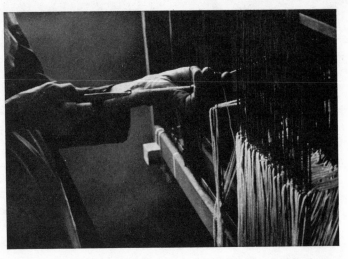

"BEAMING ON." The warp is wound onto the warp beam, one person holding the threads tight while another winds. The warp threads are kept even and of the proper width by means of the raddle, a comb-like frame the same length as the reed. (See diagram below to locate the various parts of the loom mentioned in connection with the photographs.)

THREADING THE HEDDLES. For plain weaving, using two heddle frames, the warp threads are pulled through the eyelets of the heddle cords alternately, the even threads through one heddle and the odd ones through the other. Setting up the loom for pattern weaving is a more complicated procedure.

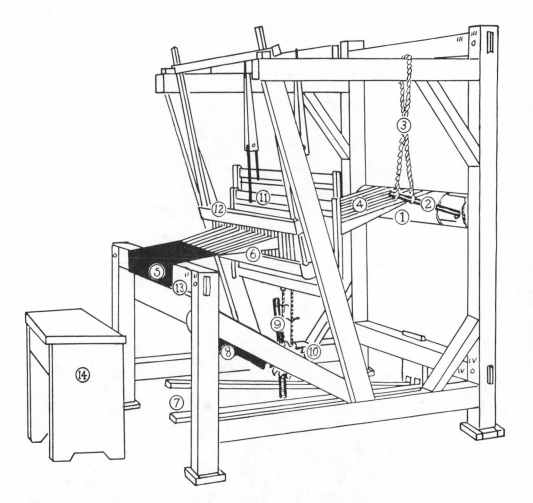

THE LOOM. (1) The warp beam, on which the longitudinal threads are wound. (2) Bar used to turn the beam when winding on the warp. (3) Rope to hold the warp at the proper tension. (4) Warp. (5) Woven material, or web. (6) Shed, the open space through which the shuttle is thrown to insert the horizontal, or weft, thread. (7) Treadles. (8) Cloth beam, on which finished material is wound. (9) Wooden bar to turn the cloth beam. (10) Ratchet to hold the cloth beam. (11) Heddle frames, strung with cords each having an eyelet in the center, through which the warp is threaded. One heddle frame is lowered by pushing down a treadle, while the other is raised by pulley action, thus creating the shed. Then the process is reversed, the other heddle being lowered while the first is raised, so that the shuttle may be thrown back in the opposite direction. (12) The reed, made up of comb-like teeth holding the warp threads. The cross piece to which the reed is attached, called the batten, swings pendulum fashion and "beats" the weft thread into position in the woven fabric. (13) Breast beam, around which the woven material slides down to the cloth beam. (14) The weaver's seat.

THREADING THE REED. The ends of the warp threads are pulled through the teeth of the reed by means of a reed hook.

THROWING THE SHUTTLE. The shuttle passes through the open space, or shed, formed by raising one heddle frame and lowering the other. For rag rugs, like the one being woven here, the shuttle consists of a narrow wooden frame on which the rags are wound. In the case of cloth weaving, the shuttle is boat-shaped, hollowed out in the center to hold the bobbin on which the weft thread is wound.

"BEATING" THE WEFT WITH THE BATTEN. After the shuttle has been thrown, the weft thread is brought into place by swinging the batten, which forces the teeth of the reed against the edge of the woven material.

MRS. MIFFLIN'S FRINGE LOOM

By ELIZABETH HAYNES

IN THE MAGAZINE ANTIQUES for June 1937 (*p. 290*), there was published a reproduction of the portrait *Thomas Mifflin and His Wife*, painted, as the signature tells us, by John Singleton Copley in Boston in 1773 (*Fig. 1*). With it is the significant statement that "Mrs. Mifflin is employing the apparatus [a tape loom] for weaving an elaborate fringe."

In the mind of anyone who likes to learn about the daily life of the colonists, this remark raises two questions: was it usual for ladies of social prominence and wealth to make their own fringe, and why did Mrs. Mifflin do it?

We know that spinning and weaving, or at least the superintendence of these tasks, were among the many duties of an eighteenth-century housewife. Martha Washington, who "directed the women in her workroom in cutting out and sewing the negroes' winter clothing" while "incessantly knitting," also made "netted fringe for counterpanes."[1] But that is a different matter. Here we are not concerned with the netted fringe, nor with fringe made with a fringing fork,[2] but only with the woven variety. For a lady of fashion to busy herself at the fringe loom while sitting for one of the leading portrait painters of her day seems to indicate that this was considered "parlor handwork." In fact the statement in ANTIQUES refers to this apparatus as "the drawing-room version of the well-known tape loom of which sundry coarser examples have been published . . ."

The handsomely-dressed Mr. and Mrs. Mifflin were wealthy people of social and political importance. Mrs. Mifflin, born Sarah Morris, was the daughter of a prominent Quaker, Morris Morris, and had married her cousin, Thomas Mifflin, in 1767. She has been described as a "lovely woman in very delicate health."[3] Her husband, a member of the Continental Congress at the time of the portrait, was to play a leading part in the events of the next decades: as first aide-de-camp to General Washington, as Quartermaster General of the Revolutionary Army, and as Governor of Pennsylvania from 1791 until his death in 1800.

In seeking the reason for Mrs. Mifflin's fringe loom, we find that English ladies had long been used to home-made fringe, and knowledge of English furnishings justifies the belief that this was woven fringe. "In 1676, Lord Keeper Guildford narrates that during his visit to Badminton he saw the Duchess in the gallery 'where she had divers gentlewomen commonly at work upon embroidery and fringe-making . . .' Gereit Jensen, the Royal cabinetmaker, in 1690 supplied '2 tables of fine Makatree with 2 engines to make fringe - £ 40.' The making of fringes, tassels . . . was a popular occupation for ladies of the 18th C."[4] As Mr. Mifflin had been educated in England, he may have suggested to his wife that she follow the English custom — or it may have been the "popular occupation" of American ladies as well.

Books dealing with home life in colonial America are, for the most part, silent on the matter of fringe but Mrs. Earle says, "A fringe loom might also be occasionally found for weaving decorative fringes; these were more common in the Hudson River Valley than elsewhere."[5] With wartime restrictions in force one could not go to the Hudson Valley (or elsewhere) to make personal search for fringe looms, and inquiries addressed to museum officials, historians, and weavers have not turned up one loom, or even any other record of one. Yet, for that matter, a special loom was not necessary for fringe. A tape loom, such as that used by Mrs. Mifflin in her portrait, was entirely practical, if properly threaded. For a fringe machine is "one in which the weft-thread is carried and detained beyond the limit of the warps, which has thus a series of loops beyond the selvage"[6] and this definition is applicable to either hand- or power-machine.

I next set out to look for drafts for fringe headings, or notations about fringe making, in old weavers' books, and, although many draft books were examined and weavers questioned, especially those who knew about old weaving, nothing of the sort has been found. Possibly it was because the heading generally used was so simple that it was not thought necessary to record it.

And so it is quite *possible* that colonial ladies made fringe. But even if it is possible, was it usual? And why, in particular, did Mrs. Mifflin? An entry in a journal or a letter written in the eighteenth century would help us here but all the journals and all the letters read to date fail to tell us. Fringe is mentioned in inventories and in letters but without explanation as to whether it was home-made or bought ready-made.

After all, not so very much was needed. American portraits rarely show fringe on dresses or on furniture but often the subject is shown against a window curtain edged with fringe. Two outstanding examples are the delightful portraits of *Colonel Benjamin Tallmadge with his Son (Fig. 2)* and that of *Mrs. Benjamin Tallmadge with her Son and Daughter (Fig. 3)*, painted by Ralph Earl in 1790. Presumably all the fringe that was needed might have been bought from local upholsterers, many of whom imported. We have the names of a dozen in New York who were soliciting "commands," among them one who advertised that he had "recently returned from London."[7] Boston, where Mrs. Mifflin sat for her portrait, had upholsterers who were advertising fringe described as "imported from London" and "just arrived."[8] In Philadelphia, there was the shop of John Ross, the husband of Betsy, an upholsterer and an active patriot who gave his life in the cause of American freedom.[9]

FIG. 1—"THOMAS MIFFLIN AND HIS WIFE." Painted by John Singleton Copley in 1773. *Property of the Historical Society of Pennsylvania. No. 33 in catalogue of Exhibition of Paintings of John Singleton Copley, at the Metropolitan Museum of Art, 1936-1937.*

FIG. 2 — "COLONEL BENJAMIN TALLMADGE WITH HIS SON." Painted by Ralph Earl in 1790. *Property of the Litchfield (Connecticut) Historical Society. No. 45 in catalogue of the Exhibition of Paintings of Life in America, at the Metropolitan Museum of Art, 1939.*

He, if anyone, would have had American-made trimmings.

But Mrs. Mifflin, it appears, made her own fringe. And, remembering the situation in 1773, we are tempted to ask if it were not due to patriotism. For the fringe seems to be of silk, and at that time, when Colonial Assemblies were passing resolutions against the use of foreign articles, and when great attention was being given to the building up of American products, silk was a "fashionable occupation."[10] Experiments in silk culture were being carried on in the South and in New England and meeting with success. That the Governor of Connecticut had the first coat made of New England silk in 1747 and his daughter the first dress, in 1750, and that President Stiles of Yale wore a gown at Commencement in 1788 made of Connecticut-grown silk, are well-known facts.[10] Now the Mifflins, being loyal Americans, probably shared the interest in silk culture and we may suppose that Mrs. Mifflin started making fringe herself because she did not wish to buy foreign articles. At least we offer this as an answer to the question of Mrs. Mifflin's fringe loom.

On the other hand, the introduction of the loom may have been the artist's suggestion, as a means of putting the sitter at her ease, as, for the same reason, he may have suggested to Mrs. Seymour Fort that she work at her tatting while posing for her portrait.[11] In this connection we recall John Hill Morgan's statement[12] that the sitters presumably went to

Copley and that some of the articles appearing in the portraits were "among the furnishings of Copley's studio."

REFERENCES

1. Ella Shannon Bowles, *Homespun Handicrafts*, pp. 89, 211. Lippincott Co., N. Y. 1931
2. Gertrude Whiting, *Tools and Toys of Stitchery*, p. 327. Columbia University Press, N. Y. 1928.
3. John H. Merrill, *Memoranda Relating to the Mifflin Family.* Privately printed 1890
4. Percy Macquoid and Ralph Edwards, *Dictionary of English Furniture*, Vol. III, p. 321. Charles Scribner's Sons, N. Y. 1927
5. Alice Morse Earle, *Home Life in Colonial Days*, p. 227. Macmillan Co. N. Y. 1898
6. Edward H. Knight, *American Mechanical Dictionary.* N. Y. 1874
7. R. S. Gottesman, *The Arts and Crafts in N. Y., 1726-1776.* N. Y. Historical Society 1938
8. George F. Dow, *Arts and Crafts in New England.* Wayside Press, Topsfield, Mass. 1927
9. Dictionary of American Biography. Vol. 16. Charles Scribner's Sons, N. Y. 1935
10. J. L. Bishop, *History of American Manufactures*, Vol. 1. pp. 359, 360. Edward Young & Co., Philadelphia, Pa. 1868
11. Property of The Wadsworth Atheneum, Hartford, Conn. Illus. in color as cover *The Art News*, Vol. XXXIX, No. 4, Oct. 26, 1940
12. John Hill Morgan, *Some Notes on John Singleton Copley, The Magazine* ANTIQUES, Vol. XXXI, p. 116, March, 1937

FIG. 3 — MRS. BENJAMIN TALLMADGE WITH HER SON AND DAUGHTER." Painted by Ralph Earl in 1790. *Property of the Litchfield (Connecticut) Historical Society. No. 46 in catalogue of the Exhibition of Paintings of Life in America, at the Metropolitan Museum of Art, 1939.*

29

II   Tasteful Household "Furnitures"

The American weaver owes a debt to the craftsmen of many cultures, in particular to the native American Indian and the Hispanic New Mexican. They brought the American weaver ancient slit tapestry techniques and brocaded construction. To the larger, later worldly influence of the Portuguese, the French, the Italians, and the Chinese, Americans owe gratitude for silk fibers and for the floral designs that became a part of their fabrics. The Flemish and the French supplied the English with master craftsmen; the English, in turn, supplied the colonies with fleece and woolens; the Indians supplied much of the world with fine spun cotton yarns; and the German and Scotch supplied many of the pattern books used in American design.

Cedric Larson's "Cloth of Colonial America," the first article in this section, brings into focus the history of the European cloth trade, the fibers, the fabrics, the trade names, the nations that controlled and produced the first cloth brought to the American shores. It is an excellent short history of this industry, particularly in England where, since the days of the Tudors, trade receipts and international leadership were balanced by the weavers and the merchants. The most versatile fiber, and one the English treasured and guarded with protective tariffs, was wool. Frequently called the "blood of England," wool was sold raw in bags or as cloth to the American colonists, and when American yeomen mastered techniques of husbandry as well as weaving and manufacturing, it was no wonder that the English showed their strong obsessive concern.

The manufacture and ownership of cloth was vital to the survival of Americans and to the independence of America. "Cloth," as Larson popularly uses the term, means all garments, coverings, and wrappings, which would include materials of wool as well as objects like carpet. Cloth was important enough in the eighteenth century for every scrap to have been used. Larson's quotation from a 1726 *Boston Gazette* advertisement demonstrates the value placed on used cloth and clothes no matter where or from whom they came. "There will be sold at auction sundry Wearing Apparel New, which belong'd to a Gentleman Deceased. Also sundry New suits of Clothes, a Parcel of Silk Stockings, also some Worsted Ditto, and sundry other Sorts of Goods." Neither a man's death nor his family's pride stood in the way of American thrift and practicality. Cloth was hard to come by and meant far more than a mere symbol of hard work or status.

Cedric Larson, like ANTIQUES authors Marion Day Iverson, Florence M. Montgomery, and Sarah B. Sherrill, discusses a particular use of cloth one often thinks of as limited to the twentieth century—the protective slipcover. Whether meant for the chair, the table, or the fine floor carpet, cloths called "druggets" protected household rarities against dirt, crumbs, and bad weather. Sarah B. Sherrill, in an article found later in this anthology (pp. 157–182), calls the protective cloth "baize" or "bays." As uniformity became the fashion in home furnishings, slipcovers played a harmonious role in the artistic scheme of a room, a point indicated by Marion Day Iverson in "Slipcovers of Past Centuries." A delightful display of slipcovers, loose and fitted, can be seen in the British prints from the Lewis Walpole Library illustrating Florence M. Montgomery's article on room furnishings. Thomas Chippendale, Iverson suggests, saw the practicality of covering silk upholstery with woolen covers.

In Franco Scalamandré's "Fabrics in Early America," one is introduced to the processes of silk weaving and silk raising. That Franklin failed to raise silkworms outside of Philadelphia, that the Moravians also failed outside of Bethlehem, and that Pinckney failed to raise silkworms of any quality did not stop Americans from having silk. Ruth Davidson's "A Glossary of French Silks" directs reader attention to the inventory of Governor John Penn as an example of the silk and damask that could be found in American households and recommends a list of the elegant fabrics from the household of Major General Edward Gibbons of Boston where ten yellow damask chairs, and velvet and damask cushions appeared along with a variety of woolens like serge, say, and perpetuana. (Fabric names such as these were used in the eighteenth century, but should not be identified with woven structures. Words, too, like "velvet" and "satin," used loosely to indicate structure or even fabric name, relate more correctly to pile and interlacing.)

The Davidson glossary of French silks includes many of the terms one might like to know about. Based on an earlier work, "Toute la Soierie Française," published in a 1958 French periodical, it is also supplemented by writings of the early twentieth-century Philadelphia textile scholar Nancy Andrews Reath. Definitions are provided for "brocading," "velvet," and the word "weave" itself (which, according to Irene Emery, is open to question), the fabric names "damask," "brocatelle," and "taffeta" (the latter is best used as a fabric name and not a weave), and the accessory techniques of appliqué, stamping, and chiné. Important men and their painterly techniques relating to the European weaving trade are also listed in the glossary —men like Gaspard Gregoire, a textile painter who applied paint directly to the warp threads before material was woven; Philippe de La Salle, considered by many to be the greatest designer-weaver in the history of silk weaving, who adored flowers and animals and with a master painter's knowledge made his weaving a fine art; and then Joseph-Marie Jacquard, the inventor of the attachment that lifted the warp threads and set the weft to weave, who eliminated a draw-loom and extra weaver, who increased production, and who introduced the easy use of the curved line to coverlet weaving.

Bed curtains were another way of using cloth both for decorative and for practical purposes. Window curtains were not hung in early eighteenth-century American houses, according to Boston and Salem household inventories quoted in Anna Brightman's article, "Woolen Window Curtains." Changes came by the 1750s when George Washington, like other men of good taste, began to order for his Mount Vernon bed chambers window and bed curtains of yellow silk and worsted damask to match the chair seats. Varieties of festoon curtains began to appear at Williamsburg and at Monticello and can be seen in illustrations accompanying Mildred Lanier's article on textile fabrics at Colonial Williamsburg and in Fiske and Marie Kimball's on Jefferson's curtains.

After 1750 window curtains became more common. The two most often-used fabrics were furniture check and harrateen. Furniture check was not, as some people have thought, something to be used exclusively in kitchen toweling. It was found in the better rooms of the Governor's palace at Williamsburg. Harrateen, like calamanco, camlet, "china" or cheyney (later to be called moreen), was a fabric name derived from a technique applied to the surface of the wool which made it resemble the fine silks. Camlet was watered and hot pressed or stamped by rollers. Cheyney or "china" was calendered. Harrateen was not listed in eighteenth-century dictionaries, although Florence M. Montgomery (p. 50) has discovered a reference to harrateen as a simple weave with a wavy surface in the Holker manuscripts of English textiles written about 1750.

"Virginia cloth" is another phrase with vague references. Listed in the Randolph inventory, it has been defined by Mildred Lanier as any cloth made of Virginia manufacture whether it is derived from wool, linen, or cotton fiber. Despite help from the dictionary-encyclopedias of Savary, Chambers, and Postlethwayt, the old cry is taken up by Anne Brightman, quoting Diderot who said, "One could fill a hundred pages with the names which are given to fabrics of the same kind." Perhaps Samuel Sewall's description of homespun as "Stubborn Wool" is not so bad a definition after all.

Suggested Reading:

Burnham, Dorothy K. and Harold B. *Keep Me Warm One Night*. Toronto: University of Toronto Press & Royal Ontario Museum, 1972.

Carus-Wilson, E. M. and Coleman, Olive. *England's Export Trade 1275—1547*. Oxford: The Clarendon Press, 1963.

Reath, Nancy Andrews. *Weaves of Handloom Fabrics*. Philadelphia: The Pennsylvania Museum, 1927.

CLOTH OF COLONIAL AMERICA

By CEDRIC LARSON

THE AVERAGE American of today, when he conjures a mental picture of an early colonist, visualizes a tousled figure outfitted in buckskin or crude homespun. Actually, only frontiersmen — and not all of them — were thus attired. The average eighteenth-century colonial family enjoyed a wide range of fabrics for wearing apparel. These fabrics constitute a broad subject, whose background involves something of the history of European clothmaking, the industrial revolution, and the commerce which flourished with the mother country save for the few years of the War for Independence.

By the time America was discovered, clothmaking in Europe had already been highly perfected. Nearly every sizable city or town had its own cloth specialty, with crafts and guilds upholding high standards of workmanship as well as of price. The looms of Flanders and the cities of central France for centuries led the Continent in quality and quantity of production, and their creations even surpassed in fineness and texture materials imported from far-off India and China. Many cloths familiar to the colonial household were named for the city or region where they had first been made.

England, since the days of the Tudors, had gradually gained the ascendancy in the sheep-raising industry; by the time of Elizabeth "to send wool to England" had become the equivalent of "to send coals to Newcastle." So weaving and cloth manufacture in the mother country got away to an early start. Both Henry VII and Henry VIII encouraged the influx into England of Flemish weavers. Craft guilds of tailors and weavers in England grew to powerful proportions, and the annual fairs at which cloth was a staple became an accepted part of civic life.

By the eighteenth century England had become the leading commercial and industrial power of Europe. The industrial revolution, which occurred between 1760 and 1790, was in no way more marked than in the development of new methods of cloth manufacture. Under the mercantilist theory of colonies, the mother country supplied the outlying possessions with manufactured products, and in turn brought raw products from the colonies. Therefore we find little cloth manufacturing within the American colonies until after the Revolution, or even the advent of the nineteenth century. But along the seaboard especially, we find every ship from the mother country bearing in its cargo a wide and attractive variety of cloths, which were extensively advertised in the papers of the colonial seaports. Hence the news sheets of colonial America offer a rich reservoir of data for the study of contemporary fabrics.

As early as 1669 the American colonies had been prohibited from exporting manufactured woolens, and a few years later such products were forbidden as articles of intercolonial commerce. Later in the eighteenth century the colonists were forbidden to manufacture hats. As this trend became more and more pronounced the colonists became largely dependent upon imports from Europe for all cloth commodities. If, therefore, a colonial housewife wished to make a new dress, or some curtains or hangings, she would eagerly scan the advertisements to note what the latest shipments from England had brought to the local merchant. That she was no stranger to varieties of cloth and could readily identify two score or more is testified by the "dry goods" advertisements with which eighteenth-century newspapers were filled.

Calthrop, a British authority on the history of dress, observed: "To see our ancestors dressed is to have a shrewd guess as to what they were — as to what they did." This is what makes interesting such newspaper advertisements as that shown in Figure 1, and a valuable source of information about contemporary fabrics.

As early as July 11, 1726, we learn from the *Boston Gazette* that there will be sold at auction "sundry Wearing Apparel New, which belong'd to a Gentleman Deceased. Also sundry New Suits of Clothes, a Box of Fine Caster Hats, a Parcel of Silk Stockings, also some Worsted Ditto, and sundry other Sorts of Goods." Lists grew longer as newspapers became larger. Twenty years later, the *Boston Gazette or Weekly Journal* for May 13, 1746, carried a fairly lengthy advertisement of Albert Dennie, advising the public of "English Goods a great Variety imported from London in the last Ships." The lists included:

Balladine sewing Silk, raw Silk, colour'd and waxed Threads, Pins, Ozenbrigs, India Dimetys, black Bombazeen and Apalene, silk Damask, Horse hair Buttons, Hair Shapes, Wadding, Linnen and Cotton Check, Velvet, and Everlasting for Wastcoats, worsted Stuff plain and flower'd, worsted Damasks, Russels, Fearnothing Great Coats, Kerseys, Druggets, Swanskins, Broadcloths, Serges, worsted & hair Plushes, Caps, Stockings, Cambricks, Shalloons, Camblets, Garlets, yard wide Linnens, bed Ticks, cotton Stockings, Chinces, Callicoes, Buttons and Mohair, Hats, Muslins, white Callicoes, Ribbands, . . . short Cloaks, Taffeties, Persians, Velvets . . .

One might quote such advertisements almost *ad infinitum*, but the above examples must suffice. Of more immediate interest is the question of what some of the most common varieties of cloth might be. In vain would we look in the pages of any modern dictionary for many of these terms.

A very widely advertised cloth was osnaburg. Spelling seemed to weigh but lightly upon the consciences of early editors, and one finds it spelled osnaburgh, ossenburgs, ozenbrigs, osnabrug, osnabrigs, osenbrigs, ozenbridge, and otherwise. This was a type of coarse woolen originally made in Osnabrück, a Prussian city in Hanover. This city had at one time belonged to the Hanseatic League and led in the manufacture of this type of cloth. Out of it the colonists would make trousers and other outer wearing apparel. Closely similar to osnaburg was a material called ticklenburg, widely advertised, which was a coarse mixed linen fabric, originally emanating from Tecklenburg, a German city near Osnabrück. When George I of Hanover ascended the English throne in 1714 a brisk commerce between England and Hanover sprang up. Textiles from Osnabrück and Tecklenburg therefore became common in England.

Another familiar material was bombasine, appearing under such orthographical variations as bombasyne, bumbazine, bombazin, bumbasine, bombazeen — all from a late Latin word denoting a silken texture. It was sometimes used by the Italians as a term for raw cotton, but was more generally applicable to twilled or corded dress material, of various combinations of silk and cotton. In black this stuff was much used in mourning.

A popular cloth for colonial dress was camlet. This was advertised in a bewildering array of spellings — camblet, chamlyt, chamlett, chamelot, chambelot, chamolet, camlott, and a host of other forms. The name was derived from two root words meaning camel's hair, which tradition says Marco Polo introduced to Europe. Hair and wool sufficed to make a fairly good imitation, and use of the material was widespread in both Europe and America until the manufacture of cheap cotton cloth undermined the market for it.

One notices the frequent recurrence of russel in colonial cloth advertisements. There are at least eight ways of spelling the name, which is said to come from Rijssel, the Flemish name for Lille, where the cloth originated. It was a wool fabric widely in favor from the sixteenth to the eighteenth century. Later russel became a sort of generic term for a variety of woolen-twilled clothing manufactured in England, such as russel-satin, russel-black, russel-silk, and so on.

Shalloon, the anglicized form of Chalons, France (where the type of material originated), was a woolen fabric of twill weave, widely employed by the colonials for linings. Tailors were wont to use it for lining coats.

Good old calico, too, graced the dry-goods advertisements of newspapers in colonial America. This term was spelled in so many ways that Noah Webster would have wrung his hands: callicutt, calecut, calicute, callicot, kalyko, calyco, callicoe, calicoe, and so on. This cloth of course took its name from Calicut,

on the west coast of India, whither an endless procession of Portuguese trading ships had sailed ever since the days of Vasco da Gama. Originally an Indian stuff of cotton, often gaily dyed, it became a staple of the English loom, generally appearing in plain, unprinted white, bleached or unbleached. At an early date, textile plants of London and the Midlands were taking all the cotton the southern colonies could produce to manufacture into many cloths, of which calico was a leader.

Every colonial store of any pretensions would carry a full line of chintz and dimity. The former, often spelled chints, chint, chince, or chinse, originally designated a stained or painted calicoes from far-off India; the Hindu word *chint* means colored or variegated. It came to mean English fast-printed cotton cloths in numerous colors, in such designs as flowers, landscapes, and the like, frequently in imitation of the Indian patterns. It was a favorite fabric for bedcovers and hangings, and even for the old-time nightgown.

Dimity (from a Greek word signifying double thread) greeted the colonial eye under a number of aliases, such as dimite, dimmety, dimmity, dimetty, demity, and dimitty. It was a heavy cotton fabric with raised stripes or fancy figures, much in demand by colonial housewives for hangings and furniture coverings and light outer garments. White dimity was widely used for gentlemen's waistcoats. (See ANTIQUES, July 1940, p. 23, and September 1940, p. 111.)

Who today could tell what a "fearnought" might be? One might hazard a guess that it was a new heavy battleship of the British navy. But no! Its only link with the sea is the fact that sailors of yore wore fearnoughts to keep out the biting winds of the north Atlantic. They were also popular in New England, where the long, severe winters rendered them a necessity. Fearnought was a stout woolen cloth for overcoats, or greatcoats. It was also used by the northern colonists for lining windows and doors against inclement weather.

Drugget was utilized extensively as a lining or protective covering for carpets or furniture. There was, in fact, a particular type of rug called the drugget. The material was chiefly wool.

In the eighteenth century, Kilmarnock signified roughly what Stetson does today. A Kilmarnock hat or bonnet was the pride of every dandy or dame in the colonies. The Scottish town of Kilmarnock was famed for its cowls (bonnets), and its woolen-spinning industry produced not only headgear but also shawls, laces, and curtains.

The cloth that made the Suffolk town of Kersey famous was a coarse, narrow fabric, woven from long wool and usually ribbed. The name also appears as kerseye, carsey, carsy, kerzie, and the like. Its sturdiness recommended it to the colonists for work clothes.

A utility cloth was kenting, said to take its name from the English county of Kent. It was a closely woven fine linen, which might be employed for napkins or tablecloths, or for straining fruit juice for jelly.

Pullicate (also pulicat) was a garishly colored material resembling a modern bandana, which originated in the town of Pulicat on the Madras coast. The English wove an imitation from dyed yarn, which was commonly made into handkerchiefs.

Who would recognize in the colonial humhum the ancestor of the modern Turkish towel? It was a coarse India cotton found only in well-to-do homes and used for general utility purposes, as toweling.

Corduroy (probably from the French *corde du roi* or "king's cord") came into wide favor in the colonies toward the latter part of the eighteenth century. Despite its name, it was of English origin, and the common type was a coarse, thick, cotton fabric worn mostly by laborers or those engaged in rough work. Varieties of corduroy widely advertised were velverett, velveteen, and thicksett.

Baize, variously called bayes, baies, bease, bayze, bays (derived from bay, the original color), was a coarse woolen fabric with a long nap, used by the colonists for sundry purposes, such as linings, curtains, and even warm articles of clothing.

Fustian, which colonial editors contrived to spell fustain, fustane, fusten, fusteen, fosten, fustion, *et cetera*, was a coarse cloth made of cotton and flax, or other mixture, generally a dark or dull color. It was a utility goods.

Duffel, duffle, or duffil (from the town of Duffel in the Belgian province of Brabant) was a coarse linen with a thick nap. Colonists employed it for purposes of hard wear, such as dressing gowns or duffel bags.

Large numbers of colonial bedrooms boasted Marseilles quilting. This material was a stiff cotton fabric, either plain-colored or printed. It was also used in waistcoats and dresses.

Three favorite linen stuffs of the colonial era were cambric, holland, and platilla. Cambric, which exists in a profusion of spellings, took its name from Kamerijk, the Flemish version of Cambray, Flanders. Originally cambric was the finest white linen for bedding, handkerchiefs, and the like, but later English imitations were of hardspun cotton yarn. Holland cloth came from the Netherlands province of that name, and in its unbleached form was advertised as brown holland. Less common was platilla, a sort of white linen said to come from Silesia and known for the fineness of its texture.

Swanskin, found on every colonial store-shelf, was a type of fine thick flannel notable for its fleeciness and warmth. It found wide sale as a woolen blanketing.

Dowlas, frequently encountered in advertisements, was a coarse linen, said to have originated in Daoulas, Brittany. It appears as dolas, doulas, dowlass, dowlace, and doulace.

Calamanco, from Latin words signifying a head covering made of camel's hair, was widely used in colonial days. It was a woolen stuff first perfected in Flanders, having a glossy surface and so woven that checks are seen on one side only. It was used as a general dress goods and utility cloth. A few of the variations are calamance, callimanco, calamanca, and calamanco.

The lowly serge, famous today for its shine, was France's gift to the world of cloth. It was a woolen fabric which has differed at different periods. In colonial days it was employed for hangings, bed coverings, and the like. Because of its durability the poorer classes bought it for use in articles of apparel. Originally it was designated by place of manufacture, as serge de Nimes, serge de Chalons. Oddly enough, the cloth called denim, known by that name both in colonial times and today, is a by-product of serge de Nimes. This was a twilled cotton fabric, usually colored, used for sturdy garments such as overalls, work-dresses, and uniforms.

Nankeen (nankein, nankin, or nanquin) from Nanking, China, was a material known to every colonial housewife. It was a cotton cloth, generally dyed yellow, which could be used for curtains or dresser cloths and combined with other materials in dresses.

Many of the advertisements in colonial newspapers simply named a cloth for the city or country in which it was manufactured; such names do not necessarily identify a type of material. For example, a cloth from Florence, Italy, might be advertised simply as Florentine; from Mantua, as Mantuan; and, again, we find Irish linens, and Russia sheeting.

The cloth advertisements which abounded in all colonial seaport newspapers, and as well in most of the news sheets of the larger towns in the interior, indicate a surprisingly advanced state of cloth manufacture two centuries ago. The fabrics cited above are merely the more common materials, and if even a year's issues of a Boston, New York, or Philadelphia newspaper were fine-tooth-combed for names of cloths, the list might be considerably augmented, although extensive research might be necessary to define some of the obsolete terms employed in these old advertisements offering cloth to our ancestors.

Upholstery Fabrics for Antique Furniture

By RUTH BRADBURY DAVIDSON

IN THE MEDIEVAL DWELLING the chairs and benches, and the chests and window sills that also served as seats, were rendered only a little less chill and hard by the loose cushions or pads, covered with leather, linen, or woolen cloth, velvet, woven tapestry, or needlework, which were laid upon them. In England, it was not before Elizabethan times that "the fashion of cushioned chayres," as one contemporary wrote, began to be general. From then on through the following century, however, we may compare the development of upholstery to the increasing elaboration of costume by puffing, padding, and ornamentation. Rich silks and damasks brightened with gold threads were imported from Italy, and fringes, galloons, and nailheads added to their effect. English industries were encouraged to meet foreign competition, and the many Huguenot weavers who fled across the Channel after the revocation of the Edict of Nantes (1685) no doubt helped to make the last years of the century the great period of English textiles.

Furniture in the William and Mary style was padded with hair or wool and covered with velvet, mohair, damask, brocatelle, camlet (a smooth woolen material), tapestry, or needlework. Chairs with the typical caned backs and seats of the period (caning had been introduced into England with the Indo-Portuguese furniture of Catherine of Braganza, wife of Charles II) were provided with feather squabs or cushions covered with silk or velvet, all in the strong, bright colors dictated by the "Florentine" taste of the late 1600's. In the American colonies at about this time a wealthy householder, Major General Edward Gibbons of Boston, had ten yellow damask chairs as well as a number of velvet and damask cushions, while in the average comfortable house there was apparently no dearth of

woolen fabrics like says, serges, and tabbies to make durable furniture coverings, warm bed hangings, and curtains. The red perpetuana—a kind of worsted—mentioned frequently in old inventories sounds like a cheerful and practical choice.

In the new world as in the old, incalculable hours of patient needlework went into making beautiful furniture covers, rare examples of which still survive. Tent stitch on canvas, imitating woven tapestry in naturalistic bird and flower patterns, and flame stitch (*point d'Hongrie*) which produced zigzag bands of strong, bright color, were long popular. Turkey work, in which strands of wool were pulled through a canvas foundation, knotted, and sheared to approximate the effect of an Oriental pile carpet, was another favorite, to judge by colonial inventories. Linen embroidered with crewel wools in "tree of life" designs obviously inspired by the painted cot-

REPRODUCTION of an eighteenth-century silk damask in a traditional Italian pattern. *Scalamandré Silks. Photograph by George D. Cowdery.*

REPRODUCTION of an eighteenth-century silk damask "in the Chinese taste." *Scalamandré Silks. Photograph by George D. Cowdery.*

AMERICAN WING CHAIR (c. 1730-1740), upholstered in damask. *Collection of Mrs. Charles Hallam Keep.* **Left**

AMERICAN WING CHAIR (c. 1740), covered with needlework of the period. *Collection of Mrs. E. R. Warren.* **Right**

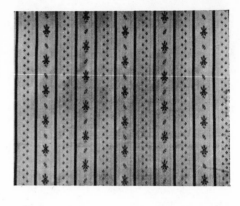

AMERICAN HEPPLEWHITE CHAIR *(c. 1785-1795)*, which is upholstered in contemporary striped satin.

NEW HAMPSHIRE ARMCHAIR in Sheraton style *(c. 1790-1800)*, covered in contemporary striped and flowered satin. *Metropolitan Museum.*

A MODERN STRIPED AND FLOWERED SATIN, suitable for use on Hepplewhite or Sheraton furniture. *Johnson and Faulkner. Photograph by George D. Cowdery.*

A MODERN BROCADE in a traditional late eighteenth-century French design, which could be used appropriately on Hepplewhite or Sheraton furniture. *Johnson and Faulkner. Photograph by George D. Cowdery.*

tons of India was used for upholstery as well as for bed and window hangings in matching sets.

Coming down to the middle of the century, we find that Chippendale, in his *Director,* advocates green haircloth or crimson damask for dining-room chairs, while he considers red morocco leather appropriate for all open-back chairs. In this period, chair seats are either removable or "stuffed over the rails" and finished with brass nails which are sometimes "done to imitate Fretwork," as Chippendale says. Velvets are still used, but damask is by far the most popular fabric for the upholstery of fine furniture. Needlework remains in fashion. Chippendale says that his "French" chairs, or chairs with upholstered backs and open arms, must be covered with "Tapestry panels or other needlework"—the word tapestry being used, as it often is today, for grospoint or petitpoint on canvas—and it appears that he supplied his clients with designs for the work. The plates of the *Director* suggest naturalistic bouquets of flowers surrounded by scrolls, *chinoiseries* with figures, or birds and flowering branches against a sketchy landscape. The work was done in a loosely twisted wool, used two strands to a needleful, or in wool or silk.

Red and green seem to have been the colors most appreciated by Chippendale and his contemporaries, with strong yellow and blue standing next in favor. References in eighteenth-century writings to "the red drawing room" or "the green saloon" may be taken quite literally, for in fashionable interiors the window curtains and furniture coverings were usually of the same stuff, which might also be stretched on the walls, while the rug and other accoutrements repeated the color. Crimson damask would have been a typical choice for a fine Chippendale room. The damask would be woven in one of the traditional Italian patterns, with large, wide-spreading forms of pomegranate, pineapple, rose, or palm leaf (motifs that go back to ancient Eastern sources) symmetrically disposed so that a line drawn down the middle of the piece would bisect the main unit of the design. Or, if the patron desired an interior "in the Chinese taste," a damask would be chosen to echo with fanciful *chinoiseries* the carved motifs of the furniture.

Later in the century, large-scale, formal patterns in textiles

give way to designs characterized by lightness and delicacy. Traditional French patterns, in which the floral motifs are arranged asymmetrically or along the undulating lines of trailing foliage, are preferred for furniture in the Hepplewhite and early Sheraton styles. Narrow stripes are popular, as often as not combined, entwined, or overlaid with flowers. Colors are light and gay, and gold and silver threads add to their bright effect. (Chairs with upholstered backs were sometimes provided with little extra flaps of the material which hung down the back and could be pulled up and over it to protect the delicate covering from face paint and hair powder.) Sheraton gives the first hint that the old fashion of using one color all through the room is breaking down in favor of what we would call a color scheme. "Blue and white, blue and black, very light blue, and yellow will harmonise," he writes in the *Encyclopedia.*

Brocaded silks and taffetas, though in high fashion, are not the only choice for upholstery. Hepplewhite says that mahogany side chairs "should have the seats of horsehair, plain, striped, or checquered, &c., at pleasure," or may have cane bottoms with cushions, the cases of which should be covered with the same as the curtains of the room. The "more elegant kind" of dining-room chairs may have seats of red or blue morocco leather, nailed to the frame with brass nails which are sometimes set in a scalloped pattern. Needlework is going out of style for furniture covering, but all through the 1700's, to judge from remains found on old furniture, a stout watered woolen rep, in red or green, is much used.

We may be sure that the prevailing English styles were followed as closely as might be in this country by the numerous upholsterers who advertised in early newspapers to "stuff"

AMERICAN WING CHAIR *(c. 1800),* covered with a contemporary English linen, copperplate printed in red in the *Apotheosis of Franklin* design. *Metropolitan Museum of Art.*

REPRODUCTION of a French linen, copperplate printed at Nantes in 1798, in a design called *Les Comédiens Ambulants. Brunschwig et Fils.*

chairs in "the genteelest and newest taste." We know from the lists of goods received by merchants of Boston, Philadelphia, and New York some of the materials that were being sold here. In Boston, in 1734, "For Present Money, Thomas Trowell, Sells Great Pennyworths of European Silks and Stuffs, as, Rich Moriello Tabbies, Florence Sattens, A blue Ground Brocade, English Damasks. . . ." *Chaneys, linceys,* and *Farrandines* were offered along with the more familiar damasks, serges, and velvets. Moreen, a stout woolen and cotton cloth which probably substituted for silk damask in more modest homes, was supplied by one merchant in black, blue, brown, Saxon green, pea green, yellow, crimson, garnet, pink, and purple. Portuguese and French products competed with English goods in our ports, while homespun, home-dyed woolens, cottons, and linens doubtless continued to fill many needs in the colonial home. Inventories of estates like those of Governor John Penn, whose gilt chairs and settees were upholstered in damask, or Mary Alexander of New York, who left her daughter "one dozen and four crimson Damask chairs and the Crimson damask window curtains . . . and yellow chairs . . . in the Blew and Gilt Leather room," give us an idea of the variety and rich abundance of upholstery textiles used in eighteenth-century America.

So far I have said little of the cotton and linen fabrics used for upholstery. Printed and painted cottons or "calicoes" were brought from India to England in the seventeenth century; Pepys bought his wife "a chint, that is a painted Indian calico, for to line her new study" in 1663. "Glazed chinces" and "India chints" were advertised in Boston in 1711 and 1712. Probably their importation was never discontinued. Cotton printing, which had been banned in England in 1721, was later allowed and encouraged, no doubt to compete with the thriving French industry, and after 1750 single-color prints, first in red or blue and then in brown, amaranth, purple, and snuff color, began to come from English looms. After the Revolution, prints like the *Apotheosis of Franklin* design illustrated were turned out especially for the American market. From France, where textile printing from engraved copper cylinders had been invented, the famous "toiles de Jouy," or "copperplate," as these printed linens were called in the advertisements, were imported in quantity. "Scotch goods" and "Irish goods" were also offered for sale early in the century; these probably included heavy linens.

Some cotton and linen was printed here before the Revolution, but the early output of the various enterprises recorded seems to have been mostly small-patterned dress goods. In

TWO CHINTZES, reproduced from old fragments that show the influence of the painted cottons of India. *Left, Ogden House,* by Brunschwig et Fils; *right, Les Épines,* by A. L. Diament.

AMERICAN ARMCHAIR *(c. 1805-1810)*, upholstered in contemporary damask of early nineteenth-century design. *Metropolitan Museum of Art.*

MODERN SATIN STRIPE, in an Empire design. *J. H. Thorp. Photograph by George D. Cowdery.*

the last quarter of the century, however, printed linens suitable for "chair bottoms" and bed furniture were offered by American printers. The distinctive blue and white dye-resist linens associated with Long Island and New Jersey, and the early American copper-plate cotton prints, usually with military or political subjects, are both prized by collectors. Domestic and imported "furniture check," in red and white, blue and white, green and white, and other colors, was used, especially for dining-room chairs and curtains, from early in the 1700's.

The change in furniture styles that came about the turn of the century naturally influenced fabric design. Plain satins, velvets, and leather set off the simple lines and dramatic decoration of late Sheraton and Empire furniture. Horsehair, which had been used since the mid-1700's, was now especially favored. Pattern in fabrics swung back to a rather stiff symmetry. Classic motifs—laurel wreaths, lyres, and columns—might be spotted regularly over a plain field, or arranged with medallions that enclosed a profile or trophy group. Stars, bees, crowns, and Egyptian motifs with Napoleonic associations were prominent. Broad stripes vied with strong, solid

colors in popularity. The printed cottons and linens used in bedrooms, however, might have neat, small-scale patterns that gave a fresh, light effect. A range of colors the eighteenth century had not dreamed of came into fashion. It is said that Napoleon always chose crimson for upholstery, while his Empress preferred the pastel tones, particularly light blue. The tradition accords with the taste of the period, which went now to strong tones of crimson, maroon, purple, gold, emerald green, and olive, now to the "off" shades of pale blue, mauve, yellow, green, or buff.

These notes may well end with a warning to those who have antique furniture to reupholster, that the best workmanship is none too good. Putting too much or too little padding on a chair seat, or losing the lines of a wing chair or sofa in the stuffing, will spoil the effect of the piece just as surely as covering it with an inappropriate fabric.

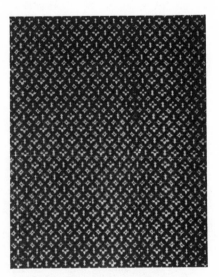

A MODERN CUT VELVET. *J. H. Thorp. Photograph by George D. Cowdery.*

AMERICAN EMPIRE SOFA *(c. 1820)*, covered in contemporary cut velvet. *Metropolitan Museum of Art.*

SLIPCOVERS OF PAST CENTURIES

By MARION DAY IVERSON

FAR FROM being a modern idea, the use of loose slipcovers for furniture has a long history. In 1611, an upholsterer named Singleton charged Lord Salisbury of Cranborne Manor, Wiltshire, for an armchair and stools of turkey work and "13 yds of yellow buckram for cases." From the expensive, delicate material of cotton or linen of the Middle Ages, buckram gradually developed into the coarse gummed fabric we know today, and references to both kinds are found in the seventeenth century. According to Roger de Felice, it was the custom in seventeenth-century France to protect seats "by means of loose covers of serge, or, in elegant interiors, of taffeta, morocco, even velvet or damask." It was an important matter of etiquette to know for whom the covers were to be removed, and for whom not.

That chair covers were used by America's early colonists is evidenced by seventeenth-century Massachusetts records. An inventory made in 1647 in the house of John Lowell of Newbury includes "1 Case for a chaire." In 1653 a wealthy Boston merchant, Captain William Tyng, had in his hall a miscellaneous assortment of chairs "all cased." The household goods of Thomas and Elizabeth Gwin of Boston included in 1669 "a dozen of chaires couered with blew . . . with Couers for chairs & Counterpaine."

One way covers may have been fastened is indicated by a William and Mary chair illustrated in Macquoid and Edwards' Dictionary of English Furniture (I, 220, Pl. XIII), which has what is believed to be the original upholstery of white taffeta and loose velvet cover with deep fringe. The cover has eyelet holes for attaching it to nails on the chair. Another method is suggested by items in bills sent to Lord Mansfield by William France in 1768 and 1770. To protect his three sofas upholstered in crimson damask there were "3 Serge Cases . . . of Crimson serge with silk strings." Two screens covered with the same damask had covers made of crimson serge finished with "Silk Ferret Tape." Chippendale also mentioned tape, which may have consisted of strings for tying on the covers, or may simply have been binding.

We cannot be certain that all chair covers mentioned separately were removable. In 1659, Harvard's first president, Henry Dunster, possessed "6 branch [embroidered] silke stolle covers and 3 such for chayres, 2 purple brancht silke covers for stooles & 2 such for great chayres." These might have referred to upholstery not then in use.

The word "case" seems to have meant either a slipcover or a cover for a loose seat cushion of an upholstered chair. The word "cover" sometimes referred to the upholstery itself and sometimes to loose covers.

Chippendale, Haig and Company used the words "cover" and "case" interchangeably, where today we would use "slipcover." Their 1772 bill for furnishing the new house of David Garrick, the famous actor, mentioned "covers" for twelve armchairs, "cases" for the bergères and sofa, "fine Crimson Serge Covers" for two bergères, and "fine Crimson Serge cases" for four armchairs. The green serge covers in his green drawing room protected silk damask upholstery of the same color. Chippendale also made cases of check—checked linen or cotton, often called "furniture check"—for "2 Chair Seats, a Cloath Chair, A Cushion & Library Stool . . . and to the Easy Chair" that he had just renovated. A large-pattern check, apparently a loose cover, appears on a chair in Love in a Village by Zoffany (1768).

Chair covers were mentioned in a letter written by Chippendale on May 7, 1773, to Sir Edward Knatchbull, who wanted four large bergères in addition to ten arm-

THE SQUIRE'S TEA, by Benjamin Wilson (1721-1788). Checked covers appear on several of the chairs. Newhouse Galleries.

JEALOUSY, THE RIVAL, by Thomas Rowlandson (1803), showing two slipcovers. Boston Public Library.

chairs previously ordered. Chippendale wrote that he would send Lady Knatchbull patterns for needlework for them that would "take some time in working . . . as the chairs can only at present be finished in Linnen. We should be glad to know what kind of Covers you would please to have for them. Serge is most commonly used but as the room is hung with India paper, perhaps you might Chuse some sort of Cotton—Suppose a green Stripe Cotton which at this is fashionable . . ."

They evidently took his advice, because when the furniture was shipped on May 19 the Chippendale establishment wrote Sir Edward that "The Chairs & Stools is stuffed in Canvas and loose Covers made out of Green Stripe Cotton, which will be a sort of finish at present & be very necessary when cover'd with needlework. . ."

For the dressing room at Harewood House, the Chippendale firm supplied chairs and sofas with green serge cases in 1773. "Fine Yellow Serge cases" for furniture upholstered in damask were made in 1775.

The Correspondence of Mary Granville (Mrs. Delaney) mentions chair covers on several occasions. On February 22, 1776, she was giving a birthday dinner at her London house in honor of the Duchess of Portland, and in advance of the occasion wrote to her niece, "I have put on all my birthday geer, new white satin, best covers on my chairs, and the best knotting furniture on my bed chamber with window curtains of the same." Two weeks later she wrote again: "I believe after all I must dunn you for your sprig'd chintz . . . for I have been obliged to add two more chairs in my drawing room, and want it to complete my set of covers, and I can't match it with anything the least like it."

Loose covers continued in use through the era of Hepplewhite and Sheraton. Hepplewhite's *Guide* tells us that "Japanned chairs should have cane bottoms, with linen or cotton cases over cushions to accord with the general hue of the chair." About easy chairs the *Guide* says, "they may be covered with leather, horsehair or have a linen case to fit over the canvas stuffing as is most usual."

Numerous advertisements in eighteenth-century American newspapers mention chair covers and cases, and it

ELIZABETH FENIMORE COOPER by an unknown artist *(1816)*. Note the slipcover on the sofa. *New York State Historical Assn.*

is possible to identify removable covers in a few of them. One of the earliest is that of Walter Rowland in the *South Carolina Gazette,* November 21, 1741. He performed "all kinds of upholsterer's work, in the best and newest manner . . . chairs stuff covered, tight or loose cases for ditto." Richard Bird, upholsterer, newly arrived in Charleston from London, let his several accomplishments be known in the *South Carolina Gazette* of September 11, 1762. Among them was "easy chairs covered and nailed or loose cases for washing. . ." In the next week's issue of the same paper, Rebecca Weyman informed her friends and customers that she made "easy chair cases for washing."

In 1765 an upholsterer named John Mason opened a shop in Charleston. According to his price list, he charged three times as much for making a cover for an easy chair as he did for a French chair (with open arms). Two years later, when he had moved to Philadelphia, Mason again advertised his prices. He claimed that he had reduced them, but his charge for an easy chair cover was twice what it had been in Charleston. The item "Making an easy chair" is followed by "Making a cover for ditto," but we cannot be sure that the covers were removable.

At Boston in 1746 there was offered for sale at vendue in the house of Charles Paxton, Esq., "Eight Walnut Tree Chairs, stuft Back and Seats covered with the same Damask [crimson], Eight crimson Cases for ditto, one easy Chair and Cushion, same Damask, and a Case for ditto. . . . At another Boston sale two years later, china silk and damask had reversed their roles. The advertisement reads "one Easy Chair yellow China with a green Damask Cover."

The *New York Gazette and Weekly Mercury* carried an announcement on August 26, 1776, that Elizabeth Evans had returned to the city and was ready to continue her upholstery work, "such as . . . wrought quilts, chair, sopha and settee cases."

The correspondence of George Washington contains two references to loose chair covers. When he was a twenty-five-year-old bachelor serving in the French and Indian War, he ordered furniture from England for Mount Vernon, which he had recently inherited. The ship *Salley* arrived in August 1757, bringing complete furnishings for the bedroom purchased for him at a London auction. Window and bed curtains and chair seats were all of yellow silk and worsted damask. Included among the furniture was "A Mahogany easy Chair, on Casters covered with ditto and a Check Case." After the General returned to Mount Vernon following the Revolution, he asked his nephew, in 1783, to inquire "of some of the best Cabinet-makers at what price, and in what time, two dozen strong, neat and plain, but fashionable, Table Chairs (I mean chairs for a dining room) could be had; with strong canvas bottoms to receive a loose covering of check, or worsted . . ."

It is clear that in the past slipcovers were not uncommon. Sometimes they were used to give a uniform appearance to a variety of chairs, sofas, and stools. They served to bring an air of informality to a room. Most generally they were used to protect handsome upholstery, but they also concealed upholstery that was shabby. It follows that even in the most carefully assembled "period rooms" today, slipcovers may be provided for the upholstered furniture, if they are chosen with an eye to appropriate color, fabric, and style.

FABRICS IN EARLY AMERICA

Textiles at the Forum

By FRANCO SCALAMANDRÉ

Members of the 1949 Antiques and Decorations Forum at Williamsburg will long remember Franco Scalamandré's genial account of a career, begun in his native Italy, which has made him one of our leading manufacturers of decorative textiles, with the interesting specialty of reproducing antique fabrics for historic restorations. They will remember, too, his generosity in letting his audience see and handle the sumptuous lengths of antique and reproduction fabrics he brought with him from his Museum of Textiles in New York. We present here excerpts from Mr. Scalamandré's informal and informative talk.

IF OLD FABRICS ARE SCARCE TODAY, it is because, throughout the ages, people have always wanted to take them away. In all the successive invasions of Europe—by the Goths, the Moors, and so on—textiles were first among the things the invaders carried off. My idea, in setting up my Museum of Textiles, was to preserve some of these old fabrics to show what was done in different countries in the past.

It is with deep feeling that I caution you about using antique fabrics in your home. American use today is so hard on them! You have to have them dry-cleaned, and after a few trips to the cleaner they are gone. If you buy antique furniture that still has some of its original covering, save that old fabric But have it put on the back of your chair or sofa, where it will be protected. . . .

Were the fabrics of the past better than those we can make today? The quality of a fabric depends, first of all, on the yarn of which it is woven. Silk has always been considered the most desirable material for decorative fabrics. In the eighteenth century, in Italy, France, and England, the new wealth and the new feeling of power which it brought with it increased the demand for silk—silk clothing and silken fabrics to furnish the beautiful, formal houses being built in the new style introduced in the sixteenth century by Palladio.

Architects and artists played an important part in the creation of these fabrics, guiding the weavers in their choice of motifs and colors. But in translating the artist's drawing into a pattern, and in drafting and setting up the loom, the weaver made changes of his own. That is true today. Weavers are no different. Jacquard designs will continue to change from production to production.

The principle of the loom also remains unchanged. There is a set of warp threads and a filler thread, "pick," or weft that crosses them. In the early years of the nineteenth century, the Jacquard method was introduced whereby strips of cardboard were intricately perforated, in connection with rods and cords, regulating the motion of the warp threads. In earlier times, this work had been done by hand, and if, as it often happened, the boy who stood beside the loom dozed off and failed to pull the cord at the right time, the design would be stretched out of shape at that point. In reproducing old fabrics we sometimes let a catch cord hold up the action of the Jacquard mechanism and elongate the design in places to simulate this effect. . . .

We use the same material today that they used in the eighteenth century for fine decorative fabrics—silk. There are interesting differences between the silks of different countries. Japanese silk, for instance, has impurities and you are apt to get unevenness with it. Chinese silk is the best in the world. Italian silk has the fewest impurities; it is 99% pure. Chinese silk is only 96% to 98% pure, but it is better because it does not fuzz. When you want to get a feeling of age, you use Italian silk.

Silk has never been produced on a large scale in America. They tried it in Virginia, but they lost about five million dollars. Silk worms are very hard animals to raise. They have to be fed for seven weeks on the leaves of a certain kind of mulberry trees. If you have two hundred trees, you can hope to produce about five pounds of silk. You do all the work of tending the trees and feeding the worms, and you get cocoons. Large ones are males, small ones females. Then comes the task of reeling the silk from the cocoon, which still contains the dead body of the worm. It is hard work, and the smell is most unpleasant. Next, you must select the eggs for mating to raise a new generation. . . . You will probably decide it is better to buy your silk than to go through all this, even though today silk costs $5.00 a pound as compared to $1.00 before the war.

The best silk yarn is called organzine. It is made of the long, unbroken length of the filament reeled from the cocoon, twisted more or less tightly for further strength. Leonardo da Vinci invented a method of twisting silk in the fifteenth century. The broken strands from the inner and outer part of the cocoon are spun like cotton to make the yarn called *bourrette*. It often happens that two silk worms spin themselves together into the same cocoon, so that the silk cannot be reeled off evenly. This gives the knotted yarn called *doppioni* (from *doppio,* double) used for rough-textured fabrics. Another kind of silk with a different luster is taken from wild or—may I say it?—bastard cocoons.

In early times, when silk was colored with animal dyes, the unevenness of the dyeing sometimes gave the fabric a horizontally striped appearance. We often imitate this effect in reproducing old textiles. Today, silk is boiled from a half to three quarters of an hour in olive-oil soap and water before being dyed, but old fabrics were dyed "in the raw" without boiling. Silk dyed this way is protected for centuries. The fabrics which we made for Colonial Williamsburg eighteen years ago were dyed in the raw and are still as good as new.

Except for brocade with a raised effect—*spolinato*—we are able to reproduce with our power machinery any of the hand-loomed fabrics of the eighteenth century. Among the old fabrics at Colonial Williamsburg which we have duplicated are: taffeta; damask (in Italy a heavy damask was used on the walls for air conditioning because it absorbed dampness in the winter and gave it back in the hot weather); lampas, a heavy, large-patterned fabric with two warps and two wefts, showing two definite colors; and brocatelle, a double cloth like lampas with a cotton or linen filler. Since the eighteenth-century hand looms could make only narrow fabrics, we have woven the silks for Williamsburg in 22-inch widths.

A glossary of French silks

FRANCE WAS A LATE-COMER among the silk-producing countries. There were guilds of silk weavers in Paris and Rouen in the thirteenth century, but even at that early date the looms of Palermo, in Sicily, had long been producing sumptuous silk fabrics in which Near Eastern and Chinese motifs were adapted to the Occidental taste. From the beginning of the Middle Ages Italy and Moorish Spain supplied rich brocades and velvets to traders from every part of Europe. It was to compete with these costly imports that Henry IV encouraged the culture of the silkworm—and, necessarily, the planting of mulberry trees throughout France—and set up *ateliers* for weaving the silk in Paris. Neither these last, nor the enterprises already in existence at Lyons and Tours, however, were able to make much headway against the flow of foreign silk until the reign of Louis XIV and the dawn of that "splendid century" in which France became the arbiter of elegance for all Europe, and her court an insatiable market for articles of luxury.

Then, stimulated by patronage at once lavish and demanding, and commanding technical and artistic skills of the first order, the French industry rose to a dominating position. The role of the designer, as distinct from that of the artisan who improvised or copied a design, was well defined in France before the eighteenth century began; Philippe de La Salle was the greatest of the many talented designers who worked at Lyons. French technicians like La Salle himself, Dangon, and Jacquard made important contributions to the development of the loom. French textiles of the late 1600's through the mid-nineteenth century reached a level of excellence that still inspires the industry today.

The glossary of French silks presented here is based on the article *Toute la Soierie Française* published in the French periodical *Connaissance des Arts* for December 1958, and we are indebted to the same source for the illustrations in black and white and in color. Many French terms, such as chenille, appliqué, and others, have passed into English usage and so are not italicized here. In other cases, the French equivalents are given in italics following the English terms. When the French term is used by students for lack of an adequate English word, it stands alone here. *The Weaves of Hand-Loom Fabrics*, by Nancy Andrews Reath, was followed in the choice of English terms.

—RUTH DAVIDSON

Appliqué. Motif or element of a design cut out of one fabric and applied on another, which serves as a background for the design. The appliqué motif, usually plain satin, is fixed in place by an embroidery stitch or by a cording that outlines it in relief. This technique makes it possible to decorate a silk textile with varied motifs that can be given added relief by a stuffing of cotton or other material pushed into the space between the appliqué motif and the ground. It was used—especially for the embellishment of draperies, since it

Detail from a Louis XIV silk fabric with appliqué chinoiserie decoration. Some of the appliqué motifs are lightly stuffed out to give them further relief.

was not practical for furniture covers—from the Renaissance to the end of the reign of Louis XIV.

Bony, Jean François (1760-1828). Designer and painter. A pupil of Philippe de La Salle employed in the Lyons factory, Bony owes his fame especially to the order he carried out for the coronation robe of the Empress Josephine and the upholstery for the furniture of Malmaison, the Empress' chateau outside Paris. The Textile Museum at Lyons preserves some of Bony's water-color drawings for textiles as well as actual silk textiles designed by him.

Bouclé. The French word means looped; in the weaving of old *bouclés* loops of metal were introduced into the fabric and pulled up so as to make a design in relief on the right side of the fabric. This technique of looped brocading was used only for velvet and brocatelle, as a fairly thick fabric was required to support the weight of the metal. It was fashionable in Italy and Spain from the fifteenth to the end of the sixteenth century, when it went out of use because of its excessive cost.

Flowered brocade,
Louis XIV period,
showing face and back
(right and wrong sides).

Brocade. According to Webster, a brocaded (*broché*) fabric. Since any fabric may be enriched in this way, however, it is well to remember that "brocade" does not serve to classify a fabric for the student.

Brocading (*brochage*). The creation of polychrome designs in slight relief on fabric of any weave by introducing extra weft threads which are used only where needed to form the design and not carried across the whole width of the fabric. These extra weft threads, to explain it another way, are interwoven with the warp threads only in small areas and are not found elsewhere in the fabric. The French word is derived from *broche*, a pointed bobbin.

Brocart. Old term for figure-woven silk fabrics incorporating gold or silver threads. The inventory of Cardinal Richelieu listed in 1653 furnishings for a bed "in silver *brocart* with crimson and white figures."

Brocatelle. The word is derived from *brocart*, which in turn comes from an Italian word of the same meaning, and designates a large and not very well-defined group of fabrics similar to lampas. Typical examples have patterns in slight relief on a satin ground; or the raised design may be satin. Their characteristic effect is obtained by the use of an extra weft or wefts, one of which is linen. (The linen weft does not show on the surface.) Used for wall hangings and the decoration of churches, brocatelle was also strong enough for furniture covers. During the Renaissance brocatelles were woven with gold threads and brocaded. The inventory of the royal furniture in 1673 illustrates their variety: "Six sets of brocatelle wall hangings, two with white grounds, two with golden yellow [*aurore*] ground, one with green ground, one with yellow and red ground."

Cannelé. Silk fabric in parts of which horizontal ribbing is simulated by short floats of warp threads. (A float is a thread that runs free for a short distance without being interwoven.) Such fabrics, sometimes enriched with gold threads, were very popular in the eighteenth century. In *cannetillé* the same weave was used for the ground, giving an effect like that of some kinds of basketwork. *Côtelé* describes a similar fabric with lengthwise ribbing.

Brocatelles: at left, *bouché,* sixteenth century; at right, brocaded, 1846.

Brocaded *cannelé,* Louis XV period.

Design in chenille on a twill ground, eighteenth century.

Catch-cord (*cordeline*). Silk, linen, or metal thread used to reinforce the selvages. Its presence facilitates describing and identifying old fabrics, when the selvages have not been cut off; the selvages of most modern fabrics have no *cordelines*.

Chenille. Thick silk thread with a short pile or nap, used in brocading or embroidery to give the effect of velvet in small areas. The word means caterpillar in French.

Chiné. Polychrome effect obtained by dyeing the threads, either warp or weft, irregularly before weaving. As the French name shows, this ancient technique was thought to have come from the Orient. *Chiné à la branche* describes silks with designs carried out on the warp threads before weaving. This method of decoration was not used in France before the time of Louis XV. Warp printing gives much the same effect today.

Damask (*damas*). A reversible solid-color fabric with a woven design that appears mat on a glossy ground on the face, and glossy on a mat ground on the back of the fabric. At first such effects were achieved with a single set of warp threads and a single set of weft threads, but damask has since been woven with extra warps and wefts and also brocaded. The name indicates its supposed origin in Damascus. Damask has been made in France since the thirteenth century; inventories of the seventeenth and eighteenth centuries list numerous varieties. Its chief uses were for wall hangings, curtains, and furniture covers.

Drugget (*droguet*). Eighteenth-century figure-woven silk fabric with a small-scale diaper pattern formed by both warp and weft threads. Widely used for men's and women's clothing, druggets also served as table and bed covers. Louis XVI fabrics with "drugget decoration" are also known.

Dyes (*teintures*). A key to identifying old fabrics. Before the nineteenth century only animal and vegetable dyes were used in France. Chemical analysis of a dyed silk thread will tell whether these or the inorganic dye substances of a later period were used to color it.

Faille. A plain cloth in which the weft threads, being much thicker than those of the warp, create a corded or ribbed effect.

Faults (*points échappés*). Faults or flaws in the weaving show up irregularly in old, hand-woven fabrics, while in textiles from modern power looms they are repeated at regular intervals.

Figure-woven (*façonné*). In textiles so described the decorative pattern is produced by the interplay of warp and weft threads, intersecting each other irregularly. Thus damasks and brocades are figure-woven; velvet may be plain or, as we sometimes say in English, fancy. The inventory of Gabrielle d'Estries in 1599 mentions a *"velours façonné de petits carreaux* [small checks]."

Genoese velvets. Old name for a *ciselé* velvet on a satin ground with large branching designs. Made originally in Genoa, these velvets were imitated in France at Lyons, Tours, and Saint-Maur from the beginning of the seventeenth century.

Gold. Gold has been used in weaving from early times. It was especially popular in the seventeenth century, and this may explain why relatively few textiles of that period survive: presumably many were burned to recover the metal. In some cases thin strips of pure gold were wound around a core of silk or linen thread; in others, pure gold was employed in wide or narrow strips.

Gourgouran. Any one of various Indian silk fabrics, either plain-colored or striped, used in the eighteenth century for curtains. These Indian silks were imitated in France.

Grégoire, Gaspard (1751-1846). Textile painter who perfected a method of decorating velvet by painting directly on the warp threads before the material was woven, thus obtaining an unusual effect of transparency. His technique was not, as has often been said, a secret, but the greatest skill and patience were required to prevent the distortion of the painted design when the fabric was subsequently woven.

Damask: face and back.

Genoese velvet.

Brocaded lampas,
Louis XV period.

Silk damask with chinoiserie design
in the style of Pillement.

Examples of *velours Grégoire* rarely measure more than twelve inches either way. They depict religious scenes after Raphael, flowers, still-life compositions, and portraits of famous men. The largest collection of Grégoire's work is preserved in the Textile Museum in Lyons. The Museum of Decorative Arts in Paris and the museums of Marseilles and Aix-en-Provence also have fine examples.

Gros de Tours. A thick, durable, corded cloth produced in quantity at Tours and popular for furniture covers in the seventeenth and eighteenth centuries. This fabric was also used for drapery and wall hangings and was often embroidered. The report on the royal furniture in 1673 mentions a set of furniture "in white *gros de Tours* sprigged with gold embroidery and flowers."

Identifying old fabrics. Note especially the width of the piece and the character of the selvages; the coloring, which depends on the dyes used (the wrong side often shows the original shades); and the presence of certain irregularities of weaving that are much rarer in fabrics woven on power looms.

Jacquard, Joseph-Marie (1752-1834). Inventor of a device (technically, an automatic selective shedding machine) that eliminated the need for a draw-boy to pull up the various combinations of warp threads as the weaving progressed, making it possible for the weaver himself to "work" the whole loom, more rapidly, by means of two treadles. This naturally brought down the cost of manufacturing figure-woven fabrics and made them more widely available. Jacquard demonstrated his invention at the Paris International Exhibition in 1800; by 1812 it had been fitted to eighteen thousand looms in Lyons. Later it was adapted to fast-running power looms.

Jardinière. Multicolored velvet with floral designs, most often on a light-color satin ground. The name suggests the flower-garden effect of many of these textiles, which were widely used in the seventeenth and eighteenth centuries.

Lamé. Textile woven with gold, silver, or other metal threads.

Lampas. A fancy compound satin, that is, a fabric of satin weave with one or more extra warps or wefts or both that are used to make a pattern. Lampas has been described as

looking like a two-color damask except that it is not reversible; its back is plain and mat. Many of the most splendid antique textiles belong to this general category. Such fabrics can be further enriched by brocading or by the use of gold and silver threads. Heavy and durable, lampas has been used since the seventeenth century for furnishing. Included in the sale of the château of Versailles was a "set of furniture in blue and white lampas . . . consisting of a large sofa, a *tête-à-tête*, a *bergère*, a small desk armchair . . . with six window curtains of the same lampas and nine similar draperies with fringes, tassels, and cords."

La Salle, Philippe de (1723-1805). The greatest figure in the history of silk weaving in France. A painter who studied with Boucher in Paris, he was also a skillful technician and made various improvements in the loom of his day. He was a designer, a weaver, and, in short, a master of the whole process by which a silk textile is created. He worked for the courts of France, Spain, and Russia, and carried out important orders for the empress Catherine II. His work is characterized by a very personal style; the compositions in which this talented painter of flowers and animals combines both realistic and conventional elements have never been surpassed. La Salle seems not to have woven velvets, but he often used chenille to give the effect of velvet in his silk textiles. He sometimes brought out parts of the design by a skillful use of black weft threads, but he rarely used gold or silver. He usually employed each color in three shades, to simulate the effect of light, shadow, and half-light. The Textile Museum in Lyons has not only a remarkable collection of silks by Philippe de La Salle but most of the artist's designs for these works.

Lyons (*Lyon*). Capital of the French silk-weaving industry, situated on the Rhône and Saône rivers not far from where Switzerland seems to bulge into the eastern side of France. The city had been an active center of the textile trade for nearly a century when Louis XI decided to establish silk looms there in 1446. The new industry grew slowly, and it was only around 1530 that Lyons began to attract enough skilled labor to compete with Italy. Colbert, the minister of Louis XIV, by regulating and encouraging the industry in the seventeenth century, gave it the impetus that eventually made Lyons the silk capital of the world. The city's textile museum (*Musée Historique des Tissus*) has one of the

45

richest collections of silk textiles and designs for silk textiles in existence.

Moiré. A close-ribbed silk fabric the surface of which has been given a characteristic watered effect by calendering, that is, by passing two pieces of the finished fabric face to face between metal cylinders, so that the threads of one piece compress those of the other; or, sometimes, by the use of engraved cylinders that impress the design on the face of the fabric. Walls covered with moiré were very fashionable in the eighteenth century, as were beds covered with this fabric. Moiré was also widely used in furnishing during the Empire and Restoration periods.

Painted silks (*soierie peinte*). Silk textiles decorated by painting (after being woven) were produced, though only rarely, in the reigns of Louis XV and Louis XVI.

Pillement, Jean Baptiste (1728-1801). Painter, native of Lyons. Pillement was one of the artists who did most to make chinoiserie fashionable. He furnished numerous designs for silk textiles.

Salembier, Henri (c. 1753-1820). French ornamental painter and textile designer. The neoclassical motifs of the Louis XVI style—urns, arabesques, cartouches, and scrolling branches—appear frequently in Salembier's designs for textiles.

Satin. Silk fabric with a smooth, glossy surface and mat back. First woven in the Orient and then in India, satin has been made in France since the fourteenth century. In both French and English the word also denotes one of the basic weaves of hand-loomed fabrics.

Selvages (*lisières*). The lateral woven borders of a piece of cloth, which finish the edge, preventing raveling, and also serve to hold the piece on the loom during weaving. Selvages aid in dating old fabrics because they differ from one period to another. In the Middle Ages a simple cord took the place of a selvage. In the fifteenth century the typical selvage was green and about three-quarters of an inch wide; it remained wide throughout the following century. In the 1600's selvages were in two colors—often green and white—and about three-eighths of an inch wide. Some Lyons velvets had a thread of silver or gold in the selvage. Since the eighteenth century, selvages have tended to be narrower. (See **Catchcords.**)

Silk. A fine lustrous filament spun by the silkworm (*bombyx mori*) in making its cocoon. An average of six hundred yards of silk can be reeled from each cocoon. Silk was cultivated three thousand years before Christ in the Orient, and Europe imported much of its supply from there until the sixteenth century. Some of the Near Eastern countries were also important sources of silk from early in the Christian era.

Silver. Silver was used like gold in weaving from the fourteenth century on; it is frequently seen in antique brocaded fabrics. However, since silver tarnishes and blackens, it was replaced in the 1800's by silvered copper. To establish the age of a silver thread, rub it against a rough surface; if copper appears, the thread, and hence the fabric of which it is a part, are post-eighteenth-century.

Stamping (*gaufrage*). Technique that reproduces a design in slight relief on the surface of a fabric by pressure. Velvet lends itself particularly well to this method of decoration, in which the length of material is passed between two heated metal cylinders, one having a design in relief, the other, the same design in intaglio. Stamped leathers and papers, as well as stamped textiles, were used in decoration from the seventeenth century.

Taffeta (*taffetas*). A tightly-woven silk textile having no right or wrong side. In French, *taffetas* also denotes the simple cloth weave. Taffeta can be brocaded or woven of several colors. In July 1699 the *Mercure de France* reported, "The most fashionable fabrics are the taffetas called perspective taffetas because they have stripes in diminishing sizes."

Tapestry. The Beauvais manufactory wove some all-silk tapestries during the eighteenth century. Silk was also used there to bring out details of the design, as it was in needlework.

Tours. Capital of the old province of Touraine, on the Loire River. Louis XI brought Italian silkworkers to the town in 1470, and until the revocation of the Edict of Nantes in 1685 numerous looms were in use there. Tours still manufactures silk.

Velvet (*velours*). Fabric with a close, standing pile on the face or right side. Velvets are woven with one or more extra warps. These supplementary warp threads pass over metal rods that pull them up into loops. A knife may then be drawn along a groove in the rod, cutting each loop open so as to make two small tufts. The resulting dense, all-over pile characterizes a solid-cut velvet. If the rods are simply withdrawn, leaving the standing loops, an uncut velvet (*velours épinglé* or *frisé*) is produced. In *ciselé* velvet, some of the loops are cut and some uncut, carrying out a design. (See also **Stamping, Genoese velvet, Grégoire, Jardinière.**)

Warp (*chaîne*). The lengthwise threads that run from one end to the other of a piece of cloth and are intersected by the weft threads that run crosswise from edge to edge.

Weave (*armure*). The arrangement, relative to each other, of the threads of the warp and weft. The three principal weaves of hand-loomed fabrics are cloth (*taffetas*), in which the warp and weft threads pass alternately over and under each other, one by one; twill (*sergé*), in which series of regularly recurrent warp threads pass in echelon under one and over two or more weft threads, producing diagonal ribs or stepped patterns; and satin, in which each warp thread passes under one and over three to five weft threads, concealing the weft and producing a smooth surface on the face of

Ciselé velvet on a satin ground, Louis XV period.

Stamped velvet with plume design, Louis XV period.

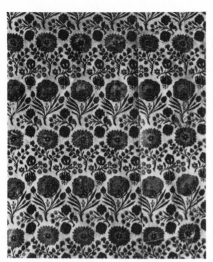

Louis XIII velvet with satin ground.

Louis XIV damask.

Silk textile by Philippe de La Salle employing chenille for the design; Louis XV period.

Directoire velvet with neoclassical design.

Lampas made for Versailles, Empire period.

Brocaded silk, Restoration period (1814-1830).

Ciselé velvet, Second Empire (1852-1870).

the fabric. It is the weave that, basically, differentiates one fabric from another.

Weft (*trame*). The threads that run across the woven textile from selvage to selvage. In weaving the weft threads are carried back and forth by the shuttle, passing under or over the warp threads as the weave requires.

Width (*largeur;* also *lé*). Dimension of a piece of woven cloth from one selvage to the other, including the selvages. This may be an indication of the age of a textile. In France, after 1666, a width of 21¼ inches was common and most fine eighteenth-century French silk textiles are found in this width, though certain silks by Philippe de La Salle were woven in exceptional widths of 27½ to 31½ inches, according to the design. Eighteenth-century Italian and Spanish silks were usually about 20½ inches wide.

47

Woolen window curtains

BY ANNA BRIGHTMAN

—luxury in colonial Boston and Salem

BY MID-EIGHTEENTH CENTURY the few wealthy New Englanders who hung elaborate curtains at the windows generally chose handsome wool fabrics which resembled fine silks. They called these textiles calamanco, camlet, "china" or cheyney, and harrateen—fashionable names that came and went with the years. These wools were watered, calendered, waved or moiréed, stamped or figured, and brocaded, to look like elegant silk fabrics. The eighteenth-century wool textiles illustrated here show patterns and weaves normally associated with French and English silk satins, taffetas, damasks, and brocades. You can think of many restored historic houses where luxurious silk textiles of similar designs have been used for authentic draperies. Now research is beginning to reveal that, although these hangings may re-create the general tone of colonial decoration, historical accuracy demands that such curtains be wool in New England mansions of the mid-eighteenth century.

In a check of over twenty-eight hundred estate inventories for the Boston and Salem areas during the first half of the eighteenth century not a single listing of silk window curtains was found. By contrast, mention of costly wool textiles became increasingly frequent as the century wore on. Thus it seems apparent that such wools were the luxury material for window curtains in mid-century New England homes.

Peter Faneuil evidently had the ultimate in fashionable furnishings in his Boston mansion house. The 1743 inventory of his estate lists two sets of matching harrateen bed and window curtains with material enough for a third; matching yellow mohair bed, chairs, and window curtains; a chintz bed and china window curtains. Notably, two of the fabrics used for Faneuil's window curtains—china and harrateen—were wool textiles of English origin, and mohair must be regarded as a similar fiber in the animal-hair family.

In ANTIQUES for August 1964 (p. 184) I reported that my survey of the household inventories of colonial Boston and Salem for three decades, 1700-1710, 1720-1730, 1740-1750, revealed that window curtains were not in common use at that time. These inventories furnish a valuable documentation of the fabrics used for window curtains by those colonists who did have them. Twelve textiles were recorded by a fabric name or specific fiber (see tabulated list). In addition, "plad," "printed," and "stript" window curtains were inventoried. Advertisements in the Boston *News-Letter* and the Boston *Gazette* through 1750 add calamanco and damask window curtains to the list.

Prior to 1740 calico and linen were the textiles used most often for window curtains at all economic levels. Camlet, cheyney (often called "china"), and harrateen, which were imported wool fabrics, increased in popularity at mid-century, particularly at the upper economic level. Over half of the inventory listings of these expensive wool fabrics are in estates valued at over £5,000, or the top ten per cent, while calico and linen are the main fabrics listed in estates with a valuation below £1,000.

Fig. 1. This scarlet waved camlet, used for hangings in the original (1747) Meeting House of the South Parish, Ipswich, Massachusetts, has crosswise grain and distinct moiré pattern. *Ipswich Historical Society.*

Fig. 2. Crimson stamped wool corresponding to eighteenth-century descriptions of figured camlet. Here the background areas have been stamped so the pattern is defined by a contrast of the dull surface against a highly glazed background. The large (over 39 inches) baroque pattern creates a handsome furnishing fabric. *Cooper Union Museum.*

A similar popularity of wool fabrics for bed curtains is clearly established by Abbott Lowell Cummings' survey of household inventories presented in his book *Bed Hangings* (1961). Between 1730 and 1740 cheyney and camlet accounted for one third of the bed hangings listed in the estate inventories of Suffolk County (Boston), Massachusetts, and advertisements in the Boston newspapers. Two decades later over half the bed curtains inventoried were cheyney or harrateen. Although a greater variety of textiles was used for bed hangings than for window curtains, the use of fine wools is common to both at mid-century.

Hazel Cummin's textile research undertaken at the time of the restoration of Stratford Hall, the Lee mansion in Virginia, revealed that a number of the textiles listed in early records were wool. Her search of eighteenth-century dictionaries and encyclopedias was a significant contribution toward the interpretation of early textiles terms. Her identification of calamanco (ANTIQUES, April 1941, p. 182), camlet (ANTIQUES, December 1942, p. 309), and moreen (ANTIQUES, December 1940, p. 286) as wool fabrics led her to conclude that wool textiles were important in the furnishing of colonial homes.

Not all eighteenth-century textiles listed in the Boston and Salem inventories are easily identi-fied. A few fabric names which were in common use at the time have disappeared without a trace. In his *Encyclopédie*, Diderot commented concerning the manufacture of wool that "one could fill a hundred pages with the names which are given to fabrics of the same kind, and which differ only in their place of manufacture."

All the available evidence indicates that calamanco, camlet, cheyney, and harrateen were luxurious and handsome imported wool fabrics. The eighteenth-century dictionary definitions, their use in colonial estates with a high evaluation, the value placed on the curtains themselves, and the surviving fragments support a picture of richness and elegance. As domestic wools were coarse and not suited to fine spinning, the colonists had to rely on imports for fine wool furnishings.

Lengthy descriptions of camlet appear in eighteenth-century dictionaries and encyclopedias by Savary, Chambers, Postlethwayt, and Diderot. Originally made of goat's hair, camlet was introduced from Persia and known in Europe from the time of the Crusades. Eighteenth-century camlets were generally made of wool, although silk or mohair was sometimes combined with the wool and occasionally the warp yarn was linen. Camlets generally had a weft grain or ribbing. This characteristic was so well recognized, Mrs.

Fig. 3. Harrateen or moreen bed curtain, c. 1750-1775, of a crimson wool which has been watered, waved, and figured. *Essex Institute.*

Cummin pointed out, ". . . that in France any surface having a crosswise rib was said to be *cameloté*; in England a waved or watered design was 'chambletted'; and coarser camlets were *grosgrains* or *grograms* in every European language."

The patterning of camlets by watering, waving, and figuring is described by Savary, Chambers, and Postlethwayt. Watered camlets were treated with a solution which gave the wool a smooth and lustrous finish when it was passed under a hot-press or calender. Waved camlets were those on which waves or a moiré effect were impressed by means of a calender (Fig. 1). Figured camlets were stamped by hot molds or rollers so that the designs appeared as shiny or glazed surfaces contrasting with the rougher wool surface (Fig. 2). The shading in these stamped figures is very similar to the two-tone effect in woven damask patterns. In fact, from a short distance it is sometimes difficult to tell whether the design of a figured wool is stamped or woven.

The use of camlet window curtains in the homes of such prominent and prosperous colonists as John Boydell and Nathaniel Cunningham confirms the impression that this was a fashionable fabric in the first half of the eighteenth century. Cunningham had "1 Sett Green Camblet Window Curtains, £15" in his "Great Parlor" and

another set at £10 in the "Great Chamber first floor" when he died in 1749. These were obviously the two most important rooms in the house as the furnishings inventoried here are extensive and costly.

Harrateen is not listed in eighteenth-century dictionaries. The identification of this fabric as an English wool moiré made in Norwich is due to the discovery of the Holker manuscript volume of English textiles (c. 1750) by Florence M. Montgomery, associate curator of textiles at the Henry Francis du Pont Winterthur Museum. Four swatches of calendered wools in this volume are labeled *harrateen*. All four are plain-weave, crosswise-ribbed fabrics with a waved, or moiré, pattern. One of the swatches has a figured vermiculated pattern in addition to the moiré. This figured and waved pattern closely resembles the background patterning of the wool bed curtain fragment shown in Figure 3. Harrateen is also described as "flowered" in eighteenth-century colonial inventories and letters. This may designate stamped patterns similar to that of Figure 3. The fabric shown in Figure 1 resembles two of the Holker swatches of harrateen. From the Holker descriptions it is apparent that harrateens were watered, waved, and figured in the manner of camlets. In fact, harrateen may well have been a fashion name for certain types of camlet.

Harrateen was one of the newest fabrics of the mid-eighteenth century. It was first advertised in the Boston *Gazette* in 1737. Between 1740 and 1750 harrateen is listed for window curtains only in the estates of Peter Faneuil and John Dennie. By the 1760's it appears more frequently in estate inventories, indicating that its popularity had grown in the preceding decades, and its continuing vogue is revealed in advertisements in the Boston newspapers.

Later generations called similar fabrics by the name moreen. This term was apparently not used in the Boston and Salem areas until 1770, although it appears at mid-century and earlier in the advertisements and records of Virginia and South Carolina.

Cheyney or "china" probably was another in the group of woolens with a crosswise grain or rib which lent itself to calendering and figuring. It is variously described in eighteenth-century inventories as watered, striped, or flowered. In the *Complete English Tradesman* (1732) Defoe simply lists "cheny" as one of the English woolen manufactures made in several places and in considerable quantity.

The exact distinctions made among camlet, harrateen, and cheyney in the eighteenth century are impossible to trace at this time. Abbott Cummings concluded that camlet was "a generic group which includes cheyney, harrateen and moreen as somewhat coarser all wool versions of the same fabric." In Peter Faneuil's inventory of 1744 both china and harrateen window curtains are listed. Fashion alone does not account for the differences in terminology.

Hazel Cummin concluded that calamanco be-

TEXTILES USED FOR WINDOW CURTAINS, 1700-1750,
in Sussex and Essex Counties, Massachusetts

	Estate Inventories			Boston Newspapers
	1700-1710	1720-1730	1740-1750	1704-1750
Wools				
Calamanco ...	—	—	—	1
Camlet	1	—	7	1
Cheyney or China ...	—	3	5	—
Harrateen	—	—	4	1
Mohair	—	—	1	—
Serge, "Stuff," or Woolen ..	1	2	—	—
Cottons				
Calico	14	11	10	—
Chintz	—	2	—	—
Muslin	1	3	1	—
Linens				
Diaper	2	2	2	—
Holland	2	1	1	—
Kentish	—	—	1	—
Linen	3	3	7	—
Miscellaneous				
Damask	—	—	—	1
Plaid or Stripe	—	—	2	—
Printed	—	1	1	—
"Work'd"	—	—	1 (?)	—
Curtains, fabrics unspecified ...	59	65	71	—

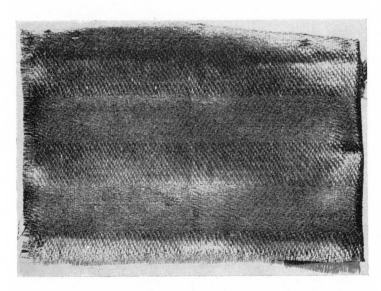

Fig. 4. Black striped calamanco, c. 1750-1800; of wool or mohair with satin stripe and an extremely high gloss. *Essex Institute.*

longed "to the great family of wool satins originating in Europe . . ." Diderot described the *calemandes façonnées* as similar to all-silk satins. Savary's description (1723), which seems to have been erroneously translated by Postlethwayt as "checquered in the warp," states that "calmande" had a twill in the warp which appeared on one side only—logically a satin weave. Apparently the name applied to a variety of wool satins, from plain or simple striped fabrics (Fig. 4) to those with decorative floral patterns similar to the silks of the day. The swatch of "wool brocade" in Figure 5 corresponds closely with the eighteenth-century descriptions of flowered calamancoes and also to flowered calamancoes in late eighteenth-century French swatch books. The pattern resembles the designs found in English and French silk brocades of the mid-eighteenth century.

Patterned wool curtains and wool textile fragments which have survived from colonial times have a design character corresponding to the European silk damask and brocade patterns of the first half of the eighteenth century. Many of the designs, like those of Figure 2, are based on French and Italian baroque patterns of the late seventeenth and early eighteenth centuries, which were popular in England for furnishing fabrics throughout the first half of the eighteenth century. Some of the English flowered wools, as seen in Figures 3 and 5, have a more rococo character, with floral details similar to French silks at mid-century. Luxurious and elegant settings obviously could be achieved with the use of such handsome fabrics. Small wonder that these textiles are inventoried in the homes of prominent Boston and Salem colonists.

Simpler wools, either homespun or imported, were used earlier in the century. The few inventory listings of serge, stuff, and woolen curtains give valuations which are low in comparison with those of camlet, cheyney, and harrateen. Samuel Sewall's *Diary* bears testimony to the practicality and sturdiness of the woolen curtains of his day. When describing the discovery of fire in his bedchamber closet, Sewall recorded: "The Window-Curtain was of Stubborn Woolen and refus'd to burn though the Iron-Bars were hot with the fire."

It is notable that silk window curtains are not listed in any of the Essex or Suffolk County inventories which I studied, although silk bed curtains and upholstery are itemized. Prior to 1750 there is only one advertisement for damask window curtains in the Boston newspapers, and it does not specify whether they are silk or wool. A fragment of damask labeled "used for draperies, 1750-1775" in the Essex Institute collections is a crimson worsted damask. By 1760 there are advertisements for silk damask window curtains. However, several fragments of damask known to have been used in New England houses, such as the one from the Moffatt-Ladd house (Fig. 6), are mixtures of silk and wool or mohair.

These inventories contain only one listing

which might be interpreted as designating embroidered window curtains. Captain John Hubbart of Boston (1740) had "1 Work'd Bed & Window Curtains, £60." Five Boston inventories between 1740 and 1750 record "work'd" or "wrot" bed hangings, but Hubbart's is the only one that lists any window hangings at all which can be related to the same room as that containing the bed hangings. Peter Faneuil's inventory with several sets of matching hangings has no window curtains that appear to have been used with his "workt Fustian Bed." The fact that no other reference to embroidered window curtains has turned up in New England records is hard to explain in view of the number of crewel-embroidered bed hangings which have survived.

Although wools were favored by the well to do, calicoes and linens are the fabrics most commonly listed for window curtains throughout the first half of the century. In estates with a low valuation (below £400) curtains, if any, are generally calico or one of the various linens such as diaper, holland, or kenting. At all economic levels calico is noted more often than any other single fabric. The fine quality of some calico is revealed through high valuation or the importance of the room in which it was hung. In 1749 John Ranchon had "6 Callico Window curtains" in the "best lower Room," and calico window curtains are listed in the "Great Room Chamber" in the

1728 inventory of Captain William Bowditch of Salem.

The calico and linen window curtains used in New England in the eighteenth century are variously described as plain, striped, "spriged," "speckled," "flower'd," or printed. According to the lists of shop goods and newspaper advertisements of the time both domestic and imported fabrics were available. "Blew & Colour Calico," "floured Calico," chintzes, printed linens, and "Stampt Dimity," were among the fabrics available in Salem in 1700. Three advertisements for Boston printers of calicoes and linens appear in the newspapers before 1722. It is impossible here to consider all the many plain and printed cottons and linens which were available to the colonists by mid-century. The inventory descriptions and the value placed on the curtains indicate that these fabrics might range from simple homespuns and small "speckled" or spot prints (Fig. 7) to more elaborate and costly English prints (Fig. 8) and Indian cottons.

Admittedly, the list of window curtain fabrics given here tells us little about their quality and

character in a particular house. Since curtain fabrics were frequently the same as those for other furnishings, bed hangings and upholstery fabrics in museums and private collections can also give clues to the nature of eighteenth-century woolens, cottons, and linens. Even then knowledge is fragmentary concerning such items as the calicoes and linens printed in Boston or the English woolens and prints imported prior to 1750.

When selecting curtain material for a historic house careful interpretation should be made of documentary evidence concerning its furnishings in relation to known facts regarding the textiles used in the locality. The list of window curtain fabrics given here, while not ruling out the possibility that other textiles were used, provides a documented basis for hangings suitable in the restoration of New England houses of the first half of the eighteenth century.

At upper economic levels the inventories indicate that the quality of the window curtains, though not the number, increased as the century progressed. The high value placed on some cottons and linens suggests that fine imported prints were popular. Clearly, the handsome English wools, treated in the manner of fine silks, are an appropriate luxury in elegant colonial New England interiors.

Fig. 7. Blue and white calico, "used just before the Revolution." The coarse weave and the mottled effect of the dark blue background suggest colonial rather than European origin. *Essex Institute.*

Fig. 8. English block-printed chintz, c. 1750, in a design of Chinese figures with buffalo and temple. Probably done in the "china blue" technique of printing with indigo. *Essex Institute.*

JEFFERSON'S CURTAINS AT MONTICELLO

By FISKE AND MARIE KIMBALL

THE TASK OF RESTORING the curtains at Monticello, lately undertaken by the Thomas Jefferson Memorial Foundation, has led to a review of all the evidence as to their material and form — evidence which, as always with Jefferson's methodical preservation of his accounts and papers, is extraordinarily rich. Collected, it throws much light, not only on the special problem at Monticello, but on the general subject of curtains in the period around 1800.

The first curtains at Monticello will have been those of the house as originally built, still far from completed in 1774, but already partly occupied before the outbreak of the Revolution, and visited by the Marquis de Chastellux in 1782. It constituted the western file of five rooms of the present house. As to these first curtains we have no records, though on all later ones used by Jefferson we have considerable information. It is indeed doubtful if he had been able to curtain all the rooms, owing to the interruption of imports during the war.

While Jefferson was in Philadelphia just after the Revolution, he took advantage of the resumption of commerce to secure some curtain materials. Over forty years later, during his last illness, he told his grandson, Thomas Jefferson Randolph, "that the curtains of his bed had been purchased from the first cargo that arrived after the peace of 1782." (H. S. Randall: *Life of Jefferson*, vol. III, 1858, p. 543.) The preliminary articles of peace had been signed November 30, 1782. Jefferson's pocket account book for 1783 shows these entries, just before he left Philadelphia for Monticello:

> April 8. paid for printed linens £ 6
> " 10. 9½ yd. linen £5-2/8; 22½ do. £7-6

While printed linens, generally, include prints from wood blocks, by 1782 there can be little doubt that what was meant was the newly fashionable prints from engraved copper plates, developed in the 1770's by Oberkampf — the *toiles de Jouy* — of which by that year the number of designs reached nearly a hundred. These were in monochrome, chiefly in red. The total yardage of these purchases of Jefferson, apparently well over forty, would have sufficed, as straight curtains, for only six or eight of the 34 then existing windows of the house. After reaching Monticello in mid-May, Jefferson left for Congress October 13, not to get back, as it proved, until after his return from France in 1789.

As Minister to France, Jefferson, in October 1784, leased a house in the rue Têtebout. One year later he took the house of the Comte de Langeac. His books reveal many purchases of textile fabrics in quantities sufficient for curtains:

1784	Dec. 20	pd.	Hôtel de Jabac for toile de Jouy (red) 621 f.
1785	Mar. 1	pd.	Barbier & Tetard marchands de Damas 1500 f
	May 20	pd.	Tetard marchands de Damas, 1593-7-6
1786	Feb. 2	pd.	Hôtel de Jabac. toile de Jouy 250 f

The most revealing account is one of March 2, 1785, with a *serrurier* who had made rods or brackets at the rue Tetebout for:

> 7 pr. lawn curtains
> red damask window curtains. 3 pr.
> blue damask window curtains. 3 pr.
> blue damask bed curtains
> red calico window curtains. 2 pr.
> red calico bed curtains. 2 sets

These same curtains are among the items listed in the contents of the eighty-six packing cases of Jefferson's goods which were shipped from Paris to Philadelphia in 1790 after his return: Six large blue damask curtains, eight medium size of the same, a drapery in two parts; six curtains and eight cords with crimson tassels; 1 bundle of mixed chintz, a piece of *toile de Jouy*, and two sets of bed hangings (*tentures de lit*). At the Hôtel de Langeac, Jefferson's red curtains had increased from three to six, and the blue ones had multiplied still more.

Although some of these curtains brought to America may well have been used in the Philadelphia house Jefferson occupied as Secretary of State, fitted up in 1790, all were doubtless taken to Monticello when he retired there in 1793.

We may assume that, on his arrival, the silk curtains were used in some of the major rooms of the then-existing house — the rooms along the western side of the house as it stands today — namely: Jefferson's room, the large central saloon, the dining room, and the bow rooms at each end — the one at the north then connected with the dining room merely by a door instead of the later arch. These rooms at this time had windows all of the same size, six feet wide to the outside of the casing, as follows: Jefferson's room and the dining room, then two each; the saloon, five; the bows, then five each. The only material in sufficient quantity for the windows of the saloon was the blue damask, of which the six large curtains and eight medium-size ones should have sufficed to make up the five pairs, or ten large curtains, needed. The six red damask curtains would scarcely have sufficed for more than four pairs of curtains then needed for Jefferson's room and the dining room.

In the Coolidge collection of drawings at the Massachusetts Historical Society is a sketch by Jefferson for two types of window curtains (*Fig. 1*). This is on a paper with the watermarked date 1794, and a known date of use, in another instance, of 1798. We believe the sketches are indeed of this period, and show the drapery of the blue and of the red curtains, respectively, on the windows as extending at this time only to a sill. By 1803, as a drawing of the house in that year shows, these windows had been cut down to the floor.

Very shortly after his retirement as Secretary of State, Jefferson began to plan a remodeling and enlargement of the house at Monticello. From this remodeling, begun in 1796, date the rooms along the eastern side, both on the main floor and on the mezzanines over them. This was the period at which Jefferson adopted the scheme of alcove beds, on the French model, both in the new

FIG. 1 — SKETCHES by Jefferson (*c. 1798*), apparently for the draping of the blue (left) and of the red damask curtains at Monticello. *From the Massachusetts Historical Society.*

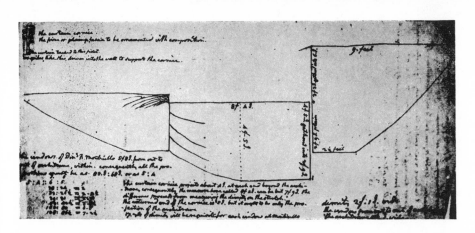

Fig. 2 — Pattern by Jefferson of dimity curtains at the President's House, with his calculation for such curtains for the dining room and elsewhere at Monticello.

1. counterpane
2. tops & vallons
   sewed together
1. single vallon
6. double do.

Here there were twelve old red curtains which it was proposed to use in the new bedrooms of the mezzanine at Monticello. As the crimson damask curtains brought home from France had been but six in number, we believe these twelve were probably of *toile de Jouy*, some of that which he had bought in Philadelphia or in France. As remodeled, they made seven pairs of window curtains and three pairs for the alcoves.

In anticipation of his final retirement Jefferson also had made in Philadelphia certain new curtains for Monticello. March 2, 1808, he wrote from Washington to John Rea in Philadelphia for "drapery for the tops of 4 windows (no curtains being desired) somewhat in the style here drawn (*Fig. 3*) of crimson damask silk, lined with green and a yellow fringe. In the House of Representatives are two small prints with drapery in this style which will give a just idea of what is desired. The architraves of the windows are exactly six feet from out to out. Thomas Jefferson asks the favor of Mr. Rea to furnish him with the above within the course of the present month."

Jefferson appended a note: "I afterwards agreed they should be of other silk and be forwarded there in a trunk from Philadelphia in a stage." Rea replied April 25, 1808:

I sent this morning by the mail stage a trunk containing 4 window draperies that you sent to me for the delay was owing to not getting damask here for which I sent to New York and Baltimore and was disappointed there likewise. They are made of the best crimson mantua which I hope will give satisfaction.
N. B. The draperies I sent on to Monticello as desired and hope they will arrive safe. The style of the drapery (*Fig. 4*)

rooms and in his own bedroom on the western side. The work progressed but slowly, as Jefferson's absences in political life were now resumed in 1797. In 1803 there were still rooms to be plastered.

Meanwhile Jefferson, in 1801, had occupied the President's House in Washington, then still unfinished, and had had the task of completing its furnishing and decoration. Here he used chintz curtains in many of the principal rooms, the only room with damask curtains (inherited from the régime of Adams) being the Ladies Drawing Room on the second floor. As in Ann Penn's fashionable house, Lansdowne in Philadelphia, in 1795, much use was also made of dimity curtains which the inventory of the President's House in 1809 lists for the large dining room and for many of the bedrooms and dressing rooms.

Jefferson used the opportunity offered by the work in Washington to take note of the methods of cutting and draping these curtains, as models for those at Monticello. In at least one instance he made a diagram (*Fig. 2*) of the cutting and draping of a curtain of the President's House. This drawing, dated January 12, 1803, shows the manner of treating one of the dimity curtains. The eight-foot-four-inch width is that of the large windows of the President's House. In a marginal calculation Jefferson has reduced the dimensions proportionally to suit the width of the dining-room window at Monticello, five feet eight inches. With dimity two feet one inch wide, he arrives at the conclusion: "17 yds. of dimity will be requisite for each window at Monticello." Thus very probably dimity was employed in the dining room and in some of the new rooms there in the principal story. We must assume that the old red damask curtains from Paris, now nearly twenty years old, were beginning to wear out, and that Jefferson planned to adopt in the dining room the Wedgwood color scheme of blue and white which prevailed there in the last years of his life.

A memorandum headed "list of red curtains" is on paper watermarked 1799 and used in the years 1804–05. It is as follows:

	length yards	breadths in each	no. of curtains	
a.	2½	1½	4	
b.		3	4	makes 12 breadths
c.	4⅔	2	4	makes 8 breadths each long enough for 2, so say 16 breadths

a. will do for 2 windows of the upper sq. room
b. 4 breadths for alcove of do.

| 8 do. | } | windows and alcove of upper S. octagon |
| 2 breadths | } | windows & alcove of upper N. sq. room |
| 10 do. |
| 4 do. | | windows of upper S Bow |
| 16 |

Fig. 3 — Sketch (*insert*) by Jefferson, sent to John Rea, for draperies of red damask for the study windows at Monticello.

Fig. 4 — Sketch by John Rea for the draperies of the study, as furnished.

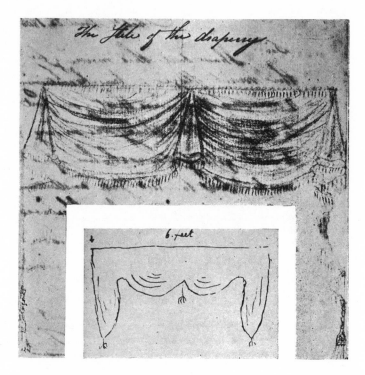

55

Fig. 5 — Sketch by Jefferson of a window drapery with calico valance, which he adapted for one of the "Square Rooms" at Monticello.

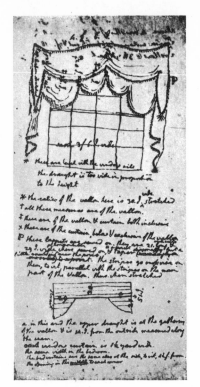

Jefferson acknowledged the receipt of the draperies on July 6, and enclosed an order on his bank for $352.67½, the amount of the bill. October 17, 1808, he again wrote Rea from Washington:

Mr. Jefferson will thank Mr. Rea to make and forward to him at this place a counterpane or coverlid of the description below . . .

A counterpane of such crimson mantua silk as the draperies which Mr. R. formerly furnished to Mr. J. 2½ yds. long and the same in width with a crimson fringe or other suitable bordering at the side and foot. No lining as it is to be lined with furs which are here; and not to be hollowed over the bolster in the French manner, but plain as is usual with us.

For what room or rooms were these draperies and this coverlet? We might suppose they were for the two new eastern "Square Rooms," each with two windows, but, as each of these had an alcove bed, why only one coverlet? And would not the coverlet with fur be rather for Jefferson himself, like the fur-lined overcoat of his later years? We conclude that these items, which Jefferson wished of crimson damask, were for the four window recesses in the small study adjoining Jefferson's bedroom — the only room in the whole house with four windows. Here, also, according to Cornelia Jefferson Randolph's plan of the house (reproduced in S. N. Randolph's *The Domestic Life of Thomas Jefferson*, 1871, p. 334; 1939, facing p. 287), was the "couch on which Jefferson reclined while studying." Very likely the fur-lined coverlet was for this. If we are right in our assumption that, at this time, there was still crimson damask in Jefferson's bedroom, it would explain Jefferson's desire to have crimson in the study, into which the bed alcove also stood open. It will be noted that Jefferson's sketch for the new draperies (*Fig. 3*) closely conforms to that of 1798 which we have inferred was for red damask curtains in the bedroom, and thus confirms that inference.

Another diagram with suggestions for curtains at Monticello is reproduced in Figure 5. Like the dimity curtains and the silk draperies, these end in points at the sill or above. This design, with striped calico valance, seems to have been measured from an executed example elsewhere, but the calculation on the back:

		yds.
alcove 4 breadths of 6	6	8⅔
2 pr. window curtains of 1½ breadth each, and 9 f	18	
2 vallons 3 yds. each	6	
		32⅔

shows how it was to be adapted to one of the bedrooms at Monticello. As an alcove bedroom with two windows with nine foot curtains this can only be one of the "square rooms" on the eastern side of the main floor. We have chosen to place these in the southerly one of these rooms, which on Cornelia Jefferson Randolph's plan of the house is called "Sitting Room," and was the room of Jefferson's daughter, Martha Jefferson Randolph.

From the time of his retirement from the Presidency in 1809 Jefferson was increasingly embarrassed financially. There was no longer money for replacements, and there were many makeshifts.

In "A list of taxable property of the subscriber in Albemarle, Mar. 1815," (*Jefferson Papers, Massachusetts Historical Society Collections*, 7th series, vol. I, 1900, p. 225) Jefferson included: *11 prs. window curtains, foreign.* On our calculation, there had been in the 1790's eleven pairs of silk ones, and, about 1805, ten pairs of red printed linen. The old silk would have been likely to wear out before the linen. Already by 1803 the red damask may have been beginning to go, for Jefferson was then canvassing its replacement in the dining room by dimity. Enough red damask survived in 1808 so that his bedroom apparently still had it (doubtless both on its single remaining window and the bed), as we have seen. By 1815, doubtless still more of the silk had gone. By the time of Jefferson's death in 1826, the red damask in his bedroom apparently had been wholly discarded for *toile*, perhaps moved down from one of the rooms upstairs.

In the unpublished inventory made after Jefferson's death in 1826 (*Jefferson Papers, Massachusetts Historical Society*), all the household linens and other textiles were assembled in one of the upstairs rooms. We note among other items the following of some relevance:

10 chintz and calico counterpanes
7 checked blue and white counterpanes
4 white knotted cotton do.
2 white homespun do.
2 dimity do.
6 sets of curtains and the draperies to 2 windows
3 curtains for the lower parts of the windows

These six sets of curtains were all that were left in the house of twenty rooms.

For the Jefferson Memorial Foundation in 1947, we have recurtained Monticello as we believe it was on Jefferson's retirement from the Presidency. Franco Scalamandré of Scalamandré Silks has given the silks needed for curtains and upholstery, in patterns specially woven for the purpose. They were cut, made, and applied by Ernest Lo Nano, with great personal interest and skill.

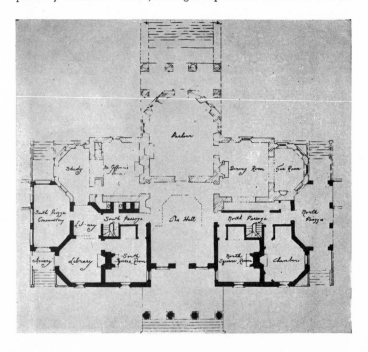

Fig. 6 — Plan of the main floor at Monticello. The original house in light hatching; the additions after 1796 in solid black.

The textile furnishings

BY MILDRED B. LANIER, *Assistant curator of textiles*

BEDDING AND TABLE linens are mentioned with greater frequency than window curtains in Virginia inventories of the eighteenth century. Neither is described in as much detail as we would like, so that the quantity and quality of other furnishings have had to be adopted as the standard for textiles. One can also resort to advertisements of the period for indications of what fabrics were used to make the "suits of curtains," "Window curtains with vallins," and other textile furnishings recorded.

Peyton Randolph's inventory listing of "492 oz Plate," fashionable furniture, "Ornamental China," and "48 Table Cloths" (twelve of which we know, from his correspondence, to have been "fine table cloths—ten quarters square, of Irish linen") gives some indication of the quality of his thirteen counterpanes, chintz bedcovers, and numerous "suits" of bed and window curtains. Among the last, "1 Sett old Blue damask Curtains . . . 2 p^r window D^o" might have been of a wool damask similar to the mid-eighteenth-century document in the Williamsburg collection reproduced for use in the Randolphs' bedroom. Flowered calamanco, watered camlets, or moreens used in several rooms in the Randolph House and Wetherburn's Tavern, together with other fashionable wool stuffs such as russels, harrateens, and tammies, formed, according to Roland de la Platière in his *Art du Fabricant d'Etoffes en laines rases et sèches* of 1776, "a considerable part of an immense quantity of light weight woolen stuffs manufactured by the English . . . in which they carry on a prodigious commerce with the rest of the world." Many examples of these textiles form an interesting part of the collection at Williamsburg.

Affluent Virginians used silks for furnishings as well as for clothing. Antique silk fabrics—bourettes, moires, and embossed half-silk, half-linen fabrics—have been used in fashioning the bed and window curtains for these buildings, in designs based on documentary evidence from pictorial sources, descriptive records, and antique furnishings in the Williamsburg collection.

The hot and humid Tidewater climate probably accounts for the astounding quantities of cotton and linen goods imported for furnishings and clothing. Customs records of exports from London to Virginia and Maryland for the year 1763 list 30,369 square yards "Cottons and Linens, printed," 49,311 square yards and 2,134 ells "Cottons and Linens, check'd," in addition to hundreds of yards of other cottons and linens such as fustians, dimities, calicoes, diapers, hollands, muslins, nankeens, seersuckers, humhums, and chintz. From the early eighteenth century, references to "Virginia cloth" begin to appear with more frequency in records of the colony, indicating the extent to which linen and wool, as well as cotton, were being grown and manufactured. Inventories and advertisements lead us to understand that the term applied to any cloth of Virginia manufacture, whether of wool, linen, cotton, or a combination of these fibers. Virginia cloth was used for table linens, bedding, clothing, and "furnitures." The Randolph inventory lists several beds with suits of Virginia-cloth curtains, one with matching window curtains.

The same inventory, dated 1776, also lists floor cloths and "1 Wilton Carpet." A 1775 deed of trust on Tazewell Hall, the Williamsburg home of John Randolph, Peyton's brother, lists with "handsome crimson Silk Curtains" and "handsome green worsted window Curtains" a "handsome large Turkey Carpet," two Wilton carpets (one described as "handsome"), and "two side Board Carpets belonging to the Dining Room." The last, listed with the contents of a closet, suggests use as protective covering

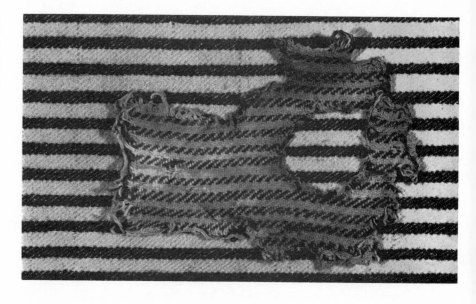

Wool blanket; American, c. 1760; 74 inches by 88. Natural and walnut-brown horizontal stripes in coarse twill weave, here illustrated with a fragment similar in color and weave found in the excavated well at the Wetherburn site. The 1760 inventory of Henry Wetherburn's estate lists 21 blankets. *Wetherburn's Tavern.*

Crewelwork bed curtains and valances; American, attributed to Rhode Island, c. 1760. Flower-filled undulating stems with exotic flowers and birds on side curtains and valances (one valance initialed *I M*) combined with backdrop, also New England; all worked with bright crewels on linen-cotton ground. The yellow twilled silk counterpane corresponds to an entry in the 1766 will of Jane Bolling Randolph: "1 fringed counterpane of best sort." *Peyton Randolph House.*

for the Wilton carpet rather than sideboard covering. This significant document reveals that in houses like those of the Randolphs, English-made carpets as well as Orientals were being used to a greater extent than had been customary in the first half of the eighteenth century. Owners ordered Kilmarnock and Scotch carpets in "large" and "small" sizes and floorcloths made to order. They did not, however, always receive them in good condition, as indicated in the much-quoted complaint Thomas Nelson Jr. of Yorktown made to his agents, John Norton & Sons of London, in 1773 about a shipment of floorcloth and anchovies: "The Cloth is injur'd by being role'd before the paint was dry." It is regrettable that so few Wiltons have survived; all records indicate that they were among the most fashionable carpets of the period.

Beds, often the most valuable item in colonial inventories, usually are listed complete with "furniture," which included feather beds, bolsters, pillows, blankets, quilts, and "ruggs," or counterpanes. The term rugg is commoner in the first half of the eighteenth century; counterpane, "counterpin," "counterpoint," and the like, occur more in the last half.

This useful and decorative item of bed furniture is usually described with a single adjective, such as cotton, fringed, fine, "chince," "work'd," or quilted. Occasionally more information is provided, as in the 1813 will of Mary Willing Byrd of Westover, who married William Byrd III in 1761. She left a daughter "the red damask bed and bedsteads belonging to it with the handsomest Virginia cloth counterpoint not worked," and a granddaughter the "worked counterpoint with bedsteads and curtains."

Illustrated here, and exhibited (with seasonal changes) in the newly opened buildings, are counterpanes of

"largest size" and "best sort," which represent the quality of the numerous listings in the inventories.

Frances Webb, the first milliner to appear in the records of Williamsburg, advertised in the *Virginia Gazette* in 1745 "Calicoes, Chintz's, printed Linnens," and on February 3, 1780, the last notice of the milliner Margaret Hunter in the *Virginia Gazette* included "an elegant assortment of the most beautiful calico and chintz patterns." Other Williamsburg storekeepers advertised quantities of these plain, checked, printed, and painted cotton and linen fabrics.

Many Tidewater Virginia families ordered furnishings directly from London agents like John Norton & Sons, using tobacco as currency. Peter Lyons of Hanover in 1771 was invoiced for "One peice of fine blue and white Copper plate Calico . . . One peice of blue grounded Cotton of a large Pattern for a Bed with suitable binding . . . One smaller peice of blue grounded Cotton of the same sort for Window Curtains with binding and Rings for the whole . . . One peice of fine dark grounded Cotton with good Colours and pretty figures" (Francis Norton Mason, *John Norton & Sons, Merchants of London and Virginia*, Richmond, 1937, pp. 190, 191).

The twentieth century has relegated cotton and linen checks to such lowly status—kitchen towels and restaurant tablecloths—that one is startled to see these very popular eighteenth-century fabrics used in formal settings. At the Governor's Palace in 1770, the inventory of the estate of Lord Botetourt listed in the "Middle Room . . . 8 Crimson damask chairs with red check covers." He, it should be noted, was only one of several royal governors to have had "check furnitures" in use there.

Dressing-table cover; probably French, c. 1760. Sheer white lawn embroidered in fine crewels in tambour technique, *i.e.,* a fine chain stitch worked on a circular frame with a hooklike device. *Peyton Randolph House.*

The Fair Lady working Tambour; mezzotint printed for Carington Bowles in London, c. 1770. The tambour frame at which the lady works is used for the type of embroidery seen in its finished form in the lawn dressing-table cover. *Peyton Randolph House.*

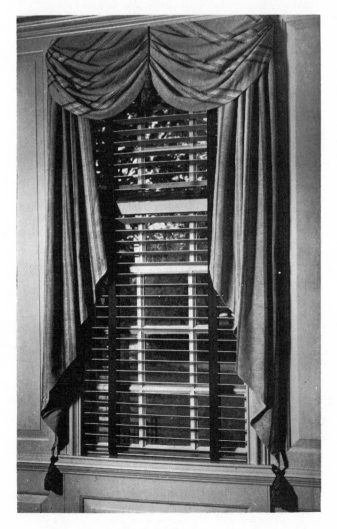

Festooned window curtains of yellow, blue, and ivory striped silk moire, lined with yellow silk bourette (both fabrics French, c. 1760). Robert Carter of Nomini Hall, having purchased and being "about to repair" the present Carter-Saunders House in Williamsburg, wrote in 1762 to Thomas Bladon of Piccadilly, London, giving the dimensions of his rooms and ordering, among other furnishings, "three pr Yellow silk and worsted Damask festoon Window Curtains for a Room 10 Feet pitch" and the same material "to Ye Seats of 18 common Chairs." *Peyton Randolph House.*

59

Counterpane, or palampore (detail); India, made for the European market c. 1700; 87 inches by 100.
Bright silks in fine chain-stitch embroidery on natural linen-cotton twill. Central flowering tree and flower-filled vases show both Eastern and Western influences.

Chintz counterpane (detail), or palampore, in painted and resist-dyed cotton; made for the Western market c. 1760; 84 inches by 105. Peyton Randolph's inventory of 1776 includes "1 Chintz Bed Cover £3," an exceptionally high valuation in comparison to "1 Marble Table £2."

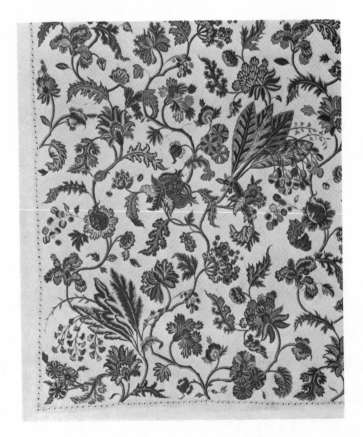

Coverlet (detail), "wrought" or "work'd" in satin and bullion stitches with laid and couched work in tawny silks on quilted linen ground; England, c. 1700; 58 inches by 74. Leaves similar to tobacco leaves are prominent among exotic flowers in the center. Three pillowberes match this coverlet; one was shown on the frontispiece of ANTIQUES in March 1963.

Crewelwork coverlet (detail),
worked in bright multicolored wools on a
napped fustian (twilled linen-cotton) ground;
New England, c. 1765; 78 inches by 89.
Wetherburn's Tavern.

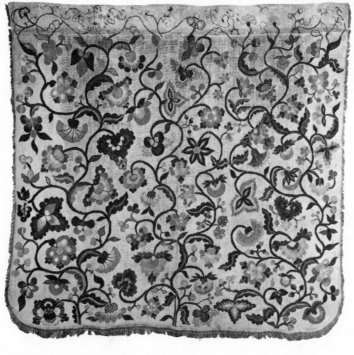

Quilted calamanco panel; New England, c. 1750; 21 inches by 35. This handsome tomato-red fragment, showing a section of lozenge-patterned border and intricately designed field pattern of people, flowers, birds, and animals, was once part of a counterpane.

Homespun woolen bed rug; New York, c. 1710; 97 inches by 79. The natural background, as well as the pattern of shaded blues, russet, and gold, has been worked in surface-covering "darning" stitches in coarsely spun two-ply wools. This wool-on-wool coverlet, which has a history of ownership on Long Island, conforms with a listing for "1 bed rugg" in the 1744 inventory of James Geddy Sr. *James Geddy House.*

Brocaded wool damask (detail); Norwich, England, c. 1765. Width 18 inches. Used as upholstery on the wing chair in the Peyton Randolph large chamber (see color plate), this represents the "flower'd calamancoes" referred to in colonial inventories. Designs of this type were derived from patterned silks. Samples of comparable wool textiles occur in two pattern books of Norwich wools at the Henry Francis du Pont Winterthur Museum that probably date between 1760 and 1790; they are listed as 18 inches wide. *Peyton Randolph House.*

Carpet; England, c. 1750. Cross-stitch embroidery in wools and silks on linen canvas; 8 feet, 9 inches by 6 feet, 5 inches. Center panel of lozenge medallion and flowers in natural colors on deep yellow ground, framed by border on soft brick-red ground. *Peyton Randolph House.*

"Fine blue and white Copper plate Calico," or chintz; England, c. 1770. This detail from a set of original bed hangings is plate printed in blue on linen-cotton ground with scenes from Isaac Bickerstaffe's comic opera *The Padlock.* The opera, based on Cervantes' novel *The Jealous Husband,* was first produced in 1768 at London's Drury Lane Theater. It was presented in 1769 in Philadelphia and New York, and in Williamsburg, on December 21, 1771, "a company of players" closed the season with a performance of it. This textile was used for many years in a house in West Chester, Pennsylvania. *Peyton Randolph House.*

Detail of hangings; *chinoiserie* chintz, copper-plate printed in red with scenes based on Jean Pillement's *Livre de Chinois* (London, 1758); England, c. 1765. The bed hangings, with valances, have an Albany history. The printed edging with which they are trimmed is like a "Striped callicoe" ordered from London in 1749 by James Alexander, merchant of New York (James Alexander Papers, New-York Historical Society). *James Geddy House.*

The mahogany four-poster curtained in the copperplate print shown above is American, c. 1790, and may well have been made near Williamsburg: it has a history of ownership there, a tulipwood headrail, and a headboard of Southern pine. Tea table and commode chair are also American, from New York, last quarter of the eighteenth century. Most of the accessories in view are English; the warming pan may be either English or American. *James Geddy House.*

Room furnishings as seen in British prints from the Lewis Walpole Library

Part II: *Window curtains, upholstery, and slip covers*

BY FLORENCE M. MONTGOMERY

A True Picture of the Famous Skreen, c. 1721. The crested pier glass and table between two tall, recessed windows provided with low seats are characteristic of eighteenth-century English interiors. The flaring box cornices of carved wood are upholstered with cloth and trimmed with fancy braid, or galloon. Hanging pelmets partially conceal the tops of the curtains, which are pulled back and up with cords. When closed, the curtains would have fallen to the floor in front of the window seats. The British Museum catalogue number of this print is BM 1710. These numbers will be given in subsequent captions where appropriate. *Illustrations are from the Lewis Walpole Library.*

The Assembly of Old Maids, dated 1743 Neat box cornices covered with cloth and edged with patterned tape conceal the tops of bunchy Venetian curtains raised to the top of the windows.

The Court at St. James's, c. 1766. Pier glasses with elaborately carved rococo frames are hung between the five long windows of a reception room at St. James's Palace. The ruffly curtains, each ornamented with three tassels, may have remained fixed in this position under their bowshape cornices. The dais with the monarch's throne at the right is covered by an elaborate canopy.

The COURT at St JAMES's.

The French Lady in London, dated 1771. The ruffled trimming of the festoon window curtain matches the lady's gown and outlandish headdress. The chair is neatly upholstered with a flat seat and precise, square corners. BM 4784.

La Françoise à Londres.
The FRENCH LADY in LONDON,
or the HEAD DRESS for the YEAR 1771
Done from the ORIGINAL DRAWING by J.H. GRIMM.

THE FIRST PART of this article demonstrated the variety of eighteenth-century bed hangings that can be identified in the British prints at the Lewis Walpole Library in Farmington, Connecticut.[1] This, the second and final part of the article, is devoted to the eighteenth-century window curtains, upholstery, and slip covers revealed in other prints from the library.

The simplest of the four basic types of window curtain consisted of two strips of cloth tacked to a lath at the top of the window and held back by tiebacks or cords. A valance, secured by brackets, concealed the tacks. Venetian curtains extended the width of the window and had no center opening. They were raised to the top of the window by cords which were run through rings stitched in vertical rows to the back of the curtain. As is the case with Austrian shades today, thin materials gathered attractively, while

65

BOARDING SCHOOL EDUCATION, OR THE FRENCHIFIED YOUNG LADY.

Boarding School Education, dated 1771. What appears to be a stiff silk curtain edged with fringe is drawn to one side of the window, which is fitted with indoor shutters. The tasseled cord is secured on brass knobs. BM 4639.1.

A GOOD STORY.

A Good Story, c. 1780. Venetian curtains are drawn to the tops of the windows in baggy drapery. A standing frill appears to substitute for a valance or cornice.

Ensign Rosebud reposing himself after the Fatigues of the Parade, c. 1782. The striped curtains, favored in the 1780's, have the usual fringed edge and center tassel. The raised window and the fact that the lady is fanning the exhausted ensign suggest that the couch is covered with a summery floral chintz slip cover. The vase of flowers in the fireplace may be painted on a fireboard. The artist, who worked for several print sellers, favored unusually busy wallpaper and carpets.

ENSIGN ROSEBUD reposing himself after the FATIGUES of the PARADE.

heavy silk damask or wool bunched. Festoon curtains, the third basic type, consisted of two vertical strips which were raised to form swags. This was accomplished by means of cords running through rings sewed to the back of each curtain in a diagonal line extending from the bottom center to the upper outer corner. The cords were secured on knobs at the sides of the windows. By the last decade of the eighteenth century French-rod curtains were favored by upholsterers, especially in major rooms for floor-length curtains which could be drawn. Thomas Sheraton described

FREDERICK elegantly furnishing a large House.

Frederick elegantly furnishing a large House, c. 1782. When closed, these festoon curtains fell to the sill. The lady holds an upholsterer's folding pattern card of cloth swatches. Several of these cards have survived in museum collections.

Stay me with Flagons, dated 1789. The loose sofa cover and window curtains are made of the same patterned chintz. How the curtain was draped cannot be determined, but it fits within the window frame. Thomas Chippendale's accounts repeatedly call for matching upholstery and window curtains (see *Furniture History*, vol. IV [1968]).

A Good Thing or Select Vestry Repast, dated 1795. The hats and walking sticks hung on the wall indicate that this was probably a room in a coffeehouse. The stiff Venetian curtains are gathered by three cords and pulleys. The single control cord is secured around one or a pair of knobs.

Stay me with Flagons, comfort me with Apples for I am Sick of Love.
London Printed for ROBERT SAYER. No. 53 Fleet Street as the Act directs 17 April 1789.

A GOOD THING or SELECT VESTRY REPAST.

A Lady putting on her Cap. – June 1795.

A Lady putting on her Cap, dated 1795. A charming, softly draped festoon curtain is pulled up under a straight box cornice which is either made of carved wood or covered with material and trimmed. These curtains may have had two parallel lines of rings and cords on each curtain to raise them high above the window sill. BM 8755.

AVARICE and CONVIVIALITY or the UNION of ELEGANCE and INELEGANCE

Avarice and Conviviality, c. 1798. These lavishly draped festoon curtains are well suited to the elegance of the room.

Nobody's at Home, c. 1800. In this simple room a festoon curtain is hung beneath a box cornice. The lower part of the window is covered with a frame on which material has been stretched for privacy or perhaps as a sun blind.

The Finishing of an Aldermans Picture, dated 1773. Like the sofa in this print, a few pieces of eighteenth-century furniture which have survived with their original covering have padding stitched down at regular intervals and buttoned to prevent the stitching from pulling through the outer layer. Generally, however, eighteenth-century upholstery was smooth. Of sofas Thomas Chippendale wrote: "When made large, they have a Bolster and Pillow at each End, and Cushions at the Back, which may be laid down occasionally, and form a Mattrass" (*The Gentleman and Cabinet-Maker's Director*, London, 1762, caption for Pls. XXIX and XXX).

Nobody's at Home.

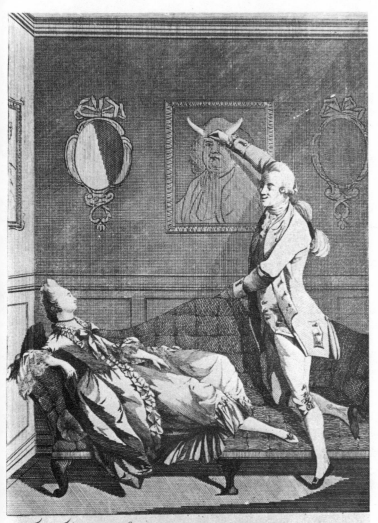

The Finishing of an ALDERMANS PICTURE
Pub.ᵈ Jan.ᵗ 1, 1773 by MDarly 39 Strand.

these curtains as having the advantage of drawing to either side of the window and not being raised off the floor when they were open. He went on to say "At present, they frequently make the French rods of satin wood, two to a window, to lap past each other about 3 inches in the centre; so that the curtain draws half on each side separately, or only half of it may be drawn at once: and when they are both drawn out, they lap over each other by means of the rod thus made, so that the light is entirely excluded in the middle."[2]

Cabinetmakers' design books indicate that upholstery was kept trim in the eighteenth century, with flat seats to side chairs revealing the carving at the base of the splat. Portraits indicate that shiny brass tacks were used along the backs and seats of chairs and sofas and resembled ornamental beading when new. Swags of shiny tacks on late eighteenth-century chairs were useful in holding down the upholstery and were also decorative. Often, narrow ornamental tape was applied at the edges of the upholstery under the tacks to cover loose threads. Silk and satin upholstery were only used in the drawing rooms and best bedrooms of the rich. When upholstering furniture in silk, Thomas Chippendale, with great practicality, provided woolen slip covers matching the color of the upholstery. Leather and horsehair were sturdy alternatives to fabric

CAP.ᵗ JESSAMY learning the PROPER DISCIPLINE of the COUCH.

Capt. Jessamy learning the Proper Discipline of the Couch, dated 1782. Fussy patterned paper and carpeting, a plain fabric at the window, and stripes on the couch belie the uniformity of patterns advocated by eighteenth-century decorators. The couch has a separate cushion and is fringed along the bottom. BM 6156.

CONJUGAL PEACE.

Conjugal Peace, dated 1782. Probably by the same artist as the print *Capt. Jessamy,* this picture shows a sofa of similar small size neatly finished with fringe. The heavy swag of drapery is the artist's invention, for there is no window. Floral wallpaper extends to the dado; the carpeting is patterned.

A Nun confessing her past Follies to Father Sly-Boots, dated 1794. The arch-back couch is fitted with a matching bolster. Note the tacks on the side chair at the left, which is perhaps covered with striped haircloth; the balls on the feet of the table and couch; and the knobs at each side of the window. According to Thomas Sheraton, "The drawing lines of festoon curtains have tassels at their ends. And opposite to this side, there should be a false line and a tassel to it, to match the right side of the window" (*The Cabinet Dictionary,* London, 1803, p. 317). BM 8585.

A NUN confessing her past FOLLIES to FATHER SLY-BOOTS.
At *Twelve.* I began to think of a Man.   At *Fourteen.* I was Violently in Love with a Man.
At *Thirteen.* I Sighed for a Man.   At *Fifteen.* I run away with a Man.
But he was a Very Pretty Man ——— therefore I hope youll Pardon me Sir.

Dido in Despair!, dated 1801. The window curtain seems to be raised unevenly, as if the two sides were hung with separate cords. A double row of tacks outlines the edges of the window seat with its buttoned padding. The dressing table has an extra ruffled apron, and the dressing glass is draped with soft cloth. BM 9752.

Temperance enjoying a Frugal Meal, dated 1792. George III's cabriole, or French, chair has neatly tacked upholstery quite in contrast to its sagging, ill-fitting slip cover, which was tied on with tape beneath the seat and at the back. BM 8117.

Celebrated Chess Match, at Parsloe's, c. 1790. Three matching armchairs are neatly slip covered in striped material finished with deep ruffled skirts.

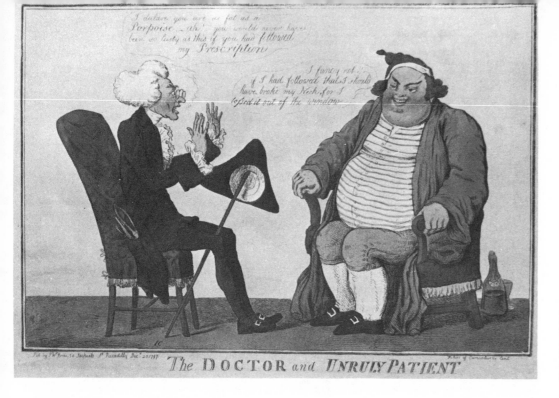

Fashion print, c. 1784. Two ample easy chairs are slip covered with striped material that matches the curtain drawn to one side of the window.

The Rival Favourites, dated 1788. The slip covers match the partly drawn Venetian curtain.

THE PROPOSAL.

THE RIVAL FAVOURITES.

upholstery. With the increasing ability of textile printers to create brightly colored chintzes and handsome patterns printed by copperplate, these washable materials along with furniture check and dimity became fashionable for all but the most elegant and formal rooms.

---

[1] ANTIQUES, December 1973, pp. 1068-1075.

[2] Thomas Sheraton, *The Cabinet Dictionary*, London, 1803, p. 298.

The CONTEMPLATIVE CHARMER.

Printed for & Sold by CARINGTON BOWLES, at his Map & Print Warehouse, No. 69 in S.t Pauls Church Yard LONDON, Publish'd as the Act directs

The Contemplative Charmer, c. 1780. The large sofa is covered with a chintz slip cover. BM 5815.

The Female Gambler's Prayer!!, dated 1801. A neoclassical side chair is covered with a cushion trimmed with wide ornamental braid and finished with a pair of tassels. BM 9796.

Domestick Amusement: The Lovely Spinner.

Domestick Amusement, c. 1764. A rush-seat armchair has a cushion tied to the stiles with bows that complement the frills and ruffles of the spinner's dress. About cushions Sheraton writes: "Amongst upholsterers there are various kinds; some for sofa seats, made to fit the seat in one length, some for backs of sofas and couches in two or three lengths, and for the ends. Cushions are also much in use for the seats of cane chairs. Cushions are stuffed with hair in a canvas case, and are then quilted or tied down, and have loose cases into which they slip" (*Cabinet Dictionary,* p. 186).

THE FEMALE GAMBLER'S PRAYER!!

III Simple "Stuffs"–From Fiber to Fabric, Plain to Fancy

Textile collections at the Farmers' Museum, Old Sturbridge Village, the Art Institute of Chicago, the Museum of Fine Arts, Boston, and individual pieces from the J. Paul Getty Museum, Virginia Museum, Minneapolis Institute of Art, Cleveland Museum of Art, the Metropolitan Museum of Art, Henry E. Huntington Library and Art Gallery, the Textile Museum, and the Smithsonian Institution illustrate the enormous range of material classified as simple weave in American museums. Though there are differences of interlacing spaces, and differences in color, the structure of feed bags, kilims, and Boucher tapestries remains the same—*one set of warps, one set of wefts.*

This section begins with the flax fiber—its product of linen and its by-product of tow. With the same demonstrative approach used at the Farmers' Museum, Virginia Parslow (pp. 76–78) recreates the details of flax preparation from seed to spool, of bobbin or quill winding, and of dyestuffs and yarn dyeing. She discusses wool and cotton and illustrates blankets and bed hangings.

Abbott Lowell Cummings' study, "Connecticut Homespun," based on a single Connecticut "public weaver," Josiah Newell, and his receipt book of dyes, adds terms pertinent to the preparation of flax fibers—"rotting," "breaking," "swincheling," "hatcheling"—each process having been spelled in many variations. With the descriptive phrase "a knot of thread," he introduces the concept of measurement. Measurement was an important tool of communication between the housewife who spun, the weaver who needed exact yardage, and the cabinetmaker who created the most valuable tool of yarn measurement— the reel. A knot, according to Alice Morse Earle in *Home Life in Colonial Days*, was forty threads going round the reel. Most reels measured between two and two and one-half yards in circumference. Richard H. Hulan's article on Tennessee textiles reprints an 1804 advertisement in which professional weaver Adam Maguire explains to customers who spun their own yarns that they needed "the cotton ten cuts to the pound." A "cut" is a woolen system for spinning based on fiber lengths and measured in yards to the pound. Typical "cuts" to the woolen or cotton pound are equal to 300 yards. "Eighteen pounds," Maguire advertised, "will make two coverlids." For an accurate account of "knots," "cuts," "yards," "skeins," and "reels," the reader should consult *The Homespun Textile Tradition of the Pennsylvania Germans*, published by the Pennsylvania Historical and Museum Commission.

The professional weaver was often a versatile craftsman. Josiah Newell and Adam Maguire, about whom the articles in this anthology on Connecticut and Tennessee weavers were written, were dyers as well as weavers, even though, as Abbott Lowell Cummings points out, the coloring of cloth was usually a separate trade. Like other professionals, Maguire also wove both "Diaper Carpets" and "couble coverlids." Ingenuity and a growing sense of production suggest the logic for grouping carpets and coverlets together in this and in other sections of the survey. Tennessee drafts offer two textual varieties that a creative weaver could accomplish without making any structural changes. A good explanation is made in the caption under Figure 4 (p. 89) of Richard H. Hulan's article on Tennessee textiles for the visual difference between two plain simple-weave fabrics. Spacing caused by a change in the number of threads inserted in one heddle, rather than by the addition of extra threads to the total web, make the patterns appear to be different. The author's alarm over the interchangeable quality of pattern names does not detract from his appreciation of the interchangeable skills of the Tennessee weavers.

Catherine Fennelly, in her discussion of the textile and costume collections at Old Sturbridge Village, discerns a dimension of American optimism and perfectionism in the history of textiles by pointing to the craze, in the early nineteenth century, for quality even in sheep. Merinos were imported and bred with American stock in the belief that they would improve the staple, the animal, the man, and—by extension—the nation. Utopian confidence in the American soil and in the labor of American hands gave Horace Bushnell a vision for his sermons—that agriculture out of doors would provide the essential family character indoors. Fennelly reminds us that it was the Reverend Bushnell who first titled the eighteenth century in America "The Age of Homespun." He was also the man who glorified the home weaver of his day, the woman who wove without remuneration or ambition. She radiated to him and to her generation a royal beneficence, "a strenuous joy."

Professional weavers and dyers could read the sermons and essays of men like Bushnell. In addition to the Bible, they read the farmers' almanacs, the weavers' drafts, and the few weavers' and dyers' instruction books published in America. *The Domestic Manufacturer's Assistant and Family Directory in the Arts of Weaving and Dyeing* (1817) demonstrates the mutuality of the two trades and the fact that Americans were able to weave dimity, block carpet, and broadcloth once imported from abroad. Jefferson's drawings of window curtains at the President's House in Washington (p. 55) calls for dimity. The Hepplewhite illustration on p. 92 recommends dimity for a tent bed. Whether dimity was conceived as a fine corded fabric like muslin and mentioned as such in the Ackermann *Repository of Fashions* in 1809, or as "a stout cotton fabric," which the *Oxford English Dictionary* of 1897 calls it, or as "a kind of coarse cotton flannel" is not clear. It was described as "a kind of linzie-wolzie" by an Italian-English dictionary of 1598. Structurally, dimity, a cloth of simple construction, refers to an interlacing technique often called "twill," which affects either a rib, a stripe, or a check. It runs diagonally or vertically according to the spacing or to the floats. Very little actual American dimity has been found, as Hazel E. Cummin emphasizes in her article on colonial dimities. Better use of the technique of structural analysis, however, might uncover what is now not recognized as American dimity.

Calamanco, discussed in another article by Hazel E. Cummin, is a fabric name for material woven from wool fiber. It has often been described as a wool satin—that is, made of the fiber wool in what is called satin interlacing, ribbed diagonally like a twill. Again, interlacings are secondary arrangements under the larger heading of structure, which is still simple—one set of warps and one set of wefts. Calamanco and dimity represent the changing tastes from the large, heavy patterns of the seventeenth century to the light, small-patterned flowers and stripes of the late eighteenth century. Calamanco has turned up with calendered effects like moreen, which originated in England. Cummin assumes that 1754 was the peak year of fashion for watered stuffs in England. The chief use of watered stuffs in England and America was as bedroom hangings. The interlacing of moreen, which is described in yet another article by Cummin, is plain rather than twill or satin, but the heavier weft yarn gives it an uneven texture.

Although visually it seems inconsistent to group elaborate pictorial tapestries with the simple weave of homespun, dimity, and moreen, tapestry weave is merely a specific way of interlacing one set of wefts. Some loom techniques changed to suit the needs of the tapestry weaver. His loom was usually upright—a high warp loom—and his main tool for inserting or weaving his threads was a bobbin instead of a shuttle. He worked from the wrong side of the fabric, and he used a cartoon instead of a draft for his working plan. The professional designer-painter was sometimes called in to make the cartoon and sometimes to weave the tapestry. In their respective articles, Ruth Davidson and Madeleine Jarry list Charles Le Brun, Francois Boucher, Jean-Baptiste Oudry, and Goya among the reknowned artists who once worked for the tapestry workshops. The Gobelin family of dyers and Colbert, the minister of Louis XVI, made the Gobelin tapestries famous by including painters, cabinetmakers, goldsmiths, and other craftsmen at Gobelins to reinvigorate weaving and unite the arts in France. Irene Emery, in *The Primary Structures of Fabrics*, cautions against using the name "Gobelin" to refer to the tapestry weave.

The Peruvian poncho, the French "Feudal Life," and the Flemish "Holy Family"—all illustrated in Christa Mayer's article, "Masterpieces of Western Textiles"—exemplify the simple tapestry weave. Mayer pictures other tapestries that represent the second structural classification of supplementary sets—which add one extra set of threads, sometimes continuous from selvage to selvage as in velvet and pile carpets, and sometimes, as in brocaded or knotted carpets, discontinuous. A good illustration of the interlacing techniques used in making tapestries—slit tapestry, weft wrapping, and supplementary wefts—are pictured in the Pickering and Landreau article, "Flat-Woven Rugs of the Middle East." Like tapestries, the kilim is a simple structure formed by numerous compact wefts and sometimes discontinuous wefts for patterning. With the latter, the construction includes either slit or unjoined and interlocked or joined weft threads. Figures 2 and 10 in the Pickering and Landreau article (pp. 124, 129) illustrate such a weave. Irene Emery offers another caution in her book against a common assumption that slits are more associated with kilim than with any other tapestry weaving.

Suggested Reading

Bronson, J. and R. "The Domestic Manufacturer's Assistant and Family Directory" in *The Art of Weaving and Dyeing* (1817). Reprint. New York: Dover Publications, 1977.

Cooper, Grace Rogers. *The Copp Family Textiles*. Washington, D. C.: Smithsonian Institution Press, 1971.

Earle, Alice Morse. *Home Life in Colonial Days*. New York: The Macmillan Company, 1898.

Emery, Irene. *The Primary Structures of Fabrics*. Washington, D. C.: The Textile Museum, 1966.

Gehret, Ellen J. and Keyser, Alan G. *The Homespun Textile Tradition of the Pennsylvania Germans*. Harrisburg: Pennsylvania Historical and Museum Commission, 1976.

Hill, J. W. F., ed. "The Letters and Papers of the Banks Family of Revesby Abbey 1704–1760," in *The Lincoln Record Society* 45 (1952): 210–217. [A documented list of of fibers, fabric names, colors, and bed furniture used in a mid-eighteenth-century English household, arranged by room.]

The textiles

BY VIRGINIA D. PARSLOW, Assistant curator, Farmers' Museum

THE FARMERS' MUSEUM is concerned not only with showing its visitors the finished products of the pioneer, but with giving them an understanding of how, and from what raw materials, the necessities of life were obtained on the frontier. Important among these were clothing for the family, furnishing fabrics for the household, and textiles and cordage for farming operations.

A small field of flax is planted each year near the Lippitt Farmhouse, where it may be seen by the visitor as it grows and blossoms and is pulled, rippled, retted, and dried. Demonstrations on the second floor of the Farmers' Museum show the processing of the flax to obtain the fiber. The operations involved, in which the original tools of the pioneer are used, include beetling and breaking to crush the inner stem, scutching or swingling to remove this broken shive, and heckling to separate the long fibers.

The heckled flax fiber is spread out in a thin web so that when it is wound on the distaff it resembles a huge cocoon. As fibers are drawn down from this holder and smoothed with dampened fingers, the revolving spindle of the flax wheel twists them into finished linen yarn and winds this onto the spool.

From the filled spool the yarn is wound onto the cross arms of the reel, which measures it into knots and skeins (the amount of yarn spun must be measured to determine the number of yards of cloth which can be woven from it). These skeins are washed and then wound on paper quills or bobbins made from elderberry stalks, placed in the shuttle, and finally woven into patterned linen cloth on the barn-frame loom.

The process of heckling the flax fibers leaves a by-product called tow—short and tangled fibers of various grades depending on the size of heckle used. The finer and cleaner grades were spun and woven into coarse fabrics for work clothing, towels, bedticks, and sacks.

The coarsest was spun into heavy yarn on a special tow wheel and laid into rope (a process occasionally demonstrated at the museum). The story of flax is thus told visually from seed to finished textile.

Flax was not the only textile fiber used by the pioneer, so sheep are to be seen in the pasture or in the fold at the farmstead. These are sheared each spring and the fleece is taken to the demonstration area, where it is picked free from burrs and tangles, carded into rolls on hand cards, and spun into woolen yarn on the great wheel.

Skeins of woolen yarn are sometimes dyed in a large copper kettle hung over an open fire at the farmhouse. The yarn is first simmered in a bath of alum dissolved in rainwater and then in a decoction of the dyestuff, in order to impart as permanent a color as possible. As in pioneer days, goldenrod blossoms, alder bark, and sumac berries are collected from the fields for producing the commonest colors. A bed of madder growing behind the farmhouse supplies a red dyestuff. Materials which the pioneer might purchase often included the dried root of madder and the ever-popular indigo; more rarely cochineal, which produced the desirable but expensive scarlet red, was bought.

Cotton was not a farm product in the northern sections of this country, but after 1800 it was readily purchasable in the form of yarn. Bed coverlets were woven of cotton and woolen yarns, and cotton was often combined with homespun linen for table linens and toweling. Cotton also replaced linen for the warp of the common material known as linsey-woolsey.

A few original textiles are used in the demonstration area as examples of various techniques, patterns, and material uses, and many more are found in their appropriate places in the buildings of the Village Cross-

Swingling and spinning flax. Swingling board and knife are used here to remove bits of broken stem from the flax fibers. Linen yarn is being spun on the flax wheel from the fibers arranged on the distaff. *Farmers' Museum.*

roads and farmstead. At both the Bump Tavern and the Lippitt Farmhouse the beds are made up with hand-woven sheets, pillowcases, blankets, coverlets, and bedcovers. Carpets, table linens, towels, and bed and window hangings show the wide variety of color and pattern in textiles available in the pioneer community.

The folk art collection, housed at Fenimore House, also includes some textiles: here the decorative rugs and the bedquilts are to be found. The rugs are in the yarn-sewn, shirred-patch, and hooked techniques. Most of the quilts displayed are of the more decorative appliqué type, but there are also pieced ones in the collection.

Hours of research insure that each tool, process, and pattern is as authentic as possible. The weaves and patterns of the original fabrics in the textile collections of the museums are constantly being studied and analyzed. These patterns are used in the fabrics woven for demonstration.

Library source material such as weavers' account books (ANTIQUES, April 1956, p. 346), old printed weaving pattern books, and newspaper advertisements help the staff to decide which types of textiles belong in the several buildings of the museum. Information from manuscripts and printed sources has also been used to determine the processes and materials used to produce the beautiful colors found in the old pieces.

Photographs on these pages by Rollins.

Spinning wool. Woolen yarn
being spun on the great wheel
from rolls produced with the hand cards.
Farmers' Museum.

Barn-frame loom. Warp-striped woolen carpeting
being woven on an eighteenth-century loom
from yarns colored with natural dyes.
Farmers' Museum.

Household and clothing fabrics. *Upper left:* Striped linsey-woolsey, once part of a petticoat. *Lower left:* Woman's blue plaid apron in empire style. *Upper right:* Young woman's blouse of hand-woven linen in blue, gold, and natural, in an eighteenth-century style. *Lower right:* blue and white linen handkerchief. *Background:* Diaper-pattern linen tablecloth, and damask table cover of cotton and blue woolen woven by James Cunningham of New Hartford, New York, in 1841.

Upper left: Rug made of strips of woolen fabric sewn to a linen background. *Upper right:* Typical example of hand-woven room-size floor coverings woven of hand-spun and home-dyed woolen yarns from about 1820 to 1860. *Lower left:* Large hooked rug. *Lower right:* Rug dated 1852, a late example of the technique of sewing loops of yarn into a background with a needle. *Fenimore House.*

Quilts and bedspreads. *Clockwise from upper left:* Quilt typical of the red, green, and white appliqué style of about 1840. Bedspread of hand-woven cotton embroidered with the cotton yarn known as candlewicking; this one is dated 1825. Pieced and appliqué quilt with embroidered detail. Quilt made up of a star-form pieced center of printed cotton with corners of appliqué woodblock chintz and quilted border. Quilted bedcover of a copperplate-printed cotton exported from England in quantity during the last quarter of the eighteenth century. *Fenimore House.*

Parlor bedroom in Lippitt Farmhouse. Original textiles shown include striped woolen carpet, summer-and-winter coverlet and rose-wheel embroidered blanket on the chest, checked linen bed hangings, and bedspread of hand-woven cotton and wool with woolen embroidery.

Connecticut homespun

BY ABBOTT LOWELL CUMMINGS

CLOTHMAKING IS AMONG THE EARLIEST American crafts. Seventeenth-century inventories mention "home made Cloth" along with imported fabrics, and later reminiscences praise the spinning and weaving skill of the early housewife. Frances Little has shown in her study of early American textiles that there were also professional weavers in the Colonies from the start; Manasseh Minor (1647-1728) of Stonington, Connecticut, is a familiar example. In a group of early Providence, Rhode Island, inventories Mrs. Little found mention of fifty spinning wheels as against nine looms, which suggests that weaving was often done outside the home. Henry Wansey, an Englishman who visited America in 1794, wrote that on Long Island the women of each family, "whenever they have any leisure, spin the yarn out of flax they themselves raise, and when they have eight or ten pounds of yarn, they send it to a public weaver, who returns it to them, wove into cloth."

The "public weaver" in some cases may simply have been an individual who possessed a loom and a knack for weaving and could thus be of service to his neighbors. Eighteenth-century account books reveal this pattern of semi-professional specialization, closely linked to the economy of the almost self-sufficient farm. Practically everyone in the community, including the artisan, farmed for a part of his living, earning the balance (often in produce) through some particular skill. The present study deals with a single family in Southington, Connecticut, whose account books show that they specialized in weaving cloth while carrying on routine farming and operating a sawmill.

Samuel Newell, the founder of the family in Southington, settled in a part of town still known as South End. His son Josiah Newell, born in 1722, came into posses-

sion of the farm after Samuel's death in 1751 and improved it with a new dwelling, recording on May 11, 1768, "then I Raisd my House." Among his children was a son, Amos Newell, born in 1762 and married in 1787 to Lucy Root, whose mother, Lucy Curtiss, was a daughter of the town's first minister. About the time of Lucy Curtiss's marriage to Elisha Root in 1764 she had made for herself (according to family tradition) the customary fine household linen. One of her towels is reproduced in part as typical of the eighteenth-century homespun product.

Amos and his father managed the farm together and at Josiah's death in 1797 Amos inherited the property,

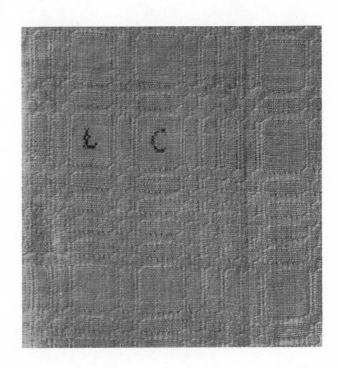

Detail of towel woven by
Lucy (Curtiss) Root about 1764.

Newell House, South End, Southington, Connecticut. Built 1768, destroyed about 1875; photograph taken about 1867.

living there until his own death in 1844. The joint day-books start on March 1, 1791, with the entry:

Elnathan Norton Dtr

to Six £ Six oz of flax	0 3 2
to Cloth for Shoes and A knot of thread	0 1 8

and on May 16 is noted "to weaving 21 2/4 yards of Linen Cloth 0 10 9." The reference to weaving "Linen Cloth" or often simply "Cloth" is the characteristic entry. Occasionally one finds accounts for the weaving of "flannel" and "Shirting," and in July 1792, there is the item "to weaving ten yds of Bed tick 0 4 7." There is seldom an item of less than ten yards, and twenty or thirty are usual. The longest single item is dated June 24, 1793, "to weaving 36 yards of linen Cloth." These entries may refer to the weaving of yarn that others had spun, or the cloth may have been produced on the Newell farm from start to finish. The site of their flax fields is still pointed out, and accounts in the 1790's credit several neighbors with assistance in the preparation of yarn, "By one days work Breaking flax," "by Spining," "By Breaking 10 pounds of wool," "By Combing 7 1/4 pounds of wool."

In addition to the accounts there is a homemade book of dye receipts consisting of several sheets of paper bound in a half sheet of newspaper published in 1784. The handwriting is probably Josiah's, and he has scribbled on the cover, apparently in getting his pen started, such phrases as "go and get some ink" and "ant my pen good." Eight receipts are reproduced here, with separations indicated and all explanatory material confined to brackets (the ninth and last, in a different hand, is nearly illegible and has been omitted):

A Recept for Colouring Snuf

Take butnut [butternut] bark and Fustick / boil it one our / then take it out and Coperis it and then Rence it well / then fling away the old dy and make it anew with red wood dye and set it with Allum / And if to red Sadden it with Butternut Liquor

Another for Colouring Snuff

Take Butternut bark of the body / make it Strong / [do] not rence it / then Set it up anew with fustic one pound to 3 or 4 yards of Cloth / add a little Redwood / set it with allum verry Strong and Close it with Potash

A Receipt for Colouring Chocolate

Take Butternut bark of the body and fustic / boil it one hour / then then [thin] it out and Coperas it once and boil it half an hour / then take out and Coperas it again and boil half an hour more / then take it out / fling away the old dyes and rence your Cloth Clean / then new vamp it again with redwood and Set it with allum and potash / Redwood 2 pounds to 3 yards of Cloth

A Receipt for Colouring Reds

Let your Cloth be white or make it a faint Butternut / then take 3 pounds of allum to thirty yards of Cloth / Boil it well / then take it Out [do] not Rence it / then Boil half a pound of Redwood to a yard of Cloth for the first Rate Colours / a qarter of apound for Common Colours / to darken it take 4 pounds of logwood to thirty yard of Cloth / then ad to the Logwood Sum Ashes or lye / use a little at a time for fear of Spotting / the more allum the Less Redwood

A Receipt to Colour Clarret

Take Butternut bark of the body and boil it one our / then take it and Copperis it / then fling away your old dy and Rence your Cloth Clean / then new vamp your dy with redwood and allum and boil it one hour / then it out and put in more redwood and allum and boil it one hour more / then potash it also / put 2 pounds of redwood to 3 yards of Cloth &c

A Receipt to Colour Scarlet

to 20 yards of Cloth take one pound of argil / put it into a barrel of soft water when boiling enter your goods boyling 4 hours / then take it out / then [add] 2 pounds of fustic when boyling enter your goods and bring them to a good yellow / then take 6 ounces of the Cream of tarter and 6 ounces of agofortis [aquafortis] Rild with quicksilver Cucheneal [cochineal] and put them all into your yellow dy and let it run [?] one our and it Shall Come to Scarlet

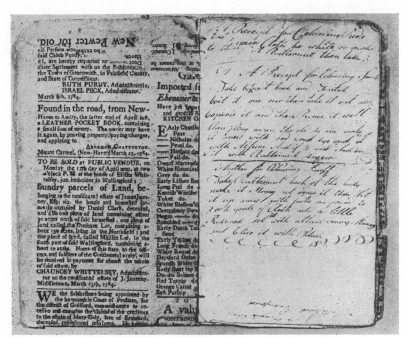

Dye receipt book of the Newell family, showing hand-written receipts bound in newspaper dated 1784.

To Colour Red

Take of the Sowerings of wheat bran to the quantity of 2 pails full of it / Stir your kittle of water / then ad one ounce of allum to a yard of Cloth / then Stur your goods for one hour / then take one pound of redwood to a yard of Cloth and put it in the Same dy / then put in your goods and bring them almost to aboil / and when it has got the strength of the dy then take agofortis to the value of half an ounce to twelve yards of Cloth / Stir it well / then put in your goods and bring it almost to a boil and it will Stand

To turn it to a Crimson put in the dy Sig out of your tub where you Liquor Cloth for fuling

A Receipt for Colouring an olive green

Take Red oak [?] bark Shumake wood older [alder] bark and Fustic and boil it one hour / tke it out / put in more of the Same and Coperis it and boil it half an hour / Coperes it again / boil it half an hour more and your Colour is finished

The only entry in the accounts for dyeing is on May 16, 1799, two years after Josiah's death: "Jacob Tyler Dtr . . . to Colouring 9 yards of Linen Cloth 0 3 0." But the use of colored yarn is implied in occasional entries for weaving "Check," as for example on July 1, 1793, "to weaving 18 yds of Check Linen 0 10 6." Checked linen was a popular homespun pattern and is mentioned often in eighteenth-century inventories. Wansey notes in 1794 that in Northford, Connecticut, "at one house where I stopped, a young woman told me that . . . the check window curtains were her own making, of flax, raised, dressed, and spun by herself and sister, as well as the bed-furniture of the house." The Newell accounts also indicate that weaving and dyeing were carried on under the same roof. In some cases, however, the coloring of cloth was practiced as a separate trade. The Marquis de Chastellux reports in 1780 that while near Hartford, Connecticut, he "went into a house where they were preparing and dying the cloth. This cloth is made by the people of the country and is then sent to these little manufactures, where they are dressed, pressed and dyed

for two shillings . . . per yard . . ."

On October 17, 1797, Josiah died suddenly at the age of seventy-five. The inventory of his estate mentions an "old Loom and tackling" and "4 yds new Check Linen Cloth." References to breaking flax in 1798 and the item of coloring the cloth in 1799 show that the clothmaking activity did not cease immediately. The accounts con-

Blue-checked linen woven by the Newell family, probably in the 1790's.

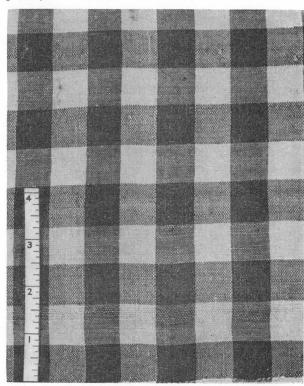

81

tinue until 1843, one year before Amos's death, but there are only two further entries for weaving, the last on June 2, 1809. One assumes from this that the weaving had been performed primarily by Josiah and gradually ceased after his death. The inventory of Amos's estate in 1844 makes no mention of a loom.

The old house was pulled down about 1875; the bulk of its contents, however, was preserved, including the account books and receipt book and the early samples of cloth here illustrated. The first, blue-checked linen, is presumably the "Check" of the 1790's recorded in the accounts, which do not mention this pattern after 1800. The second, blue-checked woolen, does not appear specifically in the accounts, but Josiah's inventory in 1797 mentions "1 Checkd woolen Shirt." The third fragment is a sample of blue resist-dyed cotton, showing one complete repeat pattern, presumably executed in this family. The familiar resist-dyed fabrics, particularly of Long Island and the Hudson River Valley, are often more sophisticated in design and more complex in color—here only one shade of blue on white. In the making of these designs the pattern areas of the white cloth are treated with a "resist" substance, generally wax or clay, perhaps applied by pattern blocks. When the cloth has been dyed the resist substance is removed (if wax by heat, if clay by washing) and the pattern appears in the original white color of the cloth protected from the dye.

The weaving tradition in the Newell family did not die out altogether. Amos Newell's oldest daughter, Olive Newell, born in 1788, grew up in her grandfather's house and seems to have learned the craft well. In 1811 she married her next-door neighbor, Stephen Walkley, and one of their sons, writing much later, recalls her many household responsibilities in that early period. It is the familiar picture of the skilled and resourceful New England housewife, and yet must owe something to her early upbringing in a house where weaving was extensively practiced. "At my earliest recollection," he writes, "our clothing as well as food was the product of the farm. We raised flax, which after being rotted, broken, swincheled and hetcheled, became flax with a residue of tow. The flax was spun on a Dutch wheel, woven by mother and bleached, for sheets and handkerchiefs. After the cotton gin was invented, about 1820, we bought cotton cloth for shirting and gave up the raising of flax . . . We kept about thirty sheep, and all our winter underclothing was made of wool, spun by the girls [his sisters] and woven by Mother . . . I remember that Mother made a blanket shawl, which took a prize at a fair in Farmington. It was all spun by the girls and dyed and woven by Mother . . . Mother used to dye the flannel for our winter shirts a bright yellow with peach leaves."

Apparently acceptance of the industrial product was slow in this rural New England town. Despite the presence nearby of the Hartford Woolen Manufactory established in 1788, and a woolen and cotton manufactory in New Haven which Wansey tells us in 1794 was "patronised by the State," there was little slackening in the traditional home production of cloth until well into the nineteenth century. And until the industrial venture proved profitable (Wansey found the Hartford establishment "hardly able to maintain itself," and the New Haven project eating up "a great deal of money"), both the village weaver and the housewife at her loom continued to play a vital role in the New England community.

Blue-checked woolen woven by the Newell family, probably in the 1790's.

Blue resist-dyed cotton, late eighteenth century (?), probably executed by the Newell family.

BY CATHERINE FENNELLY

The collections: textiles and costumes

SPINNING, DYEING, and weaving were still important household industries in rural New England at the beginning of the nineteenth century. Home textile-making had received new impetus during enforcement of the non-importation measures of the 1760's and the Revolution, and it continued to grow until after the War of 1812. Several factors account for its continuance: lack of cash in rural areas, which put much imported material out of reach of the farmer's purse; the introduction of carding mills in the 1790's, which enabled the housewife to eliminate one of the most tedious and time-consuming steps in the process; the craze for merino sheep, which gave new impetus to wool-growing; and the Embargo of 1807 and the War of 1812, which largely cut off the American market from European goods. If we are to believe both contemporary observers of the New England scene and those who looked back on it several decades later, there was scarcely a rural household that did not produce most of the textiles used by members of the family. The Reverend Horace Bushnell, in delivering a centennial address in Litchfield, Connecticut, in 1851, termed the era that preceded his the "age of homespun," giving it an apt name that still clings.

The textiles in the Old Sturbridge Village collection are representative of this age in New England: clothing, table and bed linens, blankets, curtains, carpets, and what we might today term pure decoration—a gaily stenciled window shade, painted oilcloths, fantastically embroidered or appliquéd squares, and pockets seemingly made just for fun. On looking at the collection as a whole, one is impressed by the appalling expenditure of time and effort that must have gone into making and sewing fabrics, and by the survival of so much of the product—a surprising amount in view of the proverbial New England frugality that would never allow a piece of material to be discarded until it was worn out. But New Englanders sometimes wore out before their possessions, so that the museum can today acquire the high-waisted woolen suit worn by a small boy the day he was accidentally killed at a house-raising, the exquisitely tucked and embroidered baby's cap, the glazed wool coverlet so carefully handled that it looks as though newly calendered, the appliquéd quilt guarded for a hundred and fifty years against the ravages of sun and dust.

Costumes in the Village collection range from linen shirts to silk cloaks. The few women's gowns indicate the endless variations that modified the Empire fashion, and

A corner of the textile demonstration in the Mashapaug House, with wool and flax wheels, cards, and yarn winders. The case at left displays early nineteenth-century homewoven blankets. That at right shows woven coverlets of eighteenth- and early nineteenth-century patterns. One, made in Groton, Connecticut, is dated 1833. *Photograph by Samuel Chamberlain.*

Checks and stripes in blue-, brown-, and red-and-white. The triangular-folded bandanna is cotton. The striped piece is a brown-and-white linsey-woolsey blanket initialed *A.R.* The blanket at lower left is from New Hampshire.

Checked and striped woolen homespuns. All the blankets here are from Massachusetts and New Hampshire. The stripe is a brown, yellow, and cream linsey-woolsey.

Cotton-and-wool coverlet, tan and two shades of green, found in Massachusetts. A center seam suggests that it was woven at home.

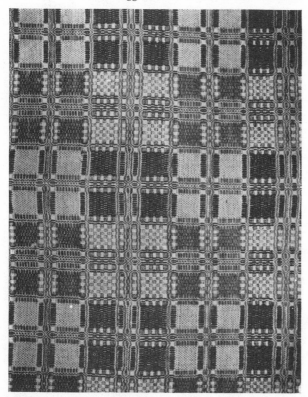

Homespun blanket, green, yellow, red, and blue plaid, found in Massachusetts.

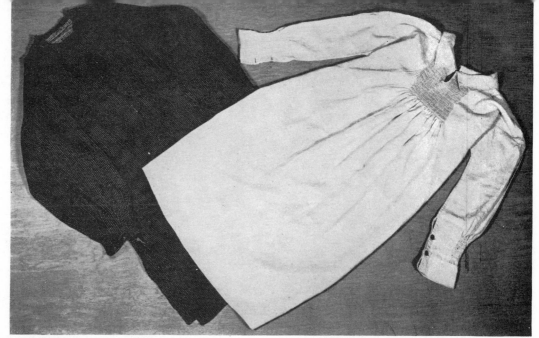

Farmer's smocks or frocks. Left, found in Vermont; indigo-and-white striped wool wtih a brown-and-white checked woolen lining; side seams are open at the bottom to allow freedom of movement. Right, found on Cape Cod; heavy white linen, smocked and embroidered at yoke, shoulders, and wrists, with pewter buttons; similar to many nineteenth-century English smocks.

Child's blue woolen suit with high waist and brass buttons. It belonged to a Spencer, Massachusetts, child who died in 1820.

Checked, indigo-dyed fabrics. Apron at left is linen, the other wool. The man's bandanna is also linen. The background is a blue-and-white wool plaid blanket.

Detail from a coverlet stenciled boldly in green, yellow, and orange on unbleached cotton. The four sides are bound in pink cotton, with the bottom corners cut out. Signed on the back *Hannah Corbin, Woodstock* [*Connecticut*].

Stenciled cotton length, thought to have been a window shade; found in New Hampshire. The urns and vases are yellow, blossoms red and rose, foliage green.

Stenciled cotton table cover, 27¼ inches square. The birds and the border swags are of particular interest. Found in New Hampshire. The colors are rose, yellow, green, brown, and blue.

exemplify the belle's lament: "Plump and rosy was my face, And graceful was my form, Till fashion deem'd it a disgrace To keep my body warm." In this *mode à la grecque* waists were high, bosoms low-cut, skirts narrow, sleeves short. But here, as in all styles, there was a decided time lag in the rural areas, and farm women tended to adapt dress fashions to their way of living. A patchwork-printed cotton dress in the collection has a high, fitted bodice, enormous sleeves foreshadowing the leg-of-mutton of the nineties, and an action-free skirt gathered at the waistline—an 1830 modification of the Empire style. Another gown, a faded pink muslin, has a narrow skirt cut straight from bodice to hem. A white cotton wedding dress has a beautifully embroidered hem, tightly gathered neckline, and long sleeves.

Here, as in every aspect of the textile collection, everyday homespun is today almost non-existent. It was worn until threadbare, then used as patches for mending. Three farmer's smocks, a few waistcoats, jackets, shirts, cloaks, and breeches comprise the limited group of men's clothing. Underclothing would seem to have been reserved to women—petticoats clumsily or beautifully quilted, chemises or shifts, and bodices. Women's indoor caps and outdoor bonnets and calashes are comparatively easy to find. Baby clothes were usually preserved, perhaps for the next baby that never arrived, perhaps for a future grandchild. Dresses for small children, boys as well as girls, are made of printed cotton. The woolens, being more perishable, have largely disappeared.

Linen was more commonly used for sheeting than cotton. Most of the sixty-odd sheets in the collection are seamed down the center, probably an indication that they were woven on narrow home looms. Those without seams are obviously imported or store-purchased, as was the cotton sheeting. Pillow cases are plain white linen. One bolster is a beautiful dark blue-and-white check. Coverlets are woven cotton or linen and wool, plain or patchwork glazed wool with the traditional pumpkin-colored backing, printed cotton, patchwork, stenciled, or candlewick-stitched. Blankets are cream-colored wool with embroidered corners or edge-stitching, checks, stripes, or plaids in several color combinations. Home weaving of blankets in checks, plaids, and stripes goes back to the early eighteenth century. Most of the blankets in the Village collection are from New Hampshire, where the Scotch-Irish tradition of beautiful weaving was strong. Tablecloths and napkins are white linen, most of them woven in a diaper or goose-eye pattern, as are many of the hand towels. Heavier towels and bed ticking are made of coarse linen or tow.

Silk seems to have been worn and used but little in country areas, or perhaps again it was used until worn out. A cotton-lined black cloak belonging to a clergyman's wife, an embroidered waistcoat, an apron, a petticoat, a few bonnets and reticules, a handful of ribbons, a shawl or two, comprise the entire silk collection.

To the uninitiated, textiles may seem at best a tenuous and elusive element in early New England rural life. Yet one has only to examine the roughness of the texture of the farmer's frock, the blend of pattern and color as expressions of a longing for beauty in the stenciled coverlet, or the exquisite, painstaking quilting on a bride's under-skirt to gain new insight into the lives and aspirations of New Englanders of the age of homespun.

Tennessee textiles

BY RICHARD H. HULAN

Field researcher, division of performing arts, Smithsonian Institution

Fig. 1. A loom of great size and complexity produced this white cotton counterpane, perhaps in Scotland (thistles appear in the pattern). Mrs. John Buchanan (1774-1831) may have had it made in Nashville, but its unusual overshot brocade weave and its six-foot width point to a highly developed textile industry. The table-top spinning wheel of black walnut, more representative of machinery available locally at the end of the eighteenth century, belonged to the same housewife. *Tennessee State Museum; except for Fig. 5, photographs are by Helga Photo Studio.*

THE DOCUMENTARY history of the textile industry in Tennessee begins with an advertisement on the first page of the first extant issue of the state's first newspaper, *The Knoxville Gazette* for January 14, 1792:

Cotton Manufactory
CUMBERLAND
The subscriber has his machines in order for carding, spinning, and weaving; and is in want of a number of GOOD WEAVERS.
The greatest encouragement will be given to such as are acquainted with the weaving of Velvets, Corduroys, and Calicoes.

John Hague
Manchester (Mero District)
Nov. 11, 1791

Both the ambitious Mr. Hague and the location of his proposed mill are unknown apart from this notice; the site of present-day Manchester was in 1791 acknowledged Indian territory. Middle Tennessee in the eighteenth century held great potential, but high risk, for the investor of industrial capital. The contrast between a settler's aspirations and the means available for their fulfillment is suggested by Figure 1. The spread and spinning wheel shown there were owned by Sally Ridley Buchanan, two-hundred-pound heroine of the Battle of Buchanan's Station (the last major Indian attack near Nashville, September 30, 1792).

It is unlikely that the spread was manufactured in Tennessee. Of the two-dozen textile plants known to have opened there by 1833, most processed only cotton and produced only yarn. A notable exception was the Nashville establishment of Adam Maguire, whose 1804 advertisement reads as follows:

Dying and Weaving

The subscriber respectfully informs the public, that he now is preparing to accomodate them in his line of business at the house of Patrick Lyons in Nashville, to wit: Dying blue on Cotton, thread and woolen: Black, red, green and yellow on woollen yarn. He will weave Diaper Carpets, Summer counterpanes and double coverlids equally as neat and good as any ever made in North America.

To make double coverlids, spin the cotton ten cuts to the pound, double and twist it, and 18 pounds will make two coverlids: one half must be well bleached, and the other dyed blue. For summer counterpanes, spin the warp 40 cuts to the pound, double and twist it, and 6 pounds will warp two; spin the filling 20 cuts to the pound, and 6 pounds of single thread will fill the two.

Adam Maguire
N. B. Those who wish to be instructed in the above branches of business will be accommodated by application as above.

Throughout the nineteenth century the cloth commercially produced in the state tended toward the simpler weaves. It was frequently for rough use (sacking for

Fig. 2. The earliest known owner of this loom was Elizabeth (Mrs. Caleb) Carman (1818-1875). It was probably made for her c. 1840; the woodwork in her house of that period is of the same native white ash as the loom. The Carman family lived on Goose Creek in what is now Trousdale (formerly Sumner) County. *Author's collection.*

Fig. 3. Homespun-cotton warp and wool weft were used by Susan Elizabeth Winningham to produce this striped blanket at Allens, Overton County, c. 1880. The colors are red, green, and pokeberry purple on a background of unbleached wool. *Collection of Mrs. L. P. Stephenson.*

cotton bales, slaves' clothing, and so on) and principally for the regional market (shirting, sheeting, jeans, bedticking, and linsey-woolsey). During this period, however, Tennessee yarns were woven elsewhere into finer fabrics. The basic fibers (flax, wool, and cotton) have been cash crops from the earliest settlement to the present time. Of lesser economic impact, but greater public interest, were the agrarian marvels: Captain James Miller (Hawkins County) raised five million silkworms in 1792; Mark R. Cockrill (Davidson County) exhibited what was hailed as the world's finest wool at the London Crystal Palace in 1851; and General William G. Harding (Davidson County) successfully raised Cashmere goats from 1859 through the 1880's.

For aesthetically satisfying Tennessee textiles, therefore, one must look beyond the early industry. A great quantity and, considering the equipment used (Fig. 2), a great variety of cloth was manufactured at home. In 1810 there were 17,316 hand looms in the state, roughly one for every six free inhabitants. Each of these produced about two hundred yards of cloth per year; eighty-seven per cent was cotton cloth, the rest wool or mixed fibers. The versatility of a housewife-weaver is shown in the list of premiums won by Mrs. A. Barnes (Sumner County) at the 1855 state fair: fine jeans, brown jeans, flannel, striped cotton cloth, cotton coverlet, linen diaper, flax linen, and tow linen.

It might well be observed that the textiles in Figures 3 and 4 satisfy a folk aesthetic, not necessarily the taste of the most sophisticated Tennessean. Still, they were the typical texiles of the region. The grim realities of poor

transportation and a chronic shortage of cash in the economy kept products of the relatively inefficient hand weaver competitive with factory goods in many communities well into the twentieth century.

Between the housewife and the factory as textile producers stands the professional hand weaver, for whom there is little documentation. Twenty-five persons are listed as weavers in the 1850 census, and there is no way to know what they wove. About one-third were men born in Great Britain, and one-third Southern widows; among the rest are a few Swiss, but (rather surprisingly) no Germans. At least one Jacquard weaver worked at Cumberland Gap before 1855; however, I know of no Tennessee-marked Jacquard spread.

The dated weaving draft is the best evidence in textile arts, short of the signed piece itself; one excellent collection of drafts from a semiprofessional weaver in Bedford County is in the Tennessee State Library and Archives (Fig. 5). This collection contains drafts dated between 1824 and 1851; it includes written instructions for making and threading a loom, and for dyeing with indigo, as well as the unusually complex six- and eight-harness pattern drafts.

Much more common are the four-harness "colonial

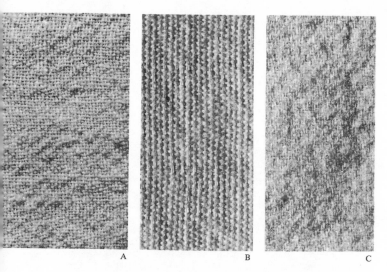

A   B   C

Fig. 4. Three white blankets with cotton warp and wool filler. A and B are plain (tabby) weave; the difference in their textures is due to the use of two warp threads in each heddle when B was woven. Both are from Wilson County, mid-nineteenth century. C is a four-harness twill weave from Faulkner's Mill, McMinnville, c. 1875. This Warren County item was marketed by Sears, Roebuck and Co. in the 1890's for $1.40 a "pair" (one blanket made of two strips sewn together). Faulkner's spinning machinery was powered by water, but the looms themselves were still hand powered when the mill closed in 1939. *A and B, collection of Lucy Barker; C, collection of Mrs. Charles Faulkner Bryan.*

Fig. 5. A booklet of pattern drafts in the Catherine Orme Williams papers, Manuscript Division, Tennessee State Library and Archives, contains this selection, "copied from Mrs. McCulloch's book, 1851." The weaver may have been Robert Scott, whose name at the end of one page of this booklet seems to indicate ownership. Various members of the Scott, Cooper, and Orme families in the vicinity of Fairfield owned the drafts; an early list of customers establishes a Bedford County origin. *Tennessee State Library and Archives.*

Fig. 6. This coverlet, whose design is usually called Tennessee Troubles (although the scene of the troubles is sometimes reported as North Carolina or Missouri), is from East Tennessee and dates c. 1850. *Collection of Mrs. David Glenn.*

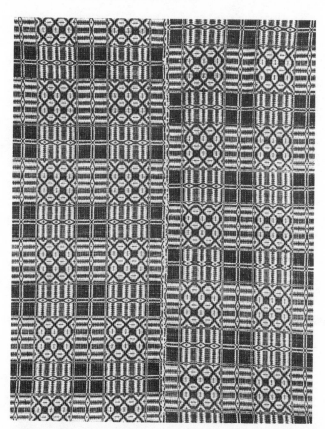

overshot" coverlets. These have been preserved and collected more than other homemade textiles because they are not only the most attractive of the average weaver's repertoire, but also the most difficult to make. One pattern with strong Tennessee associations is illustrated in Figure 6. The pattern names of coverlets and quilts are regionally traditional, and to an alarming degree interchangeable. Studies of the subject are more often romantic than scientific; here again the best evidence of the traditional name for a pattern is its draft with the name written by the weaver.

Occasionally the name of a coverlet also denotes a quilt pattern; examples are Double Bow Knot, Fool's Puzzle, LeMoyne Star, and Lovers' Knot. The quilting process (Fig. 7) lends itself to personalization by signature, date, or whatever seems important to the quilter (Figs. 8 and 9). Thus a Family Tree quilt (often in the Log Cabin pattern) may tell us the ancestry, or a Friendship quilt the social circle, of our craftswoman—certainly more than we usually know of the weaver.

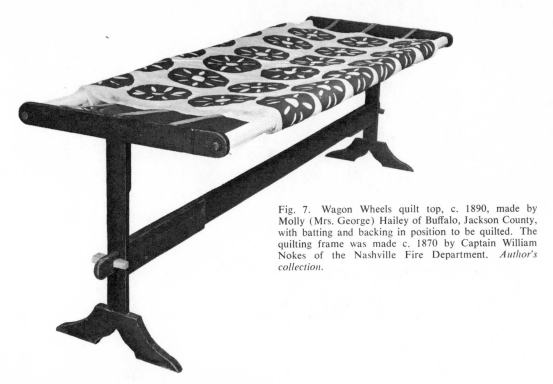

Fig. 7. Wagon Wheels quilt top, c. 1890, made by Molly (Mrs. George) Hailey of Buffalo, Jackson County, with batting and backing in position to be quilted. The quilting frame was made c. 1870 by Captain William Nokes of the Nashville Fire Department. *Author's collection.*

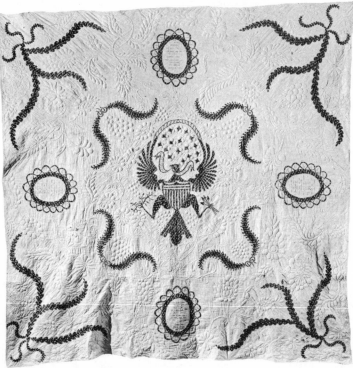

Fig. 8. The earliest and finest known Tennessee quilt. Seventeen links of chain around each oval frame the names of the states through Ohio; there are also seventeen stars above the eagle. Two poems, the first stitched in the side ovals, the second—along with signature, place, and date—in the top and bottom ones, reflect the enthusiastic patriotism of nineteenth-century America:

Long as the Stars their courses run/Or Man beholds the circling Sun/May God o'er fair Columbia reign/And crown her counsels with success/With peace and joy her Eagle bless/And all her sacred rights maintain.

O Liberty thou Goddess Heavenly bright/Profuse of bliss and pregnant with delight/Eternal pleasures in thy presence reign/and smiling plenty lead thy wanton train. Rebecah Foster/Nashville October 5/1808. *Privately owned.*

Fig. 9. Detail of Fig. 8.

WHAT WAS DIMITY IN 1790?

By HAZEL E. CUMMIN

A SERIES of studies of certain fabrics in use in America before the advent of the power loom has recently been instituted by the Robert E. Lee Memorial Foundation, in charge of the restoration of Stratford Hall, seat of the Lee family in Virginia. An outline of the first study, made with reference to the furnishing of a field bed in the Stratford nursery, is here published for the first time.

Although Stratford Hall was built about 1729, three rooms in the mansion, including the mother's room and nursery, were remodeled between about 1793 and 1805, and are being furnished in the style of that period. This was a time of much distinguished building in Virginia, especially that designed or influenced by Thomas Jefferson. And because Jefferson was meticulous in the records he kept of his work, these contain many valuable suggestions for restoration work of this period.

In the Coolidge collection of Jefferson drawings, now in the Massachusetts Historical Society library, are given directions for bed and window hangings, and among them is a sketch (No. 149f) for dining-room curtains of "dimity," dated by Fiske Kimball about 1805. This provided the necessary authority for a plan for dimity bed and window hangings in the Stratford nursery. But careful study of the notes accompanying the sketch convinced the furnishing committee that the "dimity" Jefferson intended must have been something quite different from the sheer corded dress material which is the only fabric sold as dimity in the shops today.

In the first place, the sketch is for curtains for a dining room, where privacy would have demanded something more substantial than modern dimity. Furthermore, the dimensions given are for windows of impressive proportions for which a few lengths of sheer material, "2 ft. 1 i. wide" as noted, seemed inadequate unless over-draperies were intended. But there is no mention of such draperies. Instead the directions are explicit that the dimity is to be tacked directly to a cornice of some weight and pretentiousness. Further question was raised by this note: "The curtain cornice projects about 4 i. at each end beyond the architrave, consequently the measure here called 8 f. 4 i. can be but 7 f. 7 i. the difference proceeds from *measuring the dimity on the stretch*." Obviously no "dimity" sold today would gain 9 inches across a window cornice "on the stretch." The conclusion was inevitable that the dimity Jefferson intended was an upholstery material of some kind, heavier than modern dimity, and of a very different weave.

The Stratford committee set itself the task of finding out what this material was. The first step was suggested by correspondents at the Victoria and Albert Museum of London, who wrote that, as far as they were aware, the Oxford English Dictionary description of dimity was "correct for the eighteenth-century fabric called by that name." They added, "The material sold nowadays in English shops under the name of 'dimity' is a fine corded muslin, very similar to the American variety." The Museum, they said, did not own any fabric known to have been called dimity in the eighteenth century.

The definition referred to in the big Oxford dictionary of 1897 reads as follows:

Dimity. A stout cotton fabric, woven with raised stripes or fancy figures, usually employed for beds and bed-room hangings, and sometimes for garments.

Earlier definitions are quoted from Florio, an English writer of Tuscan origin who published an Italian-English dictionary in 1598:

Dimity. Italian Dimito. A kind of coarse cotton flannel. A kind of linzie-wolzie.

These definitions prompted a canvass of a score of dictionaries, English and American, dating from the period under consideration. Since 1805, when Sam Johnson's dictionary called dimity "a fine kind of fustian," every dictionary consulted defines dimity as a "stout" upholstery material. No early dictionary, and no dictionary of any date published in England, defines it as a sheer corded stuff. A few modern American dictionaries give two definitions, thus:

Webster's *Dictionary*, 1934: Dimity. a. A cotton fabric with raised stripes or cords, used for hangings and furniture coverings, and sometimes for garments. It is of many patterns and occasionally in colors. b. A fine, thin, corded cotton fabric, white or colored, and often figured, used for dresses.

This dictionary evidence is amply supported by references in English and American literature, and by eighteenth-century newspaper accounts and advertisements. These show that dimity was in general use as an upholstery material throughout the seventeenth and eighteenth centuries, and that it was commonly "stout." Where dimity is mentioned as a costume fabric, its use as a strong, serviceable material is indicated. For example:

New Castle Court Records, 1678: Robert Hutchinson — confessed that he did take out of ye chest — one dimety wastcoate. Fielding, 1743: His waistcoat was of dimity, richly embroidered with yellow silk.

Dimity "coverings" and "linings" are mentioned frequently from 1700 on; and references to "dimity beds" are numerous after 1760. In advertisements dimity is nearly always offered along with other bed-furnishing fabrics. Thus:

Boston News Letter, March 21, 1723: To be sold at reasonable rates — striped Hollands and Ticks Bunts for beds, or bed Ticks, White Demities, flower'd and plain Fustians . . . Also . . . Bed-Camblets, Cotton Quilts, etc.

In many other references, dimity is bracketed with fustians and similar materials. This grouping recurs often enough to suggest a relationship between these fabrics other than that of general usage. A valuable account of the stout early dimity, published in France in 1760, makes this relationship clear. Here *futaine* (fustian) is described (in translation):

A kind of cloth that appears twilled on one side, and which has some relation to dimity (*basin*), although less fine.

Basin (dimity) is discussed as follows:

A twilled cloth, which must be manufactured entirely of cotton thread, in the warp as well as in the filling (*tout en chaîne qu'en trame*). There are dimities of different qualities and styles; wide, narrow, fine, medium, coarse, plain with a nap on one side; others with small imperceptible stripes without nap; and others with large stripes or bars (*rayes ou barres*), also without nap.

The account goes on to say that dimities have been made in France since 1580; that those of Troyes are the most esteemed; and that these have become so important that the Regulation of January 1701 was made especially for them. This Regulation provided, among other matters, that all dimities be made of pure cotton, without any mixture of tow, or of hemp fiber, or of flax; that the warp threads be of twisted cotton; and that the pieces sufficiently full of weft, and beaten on the loom, so as to hold up and preserve their width.

Dimities, the author continues, that come from the East Indies are white and without pile. There are two fashions of them — twilled, or *sergé*, and checked or diapered. He adds that dimities are used to make camisoles, petticoats, corsets, and counterpanes,

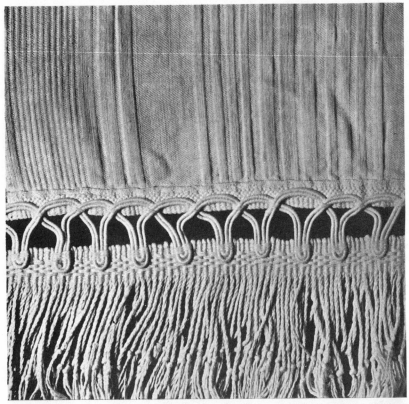

Fig. 1 (*above, left*) — Fabric of Dimity Bed Hanging (*early nineteenth century*). Part of a set from the hope chest of Susan Bayles of Acton Hall near Princeton, who married Jared Dunn of Washington in 1830. The fringe (*c. 1830*) is doubtless later than the fabric, which may have been woven long before the wedding, perhaps at Acton Hall. Note twill weave, and narrow cotton binding. *Lent to Stratford Hall by Miss Susan Coyle, granddaughter of the original owner*

Fig. 2 — Fabric of a Dimity Bed Furniture (*last quarter of the eighteenth century*). From the old Billmeyer house in Germantown occupied by one family from the time of the first owner, an eighteenth-century Philadelphia printer, until 1911. Note that the material shows a tendency to crinkle, indicating why it was measured "on the stretch." *Acquired for the Stratford nursery in May 1940*

Fig. 3 — "A Dimity Furniture for Tent Bed" (*c. 1800*). Drawing accompanied by specifications, from the trade book of Banting & Son of London. The design follows closely Hepplewhite's 1787 design for dressing a "Field Bed." *From the Metropolitan Museum of Art*

and *summer bed hangings for the country*, window curtains, waistcoats, et cetera; and that those of India (*i.e.*, white and without nap) are the most appropriate for making curtains. A photostat of the original text of this account is on file with the Stratford research.

Since dimities were so well known in 1760 that this account makes no attempt to describe their appearance in detail, we have to look further for such description. The clearest and most significant is that given by M. Bezon, Professeur de Théorie de Fabrique, in his *Dictionnaire Général des Tissus Anciens and Modernes* (1867):

The name basin is applied to various kinds of striped fabrics, whether the stripes or bands run crosswise or up and down. These bands or stripes form a kind of ribs obtained by reversal of the weave (*changements d'armures*). Thus, a group of 10 threads for a body of plain cloth (*corps de lisses taffetas*); a group of 10 threads for a body of twill (*corps de lisses sergé*), reversed on the wrong side. The twill band and the plain band form a contrast in the fabric (*forment opposition de tissus*), in such a way as to produce furrows in the twill part and a relief effect in the plain. The dimity that we describe here is the early type of this class of fabrics. *It is the old, the true dimity*, such as was made at the outset. Since then, the cloth has been altered by various combinations, and its character has been changed. As a result, many articles that now bear the name of dimity are not true dimities, but imitations.

Bezon remarks that the market for dimity, considerable in other times, has by 1867 fallen off noticeably. The decline has since continued so that today the name *basin* has virtually disappeared from general use in France.

Nevertheless, in 1924 H. Havard, in his *Dictionnaire d'Ameublement et Décoration*, still describes *basin* as: "A cotton twill cloth, used for more than two centuries in house furnishings to make linings and coverings." He adds that in the last century dimities were made in Holland and in Bruges. Those of Holland were celebrated for their fineness, and those of Bruges were known particularly by the name *Bombasin*.

A description of *Dimity* in the *Handwörterbuch der Textilkunde* by Max Heiden (1904), corresponds exactly with that given by Bezon under *Basins*, thus removing any doubt that the two names refer to the same fabric.

With these descriptions in hand, the Stratford committee set out to find a fabric that corresponded to them — a fabric, moreover, known to have been called dimity, and used for bed or window hangings in the late eighteenth and early nineteenth centuries. The Committee also wished to show that the sheer corded fabric now sold as dimity was not called by that name in the period under consideration.

The negative thesis was proved by reference to the engraved plates in Ackermann's *Repository of Fashions*, which in nearly every issue from 1809 to 1816 carried sample swatches of British-made fabrics fashionable for costume and upholstery purposes. This was the era of the great popularity of muslin as a dress fabric, and Ackermann shows literally dozens of sheer corded and checked samples of plain weave like modern dimity. But in no case are such fabrics called "dimity." They are always "corded muslins."

Thus: "A fret-work striped muslin." "An entirely new corded muslin for morning dresses." "A striped muslin or nainsook."

All these are fabrics like modern dimity, and like modern dimity they are of varying degrees of sheerness. But none are "stout." And none are recommended for upholstery purposes. At least through 1816, then, fabrics of this kind were known as muslin and not dimity; and if Jefferson had intended such a fabric for the curtains of his sketch, he would have called it muslin.

When Ackermann showed a sample intended for drapery of upholstery it was clearly identified as such. Those recommended for bed furniture are all "stout," and in addition Ackermann usually advised lining them. Dimity was too common a fabric at that time to be admitted to a place among Ackermann's "fashionable novelties." But in November 1812 a sample is shown and described thus:

. . . an entirely new article *for white beds* and other furniture, which we have been favoured with from the house of Millard in the City; . . . This handsome manufacture will be found desirable to persons who have large establishments to furnish for, as it *wants no lining*, and is sold by the piece at a very reasonable price . . .

The weave of this sample is exactly that described by Bezon, its "novelty" consisting merely of a damasklike pattern stamped into the finished fabric. The fabric itself is woven in a series of plain stripes in relief on a twill ground, each stripe being about one quarter-inch wide. On the wrong side, they are reversed to become twill stripes on a plain ground. Ackermann's does not label this fabric dimity. But in February 1809, a swatch of the same weave in a dress material of lighter weight is labeled "Bishop's Blue Bombazine." It will be remembered that Havard says the fine dimities of Bruges had become known as *Bombasins*.

From this point it was a comparatively easy matter to find examples of the same weave with the necessary documentation. The large city museums had lost all record of old dimity but happily a few historical societies in New England had not. The Wadsworth Atheneum in Hartford owns several pieces of a "dimity" bed valance from the hope chest of Mrs. G. B. Atwell of Hartford, who married in 1816. The pieces were presented by her granddaughter, who labeled them with the name she had heard her grandmother give them. The fabric is the same as the Ackermann swatch "for white beds," except that the stripes are of several different widths arranged in groups.

The Atheneum also owns a crib quilt of "dimity" embroidered with candlewick, made by Betsy Kingsbury of Hartford early in the nineteenth century. The material here is costume dimity of a quality so fine that the layman may well be forgiven for supposing it to be the same as modern dimity. But examination under a glass shows that the stripes, though only three threads wide, are woven in the same way as the Atwell valance. This piece is now on loan in the Stratford nursery. A saque or morning jacket of even finer dimity trimmed with hand-scalloped ruffles of India muslin is in the Metropolitan Museum. These are the dimities described in old accounts as *à petites rayes* (stripes) *imperceptibles*. Their quality and general appearance is no doubt responsible for the fact that corded muslins were later called by the same name.

Another documented dimity hanging is in the Essex Institute at Salem, labeled *Dimity bed curtain, 1825*. Salem at least has not forgotten dimity. Great quantities of it must have been received there during the sailing-ship era; and some still hangs on the beds for which it was brought overseas. In some houses the old curtains, no longer prized for hangings, have been used to cover bed springs or mattresses; but they are still known as dimity by the older generation, a few of whom have not heard the word applied to any other fabric. The period of great popularity for dimity bed hangings in this neighborhood was evidently between 1800 and 1820 — when Salem harbor teemed with sail, when Chestnut Street was new, and McIntire and other Salem woodcarvers flourished.

Several furnitures of earlier date and fine quality have turned up in South Jersey and Philadelphia, where, in a milder climate, the fashion for them may have become established very early (*Fig. 1*). It is not believed, however, that dimity was used unlined for bed hangings before 1760, or generally in America before the Revolution. Colonial dimity was used in other ways.

Nearly every old piece of dimity found is edged with a narrow cotton braid, probably a necessary binding for the material which was otherwise inclined to "accordion" in the midst of a breadth. We understand now what Jefferson meant by dimity "on the stretch!" We also find that these early pieces almost invariably measure "2 ft. 1 i. wide," as he recorded. A few late pieces measure 36 inches.

An interesting example of early date is shown in Figure 2, part of a bed furniture from the old Billmeyer house in Germantown. It is clear even in the photograph that this dimity is of a stouter, closer weave than those of the later period. As analyzed by an expert weaver, the "count" is 10 per cent higher than that of the next closest piece examined (*Fig. 1*). The material is still in good condition, and a full day in the sun has brought it back to its original whiteness. The herringbone stripe is an interesting variation of pattern that has not been found in any other piece. The Stratford committee believes that this furniture, which has been acquired for the Stratford nursery, dates not later than 1790.

Plans for hanging the nursery bed are now complete. In search for a contemporary design for draperies that could be appropriately executed in dimity, the committee was fortunate enough to find, in the print room of the Metropolitan Museum, an unpretentious little book that seemed almost made to order. An ordinary blank-book, titled simply *Banting & Son, London*, the volume contains some thirty or forty pencil designs for upholstery actually executed. The book is undated, and obviously covers a period of years ending about 1830. But many of the drawings are readily identifiable copies of Hepplewhite or Sheraton designs, and may be dated by these. Among them is a *Dimity Furniture for Tent Bed* (*Fig. 3*). The design is a direct copy of the engraving for a Field Bed, dated *1787*, in Hepplewhite's *Cabinet-Maker and Upholsterer's Guide*, and may be considered suitable for the Stratford nursery.

The Banting design calls for 43 yards of dimity, 70 yards binding, 2 yards calico, thread, tape, and so forth. It is interesting that when an upholsterer skilled in interpreting such designs was asked how much dimity 25 inches wide it would take to furnish the Stratford bed after this design, his estimate was for exactly 43 yards. The Stratford committee has arranged with an expert weaver to make enough additional dimity exactly reproducing the Billmeyer hangings to allow for following the Banting directions to the letter. The curtains will draw entirely around the bed, as it was intended they should do; and so the drapery will have the convincing look of serving the purpose for which it was designed, namely to keep out cold and the deadly "night air" and, in a screenless day, night-flying insects.

The bedspread to be used is, we believe, one of the rare examples of dimity *à carreaux, ou ouvres*, described in eighteenth-century accounts, and will be the subject of a later study. It is owned by Henry Wood Erving of Hartford, who has lent it for the Stratford nursery. This is perhaps the most interesting of a number of kinds of dimity used for upholstery purposes in this country over a period of more than two centuries. The Stratford committee makes no claim to have identified all of these as yet, or even the most important. But it does believe that the striped materials shown here are true dimity; and that this was the kind of dimity in use for bed and window hangings in the late eighteenth and early nineteenth centuries, the period when Ann Carter Lee's children occupied the Stratford nursery.

Note: The Stratford committee wishes to acknowledge with thanks the help and friendly interest of the several museums consulted in the course of making this study.

COLONIAL DIMITIES, CHECKED AND DIAPERED

By HAZEL E. CUMMIN

THE results of a preliminary study of eighteenth- and early nineteenth-century dimities, made in connection with the furnishing of the nursery at Stratford Hall, Virginia, were published in ANTIQUES for July 1940, where striped dimities of the period between 1789 and 1825 were pictured and described.

It will be remembered that all the documented hangings brought to light in the course of that study were of dimity in which groups of stripes of several widths were arranged in more or less elaborate patterns. Also that, with one or two possible exceptions, this dimity bore the unmistakable stamp of having been imported from either Europe or the Indies. None of it was found in the checked or diapered patterns mentioned frequently in early documents — no doubt because, by the late eighteenth century, stripped patterns had become more generally fashionable, along with other attenuated styles in furnishing.

But in the course of the study, there came to the attention of the Stratford Committee a cotton diaper bedspread embroidered with candlewick and obviously home-woven (*Fig. 1*). The owner of the piece, Henry Wood Erving of Hartford, Connecticut, said that it had been made in New England, and had always within his memory been called "dimity."

The fabric of this spread is of substantial weight, woven of un-sized and lightly twisted yarn in a typical diaper pattern, the basis of which is a twill, with the weft threads thrown to the face of the material to form the pattern. The spread is made of two breadths of this material, each forty inches wide. The effect of the material is, of course, quite different from that of the striped dimities previously described. But both fabrics belong to the same great family of twills, beloved of our colonial forbears for its enduring qualities and for the variety of patterns it embraces.

Mr. Erving was unable to furnish documentation for his spread other than that he "had always called it dimity," which of course was insufficient proof that it had always borne that name. But to those of the Stratford Committee with experience of Mr. Erving's long and accurate memory, it was evidence to warrant further study. After a fruitless search among historical societies and museums for a similar fabric recognized as dimity, proof was obtained from an unexpected source. In the Print Room of the Metropolitan Museum, the Committee came upon a volume with the title:

*The Domestic Manufacturer's Assistant and Family Directory
In the Arts of Weaving and Dying*

Comprehending a Plain System of Directions Applying to those Arts and other Branches connected with them in the Manufacture of Cotton and Woolen Goods, etc.

By J. and R. Bronson
Utica
Printed by William Williams
no. 60 Genesee Street
1817

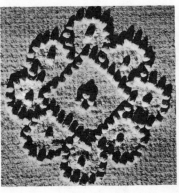 

FIG. 1 — HOME-WOVEN CHECKED DIMITY BEDSPREAD. *Left*, one motive of the spread's candlewick pattern. *Center*, detail showing the weave in actual size. Now on loan in the nursery, Stratford Hall, Virginia. *Owned by Henry Wood Erving*

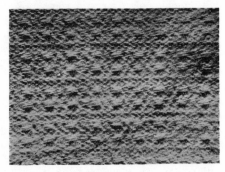

FIG. 3 — CHECKED DIM-ITY (*actual size*). Fabric woven by Edward Maag and Son after the 1817 directions shown in Figure 2. Note similarity between this material and the bedspread of Figure 1

MANUFACTURER'S ASSISTANT. 68

No. 16, Checked Dimety.

This pattern is formed with 6 treadles, and 6 wings. The first thread, is drawn on wing A, next on C, next on B, C, A, D, B, D, and so on as the draft directs; until once over, then commence again on A, as before.

There are 10 long cords, on short lams: and 26 short cords on long lams.

TREAD.

The first tread, is on treadle I, fig. 1, under the cording, next on L, fig. 2, next on J, L, I, K, J, K, and so on, until the whole tread is completed.

G and H, forms the plain bar, but if you tread I, J, K, L, only, it will form it into stripes.

Use a slaie 2 beers finer than for plain cloth, and draw 2 threads in a reed.

FIG. 2 — DIRECTIONS FOR WEAVING "CHECKED DIMITY" ON THE HOME LOOM. From *The Domestic Manufacturer's Assistant*, published in Utica, New York, 1817. *Original in the Metropolitan Museum of Art*

This little book contains instructions for weaving on the home loom a number of the staple household fabrics of its time. Number 16, on page 68, gives directions for *Checked Dimety*, including on the same page drafts for threading the loom, and for "treading" (*Fig. 2*). The Committee was able to have these directions followed by an expert weaver, with the result shown in Figure 3.

The relationship of this fabric to that in the Erving spread is apparent even to the layman. In the latter, the diamond pattern is formed by throwing the weft threads to the surface. In the material made according to directions published in Utica, a like effect is obtained with warp threads that come to the surface in the form of squares or checks. Note that the instructions for treading this material add: "if you tread I, J, K, L, only, it will form it into stripes." These stripes would be satin stripes on a twill ground, not reverse twill stripes like those shown in our previous study.

"The steps between twills and figured weaves is short," says a well-known textile handbook. "Satin really belongs to both, for it is a broken or skip twill. . . . The object [in figure weaving] is to throw a series of threads in a pattern on the face of the material, with a cross-thread at intervals, so that the floats of warp or filling may reflect the light and show the pattern clearly. . . . Diaper patterns are examples of simple figure weaving."

In translating the Utica draft, the weaver has used unsized yarn of the same weight and quality as that in the Erving spread, thus accentuating the likeness of the two materials. As they appear together, they might almost have been woven by the same hand. In both, the soft yarns and numerous floats of the pattern combine to produce a firm but not too tightly woven fabric, eminently suitable for bed furniture or hangings, and particularly for those intended for embroidery. At least one crewel-work hanging brought to the attention of the Stratford Committee is a fabric of this type.

Household fabrics which American women of the nineteenth century continued to produce at home for ordinary purposes throughout the first phase of the factory era were usually those that had served them well for the same purposes for long periods of time. Thus it seems probable that the home-loomed dimities described here were essentially the same as those *basins à carreaux, ou ouvrés*, described by Jaques Savary des Bruslons in his *Diction-naire Universel de Commerce* published at Copenhagen in 1760. In a discussion of *basins*, or dimities, Savary says (in translation):

The dimities that come from the East Indies are white and without nap. There are two kinds of them: one twilled or serge, the other checked or diapered (*les uns croisés, ou sergés, et les autres à carreaux, ou ouvrés*). Those of the Indies are the most appropriate for curtains.

What more natural than that these plain and figured dimities should have continued as staple products of the home loom long after they had been succeeded by more fashionable patterns in the imported kinds? The early records of America are full of references to them. That so little trace of surviving examples can be found today is no doubt due in part to the hard wear they received; but also to the fact that they have not for many years been recognized as dimity. Many of them may yet be discovered in collections under other classifications.

A discussion of other mid-eighteenth-century dimities, described by Savary as the products of French and Flemish looms, will appear in a later number of Antiques. The relation of these fabrics to the cottons of an even earlier period forms an interesting chapter in the history of European cotton weaving.

CALAMANCO

By HAZEL E. CUMMIN

This is the fourth in a series of studies of eighteenth-century fabrics which is being made in connection with the restoration of Stratford Hall in Virginia. The first three appeared in the July, September, and December 1940 issues of ANTIQUES, wherein certain types of dimities and moreen were discussed.

IN ANDERSON'S *History of British Commerce* (London, 1764), the following paragraph appears under the heading, *A.D. 1633:* "In neither of those Provinces (Maryland and Virginia) are there as yet any Towns of considerable Bulk or Importance. For the greater Planters have generally *storehouses* within themselves, for *all kinds of Necessaries brought from Great Britain;* not only for their own Consumption, but likewise for supplying the lesser Planters and their Servants — etc. And, whilst that kind of Economy continues, there can be no Prospect of Towns becoming considerable in either Province; which is so far a Benefit to their Mother Country, as without Towns — they must continue to be *supplied from Great Britain with Cloathing, Furniture*, Tools, Delicacies, etc. . . ."

Fortunately inventories of many of these old plantation storehouses in Westmoreland County are still preserved in the County Court House. The similarity of the "Linnen Stores" listed throughout the colonial period, to the lists of drapers' and mercers' stocks published in London at about the same time, leaves no doubt that the planters of this neighborhood obtained their "Cloathing" — and their household linens and hangings too — from Great Britain. Study of these lists leads to many fascinating discoveries.

Some of the fabrics are familiar enough to us today. Broadcloths and serges; "taffaties," damasks, and satins — of all these

there are modern versions at least approximating the old. But the names that recur most often, the names of the commoner stuffs so generally in use that no householder bothered to describe them, many of these are strange. The homely fabrics called by them have disappeared, leaving scarcely a clue by which they may be traced. And yet how to reproduce an eighteenth-century interior without them? Surely our forbears did not live all their lives among brocades and satins, any more than they dined daily off the fatted calf. It has been the effort of those who are restoring Stratford Hall to identify and restore to use some of these commoner materials which, even among Virginia gentry, must have been the bread-and-butter of their furnishings.

A fabric that appears time and again in all colonial records is *calamanco*. Westmoreland County records list it frequently. William Tyler's *Suplementall Inventory*, 1723, mentions "11 yardes calliminco." Monroe's account of the guardianship of the Watt estate, 1749–50, itemizes "To 8 yds Red Callimanco ⅖ 4 yds Tammy 21 d.... 1.7.0. To 1 pr Wom's Callamenco Shoes. To 1 best Curb Bridle .... 0.17.6." And in New England, in the Boston *Gazette* in March 1729, we find: "A Handsome Bedstead with Calimanco Curtains, Vallens, Tester, & Window Curtains, and also a Walnut Tea Table; to be sold enquire of Mr. John Boydelle." The majority of such references collected by the Stratford research date from 1720 to 1750, although an occasional one appears throughout the pre-Revolutionary period.

No satisfactory modern description of this fabric has been found. The best is that in the big Oxford English *Dictionary:*

A woolen stuff of Flanders, glossy on the surface, and woven with a satin twill and checquered in the warp, so that the checks are seen on one side only.

In the *Drapers' Dictionary* (1882) Beck states positively that this description refers to the calamanco made in his own day. For a dependable account of the colonial fabric, we must turn to earlier sources.

Sam Johnson's *Dictionary* (1st edition, 1755), says simply: "Calamanco, a Kind of woollen Stuff." Anderson mentions it as one of the "slight woollens" introduced into England by French and Flemish refugee weavers. Other contemporary English accounts, including those of the numerous trade dictionaries published about that time, are simply more or less exact translations of well-known French accounts. "It is remarkable," wrote T. C. Archer in *Wool and its Applications* (1876), "that a country like ours, more dependent than any other on its manufactures, has never attempted a systematic history of them." Certainly in the period of our interest, there were no English works on textiles or other manufactures that compare with those published in French by Jacques Savary des Bruslons in the first quarter of the century; or with the careful studies of the silk and wool manufactures made for the *Académie royal des Sciences* by MM. Paulet and Roland de la Platière (*1782–1785*).

No doubt the rigid system of manufacture inspection in force in France was responsible for this superiority of her technical records. Both Savary and Roland de la Platière were intimately associated

stands at the beginning of our period, and the other at its close.

The Savary *Dictionaire* describes *Calmande* thus, in translation: *Calmande*, called in Holland, particularly at Amsterdam, *Calaminque*. A stuff similar to that formerly called Ras d'Utrecht, which is made in the Brabant, and in Flanders. . . . The stuff is very glossy (*très lustrée*), and is made twilled in the warp (*croisée en Chaîne*); thus the twill appears only on one side, the right. It is ordinarily made all of wool. But there are some in which the warp is mixed with silk, and others in which some goat's hair is used. There are calmandes of all colors and styles; some plain and solid (*unies*); others with bands of flowers; others striped; and others watered. A great many are used throughout Flanders and the Brabant, and in France; and quantities are sent to foreign countries, especially to Spain. Calmande is appropriate for clothing, nightrobes, petticoats, upholstery (*des meubles*), and is very generally in use.

The account of Roland de la Platière, in his *Art du Fabricant d'Etoffes en Laines rases et seches*, is more detailed:

Calmande is a fabric known and regulated from ancient times; it has sustained a continuous growth, because it can be varied at will, is appropriate for an infinite number of uses, and is very serviceable. It is made a great deal in white, plain and ribbed, to be dyed in the piece. There are also made a great many kinds striped in various colors, and with flowers in various designs. The tread of calmande is precisely that of satin. (*Le pas de la calmande est précisément celui du satin.*) Five shafts, and equally five treadles, are used, of which one of the latter, pressed down, raises regu-

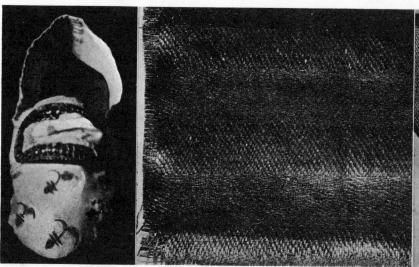

FIG. 1 — CALAMANCO SHOE (*pre-Revolutionary*). White, embroidered with red and green strawberry sprigs. *From the Concord Antiquarian Society*
FIG. 2 — PIECE OF BLACK STRIPED CALAMANCO (1750–1800). *From the Essex Institute*

FIG. 3 — PIECE OF A PINK "CALIMENCO" DRESS. Worn by Miss Dolly Adams of Concord, Massachusetts, in 1736. *From the Concord Antiquarian Society*

with this inspection, the one as inspector-general of customs and manufactures; the other as inspector of manufactures in Picardy, and later at Lyons. Savary, son of the distinguished economist, Jacques Savary (*1622–1690*), spent much of his life studying the relation of textile manufacturing to the business problems of his day. His notes, published posthumously by his brother in 1723, show a knowledge of the industry that few men of his day could have possessed. Roland de la Platière was the husband of the famous Madame Roland of the French Revolution and himself held a post for a time in the Gironde ministry. He was a member of the Académie des Sciences and one of its ablest cyclopædists. He spent years painstakingly compiling facts about textile manufacture in Europe, and was said to know more about it than any man of his time.

In Picardy, Roland had been responsible for the enforcement of eighty-five *règlements* for the weaving of "serges, druggets, baracans, callemandes (calamancoes), and other stuffs." Many of these had been instituted under the régime of Savary. In a study of eighteenth-century woolens, we cannot do better than to consult these two men, each the authority of his day, one of whom

larly four shafts at one time, while it only lowers one. . . . [There follows a detailed description of a five-shaft satin weave.] . . . From this tread there result "floats" in the warp which form the satin of the fabric; and in fact, calmande is simply a satin made of wool (*dans le fait la calmande n'est qu'un satin en laine*).

After discussing the difficulties that arise in weaving such a fabric with wool yarns, the author continues:

All this is said of the plain calmandes. In regard to those that are ribbed, of which a considerable number have been made for some time past, one can readily understand that the passage of the threads and the play of the shafts would no longer be the same, but that the ribs, being simply a reversal of the right and wrong sides (*n'étant qu'une alternative d'endroit & d'envers*), the weaving (*rentreture*) must first be reversed to produce this effect. . . . These ribs are ordinarily of equal width, and of a distance apart equal to their width; therefore the fabric has no wrong side, for all is alike from one rib to another. They may be of unequal distance apart; it is then no longer a stuff without a wrong side (*ce n'est plus une étoffe absolument sans envers*); and the right side is always understood to be that which has the most satin, that where the ribs, a little in relief as related to the ground, are larger than the spaces between them.

Calmande is made in white, ordinarily plain or ribbed, of a width of half an ell and a twelfth. . . . The calmandes of first quality are very white in comparison with the common ones, although both alike are woven in the natural color, being usually destined either to remain white, or to be dyed in full colors (*couleurs fines*), many in pale colors. Naturally one chooses the purest, whitest materials; and consequently the wools of Flanders, yellowed by poor pasturage, are not the right ones. Therefore, for the first quality, one ordinarily chooses the wool of Holland. Other wools are used for this stuff according to their fineness and strength. They are satisfactory for the medium and inferior qualities which, tawny at first, are bleached and prepared by a process to be described later.

Although a very great quantity of calmandes are made in écru, many more are dyed, striped in colors varied by all kinds of patterns. The latter do not differ at all from the others as to weave; but they are usually of commoner materials, and nearly always narrower. . . .

In France, the center of manufacture of calmande is Flanders, and particularly Roubais and its environs; however it is made in Picardy, but generally in écru in the common quality, and never striped. Flowered calmandes are no longer made there; a variety which, along with the others, they make in great quantities in Berlin, and above all in England.

The ground of the flowered calmandes is the same as ordinary calmandes: the design is made in addition on a draw-loom (*au moyen de la tire*); but this is not the place to discuss this manner of weaving; it will be treated separately. I shall content myself, for the moment, by saying that the flowered calmande, and that striped in all colors, form a considerable part of an immense quantity of light woolen stuffs (*étoffes de petit lainage*) manufactured by the English in the narrowest widths, down to 13 or 14 inches, in which they carry on a prodigious commerce with the whole world.

It is clear from this that calamancoes belong to the great family of wool satins originating in Europe, probably in the Brabant, but known in England as early as the sixteenth century. Whether they are to be thought of as wool versions of the silks brought from the south and east is a nice question that need not be discussed here. The first reference to such fabrics in English documents is to "Russel satins," concerning which the worsted manufacturers of Norwich petitioned Parliament in 1554 for some "good and politic laws," presenting that:

of late years *Russels*, called russel satins and satin reverses, had been made abroad from wools in the county of Norfolk, and being brought into this kingdom were purchased and worn, to the great detriment of the wool manufacturers at Norwich, which induced the inhabitants of that city to encourage certain foreign workmen to come to Norwich, where they were set to work, and have instructed others; so that there are now made in this same city better russel satins and satin reverses, and also fustians, in imitation of the fustians of Naples, than had been received from abroad. . . .

The petition was granted, and these stuffs appear thereafter in sixteenth- and early seventeenth-century records as "Russells," "russel satins," or "Norwich satins." They are usually described as "glazed" or "lustred." Beck says:

No mention occurs of the stuff for a long time after this. . . . But some time towards the latter part of the 18th century, it was revived, and is then described as a kind of twilled *lasting*, resembling *calimancoes*, but stouter. The glazed finish was . . . followed, and the stuff was manufactured in a wide range of qualities. . . .

Lasting was a stouter form of calamanco developed in England in the late eighteenth century for men's clothing and the tops of ladies' shoes. The French called it *Satin Turc*, and claimed to have made it earlier than the English, but not for clothing. *Russells* appear in English and American inventories of the mid-nineteenth century, and were no doubt closely related to the heavy wool satins used for window hangings in the 1860's. But how different these were, in their dull reds and Prussian blues, from the gay little calamancoes of the previous century! But each era finds a hundred ways of altering the old ones to express its own taste and feeling.

More adequately perhaps than richer fabrics, the calamancoes express the change in taste from the grandiose to the simple that was taking place everywhere in Europe in their day. Their crisp texture and polished surfaces were well calculated to satisfy the growing demand for lightness and cleanliness in household furnishings. Their cheerful stripes and unpretentious flower designs were welcome relief from the overpowering patterns of seventeenth-century stuffs. The plain kinds came in beautiful clear colors, dyed by secret processes known only to the Dutch until Van Robais went to Picardy and taught them to the Gobelins. Great quantities of these were sent to Spain, for Spain loved color. And France used her full share. The inventory of Mlle. Demarès (Paris, 1746) mentions a sedan chair lined with blue *calemande*, and a bed with curtains of blue and white striped *calamandre*. In the end, Britain became the chief center of the manufacture for the whole world. It was the last and most effective effort of her cloth weavers to stem the tide of cotton.

Several documented examples of calamanco have been turned up by the Stratford research. Three of the most characteristic are shown here. The first is a piece from a pink calamanco dress worn by Miss Dolly Adams of Concord, Massachusetts, in 1736 (*Fig. 3*). It was presented to the Concord Antiquarian Society many years ago by a member of her family, who wrote on the label that the material was "calimenco." The fabric corresponds exactly with that described by Roland. It is a light-weight stuff of satin weave, calendered to a gloss rivaling that of silk. The yarns are wool or mohair in the warp and fine wool in the weft. The color is a soft rose pink that has scarcely changed in the two hundred years since it was new.

A pair of calamanco shoes is also in the Concord Antiquarian collection (*Fig. 1*). The fabric here is white and is embroidered all over with tiny sprigs of strawberries in red and green. The shoes have no documentation other than the label *Calimanco Shoes*, attached when they were received into the collection many years ago. But the style and the design of the fabric place them well before the Revolution.

An example of dark striped calamanco (*Fig. 2*) is in the Essex Institute in Salem, labeled simply, *Damask, 1750–1800. Gift of Miss Ellen A. Stone*. Miss Ellen belonged to the old Stone family of Lexington and Watertown, and is affectionately remembered by historical societies in that neighborhood. They all knew that whatever Miss Ellen brought to them was impeccably authentic, and "really old."

This "damask" is woven exactly as described by M. Roland. The stripes are about a half-inch wide, and an equal distance apart, the satin stripes showing slightly in relief upon a plain ground. The fabric is even lighter in weight than Dolly Adams' dress, and is more highly calendered. The color is faded black.

Paul Rodier says that it was the flowered bands with which the earliest calamancoes were adorned that first gave them their name. It is beyond the ability of a mere student of American crafts to trace the derivation of that statement. But there is some reason to believe that the flowered fabric was generally in use before the plain. The evidence is a story in itself, and must wait for a later article.

SÈVRES PORCELAIN (*Louis XV period*). One of a pair of vases, in Vincennes soft paste. Shape known as *Jardiniéres à éventail*. Shown in current exhibition of Sèvres porcelain at Walters Art Gallery, Baltimore, Maryland, it is part of the largest collection in America of "the porcelain of kings"

Masterpieces of Western textiles

BY CHRISTA C. MAYER, *Curator of textiles, Art Institute of Chicago*

AMONG THE LESSER KNOWN treasures in the Art Institute of Chicago is a fine and extensive collection of Western textiles which ranks among the foremost in the United States today. Although its beginnings can be traced to the 1890's, it has been an independent unit only since 1961, when Mildred Davison was named curator of the textile collection. Until then it had grown steadily, supervised by her but under the aegis of the decorative arts department.

The origin of today's textile department was the gift of several tapestries and church vestments in the 1890's from the Antiquarian Society, an organization founded in 1878 and always connected with the Art Institute. Among its members were such individual benefactors as Martin A. Ryerson, who as early as 1894 foresaw the value of an extensive textile collection for the study of style, design, technique, and color. In 1895 he presented several hundred textiles which he had acquired in Europe the year before. Accompanying him on his travels was Edward E. Ayer, who likewise acquired textiles but gave them to the department of industrial art of Chicago's Field Museum. When the Field Museum discon-

tinued this department in 1906, the Ayer textiles were transferred, through Mr. Ryerson's efforts, to the Art Institute. Mr. Ryerson, encouraged and assisted by his wife, assembled an extraordinary private collection as well, which was bequeathed to the Art Institute in 1937. Thus, a splendid collection, ranging from the fifteenth through the eighteenth centuries, was well established.

Robert Allerton was another benefactor who traveled to Europe and returned with many treasures for the textile collection. He was concerned also with the practical aspect, and in 1927 saw the need for textile exhibition and storage space. As a result, the Agnes Allerton Textile Wing was built, and today comprises four galleries and a spacious textile study room.

A good sampling of the riches of the entire collection can be seen in the special exhibition currently on view which includes materials from most of Europe and the Western hemisphere, and covers a period of twenty centuries. It is subdivided into Peruvian textiles, tapestries, silks and velvets, coverlets, embroideries and needlework, lace, and printed textiles. The earliest pieces, dating from the first century A.D., are from Peru. Among

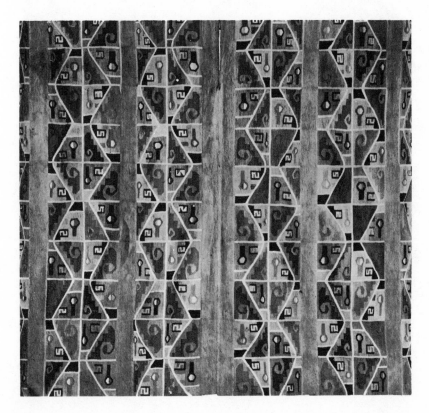

Poncho, Peruvian, from Tiahuanaco, on the south coast; 800-1100. Cotton and wool in an interlocking tapestry weave. 88 by 42 inches. *Buckingham fund.*

All illustrations are from the Art Institute of Chicago.

Fragment of a Spanish textile in Mudejar style, thirteenth century. Silk and gold foil wound around linen, in tabby weave with extra pattern wefts tied in twill weave. 23⅜ by 22⅜ inches.

Square from a German altar frontal or hanging showing the Last Supper; from Lower Saxony, late thirteenth or early fourteenth century. Linen, in tabby weave, embroidered in colored linen and silk. Recent research reveals that there are at least two companion pieces in European collections; the Art Institute's square was once probably part of an altar frontal or a large hanging to which all three belonged. 15 by 14¾ inches.

Fragment of a Hispano-Islamic textile, from Granada, Spain; fifteenth century. Silk and gold foil in satin weave with extra pattern wefts tied in tabby weave; with the inscription *Glory to Our Lord the Sultan* in Arabic. 16 by 7 inches. *Gift of Mrs. Edwin A. Seipp.*

The Feudal Life, French tapestry, probably from Touraine; c. 1500. Wool in tapestry weave. The richly dressed figures are shown out-of-doors against a brilliantly colored *millefleurs* background. 112½ by 140½ inches. *Gift of Kate S. Buckingham.*

Fragment of an Italian textile, early fifteenth century. Silk and gold foil wound around linen, in twill weave with extra pattern wefts tied at intervals to achieve a most elegant symmetrical design of chimerical animals and fanciful architectural structures. 19½ by 17¼ inches. *Gift of Mr. and Mrs. John V. Farwell III.*

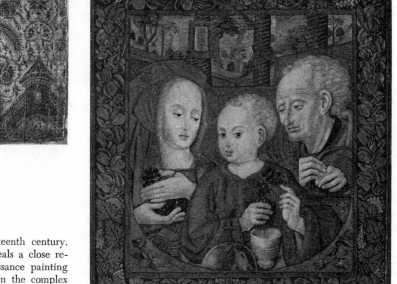

The Holy Family, Flemish tapestry; sixteenth century. Wool, in tapestry weave. This piece reveals a close relationship to Italian and Flemish Renaissance painting in scale and subject matter, as well as in the complex iconography. 28¼ by 26½ inches. *Bequest of Mr. and Mrs. Martin A. Ryerson.*

Section from an Italian altar frontal with the sacred letters *IHS;* first quarter of the sixteenth century. Silk, gold, and silver thread, with cut velvet and red and gold threads in tabby weave; further embellished by uncut loops in gold and silver thread. An example of the richest and most sumptuous of all weaves: the velvet favored in Italy during the Renaissance, enhanced here by abundant use of metal threads. 12½ by 47 inches. *Gift of Mrs. Tiffany Blake.*

Retable and altar frontal, a Spanish altarpiece originally in Burgo de Osma, made in 1468 for Bishop Pedro de Montoya. Linen, embroidered in colored silks and gold and silver metal thread. The retable shows the Madonna and Child, the Nativity, the Adoration of the Magi, and the Crucifixion. The altar frontal shows the Resurrection and six Apostles. The recently restored inscription at the top of the altar frontal reads: *O Homo Recordare Qvia Pro Te IHS Hec Tormenta Pasvs Est* (Remember, O man, that Jesus suffered these pains for thee). The inscription at the bottom, also recently restored, reads: *Resvrexit Dominvs Ivstvs Vere Et Aparvit Simoni* (The Lord is risen indeed and hath appeared to Simon). Retable, 77½ by 62¾ inches; altar frontal, 30½ by 79¼ inches. *Gift of Mrs. Chauncey McCormick and Mrs. Richard Ely Danielson.*

the European items are treasured textile fragments found in Spanish tombs during the nineteenth century but made in the thirteenth and fourteenth. The fifteenth and sixteenth centuries are represented by a delightful group of Italian fabrics and large tapestries, as well as by a number of sumptuous velvets which were often made into extraordinary ecclesiastical garments. The embroideries and needlework show another phase of the arts of textile decoration, and examples in this category range from the fourteenth through the nineteenth centuries. The eighteenth century introduced printed cottons, splendid brocaded silks, crewel-embroidered hangings, and a number of costume accessories. The nineteenth century is represented by several woven and quilted coverlets as well as by woven silks and printed cottons. The latest items were made in the 1950's. The wide-ranging and comprehensive textile collection continues to grow, largely through the generous support of donors.

This article is based on the handbook written by Miss Mayer for the exhibition *Masterpieces of Western Textiles* that opened at the Art Institute of Chicago on January 25 and will run until March 2. This special show is dedicated to Mildred Davison, who retired in the spring of 1968 as curator of textiles.

Casket, by Rebecca Stonier Plaisted; English, 1668. Scenes from the Old Testament embroidered in colored silks, gold and silver thread, and chenille on satin-weave silk, with sections worked in high relief (stumpwork). Initials *R. S.* and *I. P.* and the date 1668 worked in seed pearls. Front section shows the Queen of Sheba before Solomon; while top, back, and sides interpret episodes from the story of Abraham and Isaac. Rebecca Stonier worked on this piece for twenty years; at some time during this period she married John Plaisted. Height 15½ inches. *Gift of Mrs. Chauncey B. Borland and Mrs. Edwin A. Seipp.*

Collar; Italian, late sixteenth century or early seventeenth; linen, needle lace, *punto in aria.* An elegant costume accessory, with delightful little figures and animals. 9 by 57 inches. *Gift of the Antiquarian Society.*

Panel; French, second half eighteenth century; silk, gold, and silver thread, in warp-faced tabby weave with extra pattern and brocading wefts. 69½ by 62 inches. *Bequest of Mrs. Martin A. Ryerson.*

The Turf Inn, panel; English, c. 1780. Cotton in tabby weave, printed by copperplate in sepia. 34 by 27 inches. *Gift of Emily Crane Chadbourne.*

The Pheasants, panel; French, early nineteenth century. Brocaded silk in satin weave with additional details in fine embroidery. Designed by Jean-Demosthène Dugourc (1749-1825) of Lyons, one of the most outstanding decorative artists of his time and one of the few textile artisans known to us by name. This design was originally intended for the Spanish Royal Palace in Madrid and was woven by Camille Pernon et Cie. 94½ by 16¾ inches. Gift of Mrs. Chauncey B. Borland.

The Irish Volunteers, panel; Leixlip, Ireland, 1782. Linen and cotton in tabby weave, copperplate printed and painted. This shows the Irish volunteers, "Loyal and Determined," in Phoenix Park, near Dublin (see ANTIQUES, March 1945, cover and p. 149). 48¼ by 30¾ inches. Gift of the Illinois Chapter of the American Institute of Interior Designers.

Fragment of black and purple silk; American, 1830-1850. Cut voided velvet woven at the Harmony Society, Economy, Pennsylvania. In America sericulture was known during colonial days, although output was experimental and limited. In 1826, however, production began to be successful in this self-contained community. 18½ by 9½ inches.

European tapestry

Penelope at her Loom, French or Franco-Flemish, c. 1480-1483.
One of eight fragments from a series *The Stories of Virtuous Women.*
An area at the right is an old repair.
All illustrations are from the Museum of Fine Arts, Boston.

BY RUTH DAVIDSON

SIGHTSEERS IN EUROPE, shivering with the cold in high-vaulted stone palaces and churches even when the weather outside is clement, are often heard to ask, "How did they *stand* it in winter?" A partial answer is, with the help of tapestry—tapestry woven in long strips that were hung from spikes driven into the walls, lining the room and shielding its occupants from the chill. And after seeing some of the early tapestries preserved—in surprising numbers—in museums and historic buildings today we can easily imagine the cheering as well as the warming effect these hangings must have had with their original bright colors—the glowing reds and vibrant blues, warm browns and deep forest greens that still enliven a few rare examples and can be discovered in small unexposed areas of others—and their bold designs full of movement and narrative interest.

Tapestry, properly speaking a pattern-woven textile as distinct from an embroidered or painted fabric, has been used for many purposes in the Western world. We know from contemporary accounts that people of wealth and importance brought chests full of tapestry hangings along when they traveled, to ensure comfortable surroundings wherever they were lodged. Door and bed curtains, covers for furniture and other objects of use or beauty, parts of costumes, and even horse trappings were woven of tapestry. The origins of this craft are ancient; tapestry was made in Egypt two thousand years before Christ, in China in the T'ang period (618-906), and in the New World—in Peru—before the conquest.

Fortunately, we can study some of the most notable of surviving early tapestries in American museums, and two recent publications on the subject signal the sharp upswing of interest here. *Tapestries of Europe and of Colonial Peru in the Museum of Fine Arts, Boston,* by Adolph S. Cavallo, is the catalogue of a justly famous collection, built up over nearly a century with the express intention of presenting a survey of the art in Europe and the New World. The work appears in two well-designed volumes, handsomely presented, one illustrating sixty-six examples selected for intensive study and the other containing the full and extraordinarily interesting sections that constitute a brief history of tapestry in western Europe and Peru. *World Tapestry*, by Madeleine Jarry, appeared in an American edition earlier this year (it was published in France as *La Tapisserie*). Mme. Jarry is *inspecteur principal* of the Mobilier National de France and of the National Tapestry Manufacturers; her most recent article in ANTIQUES, *Design in Aubusson carpets*, appeared in May 1969. Her general history of tapestry, abundantly illustrated, takes in Chinese *k'o-ssu* (silk tapestries) as well as Peruvian weaving. We have drawn on both these works for this brief account of tapestry in Europe through its last great period in the seventeenth and eighteenth centuries. The illustrations reproduced on these pages are all from the Boston catalogue.

Islamic invaders are supposed to have introduced tapestry weaving into southern Europe in the eighth century. Like glassmaking, this craft seems to have been carried up the Rhine before spreading over the rest of the continent. The earliest surviving specimens of European tapestry were apparently made in the Rhineland or Lower Saxony in the eleventh to thirteenth centuries. But the great period of tapestry weaving in Europe began with the second half of the fourteenth century. At that time and for long afterward the craft, or industry, was concentrated in the central and northern parts of France and in Flanders. The looms of Paris, Arras, Tournai, and

Brussels supplied the whole continent for almost two hundred years until, with the help of French and Flemish weavers from these centers, workshops were established in Italy, Spain, England, and Germany.

The earliest suite of tapestries we have today is the marvelous *Apocalypse* of Angers, made in Paris between 1375 and 1380. Consisting originally of seven hangings, each about eighty feet long, comprising 105 pictorial panels, it was by far the most important such undertaking of its time. The surviving sixty-seven panels—long since cut apart—are admirably displayed today on the long walls of a building within the feudal fortifications of Angers, on the Loire River. This great work, illustrating with powerfully expressive images the prophecies of St. John, was designed by Jean (or Hennequin) de Bruges, so called after his native city in Flanders, and evidently inspired by contemporary illuminated manuscripts. Much of the symbolism remains obscure, and, with some unanswered questions about their history, lends these panels a certain mystery that makes them even more impressive. The tapestries were commissioned by the Duke of Anjou from Nicolas Bataille, who may have been a merchant in art goods as well as a weaver. He seems also to have been responsible for the only other tapestries that can be compared to the Angers *Apocalypse*, the *Nine Worthies* series that is one of the glories of the Cloisters in New York. Only five panels of the latter set, somewhat later in date than that of Angers, have been preserved.

These Parisian tapestries were woven on upright or "high-warp" (in French, *haute lice*)

Detail of
The Martyrdom of St. Paul,
from the series
The Life of St. Peter,
French or Franco-Flemish,
c. 1460.

looms on which the warp or set of foundation threads is stretched perpendicular to the floor. Low-warp (*basse lice*) looms hold the warp parallel to the floor. The two kinds of looms call for slightly different techniques but produce the same kind of tapestry. The weaver in either case works from the back or the wrong side of the fabric, and must either change position or use a mirror to see the front of the completed work. Weavers in the Middle Ages, like those today, followed a cartoon or working plan made—by a draftsman specialized in the technique—from the designer's sketch or painting for the tapestry.

In tapestry weaving the pattern is created by the colored weft or filling threads that are woven into the undyed warp. The worker chooses from a number of bobbins wound with yarn of different colors and weaves in one color from one side to the other of the area where that color is required, but not necessarily all the way from one edge of the tapestry to the other. For an area of another color he must release the first bobbin and take up a second, and so forth. Between sections of different colors there will be formed slits, where the warp threads are not bound together by weft threads; these may be sewed up but were often left to emphasize with a slight shadow the boundaries of the colored areas. In European tapestry the colored wefts are usually woolen yarns but silk was used with increasing frequency, alone or mixed with wool. "Gold" threads—actually silk threads wrapped with narrow strips of gilded silver—were used for especially sumptuous effects. The texture of the material and hence the style of the work depends on the coarseness and number of weft threads. Medieval tapestry, in which the weft threads run only four or five to a centimeter, is bolder and coarser than late eighteenth-century work with ten or so threads in the same space. In Europe tapestries were usually woven sidewise, that is, from side to side as they were to hang rather than from top to bottom. The height (8 to 14 feet) of the fabric thus indicates the width of the loom and makes it evident that several weavers must have worked abreast on each tapestry.

With the political and economic upheavals of the late fourteenth and early fifteenth centuries Paris lost its position as a tapestry center. Some of the Parisian weavers, following the French kings, went down the Loire River and, around Tours, Blois, and Angers, made tapestries depicting courtly life and country diversions against plain backgrounds of dark blue or rosy red scattered with flowering plants and shrubs. *Millefleurs* is the name given these delightful creations, well exemplified by the series *The Lady with the Unicorn*, now in the Cluny Museum, Paris, and *The Hunting of the Unicorn*, at the Cloisters. Other Parisian craftsmen moved to the woolen-manufacturing cities of the north, notably Arras, near the border of present-day Belgium, where they enjoyed the patronage of the rich and powerful dukes of Burgundy. Arras gave the English word arras for any woven hanging (see *Hamlet*, Act III, Scene III) as well as the Italian term *arazzo*, still in use, but only one surviving set of tapestries can be ascribed with certainty to Arras looms. Arras' rival was the city of Tournai, in Flanders, where the *Seven Sacraments* tapestry now in the Cloisters was made. A "Tournai style," developing in the mid-1400's, crowded figures into the scene until almost no room remained at the top for sky and the foreground barely accommodated a few plant motifs. Figures and faces were strikingly realistic.

At the very end of the 1400's the tapestry weavers of Brussels won a pre-eminence they were to keep all through the following century and beyond. Commissions from every part of Europe came to this city, the capital of the Austro-Spanish rulers of the Low Countries, and an industry of enormous proportions grew up.

Detail of *Two Miracles of St. Claude*, Brussels, 1500-1525.

Technique was perfected and style took new directions. Early in the period the Brussels weavers had been famous for their "golden tapestries," so called for the great quantity of gold threads that enriched their surfaces, and for such elaborate compositions as the *Glorification of Christ* (the "Mazarin tapestry") now in the National Gallery of Art in Washington, D.C. In contrast to the Gothic spirit of these works, the influence of contemporary painting, which is to say, of the Italian Renaissance, was now apparent. Brussels was called on by Pope Leo X to execute in tapestry the ten cartoons commissioned of Raphael for the decoration of the Sistine Chapel. Seven of these were completed in time for the Christmas festivities of 1519 and aroused the greatest enthusiasm when hung in Rome. Their success was in fact to alter the general design of tapestries. The medieval scheme of figures arranged in tight groups, with or without an architectural or other setting and filling virtually the whole picture, now gave way to orderly compositions in which detached figures seem to move in real space. Nudity, alternating with the draperies of classical costume, and arabesques—motifs of classical origin—were among the novelties designers of tapestry now had to assimilate as they followed the lead of such artists as the Flemish Bernard Van Orley and his followers, Lucas van Leyden, Raphael and his pupil Giulio Romano, and, in the seventeenth century, Rubens and Jacob Jordaens.

After their success with the *Acts of the Apostles* the Brussels weavers found themselves unable to fill all the orders they received. The industry in its great prosperity needed protection against frauds and imitations, and among other regulations an ordinance of 1528 required all tapestries over a certain size to show the city mark (a red shield flanked by two R's) and also the mark of the weaver or the merchant who commissioned the work. The practice spread to other centers, and though many marks have been altered or removed those that remain have enabled modern scholars to reconstruct the organization of the industry and name some of the "dynasties" of master weavers.

The history of tapestry in the late sixteenth and early seventeenth centuries is largely that of the emigration of Flemish weavers to other countries as the home situation became less favorable to luxury industries. Some of the first to leave went to Holland, notably to Delft; others found places in Sweden, Denmark, Norway, France (where a royal workshop was established by Francis I in the château of Fontainebleau), and in England, where—in its best period, from 1620 to 1636—the Mortlake factory founded by James I rivaled those of the Continent.

In 1602 two Flemish weavers, Marc de Comans and François de La Planche, went to Paris at the bidding of Henry IV, who was interested in competing with the Netherlands. They were settled on the banks of the Bièvre, a small tributary of the Seine, where the celebrated Gobelin family of dyers had had their shop, and were granted,

The Emperor on a Journey,
from the series *The Story of the Emperor of China,* Beauvais, late seventeenth or early eighteenth century.

Hunters Resting, probably after a
composition by David Teniers II (1610-1690);
Flemish, probably Brussels, 1700-1750.

these new, rebuilt quarters all the shops still weaving tapestries in Paris. To the highly organized tapestry operation were joined, in their turn, shops manufacturing furniture and decorations of every kind, goldsmiths, bronze workers, decorative painters, mosaicists, and craftsmen with all the various skills that were to embellish the royal residences and particularly the château of Versailles, where construction was soon to begin. The *Manufacture royale des meubles de la couronne*, to give this project its title, was conceived with the double purpose of glorifying the sovereign and reinvigorating the arts in France. For tapestry, it meant a new era, more splendid than anything that had gone before. The first director, the artist Charles Le Brun, himself the designer of some of the most famous tapestries made at the Gobelins, perfected a method by which highly finished cartoons, the work of artists each with his own specialty, were supplied to the weavers. But Le Brun's system left the weaver free to interpret the design in terms of his own technique, and with the colors at his disposal.

The major works of the Gobelins under Le Brun and his successor Louvois include the series *The Elements; The Seasons*, each panel of which has as a background for its allegorical subject one of the royal châteaux; *The Triumph of Alexander; The Story of the King*, which depicts not only battles and ceremonies but one scene in the Gobelins factory where objects of art—tapestries, furniture, silver, and so forth—are being shown to the sovereign; *The Months*, or *The Royal Residences*, with views of the châteaux in their extensive garden settings; *The Triumphs of the Gods*, or *The Arabesques of Raphael;* and *The Ancient Indies*, representing New World fauna and flora.

The exhaustion of the treasury by the wars of Louis XIV brought production at the Gobelins to a brief halt at the end of the century. When the shops re-opened in 1699 it was almost exclusively for the production of tapestry. Two of the new directors, the painters Jean-Baptiste Oudry, from 1733 to 1755, and François Boucher, from 1755 to 1770, exerted considerable influence on the technique as well as the choice of subject, demanding that tapestry imitate painting in all its nuances of color. The result was to alter the whole character of tapestry. The production of great decorative panels continued, however, with the *Story of Don Quixote*—so popular that it was woven nine times in twenty-four years; *The Gods*, after Boucher; the *Esther* and the *Jason* series; *The New Indies;* and *The Hunts of Louis XV*.

The royal tapestry factory at Beauvais, north of Paris, was also created by Colbert; unlike the Gobelins, it was allowed to work for private patrons and supplied wealthy members of the nobility and upper *bourgeoisie*. Its most prosperous period began in 1684 under the management of the Flemish Philippe de Behagle, and its first great success was with the *Grotesques à fond jaune,* often called the *Grotesques de Berain*

among other privileges, the exclusive sale of tapestries in France and the right to brew beer for themselves and employees. Although the continuing importation of skilled Flemish workmen at first caused alarm, French and Flemings were co-operating, within a short time, in several Parisian workshops for which designs were supplied by such artists as Philippe de Champaigne, Antoine Caron, Eustache Le Sueur, and Simon Vouet.

It was the vision of Colbert, the great minister of Louis XIV, that made the name Gobelins famous around the world. In the 1660's Colbert bought for the crown the old hôtel des Gobelins and surrounding properties and transferred to because their principal motifs are derived from Raphael's arabesques as adapted by Jean Berain I (1640-1711) though actually owing as much to the flower painter J. B. Monnoyer (1636-1699). *The Conquests of Louis the Great, The Adventures of Telemachus, The Marine Triumphs,* and especially the popular *First Chinese Set* were other series produced under Behagle. From the factory's "best period," beginning in 1722, came *Country Pleasures* and *The Fables of La Fontaine,* designed by Oudry, and six sets designed by Boucher including *The Story of Psyche* and *The Loves of the Gods.*

Certain tapestries woven at Beauvais and also at the Gobelins represent a new, eighteenth-century fashion: on a ground simulating a damask fabric garlands of flowers and other motifs —architecture, trophies, birds—surround the representation, in *trompe l'oeil* style, of a framed painting. This practical idea made it possible to produce relatively quickly and economically sets of tapestries to be made part of the decoration of a paneled room, since it was no great problem to change the dimensions of the *alentours,* or figured grounds. An example of the splendid effects obtainable is the tapestry room from Croome Court now in the Metropolitan Museum of Art. (This remarkable interior and its contents were described and illustrated in Antiques for January 1960 by Edith A. Standen and James Parker.)

Tapestry designed for covering chairs and sofas was woven at Beauvais and at the Gobelins from early in the 1700's. It was supplied in sets that usually provided medallions or unframed motifs for the backs and seats of furniture and allover patterns for other parts, and might or might not be "co-ordinated," as we should say today, with sets of wall panels.

Other centers of tapestry weaving active in the eighteenth century in France were Aubusson, southwest of Paris, and Nancy, in Lorraine. Tapestry was also made in important quantities in Munich and Berlin, Turin and Naples, London (in the Soho district), St. Petersburg, and Madrid, where Goya was a cartoon painter.

The Gobelins, Beauvais, and Aubusson factories survived the French Revolution and are still active today, as the many visitors are aware who see tapestry woven in Paris (where the Gobelins and Beauvais operations are housed together on the original site of the Gobelins factory); the two royal factories have enjoyed official patronage ever since Napoleon's rise to power. But the nineteenth century must be counted a period of artistic decline, interrupted only by the experiments of William Morris in England in the 1880's and 1890's. In our own time the craft has been reinvigorated in France by a group of gifted designers including, most prominently, Jean Lurçat, Marcel Gromaire, and Jean Picart-Le Doux, in whose work tapestry regains the force of expression that makes it an authentic art form.

Arabesques with Bust, from a series with similar elements in varying compositions; London, possibly woven by I. (Joshua?) Morris, 1700-1750.

The wealth of Boucher tapestries in American museums

BY MADELEINE JARRY

To MARK THE bicentenary of his death in 1770, the Louvre Museum devoted two special exhibitions to the work of François Boucher, painter to Louis XV. A selection of the artist's finest drawings and the best engravings after his works made up one of these displays; a group of twenty-six paintings by Boucher and a number of tapestries woven to his designs comprised the other. The two exhibitions called attention again to Boucher's role in the development of the Louis XV style. This successful young artist, who learned so much early in his career from engraving the works of the genial Watteau, became more than a painter. Bringing his fecund imagination and his technical virtuosity to bear on designing porcelains, stage sets, and tapestries as well as the painted decoration of interiors, he virtually created the new décor, all grace and elegance, in which the king lived with his favorite, Madame de Pompadour,

and which was copied everywhere in Europe and in much more distant courts.

A considerable number of tapestries were woven after Boucher's designs at the Beauvais and, later, at the Gobelins factories. But, as George Leland Hunter pointed out as long ago as 1925 in his *Practical Book of Tapestries* (Philadelphia, 1925), few are preserved in French public collections. The explanation for this is that the output of the Beauvais factory was generally not destined for the royal residences (the Beauvais pieces commissioned by the king were often for gifts) but was bought by noble and other private clients. The tapestries after Boucher's designs woven at the Gobelins in the workshop of the independent contractor Jacques Neilson (such as *The Gods*) were for the most part ordered by English lords. As a result the *Mobilier National*, or French state collection, from which most of the tapestries displayed in French museums are drawn, is not rich in tapestries of Boucher's design.

On a recent visit to the United States, however, I was struck by the number of tapestries after Boucher on view in American museums, especially in the Metropolitan Mu-

Fig. 1. Beauvais tapestry, *The Quack Doctor and the Peep Show*, from the suite *Italian Village Scenes* after François Boucher (1703-1770); the design was woven for the first time in 1736. *Virginia Museum.*

seum in New York and the Huntington Art Gallery and J. Paul Getty Museum in California. These institutions must be congratulated, as well, on showing their tapestries in appropriate settings. At the Metropolitan Museum, for instance, the tapestry-hung room from Croome Court contains a large set of furniture with the tapestry covers made for this interior (ANTIQUES, January 1960, p. 80). It is only in such ensembles that the decorative quality of Boucher's work can be fully appreciated.

Boucher's first set of tapestry designs, woven at Beauvais beginning in 1736, was entitled *Fêtes italiennes,* which has been variously translated as *Italian Village Scenes* and *Village Festivals, Italian Style.* It comprises fourteen subjects: *The Charlatan,* or *Quack Doctor; The Peep Show; The Gypsy,* or *Fortune Teller; The Hunter; Fishing; The Dance; The Luncheon; Music; Girls with Grapes; The Gardener; The Shepherdess; The Innkeeper; The Parrot;* and *The Egg Vendor.* The title of this series was intended to recall Watteau's *fêtes galantes,* or scenes in wooded parks where ladies and gentlemen strolled among statues, fountains, urns, ancient monuments, and romantic ruins.

Diderot, the encyclopedist and critic of art, did not appreciate Boucher's talents and made no effort to conceal his scorn for such pastoral pictures and their lack of realism. "Where," he asked, "were shepherds ever seen dressed in such rich and elegant clothes?" He dismissed Boucher as insincere or worse, though recognizing the artist's color sense, the variety of his palette, and his inventiveness. "That man has everything but the truth." Nevertheless, the *Italian Village Scenes* were a great success and were rewoven many times before Boucher's death in 1770. The Metropolitan Museum has nine of these, eight of which were made for Boulard de Gâtelier in 1762 and remained at the Château de Gâtelier until 1899 (Cover, Pl. I). Five tapestries from the same suite are part of the Huntington collection; from different sources, these pieces represent several different weavings. An inscription on the panel

Fig. 2.   Beauvais tapestry after Boucher's designs for the series *The Loves of the Gods,* 1749-1779. This wide piece shows two subjects: at left *Bacchus and Ariadne;* at right *Jupiter and Antiope. J. Paul Getty Museum.*

Fig. 3. *Apollo and Clytie;* Beauvais tapestry after Boucher, from *The Loves of the Gods,* 1749-1779. *Minneapolis Institute of Arts.*

jumble of disparate objects.'' The Philadelphia Museum has all five panels: *Psyche Led by Zephyr into the Palace of Love, The Toilet of Psyche, Psyche Displaying her Treasures to her Sisters, Psyche Abandoned,* and *Psyche at the Basketmaker's* (also called *Psyche at the Fisherman's).* The J. Paul Getty Museum has four of the five, lacking only *Psyche Displaying her Treasures.* The Art Institute of Chicago has fragments of one panel. The wonderfully delicate features of Psyche have often been remarked on; it may be that the artist followed the advice of his friend, the writer Bachaumont, and took as his inspiration the face of his own wife.

Boucher's designs for the *Chinese Hangings,* also woven at Beauvais, were exhibited at the Salon of 1742; several of them have been identified as small paintings preserved by the museum at Besançon. The first of this set of six tapestries was set up on the loom in 1743. The Cleveland Museum of Art has one subject, *The Fair* (Pl. II). This piece has an unusual history. It was part of the ninth set woven for the king in 1759 and given by him in 1763 to M. Bertin, minister of foreign affairs and a collector of Far Eastern art. Bertin made a gift of the tapestries to two young Chinese who were returning to the Jesuit mission at Peking. Presented by the mission to the Emperor Ch'ien Lung, the hangings were discovered in 1860 in the Imperial Palace, still in their original packing, and then dispersed. A panel representing the same subject but enlarged by the addition of supplementary figures at either side is now in the Minneapolis Institute of Art. The Philadelphia Museum has an example of the panel entitled *Fishing* with the arms of France and of Navarre on the border, indicating that it was made for the king.

Boucher's tapestry designs continued to find success, and in 1749 he made a new set, *The Loves of the Gods,* consisting of nine compositions. These were woven between 1749 and 1779, some of them as many as seventeen times. The J. Paul Getty Museum has an exceptional hanging that combines two subjects from this series, *Bacchus and Ariadne* on the left side and *Jupiter and Antiope* on the right (Fig. 2). There is an *Apollo and Clytie* in the Minneapolis Institute of Arts (Fig. 3), and the Metropolitan Museum and the Los Angeles County Museum have other subjects.

The fifth set of designs by Boucher for Beauvais was the *Operatic Fragments* (1752) which once again demonstrates the artist's skill both in grouping figures and in decorating backgrounds. The National Gallery in Washington has *Rinaldo's Dream,* and the Metropolitan Museum (Altman collection) has *Vertumnus and Pomona* from this series.

The designs for a new set of hangings undertaken in 1755 were Boucher's last work for the Beauvais factory, where his influence had been so great. The *Noble Pastoral,* or *Les Beaux Pastorales,* consisted of six subjects: *The Fountain of Love, The Flute Player, Fishing, The Bird Catchers, The Luncheon,* and *The Shepherdess.* The last of these was woven only once, and the whereabouts of that panel is no longer known. The *Noble Pastoral* was executed several times for the king, and a set of furniture covers was designed to accompany it. The suite was woven for the last time in 1778. The Huntington Art Gallery has all five existing subjects in remarkably fresh condition. There are single panels from this series in the Cleveland Museum (Fig. 4), the Boston Museum of Fine Arts (Fig. 5), and the Art Institute of Chicago (Fig. 6).

Envious of the success of Boucher's work for Beauvais,

entitled *The Luncheon* indicates that it was executed between 1753 and 1755, when Jean Baptiste Oudry and André Charlemagne Charron shared the direction of the Beauvais factory. Two of the Huntington panels depict double subjects, so that seven of the fourteen subjects are represented in the collection. The Virginia Museum in Richmond (Fig. 1), the Walters Art Gallery in Baltimore, the Philadelphia Museum of Art, and the J. Paul Getty Museum also have hangings from this series.

The second set of tapestries Boucher designed for the Beauvais factory, entitled the *Story of Psyche,* was begun in 1741. The artist had exhibited a painting at the Salon of 1739 called *Psyche Led by Zephyr into the Palace of Love.* This well-organized composition includes along with the extraordinary architecture of the palace such accessories as perfume burners, Turkish rugs, and other art objects—an abundance of ornamental elements that Diderot called ''a

Fig. 4. *The Flute Player;* Beauvais tapestry after Boucher from the *Noble Pastoral,* 1755-1778. *Cleveland Museum of Art.*

Fig. 5. *The Luncheon;* Beauvais tapestry after Boucher from the *Noble Pastoral. Museum of Fine Arts, Boston.*

Pl. I.   Beauvais tapestry *The Luncheon* from Boucher's suite *Italian Village Scenes*.
It is part of the set woven for Boulard de Gâtelier in 1762. *Metropolitan Museum of Art.*

Fig. 6. *The Bird Catchers,* from the *Noble Pastoral;* Beauvais tapestry after Boucher, with inscription (on back) *F. Boucher 1755. Art Institute of Chicago.*

the weavers of the Gobelins factory petitioned the marquis de Marigny, the superintendent of buildings, for models by this master. In 1749, with the support of Madame de Pompadour, Boucher obtained a workshop at the Gobelins, and, on the death of Jean Baptiste Oudry in 1755 succeeded him as superintendent of the factory. His direction fully justified the hopes of the Gobelins weavers. Before 1755 Boucher had given the Gobelins designs for the two large compositions *Sunrise* and *Sunset.* Now he collaborated with the painters Carle van Loo, Jean Baptiste Pierre, and Joseph Marie Vien in the production of *The Loves of the Gods.* For these Boucher supplied cartoons very similar to his compositions on this theme for Beauvais. The Walters Art Gallery in Baltimore has *Vulcan Presenting to Venus the Arms Made for Aeneas* from this set.

In 1758 Boucher began work on *The Gods,* for each subject of which Maurice Jacques supplied the *alentours* (redesigned after 1770 by Louis Tessier). *Alentours* are figured backgrounds, or surrounds, woven in damask patterns or motifs consisting of cartouches, trophies, flowers, or human or animal figures. An eighteenth-century innovation at the Gobelins, *alentours* represent one of two methods of framing the principal subject of a composition, the other being the simulation of a carved and gilded picture frame. Several English noblemen, charmed by the elegance and refinement of the designs, ordered sets of *The Gods* in shapes and sizes appropriate for overdoors and for the narrow spaces around windows or large mirrors,

so as to make a complete wall decoration. One such set, woven in the Neilson workshop for the earl of Coventry between 1766 and 1771, was intended for the latter's house, Croome Court, near Worcester. As mentioned earlier, these hangings, consisting of three large tapestries, several narrow panels, two overdoors, and covers for a set of six armchairs and two sofas, have been installed in the Metropolitan Museum, where the pictorial medallions in their *trompe-l'oeil* gilded frames on a rose-red "damask" ground can be seen to full advantage (Pl. III).

The Gobelins factory produced several other sets of chair covers after Boucher's designs. The Huntington Art Gallery has Boucher tapestries for the backs of ten chairs and two settees (Figs. 7, 8); the seats are after designs by Jean Baptiste Oudry. On the chair backs the arts are represented as children and *putti* who are sculptors, painters, and poets. The designs are reminiscent of *Children's Games,* a series which Boucher designed while he was working at Beauvais and which was interpreted there in overdoors, screens, and other small panels (Fig. 9).

It has not been possible, in the scope of this article, to do more than suggest the wealth of tapestries after Boucher in American museums, but mention should be made of the very fine series from *The Gods* now in the collection of John Paul Getty. These tapestries were woven at the Gobelins to the order of Louis XVI and presented by him in 1782 to the grand duke of Russia Paul Petrovich (later Czar Paul I) for the Palace of Pavlovsk.

Pl. II. *The Fair*, from the *Chinese Hangings;* Beauvais tapestry after Boucher, 1759.
Cleveland Museum of Art, Elisabeth Severance Prentiss collection.

Overleaf.

Pl. III. The tapestry room from Croome
Court, Worcestershire, now at the Metropolitan Museum of Art. The tapestries were
all woven at the Royal Gobelins Manufactory. Boucher designed medallions of the
four elements for the room. Visible are Ce-
phalus and Aurora, or Air, to the left of the
mantel, and Vulcan and Venus, or Fire, over
the commode.

Figs. 7 and 8. Two of ten chair backs representing the arts as children and *putti;* Gobelins after Boucher. Dating is made difficult because of uncertainty whether one or more sets of chair backs are represented. *Henry E. Huntington Library and Art Gallery.*

Fig. 9. *The Bath*
from the series *Children's Games*
which Boucher designed
for Beauvais. Date uncertain.
Cleveland Museum of Art.

MOREEN—A FORGOTTEN FABRIC

By HAZEL E. CUMMIN

This is the third in a series of studies of eighteenth-century upholstery fabrics which is being made in connection with the restoration of Stratford Hall in Virginia. The first two studies, in which certain types of eighteenth-century dimities were discussed, appeared in the July and September 1940 issues of ANTIQUES.

MOREEN appears regularly in American inventories and advertisements of the pre-Revolutionary period, and until well after the close of the Revolution. With the advent of the styles of Adam and Hepplewhite, it gave way to a fashion for lighter-weight upholstery fabrics. The change is noted in a sentence quoted by the *Oxford English Dictionary:* "She had discarded horsehair for cretonne, and moreen for dimity" — a sentence that also suggests the characteristic use of moreen as a bedroom hanging in the previous period. An inventory of the time, typical of many among American records, confirms this evidence. In the Boston *News-Letter* of August 30, 1770, "all the genteel House Furniture" of Governor Francis Bernard is advertised for sale. Of six bed furnitures included, two are moreen, and two are probably homewoven imitations of it:

1 Mohogony four Post Bedsted, with crimson Moreen Furniture, and 2 window Curtains.

1 Mohogony four Post Bedsted with Red and White Furniture Check and 3 Window Curtains.

1 Mohogony four Post Bedsted with yellow Moreen Furniture, and 2 Window Curtains. 1 sett of yellow bottom Chairs.

1 suit of Nett Curtains for a Bed with Chair Coverings.

2 four Post Bedsteads with coarse Blue Woolen Curtains.

Relegated to less important uses in the early nineteenth century, moreen was nevertheless far from becoming obsolete. Cooper in *Pioneers* (1823) arrayed one of his characters in "a petticoat of green moreen"; and for this and similar uses the fabric held its own for a quarter of a century thereafter. About 1860 it returned to fashion as an upholstery fabric, and remained a favorite for parlor curtains within the memory of many people now living. As late as 1876, T. C. Archer included it in a list of woolens which he considered "fixed fabrics" immune to the vagaries of fashion.

Yet moreen is lost to us today. Only three or four authentic eighteenth-century examples have been turned up by the Stratford study. And of these only three are documented as moreen.

Beck's *Drapers' Dictionary*, published in 1882, says of moreen:

The name of this stuff was formerly Moireen, which gives its origin more distinctly. It is an imitation of moire in commoner materials for purposes of upholstery. . . . Chintzes have at the present time nearly run this fabric out of the market. In former times when it was more in demand, a variety with embossed patterns was made by passing the cloth over a hot brass cylinder, on which were engraved various flowers or other fancy figures.

A study of earlier authorities makes it clear that the history of both fabrics mentioned by Beck has been a matter less of imitation than of independent development from a common ancestor. Jacques Savary des Bruslons (1759 edition) and Roland de la Platière (1780) both describe a watered stuff of goat's hair (*poil de chèvre*) or goat's hair mixed with wool, which, according to Savary, was given a watered surface (*auquel on a fait des ondes*) by the weight of the calender, under which it was passed many times. Savary describes another decoration called *gauffrage* in which these stuffs, like certain pile fabrics of the sixteenth and seventeenth centuries, were figured or printed with various flowers, branches, or figures (*façonnés, ou imprimés de diverses fleurs, ramages, ou figures*) by means of hot irons "that are a kind of mold, passed at the same time as the cloth under a press" (*des espèces de moules, qu'on fait passer en même tems que l'étoffe sous un presse*). This decoration, Savary says, had

previously been quite common but was used at that time (1759) only for church ornament, and for upholstery.

These watered and figured stuffs of hair are identified as moreen by M. Bezon in his *Dictionnaire des Textiles* (1867), in a passage quoting the Savary description; he says further (in translation): "The name moreen has also been given to a kind of watered grosgrain composed of a warp of double goat's hair, and a weft of three threads of worsted twisted together." The true moreen (of his own day), he tells us, was a grosgrain fabric of worsted made from Holland wool, very closely and firmly woven, watered by the cylinder, and manufactured at Leyde. A similar fabric, he says, was made of fine wools at Bradford in England. The weave of moreen is described as a taffeta weave, usually having a marked grain in the weft.

The English word for goat's hair is mohair. The word derives from the French — *mohère, moère,* or *moire* — originally used in both languages to denote the lustrous fabric made from the long silken hair of the Angora goat. In his *Dictionnaire d'Ameublement*, M. Havard describes the steps by which the word passed from these early "Moahirs of Angora" to become, on the one hand, the name for watered silks (moire), and, on the other, the name for the watered stuffs of hair or hair and wool developed in England (moireen). He says:

This word [moire] denoting a very brilliant fabric of goat's hair, was applied with us, at the close of the seventeenth century, to diverse kinds of fabrics. It seems to have referred in the beginning to several kinds of lustrous fabrics. Indeed, in the fifteenth century, we have moires of gold, of silver, and of silk (*il est question de moires d'or, d'argent, et de soie*). . . . Toward the close of the seventeenth century, we find the words *moire, mohaire, mohère, mouaire,* used to denote more especially fabrics all of silk, of grosgrain, closely woven. . . . These moires were of two kinds: plain moire, which was without watering; and watered moire. . . . Soon it was this watering, originally regarded as accessory, that became the determining cause of the name, and the word moire came to apply especially to watered stuffs (*s'appliqua specialement à des étoffes ondées*) which had received this finish by being passed through the calender. . . . Watered stuffs (*les étoffes moirées*) were much in fashion in the eighteenth century. In the present century [nineteenth] silk moire continued to be fashionable for upholstery until 1823–1835. The fashion for woolen moires (*moire de laine*) lasted appreciably longer.

Havard's description of the two kinds of early eighteenth-century moire, plain and watered, corresponds with those in an early edition of Savary (1741), and in the 1759 edition. An almost literal English translation of the Savary account appears in the Chambers *Encyclopædia* of 1741. But in the Diderot encyclopedia (*c.* 1782–1785) *la moère* is described simply as "a grained silk to which the name of moère is given because it has passed under the calender (for watering)." Thus in the third quarter of the century when, as we shall see, watered fabrics were extremely popular, the transition of the word became complete. Simultaneously in England watered mohair became moireen. The word mohair continued to be used there for fabrics of goat's hair, or of mixed hair and wool.

All eighteenth-century accounts acknowledge the English origin of moreen. The watering process seems to have originated in England, and was there brought to its highest state of perfection. Bezon, in a detailed account of "moirage," relates how the English textile trade profited from practice of the process for a full half century before it was introduced successfully into France in 1754. In that year the French government induced an Englishman named Badger to establish himself at Lyon with an English calender, bringing, says Bezon, a notable increase to the prosperity of the town. We may assume from this that the year 1754 marked a peak in the fashion for watered stuffs in this period.

before calendering appears in Figure 2, which shows the under side of the fabric. Part of a plain green moreen hanging, also owned by the Essex Institute, shows exactly this weave and texture on both sides of the cloth, which has neither watering nor pattern. This second hanging was owned in 1760 by Mrs. Samuel Philbrick of Weare, New Hampshire; and was still fastened to the tester sheet of her bed when the piece was presented to the Institute by her great-granddaughter, Miss Eliza Philbrick of Salem. Miss Philbrick's collection of old fabrics woven for her family at Weare was for many years the most interesting of its kind known to antiquarians. An example of plain watered moreen, shown in Figure 3, will be discussed in a later article dealing with the process of watering, and the results obtained at the different stages of its development.

FIG. 1 — PART OF A CRIMSON MOREEN BED HANGING (*c. 1770*). *From the Essex Institute*

FIG. 2 — REVERSE SIDE OF THE MOREEN SHOWN IN FIGURE 1. A coarse grain was necessary for the success of watering by the old process

FIG. 3 (*below*) — PLAIN WATERED GREEN MOREEN. Originally used as the lining of a chasuble

Although watered materials of hair or wool were thereafter manufactured to some extent in France, by far the greater number continued to be made in England. Combining the rich sheen of moire with the warmth and durability of Norwich woolens, these fabrics were as English as roast beef and Yorkshire pudding, and became almost as indispensable in both England and America. As has been said, their chief use in this period was for bedroom hangings. Their revival in late nineteenth-century parlors has been a cause of some confusion among collectors, since many 1860 moreens survive to snare the unwary. In color, texture, and the nature of the yarns, as well as in the watering, they differ greatly from the crisp mohair moreens of the eighteenth century; but many of them have acquired a mellowness that is deceptive. Only a few genuine eighteenth-century examples have survived.

One of the most interesting of these is shown in Figure 1. This piece is part of a crimson moreen bed hanging that belonged to Sarah (Peale) and Daniel Saunders of Salem, Massachusetts, at the time of their marriage, March 2, 1770. The hanging was presented to the Essex Institute by Miss Mary T. Saunders of Salem, labeled as it had been known in the family: *Moreen Bed Curtains*.

The fabric of this hanging is of close taffeta weave, with a grain formed by weft yarns that are heavier than the warps. The yarns are mohair in the warp, and mohair, possibly mixed with wool, in the weft. The surface of the cloth has been watered and stamped, as described by Savary, with a flower pattern similar to those of contemporary printed cottons. The unevenness of the yarns

Flat-woven rugs of the Middle East

BY W. R. PICKERING AND ANTHONY N. LANDREAU

KILIM, SOUMAK, VERNE, SILE are all terms which have been used to designate various flat-woven, or non-pile, rugs, bags, covers, tent hangings, and animal trappings made throughout a vast territory stretching from Asia Minor east to Samarkand, and south from Baku to the Persian Gulf. Pieces in these and related techniques could be made with sufficient strength to survive in the nomad's caravan and tent as well as in the villager's hut, or with a delicacy suited to the finest palaces of Islam. But in addition to their utilitarian value, these pieces possess considerable decorative appeal. While lacking the depth of color found in pile carpets, the kilim, for instance, has a bright sharpness which is complemented by the angular designs employed and further enlivened by the slit construction of the weave. Soumaks, with their surfaces of solid brocading, have a brilliance found in no other weaving. And the pieces of mixed techniques, especially those with motifs in relief upon a plain-weave base, possess an exciting clarity of design and richness of detail rarely excelled among Near Eastern textiles.

In spite of these impressive artistic, decorative, and utilitarian credentials, a relatively limited amount of research has been done on flat weaves, so that classification of flat-woven material still has few guidelines. The current exhibition of such rugs at the Textile Museum in Washington, D.C., has been arranged using type of weave as the main criterion, rather than geographical origin, which is generally the chief factor considered in dealing with pile carpets. Several main groupings emerge from this technical approach. First come kilims (in tapestry weave, which is reversible), then Soumaks, the various other compound weaves and brocaded rugs, embroidered rugs, and, finally, those of mixed techniques (which can include all of the above as well as pile). Geography is an important but secondary consideration, because the lack of adequate records has made it difficult in many instances to determine national, or even regional, origins.

The term kilim has frequently been used to designate all nonpile rugs of the Middle East. However, it can be used to refer quite precisely to tapestry-woven rugs as distinguished from rugs of different construction, particularly Soumak and knotted pile rugs. Tapestry weaving generally involves two fundamental ways of working: closely packing the wefts which hide the warp, producing areas of solid color; and weaving independent, discontinuous wefts, each of a different color, back and forth within one pattern area (Fig. 1). Most Middle Eastern kilims are weft faced (that is, the wefts hide the warps) and are in plain weave with discontinuous wefts. The term plain weave is used to describe the simple interlacing of warp and weft, with each weft passing alternately over and under successive warp units. Plain weave, therefore, refers to the order of interlacing; and tapestry weave, a technique which implies discontinuous wefts, is found in several different variations, which include plain weave or twill.

Generally speaking, tapestry-woven pieces resemble in color and design the pile rugs known to have been pro-

Fig. 1. Slit tapestry weave, showing vertical and diagonal boundaries between color areas. Weft faced. *From Irene Emery,* The Primary Structures of Fabrics (*Washington, D.C., 1966), p. 79; photograph by courtesy of the Smithsonian Institution.*

Fig. 1a. Basic structure of slit tapestry weave. *Emery, p. 79; Smithsonian photograph.*

Color plate, facing page.

Anatolian cover. Weft-float brocading on plain-weave ground; twined guard stripes at ends; braided warp fringe.
Wool warp and weft. 6 feet, 4 inches by 5 feet, 2 inches.
Collection of Arthur D. Jenkins.

Fig. 2.   Persian (Sehna) rug, slit tapestry. Note the use of slits
as a design element in the white field. Wool warp and weft.
5 feet, 4 inches by 4 feet, 1 inch. *Collection of Charles Grant Ellis;
unless otherwise noted, photographs are by Woltz Studio.*

Fig. 3.   Caucasian bag face, Soumak wrapping.
Wool warp and weft. 2 feet by 1 foot, 9 inches.
Collection of Harold Mark Keshishian.

Fig. 4.   Basic structure of progressive weft wrapping, used in
Soumak wrapping; over two warp units and back under one.
Emery, p. 214; Smithsonian photograph.

Fig. 5. Caucasian rug; allover countered Soumak brocading, knotted warp fringe. Wool warp and weft. 6 feet, 3 inches by 5 feet, 7 inches. *Collection of H. McCoy Jones.*

duced in certain regions (though the variety of designs in some rugs shows that the nomads who wove them were familiar with rugs made elsewhere). This is particularly true of kilims, so that pieces from the Sehna (Fig. 2) and to a lesser extent the Shiraz districts in Persia are easily recognized. Bold coloring and sharply angular designs distinguish kilims from the Caucasus, and the few available Turkoman kilims are rendered unmistakable by the famous Turkoman madder red. Nevertheless, unsolved problems remain in regard to the considerable number of pieces which were evidently made by nomadic or semi-nomadic peoples unrestrained by the borders of Turkey, the Caucasus, and Persia, and which possess characteristics of more than one country. These are sometimes referred to as Kurdish, an often meaningless label since many nomadic tribes in addition to the Kurds inhabited broad sections of all three regions depending upon where the political borders happened to be fixed at any given time. Kilims were also produced throughout the Balkans. Examples from Bosnia, Serbia, and Bulgaria have their own coloring, while they employ designs used in Anatolian and Caucasian weaving.

A second technique found in flat-woven rugs is Soumak (Fig. 3). Soumaks fall into two basic types. The first may be called Soumak wrapping, in which the weft is wrapped around the warp (Fig. 4), rather than passed in and out between the warp strands as in the tapestry-woven kilim. Soumak wrapping is a kind of progressive weft wrapping, and is often mistaken for other weaving structures. In Soumak the sequence of the progressive wrapping of warp by weft is consistently forward over and back under and around, with a span ratio usually of two to one. The wrapping in Soumak may be plain—that is, the rows of wrapping wefts all have the same direction of slant; or countered, with the direction of slant reversed from row to row.

The second kind of Soumak work is called Soumak brocading (Figs. 5, 6). In it, wrapping wefts are supplementary to ground weave (commonly plain weave) and are usually discontinuous, as in tapestry weave. This is one of the many compound weaves found in Middle Eastern textiles. Compound weaves are those that are composed of more than one set of either warp and weft elements or both. In Soumak brocading the weft ends hang loose at the back of the work. In one variation of Soumak the reverse face is used as the front, and is often referred to as reverse Soumak (Fig. 7). Soumak brocading is sometimes confused with embroidery. Although

Fig. 6. Beluchi rug. Allover Soumak brocading; panels separated by bands of weft-faced plain weave; weft-float weave stripes across plain-weave aprons. Wool warp and weft. 9 feet, 1 inch by 5 feet, 3 inches. *Collection of W. R. Pickering.*

Soumak is not embroidery but weaving, there is close structural similarity to stem-stitch embroidery, which often looks like Soumak brocading on both sides. Also, there is no structural relationship between Soumak and Kashmir shawls with which Soumak has been erroneously identified, probably due to the fact that in both, weft ends are left hanging on the back. Brocaded textiles, Soumak and other types (Fig. 8, color plate), represent several kinds of compound weaving; and they include one of the principal groups of flat-woven rugs from the Middle East.

The name Soumak is usually said to be a corruption or abbreviation of Shemakha, one of the southeastern Caucasian towns where weft-wrapped rugs are thought to have been made. Despite the fact that weft-wrapped textiles have a long history and are found in many places, including Persia, Turkestan, and possibly Kurdistan or Anatolia, the Caucasus is often said to be the place of origin of the Soumak technique and it has often been wrongly assumed that most or all of the Soumak rugs were made in the Caucasus. But, although the Soumak technique was employed throughout the Middle East, the Caucasus is the major source of nineteenth- and twentieth-century Soumak rugs. Like the pile carpets of this period, they were produced in large numbers for export and contain field designs and color combinations typical of rugs made in the eastern and southern districts of the Caucasus. Perhaps more exciting than the Soumak rugs, however, are the bags, animal trappings, and tent decorations; for the Soumak technique is particularly suited to these smaller pieces and, when well conceived and executed, produces brilliantly colorful and powerful results.

A number of other types of Middle Eastern compound-weave rugs (Fig. 9) are found, as well as many textiles in which several techniques, including pile, are used together in a single piece (Fig. 10). One technique which occurs in Middle Eastern textiles, either alone or in combination with various weaves, is embroidery. Strictly speaking, embroidery is not weaving but decorative needlework, composed of accessory stitches and worked into an already complete ground fabric. However, confusion seems to exist in rug literature, where several weaving structures have been called embroidery. In fact, embroidery is not always distinguishable from weaving. We have already mentioned the possible confusion between stem-stitch embroidery and Soumak brocading. Flat-woven rugs have been referred to as flat-stitch rugs or stitched tapestry work and have been described as woven with a flat stitch. However, while embroidery is always needlework, the use of a needle does not of itself produce embroidery. The important factor in describing textiles is the weaving structures involved and not their implementation. While a needle may be used in the production of such structures as Soumak, brocading, and even tapestry, as long as the structure is produced during the weaving process it is not embroidery; and the structure of a Soumak rug, for example, remains the same whether a needle was used or not. It is often difficult to tell how a completed fabric was produced.

Among the other terms that are commonly bandied about in connection with flat weaves are Silé and Verné (see ANTIQUES, March 1969, p. 373). These terms may have come from the names of Caucasian towns, although their exact geographic locations are obscure. Verné is

Fig. 7. Detail of a fabric patterned by a free arrangement of extra weft floats on a plain-weave ground.
Emery, p. 142;
Smithsonian photograph.

Fig. 7a. Opposite face of Fig. 7 showing the reverse pattern produced by the supplementary wefts which float on this face when not floating on the opposite one.
Emery, p. 142; Smithsonian photograph.

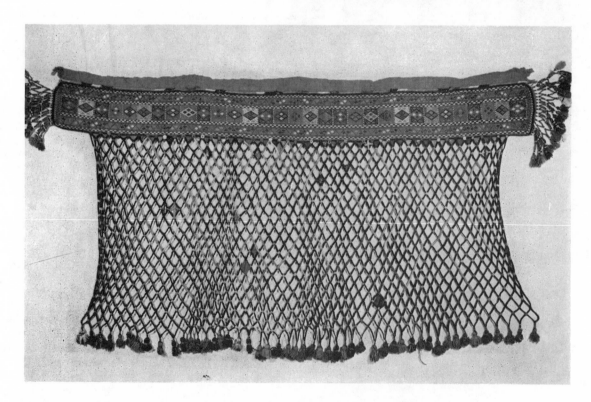

Fig. 8. Caucasian (?) animal trapping. The band is of weft-float brocading on plain-weave ground, with wrapped warp fringe. Attached to the band is a lattice of narrow flat braids; tassels added. Wool warp and weft. Over-all dimensions: 6 feet, 3 inches by 3 feet, 3 inches.
Collection of Mrs. Howard T. Karsner.

often cited as being near Shusha. Others say the Silés are made in the Baku district, Vernés in the Karabagh district. Lack of agreement makes futile the use of these terms to denote particular provenance. To add fuel to the fire, many of those who discuss rugmaking use Silé and Verné as terms for weaving structures. These rugs have been variously described as brocaded, embroidered, types of Soumak, related to Soumak, and a sort of herringbone weave. Upon examination, textiles with an S-shape stylized dragon design (characteristic of Silés) prove to be Soumak brocading; pieces with angular bird and animal patterns (often found in Vernés) are either Soumak or other brocading or a combination of more than one kind. It seems evident that neither Silé nor Verné serves to designate a particular weaving structure.

The rugs shown here probably all date from the same general period: from the middle of the nineteenth century until well into the twentieth. While the knowledge of flat weaves remains spotty, it is nevertheless increasing as more and more interest develops. As additional collectors enter the field, the blank spaces will be filled in. New approaches to classifying flat weaves will be found. Indeed, one of the most appealing aspects of the subject is that while it remains confused and uncertain, for that very reason it is filled with excitement and adventure. This is truly one of the last frontiers of Oriental rug collecting and major discoveries still lie ahead for those scholars and collectors who are willing to explore it.

This article is based on the catalogue by Anthony N. Landreau and W. R. Pickering for the exhibition *From the Bosporus to Samarkand, Flat-Woven Rugs,* which can be seen until September 27, 1969, at the Textile Museum in Washington. It will then be circulated by the Traveling Exhibition Service of the Smithsonian Institution. The catalogue is available from the Textile Museum, 2320 S Street, N.W., Washington, D.C.; $9.50 hard covers, $6.50 paper covers.

Fig. 9. Persian bag, weft-faced complementary weft-pattern weave; tapestry-woven back with tufts laid in; weft-twined ends, flat braided handle; square braided warp tassels twined into fabric; binding stitches at seams. Wool warp and weft. 11 inches by 11 inches. *Ellis collection.*

Fig. 10. Persian(?) bag face, slit tapestry weave and pile (Ghiordes knot). Wool warp and weft. 4 feet by 4 feet, 6 inches. *Textile Museum.*

IV   The More Complicated Construction

Many of the most popular eighteenth- and nineteenth-century textiles were woven in what is called supplementary set construction. Overshot coverlets, bed rugs, brocaded and velvet cloth, soumak and Aubusson rugs, Turkish, Persian, Axminster, Wilton, and Brussels carpets—despite many variations—are all supplementary structures, *each type having an extra set of warps or wefts, the wefts being either continuous or discontinuous, flat or pile*. The "coverlet," a general term for bed covering, suggests even more techniques than that which can be woven—quilting, appliquéing, stenciling, embroidering, and piecing. Florence Peto conceives her photographic survey on quilts and coverlets in this broad sense, illustrating two coverlets—among many—of particular interest to the weaver. Figure 2 (p. 132), though not structurally identified, is most likely of supplementary or extra-weft construction. Figure 4 (p. 133), the "Snowball and Star" design, is double-cloth, an example of complementary structure, a term explained in the last section of the present anthology.

"Kentucky's Coverlets," by Lou Tate, is a smorgasbord of delightful overshot and other extra-float designs. Figure 9 (p. 138), a "summer-and-winter" coverlet, illustrates two concepts that are often misunderstood: (1) that "summer-and-winter" is not a different class of weave from other extra-float weft types; and (2) that while remaining a supplementary structure it can still be woven with a Jacquard mechanism which is usually associated with the complementary or double-cloth structure.

If inventories are a good indication of the state of the weaving trade in the past, supplementary set weaving was not much of a home craft, except in the South—and even there it was not meant for sale. Early Rhode Island inventories examined by Abbott Lowell Cummings disclose ratios—like nine looms to fifty wheels and four looms to eighty-two wheels—that reinforce the beliefs that yarns were spun at home and that more complicated cloth was loomed in shops, even in the year 1675.

Another cover for the bed was the rug. Used over a coverlet, instead of a coverlet, or even instead of a bed itself, it was made of wool or coarse hair. Many twentieth-century textile enthusiasts associate a bed rug with needlework. But to Sandra Schaffer Tinkham in "A Southern Bed Rugg," it is as properly associated with woven knots. She cites examples from the Museum of Early Southern Decorative Arts and in the collections at Colonial Williamsburg. Marion Day Iverson in "A Bed Rug in Colonial America" adds "Ruggs" to the list of necessities like blankets, sheets, and bolsters used for the first sailing of the Massachusetts Bay Company, seventeenth-century inventories having made distinctions between woolen and worsted rugs and "Cotton wool and also Sheeps wooll."

Like coverlets, brocaded cloth was made with flat extra-weft floats. Like bed and tufted rugs, brocading was discontinuous weft threading not going from selvage to selvage. Brocading is most often found in tapestry or in cloth for upholstery and costume. Gertrude Townsend illustrates four brocaded gowns in her article on eighteenth-century costume.

The story of floor carpets in America could fill the pages of this survey with technical, historical, and symbolic references from around the world. The Oriental carpet has intrigued the enthusiast of things "American" because, in its use in America, it inspired the American designer and craftsman. Early Americans did weave small druggets, list or rag, Venetian, striped, and tufted rugs for the floor. They embroidered, shirred, sewed, and hooked rugs too. But it was not until Oriental carpets were imported and until English copies from places like Axminster (Devonshire), Moorfields, Wilton, and Kidderminster arrived that Americans were able to weave much more than a heavy coverlet for the floor.

William Claverly is supposed to have manufactured the first American rug in 1775, even though John F. Watson declares to the contrary in *Annals of Philadelphia* (1830) that carpet manufacturing was not introduced to America until after the Revolutionary War. William Peter Sprague was advertising Axminsters and ingrains in 1794. Isaac Macaulay began weaving Brussels carpet in Philadelphia in 1807. According to the inventories quoted in Sarah B. Sherrill's article "Oriental Carpets in Seventeenth-Century and Eighteenth-Century America," English Wiltons were in America at least by 1792. Axminsters, according to Charles Hummel, were advertised in South Carolina in 1774.

Axminsters, Brussels, and Wiltons were constructed with different kinds of supplemental sets: Brussels, with an extra *warp* woven over rods to form loops; Wilton, the same as Brussels except with the loops cut; and Axminsters, with extra *wefts* hand-knotted to form a pile similar to Oriental carpets and to the so-called "Turkey work" of the seventeenth century. Axminsters were floral rather than geometric and were inspired by the Greco-Roman aesthetic, like all the furnishings of the period between 1780 and 1830. Axminsters were woven on upright or vertical looms as were tapestries.

In Sarah B. Sherrill's discriminating analysis of Oriental carpets, distinctions are made between Orientals called "Turkish" carpets—found in American portraits and alluded to in American letters—and English Axminster and "Turkey work" copies. One way of determining the difference between the loom-woven and needleworked pieces—a problem Sherrill, like other scholars, wrestles with—is suggested by Lee Clawson of the Philadelphia College of Textiles and Science. When Turkey work is woven, only the weft threads are disturbed and seem wavy. When done on an embroidery frame—providing equal tension—both warps and wefts show a wavy disturbance from the intrusion of a needle. Sherrill also uncovers for the reader several domestic habits of our American forefathers—putting carpets on the furniture, placing covers on the carpets, and rubbing lemon or sorrel juice and hot white loaf crumbs on the stains that were made by food and by weather seeping under the door. At least London, Sherrill reports, had "scowerers" for those who failed with the lemon juice. Additional tips on eighteenth-century housekeeping practices, a subject on which curators would still like to see further research done, can be found in Rodris Roth's book, *Floor Coverings in 18th-Century America.*

In "Some Peasant and Nomad Oriental Rugs," Maurice S. Dimand writes a short, but comprehensive, overview of Oriental carpets. He puts the "Turkish" carpet into its earlier sixteenth- and seventeenth-century context of peasants and nomads, making our Turkish "originals" the peasant copies of rugs belonging to their Persian shahs and Turkish sultans. (For an article on palace carpets, see Richard N. Gregg, "Persian Palace Rugs in Oshkosh" *Antiques* 89 [May, 1966]: 718–723.) Dimand compares the Persian weaver favorably to the tapestry weaver of Beauvais, although most of what turns up in American and European paintings appear not to be palace rugs, but peasant varieties of Turkish rugs made in Anatolia.

Central Asian Turkoman rugs were woven as tribal tent furnishings. Christopher Dunham Reed, in his article "Rugs of Turkestan," points to the excellence of Turkoman craftsmen, who, as it turns out, were really craftswomen. Despite weaving equipment which was primitive and portable, such craftswomen were among the most accomplished of Oriental weavers, mastering the straight line, tying 500 knots to the inch, and working provincially for the tribe and not for the export market. In many ways the Turkoman craftswoman is reminiscent of the American weaver in the South. A graphic analysis of the number of knots per square inch, as well as of knotting types and weft character which best distinguish between rugs of different tribes, can be found in Walter A. Hawley's book *Oriental Rugs Antique & Modern.*

The Transylvanian carpets found in churches between Hungary and western Romania have been a puzzle to American scholars. Like others, H. McCoy Jones, in "Early Influences in Turkish Rugs," assumes that Anatolian weavers made these carpets, but poses the question of whether the weavers worked in Anatolia or were sent to the Transylvanian region for rugweaving purposes. Jones and Sherrill both mention the religious character of Turkish prayer rugs—the Islamic, Judaic, and Christian content—but a scholarly book is surely needed to cover this important subject.

Harold M. Keshishian's article, "Rugs of the Caucasus," suggests that Caucasian rugs have had less scholarly attention than either Persian or Turkish rugs. His account of the three republics of the Soviet Union which comprise what is known as the Caucasus—Georgian, Armenian, and Azerbaidzhan—is fascinating history and gives the Russian weaver great dimen-

ion. With the exception of a few French-inspired rugs ordered by Russian officers, rugs of the eighteenth-century Caucasian weavers were small and were considered unimportant. Keshishian explains that despite similarities with the palace weavers— Turkish knots, wool warps, and the stylized horses, peacocks, and flowers of the Persians—Caucasian weavers had no wealthy court patronage. They wove for one another and for the Christians among them who wanted animals, human figures, and cruciform motifs which the Christian Armenians and Georgians also provided.

The Spanish armorial rug, shown in Plate I (p. 215) of Sarah B. Sherrill's second article, "The Islamic Tradition in Spanish Rug Weaving," has its roots in the art of Islam and the Christianity of Spain. A blend of traditions is illustrated in the fourteenth-century "Synagogue" carpet with a gabled motif that has suggested to some Jewish liturgical scholars the Ark of the Law. The Spanish made their own versions of other weaving from the East. They interpreted the Transylvanian carpet and the Anatolian Ushak derived from the Persians. After the seventeenth century, as Sherrill points out, Renaissance motifs and the Western influences became dominant.

Suggested Reading

Cole, Arthur and Williamson, Harold. *The American Carpet Manufacture: A History and an Analysis.* Cambridge: Harvard University Press, 1941.

Cummings, Abbott Lowell. *Rural Household Inventories 1675–1775.* Boston: The Society for the Preservation of New England Antiquities, 1964.

Erdmann, Kurt. *Oriental Carpets: An Essay on Their History.* Translated by Charles Grant Ellis. London: A. Zwemmer, Ltd., 1960.

Hawley, Walter A. *Oriental Rugs Antique & Modern.* New York: Dover Publications, Inc., 1970.

Hummel, Charles F. "Floor Coverings Used in 18th-Century America." In *Irene Emery Roundtable on Museum Textiles 1975 Proceedings.* Edited by Patricia L. Fiske. Washington, D.C.: The Textile Museum, 1975.

Jarry, Madeleine *The Carpets of Aubusson.* Leigh-on-Sea: F. Lewis, 1969.

———. "Design in Aubusson Carpets," *Antiques* 95 (May, 1969): 702–707.

Little, Nina Fletcher. *Floor Coverings in New England Before 1850.* Sturbridge, Mass.: Old Sturbridge Village, 1967.

Roth, Rodris. *Floor Coverings in 18th-Century America.* Washington, D.C.: Smithsonian Institution Press, 1967.

Von Bode, Wilhelm and Kuhnel, Ernst. *Antique Rugs from the Near East.* Translated by Charles Grant Ellis. Plainfield, N.J.: Textile Book Service, 1970.

Weibel, Adèle Coulin. *Two Thousand Years of Textiles.* New York: Hacker Art Books, 1972.

QUILTS AND COVERLETS

From New York and Long Island

By FLORENCE PETO

ALL of the quilts and coverlets here pictured in company with brief notes were made in or near New York City. Their range of dates is from the 1780's to 1853. In so far as may be judged from a study of these examples, and others more or less similar, the domestic art of quiltmaking in the New York zone developed no marked individualities of design or technique during the period in review. Thus, for instance, the district has yielded nothing, either in originality or in richness of effect, comparable to the splendid eighteenth-century hooked wool bedspreads of the Connecticut Valley (see ANTIQUES for November

FIG. 1 (*right*) — FRENCH KNOTS ON HOMESPUN LINEN: WHITE (*dated 1800*)

The foundation material, woven on a narrow loom, sewed in three strips and embroidered by hand. The cornucopia filled with flowers or fruits, symbolizing abundance, was a favorite decorative motive in the early 1800's. Happily Marcy Huntting of East Hampton, Long Island, who made this coverlet, inscribed her own name and that of her place of residence on her handiwork and added the date *December 1800*. Marcy was born in 1781. Hence she was nineteen years old when she completed her bedcover.
Owned by a descendant, Mrs. Etta Hedges Pennypacker

FIG. 2 (*below, left*) — WOVEN COVERLET (*late eighteenth century*)

Made in two strips on a simple four-harness loom; flax warp with wool filling. In design, if not always in fact, wool coverlets exhibiting such geometrical patterns antedate by many years the more elaborate double-

faced coverlets whose decorative motives include involved scrolls and attempts at pictorial representation. The present piece is the work of Ida Stillwell of Gravesend, Long Island, and was probably made about 1786, when the young woman was twenty years old. She was twice married, the second time to Jacobus Voorhees.
Owned by a great-grandnephew, James Voorhies

FIG. 3 (*below, right*) — "STAR OF BETHLEHEM": PATCHWORK AND APPLIQUÉ

Delicate border design, chain edging, and graceful vases recall eighteenth-century design. Sunflower strip and diamond patchwork are distinctively of the 1800's. Ascribed to Mary Totten of Staten Island, who was born in 1781. It seems reasonable to place the date of this piece in the neighborhood of 1810. The appliquéd pattern shows an interesting mixture of printed flowers cut from English chintz and silhouette leaves of formally figured calico. *Owned by a collateral descendant, Miss Ella Butler*

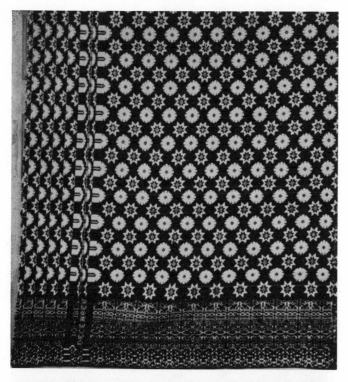

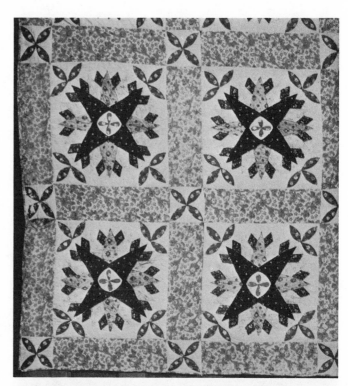

FIG. 4 (*upper, left*) — "SNOWBALL AND STAR" DOUBLE-WOVEN COVERLET

Made for Maria Kouwenhoven of Flatlands, Long Island, who was born in 1805. Maria's name and the date, *December 10, 1817*, are woven into the border. The coverlet is made of two strips seamed together. For an American coverlet of this type this date is very early.

Owned by a great-granddaughter, Mrs. Bernard Bennett

FIG. 5 (*upper, right*) — "COMPASS" OR "CHIPS AND WHETSTONES" QUILT

An involved patchwork pattern in calicoes on a homespun ground. Like most quilts made by the practical Dutch women, heavily padded for warmth and hence lacking fine stitchery in the quilting. Said to have been made by Cornelia Van Sicklen of Flatlands prior to her marriage in 1828 to Jacobus J. Voorhies.

Owned by a great-granddaughter, Mrs. Phoebe Voorhies Lott

FIG. 6 (*lower, left*) — "WILD GOOSE CHASE" QUILT

A seemingly unimaginative pattern until the long strips of triangles are seen to represent flocks of wild geese winging their way above the Long Island marshes. Johanna Bergen of Bergen's Island, Flatlands Bay, records in her diary (*1825–1829*) "grate flight of geese. I have seen 17 flocks." Johanna made the quilt here pictured.

Owned by a great-granddaughter, Mrs. Jane Voorhies Lyman

FIG. 7 (*lower, right*) — "TRIPLE STAR" LINEN AND CALICO QUILT

A curious item credited to a man, Obadiah Smith of Smithtown, Long Island, who was a successful farmer, a musician, and, because of a crippled wife, a handy man about the house. The most remarkable feature of his quilt is its star and swastika border. Probably made late in Obadiah's life, perhaps in the 1830's or 1840's.

Owned by a great-granddaughter, Mrs. Edith S. R. Scott

FIG. 8 — "GRAPEVINE AND OAK-LEAF" QUILT

Made by Elizabeth Glover of Brush Neck Manor, near Sag Harbor, Long Island. Born in 1824, Elizabeth began working her quilt when she was eleven years old. She worked her daily stint on this opus during a period of some years. It was finished in time to be placed in her dower chest. But the patient seamstress did not live to use it. Shortly before the date set for her marriage, she died of bronchial trouble, when she had barely passed her twenty-first year.

On loan, Whaling and Historic Museum, Sag Harbor. Owned by a grandniece, Mrs. Miriam Foster Gates

1934, *p. 169*). The latter items, however, are in a class by themselves. Something of their influence seems to have been carried over from New England into rural communities in central New York State, but apparently avoided metropolitan neighborhoods. Even though the pieces here illustrated betray no conscious or unconscious adherence to a particular local tradition in design and workmanship, they may each boast a reliable pedigree, and may be dated with reasonable accuracy. As a group they illustrate certain trends in design

FIG. 9 — A WHIMSEY IN APPLIQUÉ

Made in 1853 by Irene B. Forman, who was properly brought up in a brownstone house on the corner of Lexington Avenue and 23 Street, New York City. The piece is made up of 56 appliquéd blocks of highly ingenious designs executed in bright-colored calicoes. Background of designs and intersecting strips are white muslin. Irene, who ultimately became Mrs. Purdy, was a resourceful person. When financial difficulties overtook the family, she turned the brownstone mansion into a boarding house, which she operated successfully for some years.

Owned by a descendant, George Read

FIG. 10 — PRESENTATION QUILT

Presented in 1843 to Joshua K. Ingalls, a lay preacher in Southold, Long Island, by appreciative womenfolk of his congregation. Each appliquéd block, a wreath or floral design on a white cambric background, was a separate donation. When all were finished, they were sewed together, padded, and quilted. The half squares along all four edges of the quilt are filled by blue-purple clusters of grapes and green leaves. Some one person of taste must have directed the undertaking, for the individual offerings are, on the whole, well related in scale and pattern. One or two of the sisters, however, appear to have had ideas of their own. Each block is signed inconspicuously in indelible ink with the name of the woman who made it. Less elaborate "Friendship" quilts are sometimes made today.

Owned by Mrs. Charles Ingalls

and workmanship that were manifested decade by decade almost simultaneously in almost every locality in the United States. The telepathic process by which new ideas in household handicrafts were transmitted long before the days of women's magazines and women's pages in the daily and Sunday newspapers is yet to be explained. But apparently it worked rapidly and efficiently.

(Figures 3, 9, and 10, courtesy of the Art Service Project, W.P.A.; Figure 5, courtesy of the Photographic Division, Federal Art Project, W.P.A.)

Kentucky's coverlets

BY LOU TATE

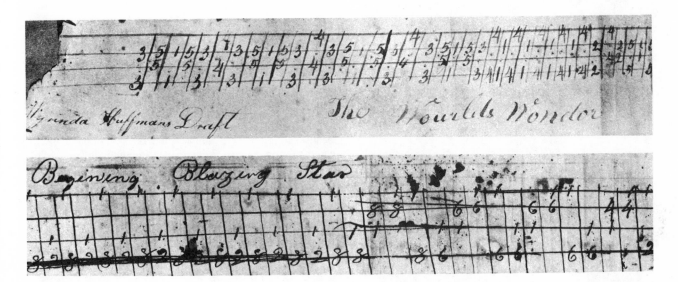

Fig. 1 The drafts of patterns used by early weavers were written on narrow strips of paper and stored as small rolls. Old patterns were usually written in a short form rather than in the thread-by-thread versions often used by modern weavers. Early coverlet weavers could read diverse forms of weaving shorthand, as the two samples shown here indicate. Wyrinda Huffman's (d. 1844) draft used a numeral placed on the line representing the harness to be threaded to indicate the number of times to repeat the threading of the harness pairing. The Blazing Star draft was written c. 1800 in the precise Scottish form of weaving shorthand. The number one indicates the first harness of the pair and the second numeral indicates the other harness of the pair as well as the number of threads in the sequence. *Except as noted, illustrations are from the author's collection and photographs are by Helga Photo Studio.*

Fig. 2. This coverlet is woven of blue and red wool on a natural cotton warp in the pattern known as Nine Chariot Wheels. *Collection of Lois Olcott.*

PIONEER WOMEN coming to the western territory of Kentucky about 1775 brought with them their precious patterns for woven coverlets. These were carried as tiny rolls of paper on which were carefully handwritten the drafts of the coverlet patterns (Fig. 1), which had been passed on to them by friends and relatives on the East Coast or by their forebears in Europe. Although these first settlers could not travel with the huge looms needed for weaving, they treasured their drafts against the day when new looms could be built.

Every household required at least one weaver to produce its cloth, including linens and clothing. Tow cloth and cotton bags were woven to barter for dyes, paper, and other supplies in the New Orleans market. Thus, it was some years after the settlers were established that women could spare the many hours needed to weave a coverlet. The period of creative coverlet weaving in Kentucky dated from

Fig. 3. This coverlet pattern combines Double Chariot Wheels with the rarely seen Double Squares. It was finely woven in Culpeper County, Virginia, on butternut-color and madder-dyed red wool on natural cotton. *Collection of Ruby Henry.*

about 1790 until 1820. While one weaver could probably keep a household supplied with textiles, five to ten spinners were needed to keep each weaver supplied with threads. Because children were adept spinners they often helped keep the family weaver going. Since spinning was so much more time consuming than weaving, the introduction of power spinning mills meant that much more time could be devoted to weaving, and even women who wove tow into rough cloth for bagging could earn more money by buying their yarns. Although Kentucky women were adept in the use of local plants to make dyes for the household linens, they bought Bengal indigo whenever possible to provide a blue that was more intense and colorfast than the dye derived from the South Carolina or locally grown indigos. Similarly cochineal, known as Spanish red, made of the dried bodies of tiny insects that were raised on plantations in Mexico, was preferred to home-grown madder.

Women who bartered their raw cotton and wool for finished yarns found that they had more time for finer weaving and could now weave for their own pleasure. Most household weavers could thread their looms for the plain weaving of household textiles, but only about one in ten was able to cipher and thread a coverlet draft. Therefore, many a coverlet weaver needed a skilled assistant for those tasks. These valued coverlets were seldom woven for sale.

A wide variety of patterns was possible on the four-harness loom used to make overshot-weave coverlets. Simple patterns were developed and combined into new designs. Nine Chariot Wheels was one of the early variations of the wheel motif (Fig. 2); another, rarer one was Double Chariot Wheels with Double Squares (Fig. 3). Bachelors Button, a very old snowball motif, was combined with squares to form Nine Snowballs (Fig. 4) and with chariot wheels and squares to form the pattern known as Eastern Wheels (Fig. 5).

Often old patterns were renamed or new patterns devised and named in honor of current events. Federal City (Fig. 6) and Federal Knot (Fig. 7), for example, reflect stories reaching Kentucky about the new Capitol in Washington which Congress formally occupied in November 1800.

Fig. 4. This coverlet, a variation of the Bachelors Button pattern, is woven with indigo-dyed blue wool and cochineal-dyed red snowball motifs on natural cotton.

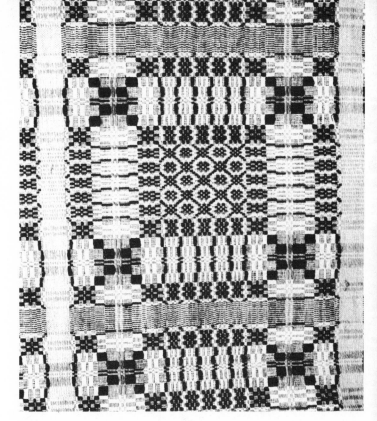

Fig. 5. Eastern Wheels combines three patterns: Bachelors Button as the central motif, four emphatic Chariot Wheels, and a finely designed square. The combined pattern was developed along the Cumberland River in central Kentucky. *Collection of Frances Richards; photograph by Alan Kelley.*

Fig. 6. Coverlet in the Federal City pattern. This pattern is "threaded on opposites." Designs in opposites were popular with early weavers because the same warp could be used for weaving blankets and dimity counterpanes.

Fig. 7. Coverlet in the Federal Knot pattern, an opposites design which lends itself to striking colorings. This one is skillfully woven of logwood-dyed black and cochineal-dyed red wool on fine natural cotton. The center seam is not visible.

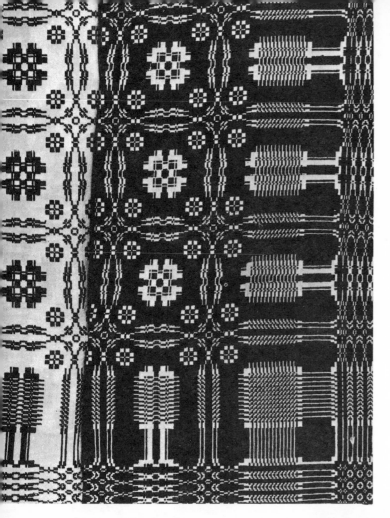

Boneyparte's March Across the Rockies recalls rumors reaching Kentucky from New Orleans about Napoleon's intention to establish a Western empire from a base in New Orleans. Boneyparte's Retreat and Wellington's Army on the Field of Battle recall Jefferson's Louisiana Purchase of 1803 and Napoleon's subsequent downfall. Jackson's Purchase was a coverlet pattern created in 1818 to commemorate the Treaty of Old Town in that year, in which Andrew Jackson persuaded the Chickasaw Indians to cede their lands on either side of the Tennessee River to the United States.

Professional weavers had little impact on weaving in Kentucky for, although they came to the state, they usually either passed through on their way to the Northwest Territory or discovered that they could earn more income by managing power mills and so gave up weaving double-weave and Jacquard coverlets. Double-weave coverlets were woven on a loom having as many as sixteen to twenty-four harnesses. The coverlet in the Whig Rose pattern with Pine Tree border (Fig. 8) has a warp of indigo-dyed blue wool and a second warp of white cotton so that the coverlet has a light and a dark side. Sometimes the second warp was composed of wool of two or three colors. Itinerant weavers produced coverlets in the double weave in Kentucky from about 1790 to 1850.

Fig. 8. This coverlet was woven in double-geometric weave by an itinerant professional weaver on a twenty-harness loom. The pattern is Whig Rose with a Pine Tree border. One warp is indigo-dyed midnight-blue wool; the other is coarse white cotton.

Fig. 9. C.L. Kean, who signed this summer-and-winter weave Jacquard coverlet, formed the pattern with a single warp of white cotton and weft of colored wool. The Rose and Eagle border was a favorite in Kentucky. Kean used house borders, as shown here, as well as vine and flower borders. The central motif, showing an acorn on the Compass Star, is rather rare. *Liberty Hall.*

138

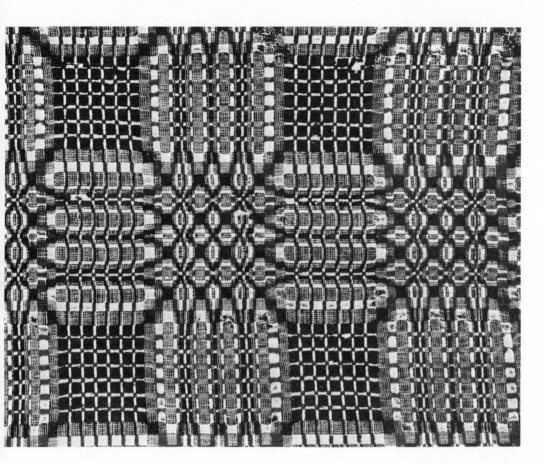

Fig. 10. This coverlet, in the Double Bowknot pattern, was woven of the deepest indigo-dyed blue wool on fine natural cotton at the Vermilion plantation near Harrodsburg in the early nineteenth century. There were many variations on the bowknot or leaf design since the motif lends itself to many changes. *Collection of Lois Bell.*

Jacquard looms were introduced to the United States from France in the 1820's. A series of punched cards controlled the elaborate Jacquard patterns of flowers, medallions, and birds. The complexity of the patterns and the looms required the services of a designer, a card maker, a threader, and a weaver. Jacquard weavers in America usually acquired their patterns from Scotland and France. Although early Jacquard coverlets were double weaves, the summer-and-winter weave using a single rather than a double warp, soon predominated because it was easier, quicker, and less expensive to weave. Most of the Jacquard coverlets found in Kentucky were bought from steamboats, which served as floating department stores. Some of these Jacquard coverlets were mill woven as early as 1834, usually in Ohio, Pennsylvania, or New York. Of the Kentucky Jacquard weavers the best known were D. Cosley, H. Wilson, F. A. Kean, and C. L. Kean (Fig. 9), who were active in Kentucky and Indiana starting in the late 1830's.

Fig. 11. Coverlet in the Pine Bloom pattern. This was a favorite design and most draft or coverlet collections have at least one variation. The drafts do not vary greatly, but many subtle color variations may be developed.

139

The bed rug in colonial America

BY MARION DAY IVERSON

THE AMERICAN COLONISTS possessed a great many rugs, and in the records they left us we find ample proof that these were used for bedcovers. Take, for instance, the "240 yards ruggs for beds" that came to Massachusetts in the cargo of the *William and John* in 1636. Or consider the "Eleven featherbeds or downe . . . also blankets and Coverletts and Rugs every [way] compleat to furnish so many beds" in the house of President Henry Dunster of Harvard in the 1640's. Notice too the bed with "One suit of good curtains . . . one Rugg, one Quilt, one pair of Blankets" bequeathed in 1721 to a young Virginia girl named Mary Ball. Eventually Mary became Mrs. Augustine Washington, and as late as 1792 her son George ordered green rugs along with rose blankets for the new executive mansion in Philadelphia.

The bed rug had a long history in northern Europe before it came to America. According to the comprehensive and handsomely illustrated book *The ryijy—rugs of Finland* brought out by Professor U. T. Sirelius in 1924 and translated into English a year later, the Finnish rugs were essentially bed coverings, but sometimes they adorned the walls of the dwelling on festive occasions. He found evidence that the rugs were in use in the fifteenth century, but the etymology of the Finnish word *ryijy* suggests that their origins were even earlier.

Several ancient bed rugs can be seen today at the Norsk Folkemuseum near Oslo, and there are others in the Hanseatiske Museum on the water front at Bergen, Norway. This house and its furnishings look much as they did when they belonged to a Hanseatic merchant. The built-in beds are short and consequently their early rugs are small.

The English word rug is probably of Scandinavian origin, says the *Oxford English Dictionary*. *Rugga* or *rogga* in a Norwegian dialect meant coarse coverlets, while *rugg* in Swedish referred to ruffled or coarse hair. In sixteenth-century Britain the word rug had two meanings; it was "A rough woollen material, a sort of coarse frieze" used for mantles and cloaks in winter; and it was also "A large piece of thick woollen stuff (freq. of various colours) used as a coverlet . . ." From this dictionary we learn that the expression "snug as a bug in a rug" goes back to the eighteenth century, when the rug was a bedcover.

While rugs are found in English farm and cottage inventories they also are noted in more luxurious surroundings. At Knole in 1624 there was a white rug for a bed that had "curtains of crimson and white taffeta, the valance to it of white satin embroidered with crimson and white silk and a deep fringe suitable." At Chelmsford Daniel Lluellan used rugs to show partiality when he made his will in 1663: one of his "best white ruggs" was to go to one friend, one of his "worst white ruggs" to another.

The American colonists brought rugs with them when they crossed the Atlantic and, as we already have seen, they also imported them. Future Maryland residents were advised by Lord Baltimore to take "one Rugg for a bed" and a "course Rugg" to use at sea. Before leaving England the Massachusetts Bay Company planned the essential requirements for one hundred men. Included were "50 Ruggs, 50 peare of blanketts of Welsh cotton, 100 peare of sheets, 50 bedtykes & bolsters."

In March 1630, while John Winthrop waited aboard the *Arbella* for favorable winds to begin his voyage to the New World, he wrote a farewell letter to his wife, who had remained at Groton in Suffolk. He assured her that their two young sons slept "as soundly in a rugge (for we use no sheets heer) as ever they did at Groton, and so I doe myself (I prayse God)." In September, even before he had experienced his first New England winter, Governor Winthrop wrote his son John to bring "a store of Coarse rugges, bothe to use and sell" when he came to America.

Meanwhile the men at Plymouth Colony had bought some of the "many Biscay rugs" in the cargo of the French ship that had been cast away on the coast of Maine in the spring of 1626. Besides making use of them for themselves the Pilgrims learned that the Indians especially wanted "coats, shirts, rugs and blankets, biscuit, pease, prunes &c." Governor William Bradford tells of these transactions in his history and also about the "two packs of Barnstaple rugs" that arrived aboard the *Friendship* in 1631. It had sailed from the port of Barnstaple in Devon. The Pilgrims were charged £75 for the hundred rugs in the two packs; in fact, through the perfidy of their agents they were charged for them twice over.

In addition to the Biscay rugs from France the colonists also received Bilbao rugs from Spain. John Pynchon, on the western frontier of Massachusetts in 1659, sold "2 yards Bilboe rug" to an Indian chief. At Boston ten years later "one bilbo rug" was listed with the bedding of Elizabeth Gwin. For the most part, however, rugs came from Ireland and England. The ship *George* brought "9 Irish ruggs for beds" to Massachusetts in September 1636. Governor George Wyllys of Hartford purchased Irish rugs "for the servants" before 1644. The British were importing both Irish and Polish rugs in 1660, but exporting only "Irish Ruggs for beds, and by the yard" (the latter may have been used for the numerous shag mantles and cloaks worn by the colonists). The importations continued until at least the 1770's, when Bristol rugs and Torrington rugs were advertised at Williamsburg, Virginia.

Twenty families of experienced clothmakers from Yorkshire settled at Rowley, Massachusetts, in 1638, and a score of years later Samuel Maverick wrote that these Yorkshiremen were "makeing Cloath and Ruggs of Cotton Wool, and also Sheeps wooll." As early as 1643 wool was brought to Massachusetts Bay from Bilbao and Malaga, Spain. The "Cotton Wool" came from the West Indies.

Occasionally there are records of rugs made in the home, like the "three home made ruggs" owned by Jenkin Davis of Lynn, Massachusetts. (When he made his will in 1661 his "Joyners tooles" were to go to his son John after John had worked with them long enough to pay the debts of the estate.) However, I have discovered nothing new about the wool-on-wool coverlets or rugs illustrated in ANTIQUES through the years. A study of inventories in the localities where they were made might prove rewarding.

There seems to be little in their appearance to differentiate rugs from blankets. Both were made of wool or cotton, both came in a variety of colors and patterns. Rugs were appraised and sold singly, while blankets often were in pairs. Sometimes the rugs in a household were of higher value, at other times the blankets; the blankets usually outnumbered the rugs.

Even though appraisers seldom bothered to describe the rugs (or anything else), by careful perusal we learn a little about their textures, colors, and patterns. A son of Elder Brewster possessed "3 shagg Ruggs" and "3 plaine Ruggs" in 1650. Nathaniel Harrison of Virginia had "6 Yarn Ruggs" in 1728. Many owned worsted rugs, and Hilliard Veren Jr., who died at Barbados in 1680, had a worsted thrum rug among the furnishings of his Massachusetts home. Thrum, the end of a weaver's warp thread, sometimes meant tufted or fringed. Rugs often were called coarse, but occasionally were spoken of as fine. In 1729 "fine Rugs" (perhaps coarse too!) were for sale at Boston. A sergelike material called say could not have been very coarse: in 1649 the Reverend Thomas Hooker of Hartford had curtains and valances for a bed that were "of greene say, and a rug of the same, with window curtains." Mr. Hooker's rug seems to have taken the place of a coverlet. Perhaps the same was true of one of President Dunster's eleven beds at Cambridge that had "a blue serdge suite very rich and costly, curtaines and valances laced, and fringe, and a blue Rug to the bed." And at the end of the eighteenth century William Grosvenor of Tolland, Connecticut, owned "one Rug coverlid."

Cotton rugs were less common than woolen ones and silk rugs rarer still. In Virginia John Bly paid £3 for a "silk rugge" about 1644. Silk rugs were the most expensive

ones in the shop of Edward Wharton of Salem, Massachusetts. In 1677 he had for sale rugs varying in price from four shillings eightpence ("1 cabbin Rugg") to three pounds ("1 large silk Rugg"). "Country" and cradle rugs were sold by weight at fourteen shillings a pound. Cabin rugs were owned by mariners like Nicholas Tucker of Marblehead who had one in 1664 and also was "heir of third of boat."

When the colors are mentioned in the personal inventories they usually are bright and gay rather than "sad." Green was favored. In the Essex County, Massachusetts, probate records between 1635 and 1664 there are at least twenty-one green rugs and seven red, seven blue, two white, and one yellow. Often a household had rugs of several colors. In 1668 William Law of Rowley had "one greene Rug & one blue one . . . one yellow cotton Rug . . . one Red & one blew blanket . . . one paire of white cotton blankets . . . one bays blanket . . . one greene English Rug" and several other blankets. He also owned a cotton loom.

The designs of the rugs are particularly elusive. John Winthrop Jr. received "Mingle coulrd checkered rugs, partly tawny, but the most are wholly red" from England in 1634. A "mingell Coulered Rug" was also in the home of a deacon of the church at Cambridge in 1672. When Captain Miles Standish and others made the inventory of Stephen Hopkins in 1644 they listed a yellow rug and a green one and also "2 checkr blankets." At Salem in 1685, Captain George Corwin's "worsted Stript Ruge" and his "Stript blanket" probably were striped. In all, the captain had twenty-one rugs; three were described as red, one as green, one as sad colored, and one as a silk cradle rug.

A "fine spotted rug white" was owned by a York County, Virginia, family in 1718. "Spotted Ruggs, good green & blue worsted and yarn ditto" of various sizes were advertised in Boston in December 1760. "Very good coloured and spotted Rugs" were for sale at Williamsburg, Virginia, in January 1776. A decade earlier "green and blue embossed lincey rugs" had been advertised there.

The bed rug seems to have gone out of fashion about the beginning of the nineteenth century. In *The Customs of New England*, published in 1853, Joseph B. Felt observed that rugs as bedcovers had been "little known among our furniture for the last half century . . ." The first reference to a floor rug quoted in the *Oxford English Dictionary* is dated 1810: "a little rug for your hearthstone." John Cogswell, the Boston cabinetmaker, had "1 floor Carpet" and "1 Hearth Rug" in a living room in 1818. Ten years later Noah Webster defined a rug as "a coarse nappy woolen cloth, used for a bedcover, and in modern times, particularly for covering the carpet before the fireplace."

The author is indebted to the Mount Vernon Ladies' Association for the use of George Washington's schedule of payments for blankets and rugs in 1791 and 1792, and to Colonial Williamsburg for the York County, Virginia, reference and for the advertisements in the *Virginia Gazette*.

Mrs. Iverson's sources include: ANTIQUES, April 1952, p. 323; *Archaeologia Americana*, III, pp. 6-7; J. Gardner Bartlett, *Gregory Stone Genealogy*, p. 62; William Bradford, *Of Plymouth Plantation 1620-1647*, ed. Samuel Eliot Morison, pp. 182, 202, 243; George F. Dow, *The Arts & Crafts in New England 1704-1775*, p. 155, 170; George F. Dow, *Every Day Life in the Massachusetts Bay Colony*, pp. 253, 257, 262-269, 270-283; *Essex County* (Massachusetts) *Probate Records*, I, pp. 358, 454; II, 110-111; III, 363; *Guide to Open Air Museum, Norske Folkemuseum*, p. 4; Clayton C. Hall, ed., *Narratives of Early Maryland*, p. 94; Sylvester Judd, *History of Hadley* (Massachusetts), p. 119; Mayflower Descendant, II, pp. 15, 206; Mount Vernon, "Sundries—bo't on account of G W," photostatic copy; *New England Historical and Genealogical Register*, XXXIX, p. 37; *Old-Time New England*, July 1934, pp. 31-32; April 1936, p. 143; Victoria Sackville-West, *Knole and the Sackvilles*, p. 95; *Suffolk County* (Massachusetts) *Deeds*, VI, p. 30; Tolland, Connecticut probate records, December 1798; *Virginia Gazette*, September 1766, September 1771, January 1776; *Virginia Magazine of History and Biography*, VIII, p. 285; XIII, 53, 57; XXXI, 372; George Leon Walker, *Thomas Hooker*, p. 182; William B. Weedin, *Economic and Social History of New England*, I, pp. 144, 176-177; *Winthrop Papers*, II, pp. 224, 314; III, pp. 150, 288, 310; *York County* (Virginia) *Orders, Wills*, XV, 421-425.

Kitchen chamber of the Crowninshield-Bentley House in Salem, Massachusetts, showing a bed rug made by Mary Avery of North Andover, Massachusetts, in 1722. The 1761 inventory of Captain John Crowninshield, builder of the Crowninshield-Bentley House, lists a "rugg" in the bed equipment for this room. Wool on linen with bold floral design in center, chevron border, rounded corners; similar in design and texture to some of the so-called wool-on-wool coverlets. *Essex Institute.*

A Southern bed rugg

BY SANDRA SHAFFER TINKHAM

Overleaf.

Wool bed rugg, 1770-1820. This bed rugg, an apparently unique example with embroidered knots, has a long history of family ownership in northern Virginia. 84½ by 66 inches. *Association for the Preservation of Virginia Antiquities, John Marshall House; gift of Miriam K. Richards.*

IT WOULD APPEAR from documented sources, and contrary to current opinion,[1] that the bed rugg was a common eighteenth-century bed furnishing in the South as well as in New England. In the York County, Virginia, inventory records, for example, bed ruggs are listed throughout the century. John Marot's inventory of 1717-1718 lists "1 bed 1.5.0 . . . 2 pr. blankets 2.4.0 . . . 1 bed 2.0.0 . . . 1 Rugg 1.0.0 . . ."; James Geddy's 1744 inventory lists "1 Settee, Bedsted, Bed Rugg &c 30/0 . . . 1 Trundle Bed Rugg Blanket & Sheet 20/"; Governor Norborne Berkeley Botetourt's 1770 inventory lists "1 bed Carpet . . . in the Chamber over the dining room" and "in His Lordship's bed chamber . . . 1 bed Carpet."

The Association for the Preservation of Virginia Antiquities has recently acquired a bed rugg that seems to be unique (color plate). It has a long history of family ownership in northern Virginia (Loudoun County), and probably was made between 1770 and 1820. The width of the bed rugg, which is made of natural unbleached wool, consists of two selvage widths seamed together with natural unbleached wool. The warp ends are roll hemmed.

Embroidered rather than woven knots cover the entire surface and define the pattern.[2] Since some knots span the seam, it would appear that they were applied after the piece was seamed. The ends of each knot have been cut, giving the rugg a very shaggy appearance (see detail). The embroidery was probably done on a frame with either a needle or a hook. Against the natural-color background are knots of dark blue, light blue, salmon pink, pale pink, a faded blue-green, and a faded tan-yellow.

Bed ruggs with woven knots are known. An example dating from between 1741 and 1743 is owned by the Faith Trumbull Chapter of the Daughters of the American Revolution in Norwich, Connecticut.[3] Colonial Williamsburg owns a Welsh rugg dated 1807,[4] and the Museum of Early Southern Decorative Arts has an example with a Virginia history.[5] The bed rugg illustrated here, however, with the embroidered knots seems to be a singular example of this technique[6] and is an interesting example of folk art expression in textiles both in its design and execution.

---

[1] Wadsworth Atheneum, *Bed Ruggs/1722-1833*, Hartford, 1972, p. 8.

[2] Technically, the bed rugg has twenty-three warps and wefts per square inch; the twist of all yarns is Z2S; the weave of the foundation fabric (or blanket) is a 2/2 balanced twill. The embroidered knots consist of four strands of Z2S ply wool; the knots are in offset rows approximately ten wefts apart and nine warps apart. The knots are constructed on sets of six warps, and the yarns are slipped to the back of each pair of outer warps and brought to the surface.

[3] *Bed Ruggs/1722-1833*, No. 5, p. 29.

[4] Accession no. 1972-369.

[5] *Museum of Early Southern Decorative Arts*, Winston-Salem, 1970, illustration on p. 25.

[6] Compare to No. 24 in *Bed Ruggs* catalogue. This bed rugg, from Canada, has knots embroidered in parallel rows.

Surface detail of bed rugg shown in the color plate.

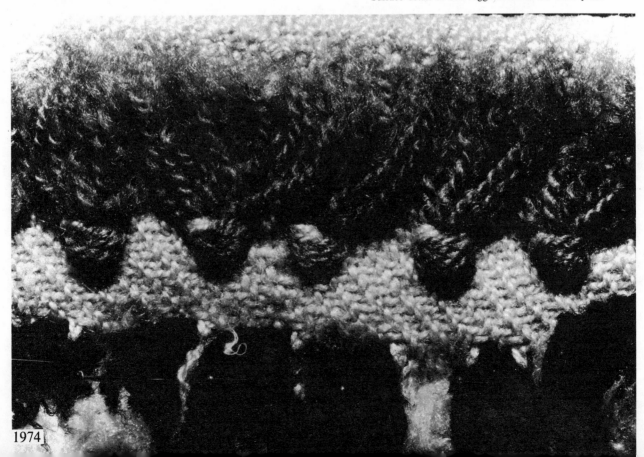

Fig. 1 — HAND-WOVEN TUFTED RUG (*1850–1857*)

Woven, on a hand loom, of domestic, dyed woolen yarn. Each tuft is twisted about two warp threads, and the whole row of tufts beaten with the comb as in Persian rug making. In this rug there is one shoot of a tapelike weft between each two rows of tufts. The next row of tufts is tied on the alternating two warp threads. Size, 30 by 60 inches.

Courtesy of Mrs. George Goodhue

Two Hand-Woven Tufted Rugs

By LOUISE KARR

THE two rugs here illustrated represent an interesting experiment in weaving. Both are from the south central part of New Hampshire, but from different towns, and, since they were evidently woven on different-sized looms, are not likely to have been done by the same person. In date, they belong to the mid-nineteenth century. I do not remember ever having seen any other rugs quite like these. Neither have I encountered descriptions of similar work in the various writings on the subject of hooked and other domestic rugs.

The method of their making would appear to have been inspired by Turkish or Persian rug work, and this in spite of the fact that in design they are Victorian, both displaying adaptations of the Horn of Plenty, so universally characteristic of Queen Victoria's early reign.

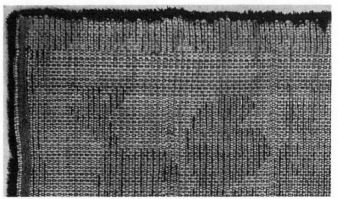

Fig. 2 — BACK OF RUG OF FIGURE 1

Detail of one corner, showing alternating row of tufts taken (twisted) around two warp threads, and the holding weft after each two rows.

The larger rug (*Figs. 1 and 2*) is the property of Mrs. George Goodhue of Hancock, New Hampshire. The Goodhue family have been long established in Hancock, and are distantly related to Mrs. Calvin Coolidge. The maker of the rug was Mrs. Goodhue's mother, who, it is thought, wove the piece as part of her wedding outfit. But where she learned the trick of such work, nobody seems to know. Her husband's aunt, Miss Ann Tuttle of Hancock, was, in her day, a notable weaver; and, as she owned the only loom in the vicinity, she was called upon to supply the surrounding country with the fruits of her handicraft. She was particularly celebrated for her woven quilts, which were in constant demand. It is not impossible, therefore, that, like many another ingenious Yankee, she decided to try her skill at something new

Fig. 3 — HAND-WOVEN TUFTED RUG (*prior to 1850*)
From New Ipswich, New Hampshire. In this rug, there are three shoots of a tapelike weft between each two rows of tufts. Size, about 26 by 60 inches.

and difficult and thus evolved a method for making hand-tufted loom rugs. In such case she may well enough have imparted her secret to her prospective niece-in-law.

All this, of course, is pure surmise. But Mrs. Goodhue is quite certain that her own mother wove the rug of our illustration, and perhaps yet another which, at one time, belonged to a grandmother. There were still other such rugs in Hancock. Stephen Van Rensselaer of Peterborough owns the fragment of one which for a long time did forlorn duty as a mat before a refrigerator until it was rescued, cleaned, and restored to polite uses. Investigation might bring still more to light.

Careful examination of the Goodhue rug leaves no doubt that it was made on the same principle as Oriental rugs. A tuft of three or four strands of homespun, hand-woven wool was twisted, from the front, around two warp threads — these latter of a sizeable cord — and then brought front again. Being fairly bulky, they would hold in place without the additional twist necessary in Oriental work. A whole row of tufts was completed; then a weft thread, looking much like a narrow tape, but possibly a strip of woolen cloth, was thrown across the warp and beaten down with the comb. In the Goodhue rug, this weft appears to have been thrown only once; but, probably, the next row of tufts, twisted around the alternating two threads, started from the same place, and the weft thread was then thrown back, as all the tufts list in the same direction. The effect is smooth and rich, the shearing having left half an inch or so of tufts.

The colors of this rug are especially bright, for the piece has always been well cared for. The cornucopias are in shaded reds, a dark shade predominating. The flowers are of different hues — blues, yellows, pinks, and reds. The border is worked out with black, reds, and touches of other colors. The groundwork is the natural, undyed wool.

The rug of Figure 3 came from New Ipswich, New Hampshire. Mrs. Hardy, its former owner, could give little of the rug's history, except that it was "very old." Indeed, it seems to be somewhat older than the Goodhue example. The colors are softer and it shows signs of wear. It is woven on a narrower loom and is longer in proportion to its breadth.

The colors, perhaps through fading, are very pleasing, a large amount of tan having been used, although the cornucopias are red and the flowers of various colors. The introduction of threads of tan into each tuft of natural color in the groundwork gives an agreeable effect. In this rug, the weft binding thread is thrown three times back and forth, and crowded very firmly by the comb, so that the weave appears to be as close in this rug as in the other.

Though the two rugs are similar, there would seem to be no connection in their origin. Hancock and New Ipswich, while not far apart geographically, are separated by hills, and the road between them is roundabout. Probably there was, at one time, however, a fashion, more or less local, for doing this sort of thing. The method of making seems in no way related to that of the hooked rug. The tufts could easily have been twisted around the warp threads by the fingers — more easily than by using a hook.

Both of the rugs described are charming examples — far more so than the photographs indicate. If there are more of the kind to be found in New Hampshire or elsewhere, I should be delighted to know about them and their history.

146

EIGHTEENTH-CENTURY BROCADE COSTUMES

Some French and English Costumes in the Elizabeth Day McCormick Collection

By GERTRUDE TOWNSEND

ANY CONSIDERATION of costume, present or past, must necessarily include an examination of the fabrics of which costumes are made, whether the material is plain, ornamented with patterns woven on the loom, or, as is the case in embroidery and printed fabrics, with the pattern added after the weaving has been completed. Comparisons of changing fashions in both fabric and cut bring out clearly the interdependence of the designer and manufacturer of textiles and the tailor or dressmaker who makes these textiles into finished and wearable garments.

Prior to 1800, brocades were of major importance in European costume. Since then their use has dwindled, though during a part of the nineteenth century brocades produced on the Jacquard loom, frequently with designs adapted from eighteenth-century models, were used to a limited extent in making the gowns of that period.

Although the history of silk weaving in France can be traced back to the thirteenth century, Italy long retained the lead it acquired during the twelfth century when, under Roger the Norman, silk weaving was introduced into Sicily from Greece. It was in the reign of Louis XIV that Jean-Baptiste Colbert, who controlled not only finances but public works, agriculture, and commerce, succeeded in bringing prosperity and prestige to France through the development of her manufactures, and in making her a leader in the manufacture of fine silk weavings. The latter achievement was not, however, the result of new and untried ventures. Royal decrees recorded by Henri Clouzot in his valuable contribution to the history of the silk industry, *Le Métier de la Soie en France* (Paris, n.d.), demonstrate the importance which has long been accorded to the silk industry in the economy of France.

An important step had been taken in 1466 when Louis XI, seeking to halt large expenditures of money outside France, particularly in Italy, for the purchase of silk fabrics, offered many privileges, including exemption from taxes, to tempt master weavers from Italy to settle in Lyons, where they would teach as well as practice their craft. But the cost of this experiment devolved on the people of Lyons alone, and Louis, annoyed by their reluctance to benefit by his far-sighted plans, decided a few years later to move the weavers from Lyons to Tours, again at the expense of the people of Lyons. Though Tours as a center of weaving never attained first importance, silk weaving continued to be practiced there to some extent up to the present time. In spite of this set-back to silk weaving in Lyons, the city's original rights and privileges as the only entry and chief depository of foreign silk, both raw material and woven fabrics, and as a center of the silk-weaving industry in France, were con-

AMONG many and beautiful costumes in the Elizabeth Day McCormick Collection, the gift of Miss McCormick to the Museum of Fine Arts in Boston, a group of four French and English gowns has been chosen for study and illustration here as characteristic examples of important fashions in fabric and cut during the eighteenth century.

firmed by Francis I in the year 1536.

But even with royal patronage, the industry was still struggling unsuccessfully against the competition of Italy when Colbert took office. Under his carefully planned economy the quality of the brocades and velvets produced in France was greatly improved and thereby the prestige of French weavings greatly increased. Every step from the preparation of the raw material through the finished product was carefully regulated. The bewildering extent to which weavers were governed by complicated regulations can be seen in the specifications given in the *Dictionnaire Universel de Commerce,* compiled by Jaques Savary des Bruslons, *Inspecteur général des manufactures, pour le Roy, à la Doüane de Paris.* The king whom Savary served as Inspector of Manufactures for the Customs of Paris was Louis XIV, whom he survived by only one year.

While an understanding of these complicated regulations would require a thorough study of the progress which had been made in the development of the loom, it should be mentioned here that the invention in Lyons, during the first quarter of the seventeenth century, of an improved drawloom, the *métier à la grande tire,* by Claude Dangon, made possible the execution on the loom of designs which were both large, and drawn with delicate and elaborate details. However, technical improvements alone could not have given the French textile industry the place of honor it has so long held. The designer's contribution to the prosperity of the industry was fully recognized. In the section of the *Dictionnaire Universel de Commerce* devoted to Lyons and its industries, the artist who designs for the loom is called the soul of the silk weaving industry: "Un excellent Dessinateur est dans Lyon un artiste essentiel, & comme l'ame d'une fabrique."

Among those artists whose designs contributed to the renown of the silk industry in France during the eighteenth century perhaps the best known is Jean Revel *(1684-1751),* celebrated both for his suave patterns of fantastic flowers, fruit, and foliage, and for several technical innovations including a method of intermingling two tones of silk, called *berclé* or *points rentrés,* to produce a more subtle shading than had hitherto been possible.

One of the gowns in the Elizabeth Day McCormick Collection is a magnificent example of the style of French brocade usually attributed to Jean Revel. It is of unusually rich and handsome brocade, with exotic fruit and flowers woven with fresh warm colors to suggest high relief, on a ground of dark brown satin — a brown which in some lights appears to be deep purple *(Figs. 1, 2).* The rich pattern of the brocade is displayed to full advantage by the ample folds of this gown, a *robe à la française à plis Watteau,* in-

FIG. 1 — BROWN BROCADE GOWN *(French, second quarter eighteenth century).*

FIG. 2 — DESIGN of exotic fruits and flowers on brown satin, of the gown shown in Figure 1.

FIG. 3 — DESIGN of ivory brocade gown worn by the Duchess of Chandos, shown in Figure 5.

FIG. 4 — DESIGN of French gown in Figure 7. Ribbons and flowers on ribbed white silk.

tended to be worn over paniers, with pleats hanging from the back of the neck and with a matching underskirt, visible in the front. The gown probably dates from the second quarter of the eighteenth century.

In the earlier form of this style, there were loose folds, not pleats, hanging from the shoulders, which disappeared in the fullness of the skirt; the skirt extended over a more or less bell-shaped petticoat. The later panier was somewhat flattened in front and behind. It is the earlier style represented by Watteau from which the name "Watteau pleats" is derived. The sleeves of the gowns Watteau painted were generally rather full and pleated vertically. A few years later a variation of the *robe à plis Watteau* appears in paintings by Troy. In one, dating from about 1730, we find the straight sleeve like that of the dress under discussion, but finished with bands or folds of the same material over the elbow, rather than the shaped double ruffle with which the brown sleeves are ornamented. The double ruffle was apparently used as a finish for sleeves during a considerable part of the second and third quarters of the eighteenth century.

Ironically enough it was by an act of the French king, Louis XIV, who had done so much toward furthering French industry, that Lyons and Tours were robbed of many of their ablest silk weavers, and that for almost a century English silk weaving attained considerable importance. The revocation of the Edict of Nantes in 1685 drove many of the finest artisans of France into exile. Silk weavers from Lyons and Tours settled in considerable numbers to the east of London, outside the city wall in the district called Spitalfields, now a part of London. Although some French Huguenot weavers settled first in other parts of England, the fame of Spitalfields silks drew so many of them eventually to London that the name Spitalfields has been adopted generally as the designation for English brocades of the eighteenth century. In 1931 there were a few silk weavers still living in Bethnal Green weaving small pieces such as handkerchiefs, ties, and scarves which were sold as Spitalfields silk. In passing it may be said that the greater number of brocade gowns of the colonial period in America which I have examined are made of Spitalfields silks.

The English gown of Figure 5 comes with a very credible tradition that it was worn by the third wife of the Duke of Chandos, daughter of John Vanhattan, Esq., and widow of Sir Thomas Daval, Kt. The marriage between the Duke of Chandos and Lydia Catharine took place in April 1736. The brocade of which this gown is made is woven with gold as well as silk in a design of fruits and flowers on an ivory ground (*see Fig. 3*). The use of gold in a Spitalfields brocade is unusual, but the character of the design, the weaving, and the technical peculiarities of the selvage, all point to an English origin.

In the study of *The Silk Weavers of Spitalfields and Bethnal Green* by A. K. Sabin, published by the Bethnal Green Museum in 1931, a catalogue with illustrations of a few of the

FIG. 5 — GOWN worn by Duchess of Chandos (*English, c. 1725-1750*).

All illustrations are from the Elizabeth Day McCormick Collection at the Museum of Fine Arts, Boston.

FIG. 6 — BROCADE GOWN (*English. c. 1725-1750*). The design — woven in strong colors — is a fanciful landscape.

original eighteenth-century designs is included. Fortunately in February 1931, shortly before this account of Spitalfields weavers appeared, I had opportunity to go through some of these designs, then in the Victoria and Albert Museum in London. My brief notes taken then include mention of one design (5973.19) which I do not find in the catalogue, but which was accompanied by original descriptive notes mentioning gold. This is dated *1720* and bears the name of *Mr. Monceaux*, with the following: "This ground is half Padushy and half Mantua, the red flowers for frosted gold and the yellow for plain, ye rest proper silk colours to illustrate it." There are in addition several examples of Spitalfields brocade described and illustrated in this catalogue which are woven with gold and silver thread, or sometimes with silver thread alone.

The qualities of drawing, color, and weave of Spitalfields silks, even though the weavers originally came from France, differentiate them sharply from French silks. Usually, though the designs may be described as more provincial than French designs, they have a real charm and originality and in addition the silk is of good quality and very durable. One of the peculiarities of the Spitalfields silks may be observed in the selvages, which, though they vary greatly among themselves, are in general easily distinguishable from the ribbed selvages of French brocades. They are almost always very much flatter than the French, and often have colored stripes in them. The width and placing of the stripes vary greatly, and frequently the colors on one edge of a breadth of silk differ from those on the other. Usually, too, the breadths of English brocades are narrower than those of French brocades. The selvage on the brocade from which the gown worn by the Duchess of Chandos was made is very flat, and appears to be quite plain, but there is an almost invisible line of color, different in each selvage, along the edge *(Fig. 8)*.

In style this gown is not unlike the contemporary French gown of Figure 1, in that the skirt is cut to display an underskirt, which in this case is a quilted petticoat though quite possibly originally there was an underskirt to match the gown. The back, however, does not hang free, but is fitted

FIG. 7 — WHITE BROCADE GOWN *(French, third quarter of the eighteenth century)*.

at the waist with flat pleats, a style described in France as *à l'anglaise*. The bands which finish the sleeves are reminiscent of the sleeve bands portrayed by Watteau which I have described above.

The brocade of the second of the two English gowns shown here is quite different in style from the first but equally characteristic of English weaving *(see Figs. 6, 8, and the Cover of this issue)*. The design, woven with silk in strong greens, reds, pinks, blues, and dark brown, is a combination of fanciful plant forms and trees in a landscape, a very elaborate landscape which includes houses and a bridge among its motifs.

In color and design this brocade suggests that of a gown belonging to the Victoria and Albert Museum, illustrated in color in the *Burlington Monograph on Georgian Art* (London, 1929). It is also very similar in weave, color, and general character to a gown of brocade in the Boston Museum of Fine Arts. For the purpose of dating it may be noted that the latter was worn, according to a well-established tradition, by a Mary Beck when she married Nathaniel Carter in Newburyport, Massachusetts, in 1742. The design of Mary Beck's brocade closely resembles an original Spitalfields design dated *1721,* illustrated in the Bethnal Green catalogue. Among the names of designers appearing most often in this catalogue is that of Anna Maria Garthwaite. The dates on her designs run from 1732 through 1741. One of the designs (5971.11) signed *Anna Maria Garthwaite* which I noted but which does not appear in the catalogue, I described as "tree-flowers and fruit in red, terra cotta, and black tones." I wish I had a photograph of the design before me for I am tempted, though obviously on too uncertain evidence, to attribute the design of the Spitalfields landscape brocade to Anna Maria Garthwaite.

The last of this group of four brocade gowns is a French gown of the reign of Louis XV *(Fig. 7)*. Made of heavily ribbed white silk brocaded in a design of wavy ribbons and flowers *(see Fig. 4)*, it is typical of the latter part of that monarch's reign. Each of these gowns is, in its own way, a distinguished product of the silk industry of the eighteenth century, and evokes the manners and customs of another day.

FIG. 8 — DETAILS OF SELVAGE AND BACK of each of the four brocade gowns illustrated, show difference between French and English. *From left to right:* detail of French gown of Figure 1; detail of English gown of Figure 5; detail of English gown of Figure 6; detail of French gown of Figure 7.

A pattern-woven "flamestitch" fabric

BY FLORENCE M. MONTGOMERY, *Keeper of textiles, Henry Francis du Pont Winterthur Museum*

FOR TWENTY YEARS OR MORE there has been in the Winterthur collection a large piece of what appears to be needlework in a flamelike pattern executed in coarse wools of fairly dark colors (Fig. 1); it is used as a table cover during the summer season. The pattern, though on a larger scale, resembles that of so-called flamestitch needlework, though the wools are loosely and unevenly spun, and the colors are rather dark and dull. During recent years similar material, which has been found in even larger pieces, has become rather generally used for upholstery, cushions, and window curtains in American period-room installations in both historic houses and museums. No one seemed to know exactly what this material was or where it came from, although the general idea prevailed that it was needlework made in the late seventeenth or early eighteenth century and hence suitable for rooms of that time.

Flamestitch embroidery, more properly known as *point de Hongrie* (Hungarian stitch), is worked with a needle in woolen or, more rarely, silk threads on a canvas ground. English and American examples, worked in bright, clear crewels, are seen in such relatively small pieces as orginial upholstery, fire screens, pocketbooks,

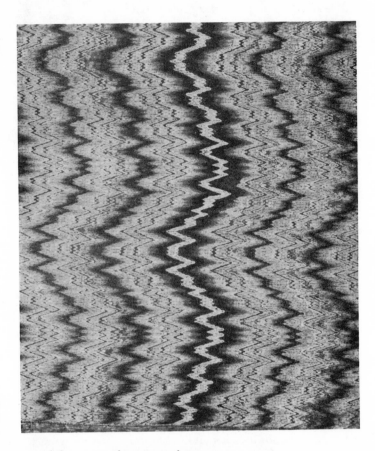

Fig. 1.   Detail of a pattern-woven wall hanging made by Duruflé at Elbeuf, in northern France; early eighteenth century.

Fig. 2.   Detail of the border of Figure 1, showing coarseness of the weave. About ⅓ actual size.

and pincushions of the Queen Anne and Georgian periods (Figs. 4, 5, 6). Of these, pocketbooks most frequently are dated, a few in the 1750's but more in the 1760's and 1770's. Though similar embroidery was done in many European countries at that time and earlier, I found it hard to believe that the over-all pattern of the large textiles mentioned had been worked with a needle instead of being woven on a loom: while proof was lacking, these textiles seemed more likely to have been pattern-woven than embroidered.

Some months ago Peter Thornton, of the Victoria and Albert Museum, kindly gave me a copy of an article he had published in *Pantheon* entitled "Tapisseries de Bergame," concerning a wall hanging recently acquired by that museum. In it he cited the French commercial dictionary by Savary des Bruslons, first published in 1723, which contained an account of wall hangings woven in northern France. Among the types listed was *point de Hongrie,* which Savary described as a sort of tapestry patterned in waves and of which he said there were two kinds: one worked with a needle on canvas, the other woven on a loom.

Upon reading that Hungarian-point hangings were woven commercially, I immediately thought of the museum's piece and went to examine it more closely. It had apparently been reworked from a larger piece, but another example in the collection (Fig. 3), still in the form of a hanging, was of the extraordinary width of ninety-five inches from selvage to selvage. This piece showed holes where it had been hooked to the wall, and it was reinforced at the top, where it would have received strain in hanging, by a heavy border or tape four inches wide. Both pieces were woven from dark brown hemplike fibers nearly covered with the loose woolen chevrons shading at regular intervals from mustard yellow to brown, dark blue, green, and rose. Mr. Thornton has suggested that the pattern is executed in some kind of brocading technique. The flamelike effect is achieved by weaving in the wefts of wool, or floats, with each shoot of coarse hempen fiber, in such a way as to form a zigzag pattern.

The smaller piece which had first puzzled me has an applied border nine inches wide in a similar flame pattern, and another one-and-one-half-inch border with repeated lettering woven in white cotton. Of several towns mentioned by Savary as centers of this tapestry manufacture, the name Elbeuf sang out, for this is one of the names on the narrower border (Fig. 2).

My letter addressed to the archivist at Elbeuf was passed around among textile people in that town of some eighteen thousand inhabitants near Rouen in Normandy for two months until it came into the hands of Charles Brisson, conservator of the museum and historian of the city. In his prompt reply he enclosed five articles that he had written for his local newspaper on the forgotten tapestry industry at Elbeuf, citing documents regarding the types and quantities of textiles made, regulations governing their manufacture, and the names of many master weavers of the area. The name Duruflé, which appears with Elbeuf in the narrow border, is that of a family of weavers registered in that town as early as 1687. Mr. Thornton suggests that a woven "signature" of this kind is an eighteenth- rather than a seventeenth-century feature. In 1911, at the time of the millennial celebration of the founding of Elbeuf, a border similar to this one was exhibited, but unfortunately its present whereabouts is not known; in fact, M. Brisson has never seen it.

In his articles M. Brisson suggests that wall hangings made at Elbeuf, Rouen, Tournai, and certain other

Fig. 3. Detail of another pattern-woven wall hanging, probably made in northern France, late seventeenth or early eighteenth century.

Fig. 4. Needlework pocketbook
with original woolen tape.
American, dated 1759.

Fig. 5. Needlework hand fire screen.
American, mid-eighteenth century.

towns were destined, not for members of royalty who commissioned the great scenic and pictorial tapestries of the Aubusson, Gobelins, or Beauvais factories, but for the lesser nobility, professional people, and the bourgeoisie, the walls of whose homes may otherwise have been adorned with paint alone. He cites another statistical work, *L'Etat de la France*, published in 1737, as stating that seventy looms for *Bergame* and *point de Hongrie* tapestries were then operated in the environs of Elbeuf, which gave work to four or five hundred people a year.

So with the kind help of others and, in fact, through their research, positive identification may now be made of at least one group of this coarse material with the bold flamelike pattern as having been woven commercially on looms in northern France and Flanders. The industry began probably in the early sixteenth century, flourished in the second half of the seventeenth, and died out about 1740.

There seems to be no reason to think that this woven material was ever made in England or America. Nor does it seem likely that it was used for upholstery, since its loose, coarse surface would make it impractical for that purpose. To date no example of American furniture with original upholstery of this sort has come to light.

It is, of course, inaccurate to apply the needlework term Hungarian or flame*stitch* to this woven fabric though we have the authority of Savary and others that it was called *point de Hongrie* in its day. We may avoid confusion between the woven material and the true embroidery by calling the one a pattern-woven "flamestitch" textile, and specifying the other as flamestitch needlework.

*All illustrations from the
Henry Francis du Pont
Winterthur Museum*

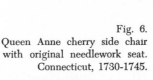

Fig. 6.
Queen Anne cherry side chair
with original needlework seat.
Connecticut, 1730-1745.

The Returning Popularity of Many-Figured Carpets

THOUGH interior decoration is, or should be, guided by certain fairly definite principles, it may follow no specific rules. Apparently the normal human eye steadfastly demands certain constants in ultimate color harmonies, in the proportion and scale of furniture, and in the distribution of plain and figured surfaces. At the same time, it tends to grow weary of any one method of securing these constants, and turns gladly to almost any scheme which, though its elements multiplied together may yield the same old total, yet presents a refreshingly novel grouping of factors.

Thus, a few years since, the decorative dictum went forth that floor coverings should be in plain colors devoid of all pattern, and that compensating liveliness should be obtained by figured draperies and furniture covers, and, on occasion, by ornamented walls. Today, I am informed, plain carpetings are no longer in high favor, and are being replaced to some extent by Oriental rugs, but more extensively by embroidered or handwoven rugs in European period designs. The embroidered pieces are usually reproductions, though French and English examples of the mid-nineteenth century survive

Fig. 3 (left) — FRENCH AUBUSSON RUG
(style of the Regency)
The large scale of the design, as well as its architectural character, accords with the somewhat massive French furniture of the Louis XIV and Regency periods

Fig. 1 (above) — ENGLISH EMBROIDERED RUG
Reproduced from an original in the Victoria and Albert Museum. Though this original is not so ancient as it would seem, its general style is of the seventeenth century, making it particularly suitable for use with old English oak and walnut

Fig. 2 (right) — FRENCH AUBUSSON RUG
(style Louis XV–XVI)
A lighter, more delicately playful, and hence more widely available rug than Figure 3. Suitable with furniture of the period from 1750 to 1785

in fair quantity. The woven rugs, particularly if in the French tapestry styles of the 1700's and 1800's, will frequently be actual specimens of their period. Seventeenth- and eighteenth-century Continental European deep-pile carpetings, seldom obtainable in the original, are now amazingly well copied.

It would be well worth while to make a study of the entire field of fascinating floor coverings now available for use in conjunction with the furniture of American, English, and European historical interiors. Far too little is known about the subject. The task of gathering the necessary material would, however, be enormous. Suffice it at the moment to present a few pictures taken from a recent exhibition held by W. and J. Sloane in their New York galleries. With one exception, the rugs illustrated are antiques of French origin; but I have endeavored to make a selection fairly indicative of the stylistic peculiarities distinguishing each of several successive decades. Although limited in scope, the group presented will, neverthe-less, afford some idea of how certain specific requirements may be satisfied without danger of serious mistake.

Fig. 4 (right) — FRENCH AUBUSSON RUG
(Empire style)
A dignified and impressive, but not too heavy, pattern that would be suitable with almost any late eighteenth- or early nineteenth-century French furniture

Fig. 5 (above) — FRENCH AUBUSSON RUG
(late eighteenth century)
Perhaps assignable to the Directoire period; but obviously inspired by an ancient mosaic floor

Fig. 6 (left) FRENCH AUBUSSON RUG
(Victorian implications)
It is no simple matter to assign exact dates to textiles. This rug may be of the late eighteenth or early nineteenth century; yet its naturalistic bouquets of flowers suggest a later time

WASHINGTON'S AMERICAN CARPET AT MOUNT VERNON

By MARIAN SADTLER CARSON

THIS IS THE STORY of three eighteenth-century American carpets, only one of which apparently is in existence today.

Some years ago, while I was studying the original furniture of the State House, now more familiarly called Independence Hall, in Philadelphia, it came to my attention that on January 19, 1794, the County Commissioners, Judge Isaac Howell, George Forepaugh, and Richard Price, while settling accounts for the enlargement of Congress Hall had paid

> Peter Sprague for Carpeting   49.9.6

Congress Hall is the most westerly building in the Independence Hall group. It was built in 1789 as a county court house, but when the Congress under the Federal Constitution selected Philadelphia as a temporary Capitol, it became known as Congress Hall. To meet an increase in membership in the House of Representatives, which sat on the ground floor, the building was extended twenty-seven feet to the south, and consequently the Senate Chamber on the second floor also was enlarged. When soon thereafter a gallery was added for spectators, the room took the form it has today.

Sprague's "Carpeting" of 1794 was for the enlarged Senate Chamber. That the original room also had a fine emblematic floor covering woven by Sprague appears from a contemporary news article in the *United States Gazette* for June 22, 1791. What he made was described as a "master-piece." The following details will show what an ambitious undertaking it must have been for the newly established "Philadelphia Carpet Manuactory":

The device wove in the last mentioned, is the Crest and Armorial Achievements appertaining to the United States. Thirteen stars forming a constellation, diverging from a cloud, occupy the space under the chair of the Vice-President. The AMERICAN EAGLE is displayed in the centre, holding in his dexter talon an olive branch, in his sinister a bundle of thirteen arrows, and in his beak, a scroll inscribed with the motto, *E pluribus unum.* The whole surrounded by a chain formed of thirteen shields, emblematic of each State.

The sides are ornamented with marine and land trophies, and the corners exhibit very beautiful Cornu Copias, some filled with olive branches and flowers expressive of peace, while others bear fruit and grain, the emblems of plenty.

Under the arms, on the *pole* which supports the cap of liberty, is hung the *balance of Justice.*

The whole being executed in a capital stile, with rich bright colours, has a very fine effect.

The seal made a lively artistic design for Sprague's carpets. It was its official significance, however, that concerned Thomson, Boudinot, and other men in official position. The practical need was to hold the warmth in the drafty rooms and corridors, and to dull the tread of heavy boots. Sprague's carpets also added life and color to the cold white paneled room, and over them walked all the patriots of the day. But the carpet was not destined to have more than a temporary place among the furnishings at Congress Hall. When the Government moved to its new seat at Washington in

DETAIL OF GREAT SEAL used as a ceiling decoration in the Senate Chamber, Congress Hall, Philadelphia. This was the central motif of both the rugs originally made for the room in 1791 and 1794, and of the rug made for President Washington, 1791. *Courtesy Bureau City Property, Philadelphia.*

1800, none of the rugs went with it. These were stored for a time in one of the upper rooms of the State House and in 1802 when Charles Willson Peale, the artist, sought to occupy most of that building for his museum, the Commonwealth of Pennsylvania moved the chairs and a few tables to Harrisburg, but sold the rugs and the other original furnishings.

But what of Sprague, this pioneer in his trade?

William Peter Sprague lived in Third Street, near Brown, about a mile north of High Street in the Northern Liberties of Philadelphia. Little can be learned of his activities. In the 1790 census he is listed as having four other male adults living with him, which suggests the possibility of apprentices. The *Gazette* above referred to said that the Manufactory "already gives employment to a number of poor women and children." He must have had not a few workmen at the looms at the time he made the carpets for the Congress, and "for various persons." His business clearly prospered, for in the 1796 *Directory* he is listed as a "gentleman." Sprague was one of the first American carpet weavers. He was an excellent artisan. The fact that his carpet has been mistaken for a French souquette, similar in weave to an Axminster, shows that his weave and his design compare favorably with contemporary French work. His carpets were woven in strips varying in width and sewn together.

The central design of the Congress carpet was notable: the Great Seal of the United States. This device has an interesting history. It was adopted in 1782 upon the recommendation of a Committee composed of Henry Middleton of South Carolina, Elias Boudinot of New Jersey, then the President of Congress, and Edward Rutledge of South Carolina. In 1795 Boudinot became Director of the Mint, succeeding David Rittenhouse, and as the son of a well-patronized silversmith he may well have had some knowledge of heraldry. As historians point out, the Seal is the design of William Barton, a Philadelphia minister, the nephew and biographer of Doctor Rittenhouse, but his sketches were materially altered and improved by Charles Thomson, of the Northern Liberties, "permanent" Secretary of the Congress. In fact, Thomson suggested the main theme—"an American Eagle, on the Wing and rising proper."

In 1897 the Mt. Vernon Ladies' Association received the gift of a handsome carpet from Mrs. Townsend Whelen of Philadelphia. While showing evidence of long years of constant service, it is still a striking piece. It may be seen at the Banquet Hall, or "new room" as it was frequently termed in Washington's day. This rug has a dull green star-studded ground, while in the large center medallion is the Great Seal of the United States. It is woven of yarn in many colors. The eagle is brown with yellow beak from which a ribbon floats with the motto *E Pluribus Unum*. It holds a green olive branch in its dexter talon, while in its sinister is a sheaf of thirteen arrows. On its breast is a shield in the national colors. The elaborately designed border around the outside is antique gold in tone. A long-necked white bird is woven in ovals in the center of each border. It is definitely not the raven of the Washington crest. The rug measures fifteen feet five inches by seventeen feet six inches. It is therefore noble in proportion as well as in spirit.

The story accompanying this gift was that it had been woven at the order of Louis XVI as a gift to President Washington, that Washington would not accept a king's gift, and hence had given it to Mrs. Whelen's grandfather, Jasper Yeates. The fact was that an examination of General Washington's correspondence did not verify the romantic portions of the story and this called for further inquiry. There was nothing to link the President with the gift of a carpet from the king of France.

AMERICAN-MADE CARPET, purchased by Washington from William Peter Sprague, Philadelphia, in 1791. *Courtesy Mount Vernon Ladies' Association.*

The news article which describes the Senate rug gives a clue to the Washington carpet, for under date of June 22, 1791, the *Gazette* stated that Sprague's "carpet made for the President, and others for various persons, are master-pieces of their kind."

A search of Washington's own account books furnishes verification of the American origin of the carpet and gives the date. With characteristic exactness the entries for April 1 to 24, 1791, are set down.

Cont^s Exp^s p^d Wm P. Sprague in part for a Carpet made by him for the large dining room   100 —

Cont^t Exp^s p^d W. P. Sprague for the Carpet in the large dining Room   114 25

Here then is the genesis of the Washington carpet. Why Washington was willing to abandon so useful and costly a furnishing when he left the Executive Mansion in Philadelphia is frankly a mystery, but evidently he did so because it was not at Mt. Vernon in 1802 when the inventory following his death in 1799 was made. Whether Yeates purchased the rug at auction when Washington sold the unneeded Philadelphia furnishings upon retiring from the Presidency, or whether that part of the story that Washington gave the large carpet to Judge Yeates is true, remains at the present time unanswered. Jasper Yeates was a Justice of the Supreme Court of Pennsylvania. A graduate of the University of that name in 1761, he acquired the most extensive law practice in the interior of the state. He became a member of the Constitution Ratification Convention of 1787 and all his life he was in close contact with Philadelphia where he was a familiar figure in the city's political, legal, and judicial life.

Thus three of William Peter Sprague's "master-pieces" are accounted for. One was described in detail in 1791, a second and larger one paid for by the County Commissioners in 1794, and now the one Washington purchased in 1791 is identified. And this carpet was in daily use in the Yeates family for about a century and today is in the one place where it should be—Mt. Vernon—not because it was there in Washington's time, but because it was bought and paid for and used by him.

Oriental carpets in seventeenth- and eighteenth-century America

BY SARAH B. SHERRILL

ORIENTAL CARPETS were extremely rare in seventeenth- and eighteenth-century America. In fact, floor coverings of any description were scarce in this country before the nineteenth century, and only a very small proportion would have been anything as special as an exotic pile fabric with a complex Oriental design. Also, not all of the rare carpets with Oriental patterns in America before the nineteenth century were actually woven in the Middle East, some were European imitations; and not many, until well into the nineteenth century, were even spread on the floor to be walked on but were more often used as table coverings. There is documentary evidence, however, that there were carpets with Oriental designs in early America. Seventeenth- and eighteenth-century American inventories, newspaper advertisements, letters, and diaries occasionally refer to "Turkey Carpets" or, infrequently and misleadingly, to "Persia Carpets."[1] The term Turkey carpet was used in a most general sense throughout the seventeenth and eighteenth centuries in Europe and America. It designated not only carpets imported from certain parts of the East but also the European versions of such carpets, woven in the symmetrical-knot technique (today commonly and inaccurately called the Turkish or Ghiordes knot) used for most pile carpets in Turkey and many in Persia. In Europe this Eastern rug-weaving technique was not only used for carpets but was also imitated in a pile fabric, known as turkeywork, used for upholstering chairs, stools, settees, and cushions from the sixteenth century onward in England. The contemporary term turkeywork was by no means used consistently to refer always to the same type of item, unfortunately for later observers among whom a certain confusion exists. The words "Turkey work" (making one word of two is a modern spelling) and "Turkey carpet" were occasionally used in a specific way in the sixteenth and seventeenth centuries to distinguish so-called Turkey carpets made in and imported from Turkey from those made in England that imitated the hand-knotted Turkish carpet-weaving technique. This helpful contemporary distinction, unfortunately rare, is found in some early seventeenth-century inventories such as that of Elizabeth, dowager countess of Shrewsbury, dated 1601, for Hardwick Hall in Derbyshire.[2] The 1602 inventory of Bridget, countess of Bedford, is quite explicit, listing "one Turkey Carpett of Englishe makinge" and "Two Wyndowe Turkey Carpettes of my owne makinge."[3] The 1614 inventory of Henry Howard, earl of Northampton, includes a great many Turkey carpets, some of them specified as "a longe Turkie carpett of Englishe worke," "a foote carpett of Turky worke," "a Turkie Cupboorde clothe," or "one foote Turky carpett two square cupboord carpettes of Turkie worke."[4] (Cupboard was a contemporary term for an

ancestor of our chest of drawers.) The term turkeywork is also used indiscriminately in the sixteenth, seventeenth, and eighteenth centuries to refer to floor, table, cupboard, chair, and cushion coverings which included pile fabrics made in England as well as in several parts of the Orient, and also to loom-woven in addition to needlework pieces with pile made by imitating the type of knot used in Turkish carpets. There is still some discussion today about how much of the European pile work called turkeywork was woven on looms and how much of it was done with a needle.[5] The large, knotted carpets made in Europe in the Turkish technique,[6] and often with Oriental designs, were certainly made on looms. There seems to be less certainty, however, about whether the knotting was done by hand on the warps of a carpet-weaver's loom or with a needle on a pre-woven fabric stretched on an embroiderer's frame in all of the smaller pieces that are described in seventeenth-century English and American inventories and advertisements as turkeywork and specified as used for cushion covers or chair and settee upholstery. Certain aspects of the history of British carpet weaving, some of which will be discussed at greater length later in this article, may perhaps be of some relevance to the matter of whether the smaller pieces, particularly those used for upholstery, may in fact be needlework. In the early 1750's several carpet-weaving establishments in England experimented with weaving large, seamless carpets with the knot used in imported Turkish carpets. This was, from the evidence of contemporary accounts, an innovation in carpet weaving in mid-eighteenth-century England. Carpets of this sort had of course been woven in England in the late sixteenth and early seventeenth centuries, but there is apparently, according to surviving evidence, a long hiatus between those and the mid-eighteenth-century reintroduction of this Turkish-knot weaving technique. In the interim, however, turkeywork chairs were made in England and are listed in numerous English and American records throughout the seventeenth century and, in American inventories, until the mid-eighteenth century. In the late seventeenth century the Cutlers' Company, for example, ordered a large number of turkeywork chairs for its new hall built in 1677 after the Great Fire of London.[7] The presumption could be made that if the weaving of large carpets in the Turkish knot, and with Turkish designs, was neglected, as it seems to have been, from the early seventeenth century until the mid-eighteenth, perhaps the turkeywork upholstery that continued to be made during that period was actually needlework.

The very general use of the word Turkey in connection with floor and table carpets or upholstery materials, whether genuine Oriental imports or European copies inspired by them, is, however, significant. Before the Revolution American colonists were supposed to import and export only via the mother country, and therefore acquired Oriental goods from England. Commercial quantities of heavy items such as carpets were usually brought to Europe by ship, and certain parts of the East, primarily Turkish Aegean and Mediterranean ports, as well as other eastern Mediterranean ports, were more accessible than others to trade by sea with Europe before the nineteenth century. An extensive study of the great numbers of European paintings that include carpets from the Middle Ages onward reveals that before the nineteenth century the overwhelming majority of Oriental carpets had Turkish designs. An exception seen in paintings is the carpets with the design often known in the trade today as Indo-Isfahan. The term Isfahan applied to this design is misleading because the

Persian examples were not made there but probably in the region of Herat (in what was then eastern Persia), primarily in the late sixteenth and seventeenth centuries. The design was also copied, chiefly in the seventeenth century and somewhat less in the eighteenth, in various parts of India for local use and for export to the West. Until the nineteenth century, many of the carpets with this Persian design that reached Europe are more likely to have been made in India, although a few Persian examples of the design may have been among those shipped to Europe from Indian ports. Given the limitations of overland travel at that early date, it is unlikely that carpets woven in Persia could have been exported to the West in the quantities indicated by the high incidence of carpets with this design in European paintings, chiefly of the first two-thirds of the seventeenth century. It is also improbable that carpets with any Persian design, including Indian examples of the so-called Indo-Isfahan, or more properly Indo-Persian, would have reached the American colonies. This design was made in very large sizes and by the mid-eighteenth century when Americans more frequently imported from England large Oriental or Oriental-design carpets to use on the floor, rather than smaller ones to cover tables, this particular type would have been out of date; and at that time, unlike today, older carpets were not sought after. The terms Persia or Persian carpets,[8] which are occasionally found in eighteenth-century documents, were therefore very likely used then (as now) in the most general sense to refer to prestigious carpets from a part of the world largely unfamiliar to Westerners, who understandably sometimes used the term Persian imprecisely for Oriental carpets in general, and still do. Other parts of the East from which carpets were apparently not imported into Europe until well into the nineteenth century (according to evidence in paintings) are the Caucasus, Central Asia, and China. Overland trade between the West and the first two regions was difficult, as it was with Persia, for large quantities of carpets. A lack of any importation of carpets from China before the nineteenth century is implied by their absence among the carpets represented in Western paintings. Not enough is known of the history of carpet weaving in China before the nineteenth century, but the earliest carpets made there seem to have been woven deep in the interior, especially at Ningsia (which was in contact with Central Asia, where carpet weaving is known since the seventh century A.D.[9]), rather than in the coastal areas (accessible to sea trade with the West) until the later nineteenth century, with the possible exception of silk carpets woven for court use. Pile-carpet weaving in Ningsia was apparently something of a novelty to the Chinese emperor in April 1697 when he visited that town. (This is the earliest-known recorded evidence of pile-carpet weaving in China.) The unfamiliarity of those who lived in the eastern part of China, as did the emperor, with such production would seem to be indicated by the comments of a French Jesuit in the emperor's party,[10] and also by the fact that when several floor carpets with pile, which the Jesuit described as similar to (but coarser than) Turkish carpets, were presented to the emperor on April 26, he was curious enough to request a demonstration of carpet weaving. Thus the term Turkey carpet came to be used in Europe because most Oriental carpets that were imported and imitated in Europe before the nineteenth century apparently came from villages and towns in western and perhaps southern Anatolia that were within easy reach of Turkish seaports.

Seventeenth- and eighteenth-century use of the terms carpet and rug (which are used interchangeably today for floor coverings) should also be clarified. The word rug (often spelled "rugg") at that time was a type of bedcover, and rugs are listed with bedding in numerous inventories, advertisements, and letters. The word rug to mean a floor (but never a table) covering has not been found in documents before the very end of the eighteenth century, and then only for a small rug destined for one particular use. Carpet was the term used for floor and table coverings before the nineteenth century, and carpets were often listed in eighteenth-century commercial papers[11] under the heading "Furniture," along with tables, chairs, and similar items. The earliest use in the English-speaking world of the word rug for a floor rather than a bed covering seems to be in an advertisement of May 22, 1799, in the *New-York Gazette and General Advertiser* in which A. S. Norwood announced a variety of floor coverings available at his carpet store including "an assortment of hearth Rugs."[12] Another early use of the word rug specifically in the context of floor coverings rather than bedding appears in 1803, again in a New York newspaper advertisement.[13] The first occurrence of the word applied to floor rather than bed coverings in the *Oxford English Dictionary* is in 1810, where it specifically refers to a rug for a hearthstone. In this country the word is similarly used in the 1818 inventory of the Boston cabinetmaker John Cogswell, who had "1 floor Carpet," valued at $6.00, and "1 Hearth Rug," valued at fifty cents, in his Back Room.[14] The word rug for a floor covering seems to have continued for at least ten years more to be used only for a hearth rug, for in 1828 Noah Webster defines a rug as "a coarse nappy woolen cloth, used for a bedcover, and in modern times, particularly for covering the carpet before the fireplace."[15]

Although inventories and advertisements indicate that carpets with Oriental designs were used in this country in the seventeenth and eighteenth centuries,[16] unfortunately for the study of the decorative arts in colonial America no carpets survive today that are known to have been in this country before the nineteenth century, in contrast to the documented genuine Oriental carpets still in some of the great country houses in England, where they have been since the sixteenth, seventeenth, and eighteenth centuries.[17] There was a much greater concentration of wealth and consequently a greater supply of imported and domestic carpets in England than in colonial America, and some of the great English families (as well as the merchants who imported carpets to sell) could and did deal directly with the East. Although there is documentary evidence that there were some carpets in colonial America that evidently had Oriental designs, those written records never describe the actual design of such so-called Turkey carpets. Paintings serve as invaluable contemporary visual documents of the decorative arts, and there are a few American paintings that can help unravel the mystery of just what specific Oriental, or pseudo-Oriental, designs were seen in those Turkey carpets so tantalizingly referred to, but not described beyond occasional indications of size, in the written records of colonial America and the first years of the new republic. Since there is only a handful of such paintings done in this country, it is helpful to extend a study of this kind to include certain English or Continental paintings that show carpets to discover what other carpets with Oriental designs colonial Americans could have obtained from England. For Oriental carpets were imported into England not only directly from the East but also at certain periods through Holland and Flanders where, in addition to the genuine article, there was a long history of local production of "tappis à la Turchesque"[18] and "Tapis de Turquie de Tournai [a Flemish town known for tapestry and carpet weaving], en fil de laine."[19] That both Eastern originals and locally made copies were available in Antwerp is specifically mentioned there as early as the second half of the sixteenth century, and a distinction is made between "des tapis de Turquie ou imitez tels."[20] Flemish weavers came to England and Ireland in the sixteenth century and wove imitation Turkey carpets there as well.[21] The fact that European carpet weavers were known to have been inspired by Oriental imports because of the great demand for these exotic floor, and table, coverings perhaps explains a few details of certain carpets in European and American paintings that some scholars today do not consider quite Oriental but which writers in the past have occasionally been too ready to assume were actually Turkish.

The few American paintings done before the nineteenth century that show interiors with carpets of Oriental design support conclusions drawn from a study of written records of the period that carpets were rare; that those with Oriental designs were rarer still; that only the wealthy owned them; and that, until at least the mid-eighteenth century, carpets with Oriental designs were used more often to cover tables or cupboards than floors. This practice was undoubtedly based in part on a desire to preserve a rare, costly, and fragile textile, but also on a custom in Europe that dated back to at least the Renaissance,[22] when carpets were spread

Pl. I.   *Portrait of an Unknown Woman,* attributed to Gerrit Duyckinck (1660-c. 1710), 1700-1710, New York City. Oil on panel. 31½ by 24¼ inches. *Henry Francis du Pont Winterthur Museum.*

Pl. II.   Medallion Ushak carpet, Ushak, western Anatolia, eighteenth century. Wool; 12 feet, 10 inches by 7 feet. *Colonial Williamsburg.*

on tables as much to preserve the carpets as to embellish a room. Textiles of several kinds were used in this manner (as seen in numerous European paintings, particularly seventeenth-century Dutch scenes of bourgeois interiors) and some were even specially shaped in the form of a cross with four short, wide arms of equal length which hung to the floor from the sides of a square table. Such a sixteenth-century Ottoman carpet with a European coat of arms, made in Cairo and now in the Communale Museum in San Gimignano, Italy, indicates the influence of European demand on Eastern carpet weaving.[23] The quality of the fabric used to cover a table followed a strict hierarchy: the more important the person destined to use the table, the more elegant the covering.[24] An Oriental carpet was one of the most elaborate table (as well as floor) coverings, and the practice of including a table (or floor) covering of Oriental design in a painting to enhance a person's status is amply demonstrated in European portraits and in a few American paintings.

Visual documentation of the use of carpets with Oriental designs does not begin in American painting until the end of the seventeenth century at the earliest and more probably only in the early eighteenth century. But one of the first Turkey carpets used in this country that is recorded in a

Pl. III. Portrait said to be of Elizabeth Franks, probably by a European artist but tentatively attributed to Justus Englehardt Kühn (d. 1717), who was born in Germany and worked in Annapolis, Maryland, c. 1708-1717. Oil on canvas, 47 by 42½ inches. *Milwaukee Art Center.*

Pl. IV. Carpet with so-called Lotto design, similar to seventeenth- and eighteenth-century examples found in churches in the Transylvanian region of Romania. Wool; 5 feet, 8 inches by 4 feet. *Metropolitan Museum of Art, gift of James F. Ballard.*

written document is a treasured table carpet that John Cogswell (an ancestor of the late eighteenth-century Boston cabinetmaker of the same name) inherited from his parents and brought with him to America when he emigrated with his family in 1635. The fact that it is given special mention in the reminiscences of three members of his household some years later would seem to indicate that a carpet of this sort was unusual at that early date in America. Until he left England Cogswell had continued the family manufactory of woolen fabrics, and apparently also inherited an appreciation of exceptional examples of weaving such as Turkey carpets. The high regard in which that carpet was held in the family is attested to in three contemporary accounts given by one of his servants, a daughter, and a nephew who lived with him.[25] That particular carpet was among the furnishings that the Cogswells were able to salvage on their unceremonious arrival in the new world from the wreck of the ship *Angel Gabriel,* in which they had crossed the Atlantic. They settled in Ipswich, Massachusetts, and some forty years later, several members of his household set down their recollections of the family's first years in America. On December 1, 1676, Cogswell's servant Samuel Haines described many of his master's possessions:

Furthermore, I do remember that my master had a Turkey worked carpet in Old England, which he commonly used to lay upon his parlour table, and this carpet was put aboard among my master's goods, and came safe ashore.

Depositions given the following spring by his daughter and nephew also made a particular point of this same carpet, which suggests that it was a cherished family heirloom. Mary Cogswell Armitage recorded on April 5, 1677, that among the items saved from the wreck at Pemequid was

also a Turkey work carpit, which was my father's carpit of his father's parler table in Auld England, & this carpit was in my father Cogswell's possession unto his dying day, & I heard it was prised in my father's inventory . . . & I never heard that my brother John had ever any Turkey made carpit; & I doe believe that he never had such a carpit.

(Perhaps their eldest brother William inherited the family Turkey carpet.) The Cogswell carpet, rare for its day in New England, was also discussed at some length in the deposition of Cogswell's nephew William Thompson, who testified on May 26, 1677,

That I lived with my Uncle & Aunt, Mr. John Cogswell, Sen., of Ipswich, and Mrs. Cogswell, about 16 years, & I did frequently see a Turkie-work carpet which they had, and I have heard them say that it was theirs in Old England, and used to lie upon their parlor table there, and that they brought it with them into this country when they came; and being this last winter in Old England, I heard my father, Doctor Samuel Thompson, say that he did well remember that my Uncle & Aunt had a Turkie-work carpet, which used to lye upon their parlour table in Old England, and took it away with them [to America].

Another early appearance of a Turkey carpet in the same part of New England is recorded in 1647 in an inventory of her estate filed by the widow Martha Coytmore, who married Governor John Winthrop in December of that year. She seems to have been well endowed with a variety of elegant textiles for domestic use, including a small Turkey carpet or cover.[26] Yet another early mention of a Turkey carpet in America is in the will dated May 17, 1673, of Elizabeth Butler of Virginia.[27] This will is also typical of

other listings that specify how such a carpet was used in this country in the seventeenth and early eighteenth centuries: the entry records a "drawing table [*i.e.* with a leaf that could be drawn out from under the top for an extension] and Turkey carpet." The 1691 Roxbury, Massachusetts, inventory of John Bowles indicates a similar use of a Turkey carpet: it lists together "a Table and a Turkey work Carpet" in the parlour, the principal room in the house, which also contained six turkeywork chairs and six turkeywork cushions.[28] The 1729 inventory, taken in Boston, of Governor William Burnet[29] lists "a small Turkey Carpett" valued at £1/5/0. Boston was one of the wealthiest towns in the Colonies in the mid-eighteenth century, and there is documentary evidence that Turkey carpets were to be seen in some of the more distinguished houses. Peter Faneuil's inventory of 1743 reveals an unusually lavish use of Turkey carpets. He had "a large Turky Carpet" valued at £35 in the parlor and three "Turky workt" carpets, one large, in the chambers, or bedrooms, worth £25, £29, and £25. In one of the chambers there was also an unspecified type of carpet valued at £15. The February 6, 1748, inventory of Nathaniel Cunningham, who lived near Boston, is also unusual in including a number of Turkey carpets: "2 old Turkey Carpets £7" relegated to the attic, "2 Turkey Carpets £4" in a small upstairs bedroom, as well as "1 fine Large New Turkey Carpet £60 [and] 1 D[itto]. somewhat worn £30."[30] Charles Apthorp's 1759 Boston inventory shows that he had a "Turkey Carpit & 3 Matts," valued together at £9/8/0 in his "Dining Room up Stairs." According to a 1774 inventory, another Bostonian, James Bowdoin, had four large Wilton carpets, two Scotch carpets, and three small undescribed carpets, as well as a small Turkey carpet in the west lower front parlor, where there was also "a small Wiltshire d[itt]o" and "a floor cloth." In his back entry there was "a large Turkey Carpett" valued at £7/7/0. That a carpet of that type was relegated to such a location perhaps indicates that it had become too worn to be used elsewhere in the house. The inventory of Andrew Belcher of Milton, near Boston, taken on February 25, 1771,[31] also lists some Turkey carpets that were apparently no longer the pride of the household. In the chamber over the parlor there were "4 old Turkey Carpets" valued at 6 shillings listed on the same line as a large trunk valued at 3 shillings, and they are totaled together at 9 shillings. A Maryland inventory of 1787, that of a well-to-do lawyer named Charles Ridgely,[32] the son of John Ridgely, of Baltimore County, also distinguishes between old and new, the difference in value perhaps indicative of size: "1 Old Turkey Carpet £6/-/-" and "1 new small Turkey carpet £2/10/-." He also owned "1 pair Turkey bed furniture etc. £22/10/-." Bed furniture was a contemporary term for bed hangings,[33] and could include a variety of the many textiles then associated with beds. The word Turkey in Ridgely's inventory may denote a fabric with pile (imitating the Turkish carpet-weaving technique, possibly with a needle). The word pair in this instance could perhaps mean a pair of turkeywork bed curtains; it seems unusual if this entry in Ridgely's inventory described a pair of bed "rugs" (the specific term in eighteenth-century inventories for a bed cover, which could be in a variety of pile and non-pile techniques, both woven and embroidered). Bed rugs, unlike blankets, were not listed in pairs. A more likely explanation of what was meant by "1 pair Turkey bed furniture etc." is perhaps suggested in a letter dated August 4, 1683, among the correspondence of the British East India Company, ordering a large number of sets of bed furniture, with detailed instructions about the desired sizes of the various components of the sets. The order not only stated that these sets were to include curtains and valances but also specified "Each bed to have two small Carpetts, 1½ yards wide and 2 yards long, each bed to have 12 cushions for chairs of the same work."[34]

Most Oriental carpets used in this country until about the middle of the eighteenth century seem to have been fairly small and were generally used on furniture rather than on the floor. By mid-century larger as well as smaller carpets were being used on the floor and are recorded in the inventories, newspaper advertisements, and letters ordering furniture from merchants in London. Newspaper advertisements in the Williamsburg *Virginia Gazette* between 1736 and 1780[35] reveal that both Turkey and English carpets could be purchased there, as in New England, new or, often, second hand at auction.[36] An advertisement in a Boston newspaper of 1754[37] for an auction, or "Publick Vendue," describes "a Parcel of valuable Household Stuff, among which are a very large *Turkey* Carpet, measuring Eleven and an half by Eighteen and an Half Feet. . . ." So-called Persia carpets were occasionally imported from England, with various English floor coverings, and offered for sale here by merchants, as mentioned above; but more often it was Turkey carpets that were advertised in Boston newspapers from 1754 to 1770, generally to be sold at "Publick Vendues."[38] That such carpets were especially treasured is indicated by an advertisement offering a reward in the *Boston News-Letter* for February 20, 1755: "Stolen out of a House in Boston, 'a Turkey Carpet of various Colours, about a yard and half in length, and a Yard wide, fring'd on each End.' Three dollars reward."[39]

Indications of size in feet and inches are not always given in contemporary written records. Some documents specify only large or small, and others refer simply to "a Turkey carpet." But some eighteenth-century newspaper advertisements contain terms denoting size or type that may need a little explanation today. London merchants who imported carpets from the East borrowed some of the words used in the carpet-weaving regions of the Near East, a few of which are heard occasionally in the trade today. Three advertisements[40] from London newspapers in the first half of the eighteenth century are fascinating for several reasons. They not only tell us about carpets that were shipped directly to London from Turkey; they also reveal that certain sizes were indicated at that time by special terms; and they designate some of the imports as suitable for use on the floor as well as on tables in certain rooms in fashionable London (or perhaps American) houses. From *The Daily Courant*, November 27, 1711:

At Captain Parker's Warehouse, in Merchant-Taylors-Hall in Threadneedle-Street, near the Royal Exchange, are exposed for Sale, a Parcel of Turkey carpets, just arrived by the Fleet from Turkey, viz Twelve fine Moschet carpets proper for Ladies Chambers or Dressing Rooms, and ninety two Pike [pile?] Carpets, some fit to cover Drawing Rooms and Chambers, others of a smaller Size to put under Beds and Tables, in Dining-Rooms and Parlours, or by the Chimneys to sit on."

From the *Daily Post*, April 3, 1724:

Imported by the last Ships from Turkey, a large Parcel of Turkey and Musket Carpets for Floors, Tables, Fire sides, &c. of the best Colours and Sizes, by Mr. John Howard and Hambleton, at the Talbot in Long-Lane by West-Smithfield, Cheaper than at any Place in England. Where all manner of Household Furniture made and sold and fine Tapestry Hangings.

From *The Country Journal or the Craftsman*, August 1, 1740:

JUST IMPORTED *And to be sold at Carpenters-Hall near Little Moorgate.* A Large and fine Parcel of SMYRNA, SEGIADYA, and other choice Turkey-Carpets: Consisting of great Variety of Sizes of lively Colours and divers curious new-fashioned Patterns. Many fine Carpets from three to four Yards square, and others from six to seven Yards long and proportionable Weadths, extremely useful for Dining-Rooms, &c with Hearth and Bed-side Carpets of excellent Patterns and Fineness.

N.B. There is several Bales of Carpets to be disposed of to those who sell again.

The terms *Moschet* and *Musket*, also found spelled *Mosquet* and *muskitto*,[41] are derived from French and Italian corruptions of the Arabic word *masgid* or *masjid* for mosque,[42] which in turn is related to another Arabic word, *sajjada* or *sagada*, meaning to worship or prostrate oneself (which is the Islamic manner of praying); the act of prostration is *sajd*. The term *sajjada* was used first in the East and then in the West to refer to a carpet of a size small enough to be suitable for use by a Moslem to pray on,[43] as the Islamic faith requires that prayer be performed on a clean place, not directly on the ground or bare floor. While any sort of textile will serve the purpose, when possible a carpet—usually of a portable size—was used, at home, during travels, or in a mosque. The word *segiadya* in the 1740 advertisement quoted above comes from the Arabic word *sajjada*, which is occasionally met with in the trade today to designate, as it (and *Moschet* or *Musket*) did in the eighteenth century, a prayer carpet.

The scarcity of carpets of any sort in the average American house before the nineteenth century is picturesquely commented on in *Annals of Philadelphia*, by John Fanning Watson, which was published in 1830, but he was reminiscing about the good old days:

The rarity of carpets, now deemed so indispensable to comfort, may be judged by the fact that T. Matlock, Esq. now aged 95, told me he had a distinct recollection of meeting with the first carpet he had ever seen, about the year 1750 at the house of Owen Jones, at the corner of Spruce and Second street. Mrs. S. Shoemaker, an aged Friend of the same age, told me she had received as a rare present from England a Scotch carpet; it was but twelve feet square, and was deemed quite a novelty then, say 60 years ago. When carpets afterward came into general use they only covered the floor in front of the chairs and tables. The covering of the whole floor is a thing of modern use. Many are the anecdotes which could be told of the carpets and the country bumpkins. There are many families who can remember that soon after their carpets were laid, they have been visited by clownish persons, who showed strong signs of distress at being obliged to walk over them; and when urged to come in, have stole in close to the sides of the room tip-toed, instinctively, to avoid sullying them![44]

It is only the inventories of colonists of a certain degree of wealth that include the rare mentions of Turkey carpets.[45] Thomas Hutchinson of Boston had a "large turkey carpet" in his parlor in 1765.[46] Another well-to-do Boston household with Turkey carpets among its other luxurious furnishings, which impressed the young John Adams, was that of Nicholas Boylston, who lived in what was easily one of the most elegant houses of his day, when Boston was one of the wealthiest towns in the Colonies. In his diary for January 16, 1766, John Adams provides a detailed picture of that house, which had more than one Turkey carpet:

Pl. V. *The Bermuda Group, Dean George Berkeley and His Entourage*, by John Smibert (1688-1751), c. 1729. Oil on canvas, 24 by 29 inches. This is a small study for or replica of the larger Bermuda Group portrait owned by Yale University. *National Gallery of Ireland, Dublin.*

Pl. VI. Carpet with double-arch design of the type found in Transylvanian churches; seventeenth or eighteenth century. Wool; 5 feet, 3 inches by 3 feet, 10 inches. *Colonial Williamsburg.*

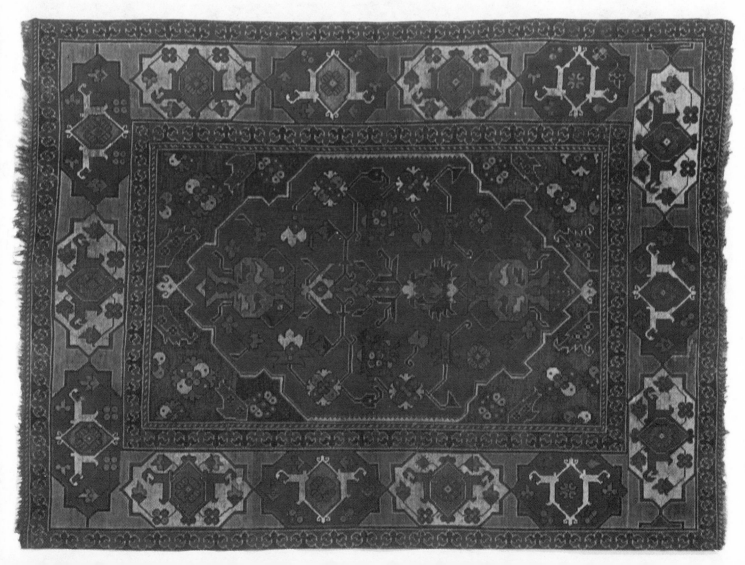

Pl. VII. *Isaac Royall and His Family*, by Robert Feke (1707-1752), 1741, Boston. Oil on canvas, 56¼ by 77¾ inches. *Harvard University Portrait Collection.*

Pl. VIII. Carpet with double-arch design of the type found in Transylvanian churches; early eighteenth century. Wool; 5 feet, 4 inches by 4 feet, 1 inch. *Philadelphia Museum of Art.*

Dined at Mr. Nick Boylstones, with the two Mr. Boylstones, two Mr. Smiths, Mr. Hallowel and the Ladies. An elegant Dinner indeed! Went over the House to view the Furniture, which alone cost a thousand Pounds sterling. A Seat it is for a noble Man, a Prince. The Turkey Carpets, the painted Hangings, the Marble Tables, the rich Beds with crimson Damask Curtains and Counterpins, the beautiful Chimny Clock, the Spacious Garden, are the most magnificent Thing I have ever seen.[47]

The Moffatt-Ladd House in Portsmouth, New Hampshire, was also unusually elegant, with a so-called "Persia Carpett" in almost every principal room, according to a 1768 inventory.[48]

Eighteenth-century Americans acquired carpets with Oriental patterns not only at auctions in this country or from merchants here who imported them from England. They also wrote to their agents in England for carpets and other elegant furnishings or, when possible, selected such special luxuries as a Turkey carpet themselves when they were in London. Correspondence of the period reveals the concern prospective buyers of Oriental carpets felt about the choice of such items, and it was decidely preferable to pick them out in person. Ordering through an agent and relying on someone else who might not have a great degree of connoisseurship in fine furnishings could be risky—and those who could afford to order such items directly from London merchants usually specified in their letters that they be of the best quality. It was far more satisfactory to do the selecting oneself, as did Benjamin Franklin, who when he was in London in 1765, received a letter from his wife in Philadelphia requesting ". . . if, as we talked before you went away, if you could meet with a Turkey carpet I should like it. . . ."[49] Franklin was certainly one to require good value for his money and had a practical concern for acquiring items of good quality as well as an awareness of fashionable furnishings, since he frequented the upper circles of society in England and France, who set the fashions. If one could acquire a carpet actually imported from the East, that was preferable; but failing that, English carpets were acceptable, and often necessary, substitutes. Franklin, still in London the following spring, wrote to his wife that he was sending "A Large true Turkey Carpet cost 10 Guineas, for the Dining Parlour."[50]

Among those eighteenth-century Americans who sent frequent orders to agents in London were various members of the Carroll fammily of Maryland. Charles Carroll known as the Barrister (1723-1783), son of Dr. Charles Carroll of Annapolis (1691-1755), wrote to one of his London agents, William Anderson, in September 1760 for various household furnishings, including "One Turkey Carpet suitable for a Room 25 feet Long and twenty Broad at about Ten Guineas/ one Ditto for a Room Twenty feet Long and Eighteen Broad at about six Guineas."[51]

Charles Carroll of Carrollton (1737-1832), son of Charles Carroll of Annapolis (1702-1782) and a Signer of the Declaration of Independence, was a man of great wealth and discriminating taste in the fine and decorative arts as well as in the art of living well.[52] He was apparently uneasy about ordering elegant furnishings through his agents in London and when requesting such items, which he did rarely in relation to the quantities of more mundane materials needed for operating his estates and plantations, he included elaborate instructions about the selection and shipping of the luxury items, and complained later when goods such as painted floorcloths were received in bad condition or were damaged because he felt they had not

been carefully packed or were of inferior workmanship. In an invoice, or order, sent to one of his agents in London on October 26, 1771, he asked for various pieces of furniture and upholstery fabrics for a room twenty feet square. He specified that the items be chosen with the scale of the room in mind, and included in his furniture order a request for

One Turkey Carpet 17½ feet long & 16 feet broad. If a Turkey carpet cannot be procured exactly of these dimensions or near it, you are desired to procure one of the best kind of Axminster, Wilton—or any other English manufactory. . . . One best painted black and white Floor Cloth 16 feet & 6½ long, and 14 feet broad—N.B. If they will stow on well, and it is a safe Package—let the Carpet and the floor cloth come over on a Rowler, or Rowlers——[53]

His father, Charles Carroll of Annapolis, begins a letter accompanying this order to their London agents:

Sir
Most of the articles mentioned in the inclosed Invoice were intended by my son to be bought by a Person of whose Judgment & Taste he has a good opinion especially the furniture. I know that a man of Industry and good sense may perform any commission of this sort to satisfaction, especially when he has the ready money (as you have) if he will take proper measures—and give himself some trouble. I know it is the common practice of our merchants to send our Invoices to the several Tradesmen—hardly ever to see the goods sent in, & should they see them, that in the uncommon articles [i.e., the special furniture ordered in this letter] they are no way competent Judges of their value—that they take a trouble to make themselves so by consulting such as are. . . . To apply with the Cash in hand, where you are not a Judge to Consult those who are, both as to Taste & value this is a certain way to increase your Business, with others & to be assured of a Continuance of mine. I must repeat what is in the Invoice, & beg you will see to the package of these goods, The shipping, and stowing of them very Carefully. . . .[54]

Nearly thirteen years after his previous order for a Turkey carpet he ordered another, on February 9, 1784, after peace had been established and he had resumed his orders to London merchants. That time, having learned from experience about certain problems inherent in some Oriental carpets, he gave specific instructions about the selection of:

1 Best Turkey Carpet 19 foot Long & 17-foot broad—
N.B. W. Johnson is requested to Examine well this Carpet to see that it is clear of puckers which Turkey carpets often have and which besides being ugly occasion them to wear out sooner in such Places—[55]

This concern about the wear and tear of such a special household item was shared by others in America fortunate enough to possess Turkey, or other, carpets. If a carpet was used where food could spill on it during tea or other meals, it might be covered with a protective crumb cloth, a term used from at least the mid-nineteenth century onward. This custom is documented in written records such as inventories and housekeeping manuals in this country from at least the late eighteenth century and throughout the nineteenth. It is also documented in such paintings as a Dutch watercolor of about 1770 (*Family of Five at Tea*, by an unknown artist) now at Colonial Williamsburg, and about 1821 in Henry Sargent's painting of a dinner meeting of the Wednesday Evening Club at his house in Boston (that painting is now in the Museum of Fine Arts in Boston). Such a covering for a carpet in England and America was usually of baize (also spelled bays), and often of a color to harmonize with the room. Baize was described by Thomas Sheraton in *The Cabinet Dictionary,* published in London in 1803, as

BAYS, or BAIZE, a sort of open woollen stuff, having a long nap, sometimes frized, and sometimes not. This stuff is without wale, and is wrought in a loom with two treadles like flannel. It is chiefly manufactured at Colchester and Bocking, in Essex. . . . This manufacture was first introduced into England, with that of says, serges, &c. by the Flemings, who fled thither about the fifth of queen Elizabeth's reign, from the hand of persecution, for their religion.
Brit. Encyclop. Bays is in breadth commonly 1½ yard, 1¾ yard, or 2 yards, and their length from 42 to 48 yards. It is much in use by cabinet-makers and upholdsterers. By the latter, bays is used to cover over carpets, and made to fit round the room, to save them.[56]

Such a protective covering was used in Aaron Burr's New York City residence, Richmond Hill, according to a 1797 inventory[57] which listed in the "Blue or drawing Room," "1 Elegant Turkey carpet" and "a Carpet of Blue Bays to cover the turkey ditto." In his dining room he had a green baize cover to be used with a Brussels carpet. Abigail Adams, according to an inventory taken in 1801, also had a green baize cover for a Brussels carpet for the dining room at the White House[58] during her short stay there. Carpets were sometimes taken up in the summer in the North as well as in the South, and this may have been as much for their protection as for comfort.

In spite of precautions, however, carpets needed cleaning from time to time. Eighteenth-century housekeeping manuals explained how to do it yourself:

To revive the colour of a Turkey Carpet, beat it well with a stick, till the dust is all got out, then with Lemon Juice or Sorrel Juice take out the spots of ink, if the carpet is stained with any, wash it in cold Water, and afterwards shake out all the Water from the threads of the carpet, and when it is thoroughly dry, rub it all over with the Crumb of an hot White Loaf, and if the weather is very fine, hang it out in the open air for a night or two.[59]

Cleaning a large carpet oneself is no mean feat, even today, and the housewife who followed the above instructions ran the risk of irretrievably bleaching the color out of the parts of the carpet she treated with lemon or sorrel juice. It was, and is, probably safer to rely on professional carpet cleaners, and their services could be obtained even in the eighteenth century. An advertisement in *The New-York Gazette, and Weekly Mercury* for December 23, 1771, announced:

Baker and Yearsley, Silk Dyers and Scowerers from London, Beg leave to inform the public in general, that they have begun their business in all its various branches, at the upper end of Maiden-Lane, near Doctor Vanburen's. . . . They . . . clean Turkey and Wilton carpets, and make the colour quite fresh.[60]

Carpets were rare and expensive enough in the eighteenth century to warrant special care to preserve them as long as possible. For the protection of valuable carpets one

enterprising blacksmith devised an ingenious mechanism. On December 7, 1799, this advertisement appeared in the *Mercantile Advertiser* in New York City:

DOOR SPRINGS.—William Carver, Horse Farrier and Shoeing Smith. . . . he makes patent springs for palour [*sic*] doors which will cause the doors to clear, the carpets, and when shut prevent air drawing under the door into the room. . . . it is presumed no gentlemen will be without them that have valuable carpets on the floors, as they are far preferable to any thing offered of the kind in this country. They are not to be perceived when fixed to the doors. He will wait on the gentlemen to shew the springs if required.[61]

The all too few paintings executed in America before the nineteenth century that include Oriental-design carpets must not be considered conclusive proof that the carpet depicted was necessarily here then or owned by the subject of the portrait, for there was a long tradition in English portraiture to confer status and dignity on the sitter by including an elegant piece of furniture or a particularly prestigious textile such as a rare and exotic carpet with an Oriental design, either on a table or on the floor. The original English oil portraits were not, however, usually seen by the American artists, who often used mezzotints of such portraits as models for an elegant pose or attribute to enhance the appearance of the subject. Although certain details in American portraits are directly traceable to English prototypes, mezzotint copies of English portraits do not show complex carpet patterns as clearly as do some English oil paintings, and not clearly enough to be of use to an American artist. Yet the carpets with Oriental designs seen in the handful of American portraits done before the nineteenth century that include such carpets are depicted carefully enough for their patterns to be identified. It seems reasonable to conclude, with due caution, that the carpets shown in these American paintings were actually in America then, since they exhibit the sort of detail that would not be transmitted at second hand through a mezzotint. It is not sure, however, whether they were studio props or actually owned by the sitters. Even if the inventories of some of the subjects of these portraits list carpets, these written records do not describe such items in sufficient detail for us to be able to state with certainty that the carpet in that person's portrait is one of those mentioned in his inventory.

It is difficult to establish which of two paintings (Pls. I, III) currently attributed to American artists was the first done in this country to show a carpet with an Oriental design. The portrait of an unknown woman illustrated in Plate I is attributed to Gerrit Duyckinck, who worked in New York City from about 1680 to about 1710. The portrait in Plate I may or may not have been painted before that illustrated in Plate III, which has been very tentatively attributed (with less confidence than the attribution of Pl. I to Duyckinck) to the artist Justus Englehardt Kühn, who was born and trained in Germany and worked in Annapolis, Maryland, from at least 1708 until his death in 1717. Genealogical research to date has not uncovered an Elizabeth Franks living in the late seventeenth or early eighteenth century in the Annapolis region where Kühn worked, nor in Philadelphia, New York, or New England. Also, the subjects of all other portraits attributed to Kühn are related to the Carroll family of Maryland, including the one signed Kühn portrait, of Ignatius Digges. Certain technical considerations, including the modeling of the face in the

Preceding page.
Pl. IX. *Jeremiah Lee,* by John Singleton Copley (1738-1815), signed and dated *JSC* [monogram] *P. 1769.* Oil on canvas, 95 by 59 inches. *Wadsworth Atheneum, Hartford, Connecticut.*

portrait in Plate III, which is more three-dimensional than in other portraits attributed to Kühn, point to the hand of an artist more sophisticated than Kühn, and to a European provenance for the work. It is in any case based on European prototypes. Furthermore, most seventeenth- and early eighteenth-century American inventories that mention a Turkey carpet, and further specify where it was used, indicate that it was spread on a table or cupboard rather than on the floor as it is in the painting in Plate III. Since such textiles were even rarer in this country than in Europe, it is likely that few were put on the floor here until sometime in the second or third decade of the eighteenth century. If the painting illustrated in Plate III is American, it is perhaps the earliest evidence we have of an Oriental carpet used on the floor in this country. If it is European, it is at least an indication, as are European paintings such as those illustrated in Plates XVII, XIX, and XXI, of other Oriental carpet designs that could have reached this country in the late seventeenth century and early eighteenth. If both paintings represented in Plates I and III are accepted as American, it is of some interest to establish which of the two is the earliest that represents an Oriental carpet here. The current attributions to specific artists working in

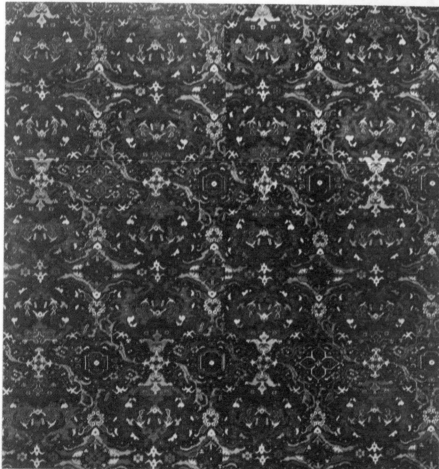

Pl. X. So-called Smyrna carpet, western Anatolia, eighteenth or nineteenth century. Wool; 5 feet, 10¾ inches by 4 feet, 2 inches. *Textile Museum, Washington, D.C.; photograph by Otto E. Nelson.*

Pl. XI. English "Turkey carpet" with an adaptation of an Anatolian so-called Smyrna design based on the eighteenth-century Ushak rendering of a provincial version of a sixteenth-century design of the imperial Ottoman carpet manufactories; probably Axminster, third quarter of the eighteenth century. Wool warp and pile, bast weft; fragment cut from a carpet at Ramsbury Manor, England; 16 feet, 1 inch by 15 feet, 6 inches. *Tryon Palace, New Bern, North Carolina; photograph by Bradford L. Rauschenberg.*

168

America indicate dates for the two paintings that are the reverse of the periods of the styles of dress portrayed in each work. The costume shown in Plate III is typical of about 1685 to 1690 and the dress in Plate I is typical of about 1710 to 1720. But it is risky to date the paintings solely on the basis of costume.

The designs of the carpets portrayed in both Plates I and III are quite recognizable as of Turkish origin, though it is not absolutely certain that both carpets were actually made in Anatolia. The painting attributed to Duyckinck shows a coarsely knotted table covering with the medallion Ushak design (Pl. II), known from the sixteenth century onward in carpets woven in Ushak in western Anatolia. In the painting it is the scalloped edge of the central medallion of the carpet design that is seen at the lower edge of the canvas. In later examples of this design the oval central medallion of earlier versions is often more angular and hexagonal (cf. Pls. II, XIII, both of which are somewhat late types). The Duyckinck portrait may show an actual Turkish import or possibly a Flemish version of the design. The way the motifs are drawn as well as the coarse knotting suggest European weaving, but the artist may have depicted an unfamiliar Oriental design carelessly. Also, most surviving medallion Ushak carpets made before the nineteenth century were large, but the table covering here appears to be relatively small. Since carpets of this design appear in a great many European seventeenth- and eighteenth-century paintings, as well as in two American ones (Pls. I, XII), we know that great numbers of medallion Ushaks were imported into Europe at that time.

The design of the carpet in the painting in Plate III is a version of one of the patterns (this one misleadingly known as the Lotto design) woven in western Anatolia, and perhaps also in the Konya region of south central Anatolia, in the sixteenth and seventeenth centuries. The main border of the carpet is shown at the lower edge of the portrait in Plate III. A similar carpet with a border even closer than Plate IV to that in this painting, with a small cross form at the center of each cartouche, is illustrated in Plate IV of Jules de Végh and Charles Layer, *Tapis Turcs Provenant des Eglises et Collections de Transylvanie* (Paris, 1925). Above the dog's back in Plate III is the side of one of the cross motifs that alternate with skeletal octagons, both of which are characteristic of the field of this carpet design. Between the girl and the dog is a version of the motif used in the carpet in Plate IV at the center of either long edge of the field between the points of two cross-shape motifs. The narrow inner guard border, which resembles a twisted rope, is similar in the carpet in the painting and in the example in Plate IV. It has been suggested[62] that some of the variants of this design (one of which is depicted in Pl. III; another, illustrated in Pl. IV) and certain others may have been woven at least as early as the seventeenth century, and have also been copied in the twentieth century, in the part of eastern Europe (which includes what is today Romania) that was from the mid-sixteenth century to the late nineteenth under the domination of the Ottoman Turks. The word Transylvanian has been used in connection with several variants of carpet designs associated with Anatolia that have been found hanging in Protestant and Catholic churches in the Transylvanian region of present-day Romania. Much more study of the carpets still in Romanian churches and museums and in Hungarian museums remains to be done before any sound conclusions may be drawn as to where the so-called

Transylvanian carpets may actually have been woven. Although weaving is known in neolithic times in the region that is today Romania, not enough is known about how far back the present pile-carpet-weaving tradition in Romania extends. It goes back at least as far, however, as a carpet in the Hungarian National Museum (Magyar Nemzeti Galeria) in Budapest that is inscribed *D: S: 1723* and has a non-Anatolian field and a border and long fringe characteristic of many Transylvanian church carpets.[63] Such contemporary documents relating to carpets imported or used in the Transylvanian region from the sixteenth century onward as have been studied to date do not shed sufficient light for firm conclusions to be drawn on either side of this controversial question. For the present it is perhaps best to reserve judgment on the matter and leave open the possibility that some of the so-called Transylvanian carpets as well as some not so-called, including several illustrated in this article, could have been made in the part of eastern Europe that was for a long time under strong Turkish influence. Carpets of the so-called Transylvanian church type with a variety of different designs are seen in a great many Dutch and some English (as well as at least two American) paintings of the seventeenth century and early eighteenth, indicating a great volume of trade in this particular category of carpet.

The first signed and dated picture with an Oriental carpet that we can be quite certain was painted in this country is by John Smibert, a portrait of the Bermuda Group, as the entourage that accompanied Dean (later Bishop) George Berkeley in 1728 from London en route to Bermuda to set up a missionary college called itself. A small version by Smibert of his large group portrait is seen in Plate V. Smibert himself was one of the group and perhaps intended to teach painting in the projected institution. They landed at Newport in January 1729 to wait for the funds Parliament had voted. Since the money never materialized, Berkeley returned from Boston to London, arriving there in February 1732. Smibert, however, remained in this country and in 1729 began the large (70¾ by 94½ inches) portrait of the Bermuda Group now owned by Yale University.[64] The considerably smaller version of this portrait shown in Plate V was owned by Dr. Thomas Moffatt, Smibert's nephew, who joined the Bermuda Group here but did not sail with the other members from London. This version may have been done as a memento for Moffatt or as a study for the larger work. The smaller canvas is of more interest than the Yale painting in a discussion of Oriental carpets because in the smaller work Smibert included more of the carpet. The carpet's border, which is not seen in the larger canvas, is, interestingly, the part of the carpet the artist depicted most faithfully. (There is no evidence that the larger canvas was ever cropped at the bottom.) The border of the carpet in the smaller version, shown in Plate V, is similar to a border frequently used with one of the several types of field design represented in so-called Transylvanian carpets (Pls. VI, VIII). This type of field design is more commonly found than the so-called Lotto pattern (seen in Pls. III and IV) in carpets depicted in European paintings, particularly Dutch seventeenth- and eighteenth-century works. The relatively high incidence of so-called Transylvanian carpets in these paintings implies a very large European importation of such carpets at that period in comparison with carpets with other Oriental designs. The border pattern of the carpet design seen in Plate VI also influenced certain carpets woven in Europe in the latter part of the eighteenth century, as we shall see presently. The motif framed by the cartouches in the border of the carpet in the smaller version of Smibert's Bermuda Group portrait is a variant of a similar motif seen in Plate VI. It is sometimes called the "turtle" motif, which is a misnomer (like other Western names for often-misunderstood forms in Oriental carpets). That motif is an angular derivation of the more curvilinear Persian arabesque form representing a pair of split, or forked, leaves on a stem in profile. The motif as seen in the smaller Smibert canvas is a further step away from the Persian original than is the motif in the carpet in Plate VI. The motif shown in the Smibert painting is a variant with four instead of two "arms," so to speak, in which the relationship with the original form of the split-leaf arabesque is all but impossible to discern. This "four-armed" "turtle" is seen in a number of Transylvanian church rugs.[65] Smibert depicted the field of the carpet on the table in both the large and small versions of the subject in a much more cursory manner than the quite meticulous way in which he portrayed the border in the smaller work. The layout of the field design of Smibert's carpet is nevertheless recognizable as one of the field designs characteristic of so-called Transylvanian church carpets: the type represented in Plate VI. The drawing of the field motifs of the carpet in the painting suggests a northwestern European version of the popular design, however, or possibly the artist may not have understood the design. The very regular stepped edging of the arch at each end of the field of the table covering in the painting is not characteristic of the drawing in Transylvanian church carpets. This may be Smibert's alteration or it may, taken together with the atypical drawing of other field motifs, betray a version of this design that was woven in northwestern Europe.

Robert Feke, on the other hand, gives a much more precise portrayal of a carpet of this type (which seems to be a genuine Eastern example, fairly coarsely woven) in his painting of the successful New England rum merchant Isaac Royall Junior and his family (Pl. VII), of Medford, Massachusetts, even to the point of showing the individual tufts of pile. The portrait, done in 1741, is clearly based on Smibert's canvas.[66] The inventory taken by Isaac Royall Junior in his father's house in Medford in 1739, the year Isaac Royall Senior died, and two years before the family portrait was painted, includes "a Turkey Carpitt" valued at £40 in "the Best Room" along with other distinguished furnishings.[67] The Royall inventory is unusual in listing not just one but three so-called Turkey carpets. The second was in "the Marble Chamber" (the best bedroom of the house), valued at £30. The third was listed as being "in the front garats," perhaps relegated there because it was worn. We cannot know for sure, of course, if any of these is the carpet in the 1741 portrait of Isaac Royall Junior with his family. No inventory of the Medford house exists for Isaac Royall Junior, as he and his family left in 1775 for England, never to return to America. The table carpet in the Feke portrait might possibly have been a studio prop of the artist, who was certainly basing his prominent treatment of this luxurious textile on Smibert's earlier Bermuda Group portrait. The only element in the carpet in Feke's painting that looks nonoriental is the outer guard border (unfortunately cut off at the bottom in this illustration), which is somewhat simplified. Otherwise the carpet is depicted remarkably exactly, compared with actual so-called Transylvanian carpets of its type (Pl. VIII).

John Singleton Copley's portrait of Jeremiah Lee (Pl. IX), done in 1769, five years before the artist went to live for the rest of his life in England, is the only painting Copley did in America that shows a carpet with an Oriental design. The year before Copley painted this portrait, Lee's imposing mansion in Marblehead, Massachusetts, was completed, and this canvas was to be hung there, with Copley's likeness of Mrs. Lee. Jeremiah Lee was one of the most prominent of the import-export merchants in his day in Marblehead and perhaps in all of the Colonies. His house, like the pair of portraits, was a symbol of his success. In portraits of this sort the furnishings depicted are not necessarily the subject's own, but may be in accord with the conventions of high-style portraiture. The ornate rococo table[68] and Lee's position beside it are derived[69] from John Vanderbank's portrait of Queen Caroline done in 1736.[70] The table is a line-for-line copy of the one in the Vanderbank painting and does not represent one of Lee's own possessions. It is taken by Copley from a mezzotint of the portrait of Queen Caroline, probably Vanderbank's greatest painting and widely known in the eighteenth century through mezzotints. That portrait does not include a carpet, however, but Copley depicts a floor covering rare and sumptuous for its time and place to embellish even further an important commission from a man set on impressing his contemporaries, first, with an unusually elegant house and, the following year, with a pair of imposing full-length portraits of himself and his wife. Such a pair of full-length portraits of an American husband and wife was extremely uncommon at that date. For this expression of his position in society Lee, or Copley, may have been inspired by the large, full-length portraits done by Smibert in 1744 of Mr. and Mrs. William Browne. Her portrait shows in the background their new mansion, Browne Hall (called by neighbors "Folly Hill"), which was built between 1740 and 1745 in Danvers, a few miles outside Salem, which is the town next to Marblehead, where Lee lived. Lee was undoubtedly familiar with this pair of Browne family portraits,[71] which are recorded in Smibert's notebook in 1734 and 1738 respectively and were completed before Mary Burnet Browne's death in 1745.[72]

Copley, in depicting his subject standing on a luxurious carpet with an Oriental design, was following a specific prestige-enhancing convention used throughout Europe, ever since Oriental carpets were introduced into the West, not only for early paintings of the Madonna and for portraits of royalty and nobility but also for portraits of the affluent members of the mercantile bourgeoisie. In his painting of Lee, Copley used the carpet as well as the ornate rococo table to create an elegant setting for the portrayal of a well-to-do American merchant proud of his social status. The source of the table in a mezzotint of a well-known English portrait has been demonstrated above; but the carpet was probably painted from life, so to speak, rather than after a black and white mezzotint, so recognizably are the colors and details of the carpet design given. It is not certain, however, if Lee actually owned that carpet, or if he or Copley perhaps borrowed it for the portrait. Inventories might be expected to shed light on whether or not the carpet might have belonged to Lee. The carpets listed in the inventories[73] taken the year after his death in 1775 and the year after his wife's in 1791, however, are not described in enough detail for us to know what the designs of those carpets were, nor to enable us to equate one of them with the floor covering in his portrait. These two inventories nevertheless provide intriguing, if inconclusive, clues. The inventory taken June 28, 1776, of Jeremiah Lee's estate includes carpets but none specified as "Turkey":

1 carpet 67½ yds @ 6/ 20.7.0
5 carpets 72¼ yds @ 6/ 21.13.6
91 yds of carpeting @ 12/
a canvas carpet 80/
and [sic] old carpet + bed rods 20/ 1.0.0
stair carpets 14/

The inventory taken of Martha Swett Lee's estate on April 29, 1792, lists in the Hall Chamber (the bedroom she used above the elaborately paneled room known as the Hall on

Pl. XII. "Lansdowne" portrait of George Washington, by Gilbert Stuart (1755-1828), 1796. Oil on canvas, 96 by 60½ inches. *Pennsylvania Academy of the Fine Arts, bequest of William Bingham, 1811; photograph by Eugene L. Mantis.*

Pl. XIII. Medallion Ushak carpet, Anatolia or Europe; nineteenth century. Wool; 14 feet, 5 inches by 8 feet, 3 inches. *Colonial Williamsburg.*

171

Pl. XIV. *A Family in an Interior,* by an unknown English artist, 1740-1750. Oil on canvas, 39 by 51½ inches. *Collection of Mr. and Mrs. Paul Mellon.*

Pl. XV. English carpet with neoclassical field design and pseudo-Oriental border based on the border of a Transylvanian church carpet, probably Axminster or Moorfields, c. 1770. Wool warp and pile, bast weft; 25 feet, 8 inches by 15 feet, 1 inch. *Winterthur Museum.*

Pl. XVI. English carpet with neoclassical field design and a pseudo-Oriental border, probably Axminster or Moorfields, c. 1770. Wool warp and pile, bast weft; 18 feet, 8 inches by 12 feet, 5 inches. *Tryon Palace, Rauschenberg photograph.*

the first floor):

1 Large Wilton floor Carpet £10 1 Small d° 3/0........11.10.0

Listed as being in the "back Western Chamber" was:

1 Old floor Carpet 12/

This mention of a large Wilton carpet could be a misleading clue in any attempt to identify the "Turkey" carpet in the portrait of Jeremiah Lee with the Wilton carpet listed in his wife's inventory. It might seem irresistible at first to draw a hasty conclusion that Mrs. Lee's Wilton carpet might be an English "Turkey" carpet and could therefore perhaps be the carpet in Jeremiah Lee's portrait because of the striking similarity between certain elements of design and color of the carpet in her husband's portrait and related elements in the carpet in Plate XI. This untenable supposition could arise in the light of the tentative but, as we shall see, incorrect attribution of the latter carpet to the Wilton factory in notes on that carpet on file at Tryon Palace Restoration in New Bern, North Carolina, which has owned the carpet since 1957. The Tryon Palace carpet (approximately sixteen feet square) is skillfully made up of three pieces cut from a large carpet that was reduced for the dining room at Ramsbury Manor, near Marlborough in Wiltshire, England,[74] apparently in the 1950's (the remainder of the carpet may still be there). The original carpet is said to have been made in the third quarter of the eighteenth century for the duke of Newcastle's princely Nottinghamshire estate, Clumber Park,[75] built between 1752 and 1767 and demolished in the 1930's. The appearance in an American portrait done in 1769 of a similar carpet with an adaptation of the same Oriental design documents the availability of such a carpet in the 1760's, and thus supports the tradition that the large carpet of which Plate XI is a part was made at about that time for the duke of Newcastle's estate Clumber Park, which was completed in 1767. The original carpet eventually reached Ramsbury Manor, which was the residence of the earl of Wilton from 1953 to 1958.[76] The confusing misattribution of the carpet to the Wilton factory seems to have arisen because of the association of the earl of Wilton with Ramsbury Manor in the 1950's and the fact that the dealer who sold the fragments that make up the large carpet in Plate XI to Tryon Palace in 1957 is said to have acquired them from the earl of Wilton, who owned and lived at Ramsbury Manor at the time. The earl of Wilton's family, however, has no connection whatsoever with the Wilton factory in Wiltshire. His family, the Egertons, have their seat at Wilton Castle in Herefordshire, and they should not be confused with the family that has at different periods taken a special interest in the Wilton factory. That is the Herbert family whose head, since 1605, has carried the two titles earl of Pembroke and earl of Montgomery. Their country seat is Wilton *House* in Wilton, near Salisbury, in Wiltshire, and also near the Wilton factory. To weave another potentially confusing thread into the story, from 1553 to 1676 the earls of Pembroke and Montgomery owned the estate on which Ramsbury Manor was built by the estate's next owner between about 1680 and 1683. After 1644 the earl of Pembroke's family had concentrated its attention on rebuilding Wilton House. The estate on which Ramsbury Manor was built passed through many hands before the 1950's, when the earl of Wilton lived there. The carpet under discussion, of which a part is seen in Plate XI, was not woven for either family, however, but for the duke of Newcastle. So the association of the earl of Wilton with

the carpet in the 1950's should not be confused with where it may have been woven. Technical analysis of the carpet and the history of British carpet weaving also exclude the Wilton factory as a candidate for the firm that made the carpet represented in Plate XI. It is not known precisely when that carpet was acquired by the earl of Wilton nor when it was installed at Ramsbury Manor; successive owners of the house often bought its major furnishings as well. The carpet was apparently not there in 1934 when C. E. C. Tattersall published *A History of British Carpets*, in which he discusses three carpets at Ramsbury Manor (which he attributes to Axminster), none of which is related to the fragment in Plate XI. If a technical analysis of the carpet in Plate XI and the history of carpet weaving in England are discouraging for any supposition that the carpet in Plate XI could have been made at Wilton, they also therefore militate against any speculation that Mrs. Lee's Wilton carpet might be the carpet in her husband's portrait.

The carpet of which part is shown in Plate XI has a traditional history that it is of English manufacture. This attribution of a carpet with a western Anatolian design to an English weaving establishment is supported by the fact that in the carpet represented in Plate XI, which is woven (fairly coarsely, about twenty to twenty-five knots to the square inch) in the Turkish-knot technique, bast is used in the weft, rather than wool. (Bast fibers include flax, or linen, as well as hemp and jute.[77]) Bast is characteristic of European carpets but not of eighteenth-century Anatolian carpets. Just as the identification of secondary woods that cabinetmakers used in parts of furniture not normally visible (because such woods were available locally and inexpensively) can help establish where a piece of furniture was made, so a close examination of the materials used in carpets can sometimes reveal where they were woven. Wool was the most suitable material for the pile (leaving aside special silk rugs and occasional touches of cotton in certain Oriental rugs), but English carpet weavers in the eighteenth century sometimes used bast fibers for the warp or weft (the "secondary," less visible elements of a carpet), unlike Anatolian weavers at that time. Too, the drawing of the design in the carpet shown in Plate XI is somewhat stiffer and more mechanical than one would expect in a carpet woven in Anatolia. The Turkish-knot technique in which the carpet in Plate XI is woven was imitated at Axminster from 1755 to 1835, as well as at Exeter and Moorfields in the second half of the eighteenth century, but not at Wilton before 1836. Also, none of the three fragments that make up the carpet shown in Plate XI is narrower than ninety-two and a half inches, and until 1836 Wilton was only able to weave carpeting in strips twenty-seven or thirty-six inches wide. Axminster seems to have been the most successful producer of English "Turkey" carpets in the second half of the eighteenth century. Thus, it seems likely that the English carpet represented in Plate XI was woven at Axminster and not at Wilton, since an eighteenth-century date for the carpet seems reasonable, as a carpet like it appears in an American painting of 1769. Thomas Whitty had established in 1755 at Axminster the first of the wide, vertical looms he installed to weave imitations of the large, seamless Turkish carpets that so impressed him in 1754[78] that he was determined to copy them. He learned about the technique and the vertical looms necessary to produce it by watching the work of French weavers who had begun coming in 1749 from the Royal Savonnerie Factory to the weaving establishment of their fellow Huguenot *émigré*, Peter Parisot, in Paddington. Parisot soon expanded and moved to Fulham where by 1753 he had a hundred weavers and many apprentices. By 1755 he was having difficulties and Claude Passavant (also spelled Passavent), another Huguenot, moved the Fulham factory to his own factory at Exeter. Once Whitty had learned the secret of making "Turkey" carpets, in April 1755 he tried his hand (and, a few months later, those of his daughters and their aunt) at making an English "Turkey" carpet with the Turkish knot and in one piece without seams, at his clothmaking factory in Axminster, in Devonshire. Whitty had previously used horizontal looms (as did the Wilton factory), on which only relatively narrow strips could be woven. The innovation was an immediate success and he enjoyed the enthusiastic patronage of noble families even before his first hand-knotted carpet was off the loom. In 1835 the Axminster factory went bankrupt (it never recovered from a fire at the factory in 1828) and the following year Wilton bought Axminster's wide, vertical looms (and hired many of Axminster's weavers who were skilled at using them) on which the Wilton factory could, for the first time, weave large, seamless, hand-knotted carpets in the so-called Turkish knot.[79] These vertical looms were from thirty-three to forty feet wide, and their upright side supports helped strengthen the structure of Wilton's old buildings. Before that Wilton had only about a dozen looms on which Jacquard, ingrain, and so-called Brussels and Wilton carpets were woven,[80] in relatively narrow strips that were then sewn together to make large carpets. The failure of the Axminster factory gave the Wilton firm the chance to diversify and expand its operations. Wilton and other English factories had been making another kind of cut pile, which the Wilton factory had apparently developed in the 1740's; but the technique was quite different from the hand-knotted, Turkish-type of knot made on Axminster's wide, vertical looms. In 1740 Henry, ninth earl of Pembroke and sixth earl of Montgomery (1693-1751), distinguished for his taste and talent in architecture, contributed to the development of the Wilton weaving factory.[81] In that year he encouraged skilled French weavers to come to Wilton, bringing with them a knowledge of how to weave so-called Brussels carpets, which originated in Belgium and of which the first English examples were woven at Wilton. Basically, the Wilton pile surface was a refinement of the loop pile characteristic of so-called Brussels carpets. In both the Brussels and Wilton techniques, pile was formed by weaving a supplementary warp over rods placed on the loom in such a way as to make loops that stood up on the surface of the carpet. In Brussels carpeting the loops were left uncut, while in the Wilton type a velvety surface was achieved by cutting the loops. Brussels carpets, as well as the Wilton type, were woven at Wilton on narrow, horizontal looms that produced strips three-quarters of a yard or a yard wide. Carpets made in the cut-loop-pile technique that was an early specialty of the Wilton factory came to be known as Wilton carpets in the eighteenth century regardless of where in the British Isles they were made, just as the term Axminster came to be used in the nineteenth century for any British carpet woven in the Turkish-knot technique developed by Thomas Whitty at Axminster.

Premiums were awarded in England in March 1757, 1758, and 1759 by the Royal Society of Arts and Sciences to encourage English production of carpets at least twelve by fifteen feet using the Turkish-knot technique that could compete with the imported Turkish carpets, and would preferably be as good but less expensive. Turkish and Persian carpets were held up as models. In 1757 Whitty tied for first place, in the first of the three competitions, with Thomas Moore of Moorfields. In 1758 Whitty tied for first with Passavant of Exeter, his only competitor. Because Whitty had already won a premium the year before, he was required to enter at least three carpets. In 1759 Whitty won first place alone. Moore and Passavant did not even enter the competition that year, and Whitty was required, as a previous winner, to enter at least six carpets. He had only one competitor, Jesser of Frome, who entered just one carpet. Two other factories besides Axminster that had wide, vertical looms on which they wove seamless carpets in the Turkish knot, many of them with purely English designs, were Exeter (which began about 1754 but apparently produced little in the decade before Passavant's death in 1776, and which a visitor in 1770 described as diminutive) and Moorfields (which was founded by 1755 and closed in 1795). Passavant signed his carpets *EXON* and also dated them. Moore often dated and signed his carpets *Thos. Moore*. Unfortunately, Whitty seems not to have signed his carpets produced at Axminster. Not much is known of the Frome factory after the March 1759 competition.

Against this background of English carpet-weaving history it is interesting to examine the design of the carpet in Copley's portrait of Jeremiah Lee. The striking similarity between that carpet and the English "Turkey" carpet illustrated in Plate XI becomes apparent on close analysis of the design and colors of the two. Copley has rendered the design of the field of the carpet faithfully enough, if somewhat crudely (although he has sketched the border pattern even more casually), for its pattern to be identified as having been based on the design of a certain type of carpet made at Ushak and other places in western Anatolia not far from the Aegean port now called Izmir but still known in the eighteenth century as Smyrna. In the eighteenth and nineteenth centuries many carpets of this and other designs were shipped from Smyrna to Europe and some were also copied there. The so-called Smyrna pattern represented in Plates X and XI itself is a provincial western Anatolian version of a much more ornate carpet design woven in the sixteenth century in the Ottoman court manufactories in Turkey and in Ottoman-dominated Cairo.[82] The English carpet in Plate XI is a close copy, in terms of color and drawing, of the version of this design that was woven at Ushak, of which several examples are known.[83] The representative of this provincial version of the Ottoman court manufactory design seen in Plate X, with its different colors and drawing, was apparently woven elsewhere in the Smyrna region. The carpet in the Lee portrait is several steps away from the Ottoman court manufactory "original," but, misunderstood as they were by the artist, the chief features of the design of a so-called Smyrna carpet (with a provincial version of the Ottoman court manufactory pattern) are apparent. In comparing elements in the carpets in Plates IX, X, and XI, it should be noticed that the direction of the design of the carpet in the painting is at right angles to the designs of the two carpets illustrated on the facing page. The dark-blue cross outlined in red on a yellow diamond by Lee's right foot may be compared with similar diamonds with crosses in red on white and in red on light blue in the English copy of an Ushak carpet seen in Plate XI. Also, the dark-blue and red polygon just above the cross in a diamond by Lee's right foot in the Copley portrait has its prototype in the English "Turkey"

Pl. XVII. *Still Life*, attributed to Cristoforo Monari da Reggio (d. 1720), signature and date 1709 unclear. Oil on canvas, 53⅝ by 39 inches. *Museum of Fine Arts, Houston; Samuel H. Kress collection.*

Pl. XVIII. Star Ushak carpet, Ushak, western Anatolia, seventeenth century. Wool; 12 feet, 2 inches by 6 feet, 7 inches. *Philadelphia Museum of Art.*

carpet in Plate XI. Although the artist has not depicted the border of the carpet faithfully enough for us to know exactly what the design of the border of the actual carpet he was portraying was, the main border of the carpet in the painting appears to be a crude version of the Anatolian stylized lotus palmette and vine pattern. The large carpet (made up of three fragments) at Tryon Palace (Pl. XI) has no borders, and the border patterns in the carpet at Ramsbury Manor from which the carpet at Tryon Palace was cut are perfunctory versions of various narrow guard stripes, with no main border. The drawing of the carpet in the Copley painting, particularly the border, would seem to point to English manufacture, although it could have been woven in Ushak. If it was English it may well have been made at Thomas Whitty's factory at Axminster because at the time that portrait was painted his factory was probably the most successful producer of large, seamless English "Turkey" carpets.

The weaving of so-called Turkey carpets in England is recorded by several American visitors, some of whom were particularly struck by the innovative technique (for England in the second half of the eighteenth century) used at Axminster, where they saw large, seamless carpets with Turkish, as well as English, designs being woven in the Turkish knot, very successfully imitating Oriental imports. One such traveler with a special interest in carpet weaving was an American named Samuel Rowland Fisher, a partner

in the Philadelphia firm of Joshua Fisher and Sons, who went to England several times in the latter half of the eighteenth century to avoid buying through agents. He noted in his journal[84] in 1767 that "Turkey Carpetts" were made at Worcester and that he visited large establishments in Kidderminster that made "Scotch, Wilton & Turkey Carpetts." By "Turkey Carpett" Fisher indicates that these were pile carpets, but not what the designs were nor whether they were narrow, strip carpeting such as that produced at Wilton in the cut-loop pile technique or the wide, seamless variety in the handknotted Turkish technique that distinguished Axminster's "Turkey" carpets, as well as Moorfields' and Exeter's, at that time.

A carpet like that in the Copley portrait of Jeremiah Lee or that in Plate XI may have been in progress when a Salem, Massachusetts, merchant named Samuel Curwen visited Thomas Whitty's factory at Axminster in 1777 and 1778. Curwen was a loyalist (but not a royalist) and chose to take refuge in England for nine years from 1775 and 1784, during the Revolutionary period. His wide-ranging travels in England are documented in his letters and in a meticulously kept diary. He went more than once to Axminster and on November 10, 1777, reports:

Here is also wrot beside his own of a peculiar construction, Turkey carpet so very like in figure color and thickness as not to be distinguished [from the genuine imported article]. They are wrote [wrought] in perpendicular looms by females, whose fingers, by use, move with a velocity beyond the power of the eye to follow. . . . There was working a most beautiful large one for the Countess of Salisbury of 36 feet square amounting to £96. From the following account he obtained the knowledge of making the Turkey carpets; an old fellow in ragged military garb stopping at his door desired to see his manufactory, always open for a 1/ fee from each visiter, a customary fee forming a fund for the labourers, divided every Christmas. The old man on being interrogated said he had wrot all over Europe in all kinds of businesses; in the Carpet way, yes, Turkey carpet, yes; from him he obtained his knowledge and now makes to as great perfection as the genuine, his carpets consist of one piece only, not like the other manufactories in widths of ¾ or ⁴/₄ [of a yard, thus twenty-seven or thirty-six inches] wide. The Wilton the next in value are 9/ apiece [per square yard], the Axminster 24/ [per square yard] as I was [told] the next day by his son who rode with my Companion and me to Lyme.[85]

The following August, Curwen was in that neighborhood again and on the seventeenth,

proceeded to Whitty carpet manufacture before noted, well known to the curious and wealthy by the name of the Axminster carpet; beside the one peculiar to himself he imitates the turkey to greatest perfection beside the elegance of the figure and shades they are closer [that is, more tightly woven] and much more substantial and are to the bigness required all wove together without seam as all others are. The price of best Wilton as told us by the young Whitty in our ride to Lyme together to be 8/ per [square] yard, of his fathers 24/.[86]

Among the apparently frequent "curious and wealthy" visitors who were favorably impressed by the Whitty carpet factory at Axminster was Abigail Adams, who accompanied her husband while he served as American minister to England. She was in Axminster nine years after Curwen's second trip there and records in her diary on July 26, 1787:

Went . . . to see the Manufactory of carpets for which this place is famous. The building in which this buisness [sic] is carried on is by no means equal to an American Barn. The whole Buisness is performed by women and children. The carpets are equally durable with the Turky, but surpass them in coulours and figure. They are made of coars wool and the best are 24 shillings a square yd., others at fourteen. They have but two prices.[87]

Mrs. Adams also described that visit to Axminster in a letter to her sister dated September 15, 1787:

The manufactory of the carpets is wholly performed by women and children. You would have been surprised to see in how ordinary a building this rich manufactory was carried on. A few glass windows in some of our barns would be equal to it. They have but two prices for their carpets woven here; the one is eighteen shillings [her diary entry, written on the day of the visit, is perhaps the more accurate], and the other twenty-four, a square yard. They are woven of any dimensions you please, and without a seam. The colors are most beautiful, and the carpets very durable.[88]

Just as the British had wanted to be able to make good domestic carpets that would undersell the Turkish imports, so in the new United States an enterprising American named William Peter Sprague, who opened the Philadelphia Carpet Manufactory shortly before 1791, aspired to make Axminster-type carpets in this country. He is reported to have made both ingrain carpets and, in June 1791, "those durable kind called *Turkey* and *Axminster*, which sell at 20 per cent cheaper than those imported, and nearly as low as Wilton carpeting, but of double its durability."[89]

Three of the examples of Gilbert Stuart's "Lansdowne" portrait of George Washington (see Pl. XII) include a carpet with the medallion Ushak design.[90] Allowance should be made for the fact that the artist seems to have simplified the carpet design; it is recognizable, however, as either a late Turkish example of the popular medallion Ushak

pattern, or a European imitation, like that shown in Plate XIII, which may have been woven either in Anatolia or somewhere in Europe. In late Turkish versions of the medallion Ushak pattern the drawing of the design became more angular, and the central medallion degenerated from a graceful oval to a squat, and even quite linear, hexagon. In the carpet in the Stuart portrait of Washington illustrated here the dark-blue spotlike motifs on a red ground (between Washington's feet) are not unlike the drawing in some late Turkish version of the stylized lotus flower and leaf motifs (usually blue on red) that fill the field between the center and corner medallions. In certain late Turkish examples these floral and foliate forms appear in a somewhat degenerate form as large, fairly regular spots rather than the more delicate and recognizably vegetal form in which they are seen in earlier versions of the medallion Ushak pattern. Again, as in the case of Plate VII, the lower edge of the portrait of Washington has unfortunately been cut off as illustrated here, eliminating part of the design of the carpet. In this case, the omitted part is important to a full understanding of the relationship between the carpet in Stuart's painting and that in Plate XIII. Stuart has represented under Washington's left foot the central medallion of the popular carpet design, but he has very much changed the motif, although it is still recognizable with its scalloped edge. He has reduced a large hexagon to a small diamond, and indicated more of the red field immediately behind his diamond-shape medallion, where one would expect to see, instead, more of the blue background of a large, hexagonal medallion. In the lower part of the portrait, which is cut off here and is therefore not seen in Plate XII, enough of the top of a yellow-rimmed pendant motif with an irregular outline immediately below the central medallion is indicated to make it apparent what the motif is. The corner quarter medallion, to which Washington's right toe points, has been simplified, and even Westernized, by the artist. An unusual Turkish example of a medallion Ushak carpet with a diamond-shape pendant motif exists in storage at the Museum of Turkish and Islamic Art in Istanbul,[91] but the pendants to the central medallion in this carpet design are normally the lobed form with an irregular outline seen in Plates II and XIII, as well as at the lower edge (which is cut off in Plate XII) of the three versions of the "Lansdowne" portrait of Washington that include a carpet. Whether Washington ever owned the carpet in his portrait is not known. Mount Vernon account books show that in 1757 and 1759 Washington purchased several Wilton carpets, including two Wilton ingrain bedside carpets; but the use of Turkey carpets (Oriental or Occidental) cannot be documented at Mount Vernon. In any case, Stuart painted the portrait in Philadelphia.

When paintings are used as documents in the study of carpets, the temptation to draw hasty conclusions must be resisted. While carpets in some paintings, judiciously deciphered, can yield valuable information, others, such as that in Plate XIV, are distinctly treacherous. This charming English conversation piece of the mid-eighteenth century portrays a carpet that is probably a European "Turkey" carpet inspired by an Oriental example, although it is not precisely like any particular known Oriental carpet design. The border is vaguely reminiscent of some Transylvanian church carpet borders, and the field, while it contains some purely European floral motifs, may have been remotely inspired by an Ushak design in a very general way. Since the architecture, furniture, and costume appear to indicate a somewhat earlier date for the painting than the late 1750's, when Thomas Whitty and others began to sell English-made Turkish imitations, the carpet in the painting in Plate XIV is perhaps Flemish. Also, the fact that it is so hard to tell whether the carpet in the painting might or might not be inspired by an Oriental design may be due to the artist's rather casual and inexact representation of the carpet. The carpet in the painting does, however, seem to be European rather than Eastern.

However remotely the carpet in the painting in Plate XIV may have been inspired by Oriental prototypes, that the border of one then much-imported type of so-called Transylvanian carpet (Pl. VI) was closely copied by English carpet weavers is clearly shown in the border of a surviving eighteenth-century English carpet (with a very English neoclassical field design) at Winterthur (Pl. XV). Some of the medallions in the border of that carpet contain a form sometimes called the ''turtle'' motif, which is also seen in Pl. VI. The carpet in Plate XVI has the same neoclassical field design as the carpet in Plate XV, and they may have been woven at the same English factory. Both have the bast weft that is characteristic of much English carpet weaving, and wool warp and pile. They are both fairly coarsely woven, with about twelve to eighteen knots to the square inch. Both are woven with the Turkish knot, and neither is woven in twenty-seven- or thirty-six-inch strips, and so could have been made at Axminster, or perhaps at Moorfields, where carpets with neoclassical patterns (some of them designed by Robert Adam) are known to have been woven. The entire carpet in Plate XVI seems, on close inspection, to be woven in one piece, without seams anywhere. The field of the carpet in Plate XV is woven in one piece, without seams, but the border is composed of three sections (the main border and each of the narrower guard borders flanking it) sewn together and attached to the field. This feature and the existence of another carpet with the same field design but a different border (Pl. XVI) would appear to indicate that this neoclassical field pattern could be ordered with a choice of different main and guard borders, which in some cases could be sewn on after the middle part of the carpet was woven. If the carpet in Plate XV was cut down at a later stage of its existence (as was the carpet represented by the fragmentary carpet in Plate XI), it does not seem likely that the border would have also been cut into three sections at that time; so the sectional borders may have been assembled at the time the carpet was first sold. The border design of the carpet in Plate XVI appears to have been derived from the type of border seen in certain Transylvanian church carpets like that shown in Plate XX. It is even more Anglicized than the border of the carpet in Plate XV, and the awkward corner solution in both carpets is not at all Oriental; but an Oriental kinship can be traced in the border of Plate XVI too. Such a relationship with imports from the East is not inconsistent with the eighteenth-century (and earlier) English practice of looking to the much-sought-after Oriental carpets for inspiration.

Because there are so few, half a dozen at the most, American paintings before the nineteenth century that include so-called Turkey carpets—made in the East or West—it can be useful to study certain English or Continental paintings for further clues as to what actual Oriental, or psuedo-Oriental, carpets would have been available to Americans in the seventeenth and eighteenth centuries, and could have been among those tantalizing references in contemporary written records to undescribed ''Turkey carpets.'' There are a great many European paintings that show

carpets, and a certain informed selectivity must be exercised in picking out those that could be helpful to the study of the decorative arts in America. The three illustrated here (Pls. XVII, XIX, XXI) may serve to widen our perspective on carpets that could have graced American tables and floors before the nineteenth century.

The Italian painting in Plate XVII shows a Turkish carpet design related to the medallion Ushak (Pls. I, II, XII, XIII), but not (according to evidence gleaned from European paintings) imported into Europe in quite as large quantities. This design is known as the star Ushak (Pl. XVIII). A closer match than Plate XVIII for the motifs in the border of the carpet in the painting in Plate XVII is a star Ushak carpet given by Joseph V. McMullan to the Metropolitan Museum of Art.[92] The border of the McMullan carpet, like that of the carpet in the painting in Plate XVII, also has the same ground color as the field. This striking pattern was a favorite in the West, and is seen in English, Flemish, and Italian paintings[93] from the first half of the sixteenth century onward, among them the still life attributed to Christoforo Monari da Reggio illustrated in Plate XVII. The design of eight-pointed-star-shape medallions alternating with diamond shapes in offset rows was woven in Ushak in western Anatolia in the sixteenth and seventeenth centuries and possibly in the eighteenth as well. The star Ushak pattern was also copied in Europe in the late sixteenth century, when three carpets were woven for Sir Edward Montagu; they are now owned by his descendant the duke of Buccleuch and Queensberry.[94] A few in this design, which were usually made in moderately large sizes, could perhaps have reached the American colonies.

Smaller carpets of so-called prayer-carpet size (those that were occasionally referred to as ''musket'' or ''segiadya'' in eighteenth-century newspaper advertisements) from western Anatolia and perhaps Turkish-dominated eastern Europe with a variety of designs that include those seen in paintings by Smibert (Pl. V) and Feke (Pl. VII) and in the portrait tentatively attributed to Kühn (Pl. III), are found in many European paintings and indicate a large Western importation of such small carpets. Two are seen in the Dutch paintings illustrated in Plates XIX and XXI. The English, as well as the Dutch, imported such carpets directly from the East, and at certain periods the English obtained them indirectly through Holland. Nicolaes van Gelder's still life (Pl. XIX) includes a carpet with a triple arch supported by thin pairs of columns, similar to the carpet illustrated in Plate XX and characteristic of one carpet design sometimes attributed without any definite evidence to Ladik, near Konya.[95] (Carpets with the coupled-column design are not as narrow as Ladik carpets characteristically are.) The design of the carpet in the painting is seen from the side, with the border of the carpet at the lower edge of the canvas. A snail is depicted crawling on one of the columns, and the spandrels above the arches are shown to the left of the roses draped over the edge of the table. In the carpet in Plate XX the three large, curved, serrated leaves in the blue spandrels above the arches are unusual; normally there are two such leaves in that position in this design. Some of the carpets preserved in Transylvanian churches have a similar field design.[96] The triple-arch, coupled-column pattern is ultimately derived from one of the sixteenth-century Ottoman court prayer carpet designs,[97] of which the later Anatolian versions, and those found in Transylvanian churches, are provincial adaptations.

Pieter de Hooch's domestic scene of a musical gathering

Pl. XXI. *The Music Party*, by Pieter de Hooch (1629-1681), c. 1665. Oil on canvas, 39½ by 46⅞ inches. *Cleveland Museum of Art.*

Pl. XXII. So-called Ghiordes prayer rug, Ghiordes, western Anatolia, probably early nineteenth century. Wool; 6 feet by 4 feet, 4½ inches. *Collection of Charles Grant Ellis, Nelson photograph.*

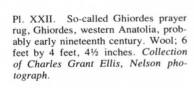

179

illustrated in Plate XXI shows a very precisely depicted carpet with a type of single-arch design found in some Transylvanian church carpets and also in Turkish Ghiordes prayer carpets such as that illustrated in Plate XXII. The carpet in the painting is draped over the table so that the yellow border and the top of the field design with an orange and red oblong panel above the arch are seen. The colors and the less crowded rendering of the border design of the carpet in the painting are more characteristic of the Transylvanian church carpets with this design than of Ghiordes prayer carpets.[98] The patterns of both the field and border that are typical of this variety of Transylvanian church carpet as well as of the Ghiordes prayer carpet represent provincial versions of a design directly or indirectly derived from a more ornate carpet design made in sixteenth-century Ottoman court manufactories with a single arch supported by two columns, one at each side, and a border of alternating palmettes and rosettes with pairs of curving leaves above or below them. The border was also used with other Ottoman-court-manufactory field designs.[99] The wide, flat-woven end finish of the carpet in De Hooch's painting, with its long fringe, is typical of some of the many so-called Transylvanian carpets. Such long warp ends were often yellow or red, a feature of rugs seen in northern European paintings of the seventeenth and early eighteenth centuries.

That useful source of information on the decorative arts, Thomas Sheraton's *Cabinet Dictionary*, published just after the close of the eighteenth century, sums up the contemporary view of carpets for fashionable houses in England, and in America among those who followed England's lead in such matters:

Carpets of various manufactories, have been a leading article of a well furnished house, for some years past. I cannot, from present information, find the aera [*sic*] in which carpeting was first invented: but from some citations of Shakespear, they seem to have been in use at that time. The Persian and Turkey carpets, are those most esteemed. The Parisian carpets are a tolerable imitation of these. But besides the Persian, Turkey, and Parisian carpets, there are the following sorts, which have their names [not so in all cases] from the places where they are manufactured; as

Brussels carpet, the metropolis of the dukedom of Brabant. [the technique originated there and was later adopted in England]
Kidderminster—a town in Worcestershire.
Wilton—a town in Wiltshire.
Axbridge—in Somersetshire. [Sheraton may have meant Axminster, which is in Devonshire.]
Venetian carpet, generally striped [a type of ingrain]. And Scots carpet [Scotch, or ingrain], which is one of the most inferior kind.[100]

Relatively few Americans in the seventeenth and eighteenth centuries were fortunate enough to possess carpets with Oriental designs. Those who could afford such luxuries acquired them, before the Revolution, indirectly, via England. From the evidence of paintings, carpets were imported into Europe before the nineteenth century from only those parts of the East, chiefly Turkey, that were accessible to sea trade. Paintings also show that these colorful imports were imitated and their designs were adapted in Europe in an attempt to satisfy the great demand for these decorative floor coverings and to supply locally made substitutes for the expensive imports. The few references to so-called Turkey carpets in contemporary documents give all too little information about the specific patterns that would have been seen in such carpets. Paint-

ings of the period, however, provide valuable clues in the study of this aspect of the decorative arts used in seventeenth- and eighteenth-century America. Carpets with Oriental designs never went out of style in the seventeenth and eighteenth centuries and were very highly prized in both England and America to complement all styles of furniture from Elizabethan and Jacobean through the late eighteenth-century neoclassical. They provided not only protection against cold and noise but, for the lucky few, a sybaritic luxury and a touch of exotic color.

I would welcome information about additional seventeenth- and eighteenth-century written references to Oriental carpets or carpets with Oriental designs (usually referred to then as Turkey carpets) in this country as well as information about, and slides or photographs of, other paintings (American or European, particularly those done before the nineteenth century) that include such carpets.

[1] Abbott Lowell Cummings, *Rural Household Inventories, 1675-1775* (Boston, 1964), p. 245 (1771); George Francis Dow, *The Arts and Crafts in New England 1704-1775, Gleanings from Boston Newspapers* (Topsfield, Massachusetts, 1927), pp. 92 (1763), 119 (1761), 170 (1761); Rita Susswein Gottesman, *The Arts and Crafts in New York, 1726-1776* (New York, 1938), p. 126 (1774).

[2] C.E.C. Tattersall, *A History of British Carpets* (Essex, England, 1934), p. 40; and May H. Beattie, "Antique Rugs at Hardwick Hall," *Oriental Art*, Summer 1969, pp. 52-61; and Beattie, "Oriental Carpets at Hardwick Hall," *Country Life Annual*, 1961, pp. 98-103.

[3] Tattersall, *History of British Carpets*, p. 41.

[4] Tattersall, *History of British Carpets*, pp. 42-43.

[5] The so-called Turkish knot can be made equally well woven on a loom or worked with a needle on a coarse canvas (or even, in some cases, silk) foundation. There are varying opinions among authorities as to whether all of the smaller pieces of English and American turkeywork usually used for upholstery were worked by needle or woven. Large, knotted-pile carpets should not be classified with smaller pieces of turkeywork used as upholstery, and in a discussion of techniques these should be considered separately. Also, in eighteenth- and even early nineteenth-century documents the words "work" and "workt" often refer to embroidered fabrics, wrought with a needle (see *Bed Hangings, a Treatise on Fabrics and Styles in the Curtaining of Beds, 1650-1850*, compiled by Abbott Lowell Cummings, Boston, 1961, pp. 37, 38). Irene Emery (in *The Primary Structures of Fabrics*, Washington, D.C., 1966, p. 245) states that "the sewing method was used in the seventeenth and eighteenth centuries to imitate 'knotted carpets' in the needlework known as 'Turkey work.'" Georgiana Brown Harbeson (in *American Needlework*, New York, 1938, pp. 41-42) also calls turkeywork needlework; she explains how it was done by colonists, and distinguishes the American technique from that of work imported from England as the latter is described by Tattersall in *History of British Carpets*, pp. 51-52. (This is perhaps a dubious distinction.) Two other books that also describe how turkeywork was done with a needle for upholstery (by professional embroiderers and by skillful amateur needlewomen working at home) are Therle Hughes, *English Domestic Needlework, 1660-1860* (New York, 1961), pp. 32, 46, 105; and Frances Little, *Early American Textiles* (New York, 1931), p. 171. Hughes also states (p. 105) that "Sometimes the formalised flower patterns associated with this work [turkeywork] are surrounded by coarse cross stitch, suggesting amateur work." Apparently the pile was an additional decorative stitch, done with a needle as was the cross stitch. Mary Symonds and Louisa Preece in *Needlework through the Ages* (London, 1928) also indicate that a mixture of different embroidery stitches sometimes appears in the same piece of work, among them turkeywork pile: "Some pieces of Turkey work were evidently woven on a loom [the authors are apparently referring to carpets], but much of it is true embroidery on a very coarse canvas, easily observable on examination. The entire surface might be covered with pile work, or the pattern only in pile with the background in a large cross stitch, frequently on black or dark brown silk" (pp. 268-269). Symonds and Preece also discuss and illustrate the turkeywork covering of chairs at Holyrood Palace that have a pile pattern on a flat black silk ground (p. 281, Pl. LXIII). Tattersall (in *History of British Carpets*, pp. 51-52) makes the only case against needlework, which he based on technical considerations with which some scholars today, and in the past, who have examined turkeywork closely would not necessarily agree. More technical study remains to be done by those well versed in both weaving and needlework skills, comparing a large number of examples of turkeywork used for upholstery to determine whether or not all of it was done with embroidery needles. The so-called Persian or Sehna knot (used elsewhere in the East as well as in Persia) was not used in English carpet weaving or turkeywork.

[6] Four late sixteenth-century carpets (one dated 1584, another 1585) owned by the Duke of Buccleuch and Queensberry, a descendant of Sir Edward

Montagu for whom they were made, with remarkably exact renderings of two well-known sixteenth-century Turkish designs, are either of Flemish or English manufacture. One is in the so-called Lotto design, the other three are in the star Ushak design (illustrated in Tattersall, *A History of British Carpets*, Pls. II, III top, and IV top). Documents indicating Flemish and English imitations of Turkish carpets are cited in May H. Beattie, "Britain and the Oriental Carpet," *Leeds Art Calendar*, No. 55 (Leeds, 1964); Tattersall, *History of British Carpets*; Bertram Jacobs, *Axminster Carpets (hand-made), 1755-1957* (Leigh-on-Sea, 1970); F. Fredricx, "Tissus importés et exportés par Anvers au XVIe siècle," *Textilis* (Ghent, March 1968) pp. 13-20; and Fredricx, "Anciens tapis d'Occident, tapis oubliés," *Textilis* (August 1965), pp. 15-18.

[7] Hughes, *English Domestic Needlework*, p. 133.

[8] Dow, *Arts and Crafts*, p. 92 (1763), p. 119 (1761), p. 170 (1761); Thomas Sheraton, *The Cabinet Dictionary* (London, 1803; reprinted New York, 1970), Vol. I, p. 132; Cummings, *Rural Household Inventories*, p. xxxii (an example in New Hampshire, 1768). Also out of date by that period—and in any case hardly likely to have been obtainable by the early American colonists or their parents—were the Persian, silk, so-called "Polonaise" carpets (some of which were enriched with brocading in silver or silver-gilt threads) acquired by some titled European families in the seventeenth century. That Persian design almost never appears in European paintings. Rare instances of carpets with two other Persian designs, very likely made in India and exported to Europe in the East India trade, are depicted in two European paintings in the Prado in Madrid: Juan de Pareja's *The Calling of St. Matthew* of 1661, and *The Virgin and Child Worshipped by St. Louis, King of France*, by Claudio Coello (c. 1630-1693). These, like the "Polonaise" carpets, are too exceptional and, like those and carpets with the so-called Indo-Isfahan design, too early, among the numbers of Oriental carpets to reach Europe to support a belief that there were any carpets woven in Persia in American houses in the seventeenth and eighteenth centuries.

[9] Hans Bidder, *Carpets from Eastern Turkestan* (New York, 1964), pp. 19-20.

[10] "Septième Voyage du Père Gerbillon à Ning hia fait à la suite de l'Empereur de la Chine en l'année 1697," Jean Baptiste du Halde, *Description géographique, historique, chronologique, politique, et physique de l'Empire de la Chine et de la Tartarie chinoise* (Paris, 1735), Vol. IV, p. 372; and quoted in part in Beattie, *The Thyssen-Bornemisza Collection of Oriental Rugs* (Castagnola, Ticino, Switzerland, 1972), pp. 73 and 74, n. 1.

[11] In his Letter-Book of 1771-1833 (unpublished ms. in the Arents Collection, New York Public Library), Charles Carroll of Carrollton (1737-1832) distinguishes between rugs (or ruggs) and carpets (including "Turkey carpets"). The eighteenth-century Boston newspaper advertisements listed in Dow, *Arts and Crafts*, also indicate what was specifically meant by the terms carpet and rug at that period.

[12] Gottesman, *The Arts and Crafts in New York, 1777-1799* (New York, 1954), p. 151, No. 485.

[13] Gottesman, *The Arts and Crafts in New York, 1800-1804* (New York, 1965), p. 156, No. 384.

[14] The inventory is listed in part in Joseph Downs, *American Furniture, Queen Anne and Chippendale Periods* (New York, 1952), under the entry for No. 227; also cited in Marion Day Iverson, *The bed rug in colonial America*, ANTIQUES, January 1964, p. 108.

[15] Downs, *American Furniture*, entry for No. 227; Iverson, *The bed rug in colonial America*, p. 108.

[16] In addition to the inventories and advertisements cited in this article, the presence of Turkey carpets in New York in the early eighteenth century is indicated by inventories quoted in Esther Singleton's *Social New York Under the Georges, 1714-1776* (New York, 1902), pp. 58 (a 1705 inventory listing "three Turkey-work carpets") and 60 (a 1718 inventory also listing "three Turkey-work carpets").

[17] One such instance is documented in the 1601 inventory of Hardwick Hall, which lists numerous Turkish carpets (chiefly used on tables and cupboards) and distinguishes between them and "Carpets of Turkey work," with pile resembling that of Turkish carpets but made in the West. See Beattie, "Antique Rugs at Hardwick Hall," pp. 52-61; and Beattie, "Oriental Carpets at Hardwick Hall," pp. 98-103. Other English country houses with Oriental carpets that have been there since an early date are Berkeley Castle, Montacute, Knole, and the Red Lodge, which is part of the Bristol City Art Gallery.

[18] Ludovico Guicciardini, *Descrittione* (Antwerp, 1567), cited in Fredricx, "Tissus importés," p. 16.

[19] A 1524 will, referred to in Fredricx, "Tissus importés," p. 18.

[20] "Guicciardini's Description of the Trade of Antwerp, 1560," *Tudor Economic Documents*, ed. Richard Henry Tawney and Eileen Edna Power (London, 1924), Vol. 3, p. 155; and quoted in part in Beattie, "Britain and the Oriental Carpet," p. 11.

[21] Beattie, "Britain and the Oriental Carpet," pp. 10, 11; Sheraton, *Cabinet Dictionary*, Vol. I, p. 40.

[22] Fredricx, "A Propos de quelques tapis de table du palais Mazarin," *Textilis*, April 1959, pp. 15-20.

[23] Kurt Erdmann, *Seven Hundred Years of Oriental Carpets*, ed. Hanna Erdmann and trans. by May H. Beattie and Hildegard Herzog (Berkeley and Los Angeles, 1970), Fig. 253.

[24] The ancestor of our table was the medieval plank of wood on sawhorses, which required a covering of some sort. The French word *bureau* for desk derives from one of the types of fabric used in fourteenth-century Europe by bankers to cover tables that were used for counting money; this was a coarse, brown wool cloth, sometimes striped, known as *bure* or *bureau*; the word gradually became used for worktables that would be covered with a cloth. (Fredricx, "A Propos," p. 16.)

[25] Ephraim Orcutt Jameson, *The Cogswells in America* (Boston, 1884), pp. 11-12; and quoted in part in Cummings, *Rural Household Inventories*, p. xvi.

[26] Little, *Early American Textiles*, pp. 219-220.

[27] On record at Essex Courthouse. In W. G. Standard, "Abstracts of Virginia Land Patents," *The Virginia Magazine of History and Biography* (July 1895), Vol. 3, p. 64; cited in Rodris Roth, "Floor Coverings in 18th-Century America," *United States National Museum Bulletin 250, Contributions from the Museum of History and Technology*, Paper 59, pp. 1-64 (Washington, D.C., 1967), p. 4.

[28] Cummings, *Rural Household Inventories*, p. 55.

[29] I am indebted to R. Peter Mooz for information about the Boston inventories for Governor William Burnet (1729), Peter Faneuil (1743), Charles Apthorp (1759), and James Bowdoin (1774).

[30] Suffolk County Probate Books, Vol. 42, pp. 155-164; cited in Roth, "Floor Coverings," p. 4.

[31] Cummings, *Rural Household Inventories*, p. 245.

[32] Hall of Records, Annapolis, Maryland, Box 33, Folder 2. I am indebted to Gregory R. Weidman for bringing this inventory, and others, to my attention.

[33] Cummings, *Bed Hangings, passim*.

[34] Quoted in Hughes, *English Domestic Needlework*, p. 122.

[35] See Roth, "Floor Coverings," p. 6, n. 8.

[36] Alfred Coxe Prime, *The Arts and Crafts in Philadelphia, Maryland and South Carolina, 1721-1785* (Topsfield, Massachusetts, 1929), and *The Arts and Crafts in Philadelphia, Maryland and South Carolina, 1786-1800* (Topsfield, 1932), *passim*.

[37] *Boston Gazette*, March 26, 1754; cited in Dow, *Arts and Crafts*, p. 113.

[38] Dow, *Arts and Crafts*, pp. 113, 116, 119, 121, 124, 128.

[39] Dow, *Arts and Crafts*, p. 114.

[40] From an unpublished typescript of excerpts from London newspapers in the research papers of Robert Wemyss Symonds at the library of the Henry Francis du Pont Wintherthur Museum. I am indebted to Karol A. Schmiegel for bringing these three advertisements to my attention.

[41] The term "muskitto Carpett" is found in a 1612 book of accounts at Hardwick Hall in England, which also records the purchase over the years of other Oriental carpets; cited in Beattie, "Antique Rugs at Hardwick Hall," p. 60.

[42] Various spellings of the Italian word for mosque (mesquita, mosquita, or moskyta) are used in Richard Hakluyt, *Hakluyt's Collection of the Early Voyages, Travels, and Discoveries, of the English Nation* (London, 1598-1600; reprinted London, 1809-1812), ad cited in Beattie, "Antique Rugs at Hardwick Hall," p. 61.

[43] A discussion of the term *sajjada* and citations of its use in fourteenth-and early nineteenth-century texts is given in Richard Ettinghausen's essay "The Early History, Use and Iconography of the Prayer Rug," in the exhibition catalogue entitled *Prayer Rugs*, published by the Textile Museum (Washington, D.C., 1974), pp. 10-25.

[44] John Fanning Watson, *Annals of Philadelphia* (Philadelphia, 1830), p. 185.

[45] Rodris Roth surveyed inventories of the Boston region for selected years in the mid-eighteenth century and found very few that included floor coverings at all, and of those, even fewer that specified Turkey carpets ("Floor Coverings," p. 7).

[46] Massachusetts Archives VI, p. 301; cited in Cummings, *Rural Household Inventories*, p. xxxii.

[47] *Diary and Autobiography of John Adams*, ed. L.H. Butterfield, asst. eds. Leonard C. Faber and Wendell D. Garrett, Vol. 1, *Diary 1755-1770* (Cambridge, Massachusetts, 1961), p. 294.

[48] New Hampshire Archives, Court Files, case no. 25135; cited in Cummings, *Rural Household Inventories*, p. xxxii.

[49] Letter from Deborah Franklin to Benjamin Franklin, Philadelphia, fall of 1765. In Edward Riley, "Franklin's Home," *Transactions of the American Philosophical Society*, 1953, new series, Vol. 43, part 1, p. 153.

[50]Letter from Benjamin Franklin to Deborah Franklin, London, April 1766. In *The Writings of Benjamin Franklin*, ed. Albert Henry Smyth (New York, 1905-1907), Vol. 4, p. 450.

[51]"Letters of Charles Carroll, Barrister," *Maryland Historical Magazine* (December 1937), Vol. 32, p. 367.

[52]See ANTIQUES for October 1975, pp. 736-743.

[53]Charles Carroll, Letter-Book 1771-1833.

[54]*Ibid.*

[55]*Ibid.*

[56]Sheraton, *Cabinet Dictionary*, Vol. I, p. 40. The 1952 unabridged edition of *Webster's Dictionary* describes baize in much the same way Sheraton did: "A coarse woolen stuff, with a long nap, sometimes frizzed on one side, without wale, and woven with two treadles, like flannel." Webster's *Third International Dictionary* indicates that the coarsely woven woolen or cotton fabric was "napped to imitate felt." The name apparently comes from the fabric's original bay, or chestnut, color.

[57]Cited in Roth, "Floor Coverings," p. 28.

[58]*Ibid.*

[59]*The Toilet of Flora* (London, 1775), cited in Roth, "Floor Coverings," p. 54.

[60]Gottesman, *Arts and Crafts, 1726-1776*, pp. 284-285.

[61]Gottesman, *Arts and Crafts, 1777-1799*, p. 206, No. 676.

[62]The most recent published discussion of the variations of this design and the several places it may have been made is in Charles Grant Ellis, "The 'Lotto' Pattern as a Fashion in Carpets," *Festschrift für Peter Wilhelm Meister* (Hamburg, 1975), pp. 19-31. On page 23 Mr. Ellis makes a provocative suggestion about a possible eastern European origin for certain varieties of the so-called Lotto design and, by implication, of other carpet designs in the Turkish manner.

[63]Illustrated in Radisics Elemér, *Magyar Lélek Magyar Munka* (Budapest, 1943), p. 84. This carpet was woven in Transylvania, part of which, at the time this book was published, had been assigned to Hungary.

[64]For detailed information about Smibert's two canvases of the Bermuda Group see Henry Wilder Foote, *John Smibert, Painter* (Cambridge, Massachusetts, 1950) and *The Notebook of John Smibert*, with essays by Sir David Evans, John Kerslake, and Andrew Oliver (Boston, 1969), *passim*.

[65]Two are illustrated in Jules de Végh and Charles Layer, *Tapis Turcs Provenant des Eglises et Collections de Transylvanie* (Paris, 1925), Pls. XIII, XIV; another, in Joseph V. McMullan, *Islamic Carpets* (New York, 1965), No. 88; yet another is in the Black Church, Braşov, Transylvania, Romania (unpublished).

[66]See Foote, *Smibert*, pp. 117-118.

[67]Cummings, *Rural Household Inventories*, p. xxviii; the contents of the entire inventory (which is on file in the Probate Court in East Cambridge, Massachusetts) are printed in Gladys N. Hoover, *The Elegant Royalls of Colonial New England* (New York, 1974), pp. 31-38.

[68]The design of this table leg derives from a plate in Nicolas Pineau's *Nouveaux Desseins de Pieds de Table*, which was plagiarized by Batty and Thomas Langley in *The City and Country Builder's and Workman's Treasury of Designs* (London, 1740). *Cf.* side table illustrated in Desmond Fitz-Gerald, *Victoria and Albert Museum, Georgian Furniture* (London, 1969), No. 42.

[69]I am grateful to Mr. Mooz for bringing the Vanderbank portrait to my attention as an influence on the Copley portrait of Jeremiah Lee.

[70]Illustrated in Ellis K. Waterhouse, *Painting in Britain, 1530-1790* (London, 1953), No. 100.

[71]Again, I would like to thank Mr. Mooz, for pointing out the Smibert portraits of Mr. and Mrs. William Browne as a possible precedent for Copley's paintings of Mr. and Mrs. Jeremiah Lee.

[72]Foote, *Smibert*, pp. 138-140. The portraits of Mr. and Mrs. William Browne are listed in *The Notebook of John Smibert* as No. 92 and No. 158; see pp. 92, 95, 110, and 114.

[73]Photocopies of the inventories and wills of Mr. and Mrs. Jeremiah Lee are kept at the Lee House in Marblehead. The originals are filed at the Probate Court of Essex County, Massachusetts, in Salem.

[74]Jacobs, *Axminster Carpets*, p. 49, Pls. 27, 35. See also Christopher Hussey, "Ramsbury Manor, Part II," *Country Life*, December 14, 1961, p. 1526.

[75]See records at Tryon Palace Restoration, New Bern, North Carolina; and Jacobs, *Axminster Carpets*, p. 49.

[76]Hussey, "Ramsbury Manor, Part III," *Country Life*, December 21, 1961, p. 1580. See also Hussey, "Ramsbury Manor, Part I," *Country Life*, December 7, 1961, pp. 1376-1380; and Oliver Hill and John Cornforth, "Ramsbury Manor, Wiltshire," *English Country Houses, Caroline, 1625-1685* (London, 1966), pp. 178-183.

[77]"The stem structures of dicotyledonous plants provide bast fibers—notably *flax* (linen); also jute, hemp, ramie, apocynum, nettle, et cetera" (Emery, *Primary Structures*, p. 5).

[78]Cited in Bertram Jacobs, *The Story of British Carpets* (London, 1968), pp. 20-26; also in Jacobs, *Axminster Carpets*, pp. 21-26; and in Tattersall, *History of British Carpets*, pp. 67-69.

[79]Tattersall, *History of British Carpets*, pp. 74, 170.

[80]Jacobs, *Axminster Carpets*, p. 60.

[81]Tattersall, *History of British Carpets*, pp. 120, 170.

[82]Kurt Erdmann, *Oriental Carpets*, trans. by Charles Grant Ellis (Tübingen, Germany, 1960), Nos. 129, 136.

[83]There is one eighteenth-century example attributed to Ushak at Hearst Castle, San Simeon, California; another is at Berkeley Castle, England; and there are three more in the royal palace in Stockholm. I am grateful to May H. Beattie and Charles Grant Ellis for bringing these to my attention and for sharing with me their technical notes on these carpets as well as on the carpets illustrated in Plates XI, XV, and XVI. The San Simeon, Berkeley Castle, and Stockholm carpets are all made entirely of wool, including the weft (which is bast in the carpets in Pls. XI, XV, and XVI). The knot counts per square inch for the five Ushaks are thirty-six to fifty-six in the San Simeon example (it is unevenly woven), thirty-three in the Berkeley Castle example, and twenty in all three Stockholm examples.

[84]Samuel Rowland Fisher [ms. diary, First Trip to England, 1767-1768], *The Diaries of Samuel Rowland Fisher, 1745-1834*, owned by the Historical Society of Pennsylvania (Am. 0652-11); also on microfilm in the Joseph Downs Manuscript Collection at the library of the Henry Francis du Pont Winterthur Museum (M-296). It was quoted in a lecture by Charles F. Hummel.

[85]*The Journal of Samuel Curwen, Loyalist*, ed. Andrew Oliver (Cambridge, Massachusetts, 1972), p. 412.

[86]*Ibid.*, p. 473.

[87]*Abigail Adams' Diary of A Tour from London to Plymouth, 20-28 July 1787*, in *Diary and Autobiography of John Adams*, Vol. 3, pp. 206-207.

[88]Letter from Abigail Adams to Mary Cranch, London, September 15, 1787, in *Letters of Mrs. Adams, The Wife of John Adams*, ed. Charles Francis Adams (Boston, 1840), p. 383.

[89]*New-York Magazine; or, Literary Repository* for June 1791, No. VI, Vol. II, pp. 311-312; in the William L. Clements Library; and on microfilm in the Henry Francis du Pont Winterthur Museum, Joseph Downs Manuscript Collection (M-353); also cited as from the *Pennsylvania Gazette of the United States* in Roth, "Floor Coverings," p. 44.

[90]Besides the portrait in Plate XII, the other two examples of Stuart's "Lansdowne" portrait of Washington with the carpet are in a Scottish private collection and at the Brooklyn Museum. Stuart had hoped to provide for a comfortable old age with the engraving rights of this portrait, which were, maddeningly for him, pirated. For a discussion of the circumstances surrounding the execution of the original and first replica of the portrait, see Robert C. Alberts, *The Golden Voyage, the Life and Times of William Bingham, 1752-1804* (Boston, 1969), pp. 290-293. For a complete discussion of the three versions of this portrait that have the carpet, see John Hill Morgan and Mantle Fielding, *The Life Portraits of Washington and their Replicas* (Philadelphia, 1931), pp. 223, 238, 260-262, 355-359.

[91]I would like to acknowledge my debt, once again, to Mrs. Beattie for bringing this carpet, also, to my attention.

[92]McMullan, *Islamic Carpets*, No. 67.

[93]One is seen in the portrait by Paul van Somer I, dated 1614, of *Edmund, Third Baron Sheffield, First Earl of Mulgrave*, now at Colonial Williamsburg (illustrated in Mildred B. Lanier, *English and Oriental Carpets at Williamsburg*, Williamsburg, 1975, No. 26A). The carpet in that painting is somewhat freely rendered by the artist and may be an English or Flemish imitation.

[94]Tattersall, *History of British Carpets*, Pls. II, III top.

[95]See Beattie, "Coupled-Column Prayer Rugs," *Oriental Art*, Winter 1968, particularly pp. 251-255.

[96]Beattie and Ellis as quoted in *Prayer Rugs*, p. 54. A carpet with this design (and border motifs drawn in a similar, not particularly crisp, manner) found in the Protestant Church in Braşov, Transylvania, is illustrated in Végh and Layer, *Tapis Turcs*, Pl. XXV.

[97]See *Prayer Rugs*, No. I.

[98]One Transylvanian church carpet with colors and a border similar to those of the carpet in the De Hooch painting is illustrated in Végh and Layer, *Tapis Turcs*, Pl. XVIII. Another similar carpet is in the Black Church in Braşov (unpublished). The particular form of the oblong panel above the arch in the carpet in the painting is seen in Pl. XIX in Végh and Layer.

[99]The Ottoman court manufactory prototype for the field and border is seen in Erdman, *Oriental Carpets*, No. 138. A similar prototype for the border alone is seen in Erdman, *Oriental Carpets*, Pl. VII and Nos. 129-132.

[100]Sheraton, *Cabinet Dictionary*, Vol. I, p. 132.

The Turkey carpet in early America

BY JOSEPH V. McMULLAN

Top. Late seventeenth-century "Transylvania" rug of the best type, showing cartouche alternating with eight-point star in border. Red ground; details blue, white, and yellow.

Middle. *Dean Berkeley and His Entourage*, by John Smibert, 1729. *Yale University Art Gallery.*

Bottom. *Isaac Royall and Family*, by Robert Feke, 1741. *William Hayes Fogg Art Museum.*

Opposite page. Eighteenth-century "Transylvania." Note that the star has been dropped from the border design. Beige ground; details red and blue.

All rugs illustrated are in the author's collection.

DURING THE GOLDEN AGE — from about 1520 to about 1820 — of domestic architecture and decoration in England and on the Continent, Asia made two significant contributions to household adornment in the western world: China trade porcelain (miscalled Oriental Lowestoft) from Asia East, and "Turkey" carpets from Asia West. The first gave a light, gay touch to drawing rooms and bedrooms, and lovely settings for the table. The second brought abstract design and clear, well-balanced color to the floor, the foundation of any room. Together the two added beauty and richness to interiors, providing a wonderful complement to polished woods, painted or paneled walls, colorful draperies and upholstery, so that the whole achieved the coherence and balance which mark true sophistication.

Carpets and rugs came westward in the sixteenth century, followed by porcelain in the seventeenth and eighteenth. Both disappeared about 1820: the porcelain forever, doomed by trade restrictions in China and the development of extensive porcelain industries in Europe; the rugs, temporarily eclipsed by the Jacquard loom and protective tariffs, until the revival of interest in the 1870's.

Henry VIII first introduced the carpets and rugs of the Orient to the English-speaking world. He knew of them, wanted them in quantity, and got them, as he did his wives. Tangible evidence of their arrival (it took Cardinal Wolsey's connections and the Venetian caravels) appears in a familiar Holbein picture of Henry, who takes his proud stance on a Turkish carpet of the "Ushakh" type — one of the group which enriched the floors of his newly-erected palace at Hampton Court. As the sixteenth century progressed England widened her trade connections with the East, and British nobility emulated the monarch. The Montagues still possess a Star Ushakh which has come down through the family from at least 1580. Dur-

ing Elizabeth's time, and somewhat later too, normal supplies were supplemented by loot from unfortunate Spanish, Portuguese, and Dutch trading ships.

Regardless of place of origin, virtually all of these rugs came to Europe by way of Turkey and hence were universally known as "Turkey" carpets. Most were of Turkish origin, but many came to Turkish ports from the Caucasus and Persia. Curiously enough, the early China trade brought no rugs to Europe. Few, if any, reached Canton or any other accessible trade port during that period, and the rugs known as Chinese were actually Mongolian. Rugs of Central Asia and Chinese Turkestan, so-called Bokharas and Samarkands, were likewise unknown to the West until practically our own times. These types, therefore, whether of the period or not, form no essential part of our subject.

In America the colonists who acquired wealth in the seaport towns and on the great plantations of the Tidewater, and their successors in the new Republic, formed a group with the means, the taste, and the connections to follow the new trend. They built fine homes and filled them with beautiful furnishings — and they imported Oriental rugs. Inventory after inventory mentions Turkey carpets, and we know with certainty that they were here and keenly appreciated. But not one documented piece of the late seventeenth century, the entire eighteenth, or even the early nineteenth century has come to light in an American family. That being the case, how can we know what they were like?

Frescoes and other pictures from the twelfth century on provide us with ample evidence as to the rugs known in Europe. The Venetian school shows them repeatedly, and Carpaccio introduces no less than eleven in a single picture. Holbein, Lorenzo, Lotto, the Memlings, Vermeer, and many others show rugs continuously, down to Zoffany at the end of the eighteenth century. The examples pictured were usually the "latest" thing, so an excellent chronology of design and color for a period of about five hundred years can be compiled from them.

But America was not Europe. What visual evidence have we of our own Turkey carpets?

Fortunately the evidence does exist, in four well-known American paintings by important artists portraying important subjects. In 1729 Smibert painted Dean (afterward Bishop) Berkeley in a group about a table covered with a Turkey carpet. A few years later, in 1741, Isaac Royall had his family painted by Robert Feke in a similar grouping. The rugs in these paintings are Turkish, of the type known as "Transylvania," and the patterns differ only in detail. The way these Transylvanias are displayed, in the most prominent position possible, indicates how greatly they were prized. The Transylvania rugs shown here, with the rugs in the paintings, provide an interesting chronology. A fine early (seventeenth-century) rug displays a characteristic cartouche alternating with eight-point star in the border. Later examples drop the star. The type dies out at the end of the eighteenth century; a splendid late specimen is illustrated.

Before the Revolution Oriental rugs had to come through England, but after 1784 the new country was able to take its own risks and trade direct. Even as early as 1768, when Colonel Jeremiah Lee, builder of the great Lee Mansion at Marblehead, had his portrait painted by Copley, the supply had become more accessible. Colonel Lee is shown standing on his rug, which probably came

through Smyrna. Stuart's "Lansdowne" portrait, painted in 1795, shows Washington standing on an Ushakh rug.

So much for the background. How can one find correct rugs for fine early American interiors today? The Orient is stripped of good old pieces, but suitable rugs do become available from time to time in this country. It is important, of course, that the buyer know which rugs are "suitable." Until recently it was practically impossible even to see carpets of the kind used in early America, but now examples of correct design and period in a proper setting are on public exhibition at the Henry Francis du Pont Winterthur Museum, Wilmington, Delaware (several of these may be seen in color in ANTIQUES, November 1951, and in Joseph Downs' *American Furniture: Queen Anne and Chippendale Periods,* 1952); at Colonial Williamsburg in the Governor's Palace, Brush-Everard House, and Wythe House; in some of the houses at Old Deerfield, Massachusetts; in several furnished old houses under the care of the Philadelphia Museum of Art; and in the American room sections of the Brooklyn Museum, the Metropolitan Museum of Art in New York, the Museum of Fine Arts, Boston, the St. Louis Art Museum, and the Art Institute of Chicago. Several other institutions display early rugs which are properly identified, though not shown in period settings: the James F. Ballard collection, now divided between the St. Louis and Metropolitan museums; the Philadelphia Museum of Art; the Boston Museum; the Art Institute of Chicago; the William Rockhill Nelson Museum of Kansas City; and the De Young Museum in San Francisco.

Visitors to Boston will have an opportunity to observe, throughout this month, probably the largest and most varied collection of authentic Turkish rugs from the sixteenth century down to the early nineteenth which has ever been gathered together under one roof. In Harvard's Fogg Museum in Cambridge, they form part of a comprehensive exhibit, *The Turks in History,* which covers a period of about a thousand years.

Listed below are a number of sound books and catalogues recommended especially for their coverage of Turkish, Caucasian, and Persian rugs of the seventeenth, eighteenth, and early nineteenth centuries.

For authentic period rooms the rugs as well as other furnishings must, of course, be actually of the period. For use with antiques in homes, however, later rugs are permissible, and fortunately superior examples in excellent harmony with early interiors can still be procured. They are the honest productions of the nineteenth century under a variety of trade names, such as Daghestan, Sumakh, Shirvan, Karabagh, Derbend, Kazakh, and others from the Caucasus; Bergamo, Ladikh, Konia, Ushakh, Melas, and Makri from Turkey; Mongolian (usually called Chinese) and Samarkand (eighteenth-century as well as nineteenth) from Central Asia; Joshaghan, and Heriz from Persia. Many of these names are indicative only of type and source, not of style and period like, for instance, Chippendale and Hepplewhite in furniture. If they offer any analogy to furniture designations it is to place names like Newport or Philadelphia, in relation to eighteenth-century American furniture.

The real fitness of a rug depends not on the label but on good design, good wool, sound vegetable dyes, and clear, solid color. Reasonable study of examples in museum collections, supplemented by careful reading of good books and catalogues, should soon dispel the aura of mystery which has so long enveloped the subject and should give the student a knowledgeable appreciation of the rugs that belong with other antiques in the finest interiors. Like the quest for any antique, it is a matter of search plus knowledge.

Left. *Colonel Jeremiah Lee* by John Singleton Copley, 1768.
Wadsworth Atheneum.

Right. *George Washington* by Gilbert Stuart, 1795. The "Lansdowne" Washington (replica).
Brooklyn Museum.

Late eighteenth-century Bergamo rug from eastern Turkey. This design is practically duplicated in many Caucasian rugs of the nineteenth century, though usually without the stylized ducks. Gold ground; principal details red and blue, white in border and cartouches.

Early nineteenth-century flat-woven Sumakh. The effulgent star design within the medallions has been in continuous use since the fifteenth century. Multicolor, with a wide range of shades.

The duplicate of this well designed mid-nineteenth-century Kazakh, with its highly stylized floral details, is in the Metropolitan Museum of Art. Deep red ground; details in blue and red; strong accents in white.

BIBLIOGRAPHY

Antique Rugs from the Near East, Wilhelm von Bode and Ernst Kuhnel. Weyhe, New York, 1922; third revised edition. The fundamental handbook on the subject.

Masterpieces of Oriental Rugs, Werner Grote-Hasenbalg. Brentano's, New York, 1922; translated from the German. Many plates in color, brief but good text, dates almost always accurate.

Tapis Turcs, Turkish Rugs from the Churches and Collections of Transylvania (Hungary), I. de Vegh and Ch. Layer. Hungarian Museum of Decorative Arts, Paris, 1925. Thirty plates, all in color; brief text in French. Dating reliable.

Altorientalische Teppiche in Siebenburger (Hungary), Emil Schmutzler. Carl W. Hiersemann, Leipsig, 1933. In German; fifty-five plates, all in color. Dates reliable.

Oriental Rugs and Carpets, Arthur Urbane Dilley. Scribner's, New York, 1931. An indispensable book — especially Chapters I, II, III on background, Chapter VI on Turkish rugs, Chapter VII on Caucasian.

A Handbook of Muhammadan Art, Maurice Sven Dimand. Metropolitan Museum of Art, New York, 1944. Without a peer for general information on Islamic art.

Catalogues:

Loan Exhibition of Oriental Rugs and Carpets from the Collection of J. F. Ballard. Metropolitan Museum of Art, New York, 1921; Minneapolis Institute of Arts, 1922. Dates unreliable, in general about one hundred years early.

A Loan Exhibition of Early Oriental Carpets, Arthur Upham Pope. Chicago Arts Club, Chicago, 1926. Brilliant introduction and lucid descriptions. Selected bibliography with critical comment.

The date on this boldly effective Kazakh, A.H. 1212, is equivalent to our 1797. Rugs of this type are much more plentiful in today's market than good Turkish examples. Blue ground; details in red and blue on white.

186

Rugs of Turkestan

BY CHRISTOPHER DUNHAM REED

MANY HOMES in which Oriental rugs are found contain one or more Turkoman examples, yet less is known of them generally than of any other kind of Oriental rug. When they first came to this country, about eighty years ago, they were orphans whose background was unknown, and they have suffered a general neglect ever since. The name Bukhara, after the city where many rugs reached market, is applied indiscriminately to all Turkoman rugs, and often to this imprecision the utterly meaningless terms Royal and Princess are prefixed. Museums pay scant attention to Turkoman rugs, books on the subject are few and out-of-print, and rug dealers, many of whom know better, do little to correct confusion.

In an attempt to further the appreciation and the collecting of these extremely interesting weavings, the Fogg Art Museum of Harvard University is presenting in January and February an exhibition of fifty-two representative Turkoman pieces, some of which are illustrated here and on the frontispiece of this issue. They were made in one of the least civilized parts of Asia, a bleak expanse stretching eastward about 1,400 miles from the Caspian Sea to the western portions of Chinese Turkestan, and southward from Siberia through Afghanistan and parts of Persia. Across large reaches of this vast and mostly barren area, the Turkoman tribes roamed at will in search of adequate pasturage for their flocks, coming in contact (often violent) only with other Turkoman tribes.

Members of the numerous Turanian race, of which the Mongols were the easternmost branch, the Turkomans clung to their nomadic, simple life far more tenaciously than their cousins to the east. Refusing to settle down, to erect permanent buildings, or to engage in the various civilizing activities of the city dweller, they continued their unfettered existence until the Russian conquest in the second half of the nineteenth century.

The nomadic Turkomans apparently kept no written record of their affairs, and what may be told of their history is largely either legend or surmise. Of their character, literary romances provide the most copious, if not the most scholarly, anecdotes, and it is enough of this sort of documentation to note that in Morier's *Adventures of Hajji Baba* it was said of the Turkomans that "none but an eater of lions ever came unhurt out of their clutches." Now the collective farm has appeared in Central Asia, nomadism is virtually extinct, tribal loyalties have vanished, and the Turkomans call each other comrade.

In the era in which the best rugs remaining to us were made, the nineteenth century, the Turkomans were still a nomadic people. Sheep, goats,

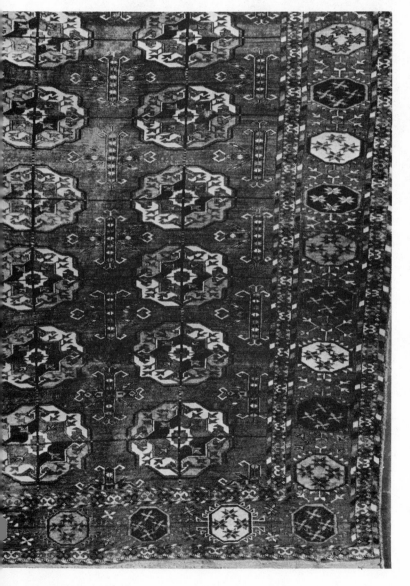

Tekke rug (detail). Guls in the shape of flattened octagons quartered by narrow lines running the length and width of the field characterize a variety of rug long popularly called "Royal Bukhara." Size, 9 feet, 5 inches by 6 feet, 9 inches. *Museum of Fine Arts, Boston.*

Ersari saddlebag face. Medallion forms are rare in Turkoman rugs, and their appearance in Ersari work may indicate the influence of Persian design upon the weavers. The ground color of the field is rust red; that of the border is green. Size, 5 feet, 3 inches by 1 foot, 10 inches. *Collection of Mr. and Mrs. Gerald A. Peterson.*

Chodor saddlebag face. The motif of two bird-like creatures confronting a tree, seen in miniature in this bag face, appears in the so-called Marby rug, a fifteenth-century piece from Anatolia or the southern Caucasus. The Chodors were a subdivision of the Yomud tribe. Size, 3 feet, 5 inches by 1 foot, 2 inches. *Collection of Jerome A. Straka.*

Baluchi pillow face (detail). The Baluchi people, living to the south of Turkestan, were not Turkomans but wove rugs predominantly Turkoman in feeling. The field of this piece is blue, not the familiar Turkoman red. A date, which appears to correspond to the year 1904 in our chronology, was woven into the rug. Size, 2 feet, 8 inches by 1 foot, 7 inches. *Collection of Mr. and Mrs. Stephen D. Paine.*

Yomud saddlebags. This complete pair of saddlebags is gay and lively in color and bold in design. The Yomuds had a particular fondness for diamond forms and sometimes drew quite elaborate ones. Size, 3 feet, 4 inches by 1 foot, 6 inches. *Collection of H. McCoy Jones.*

and camels were the most important possessions of a tribe, and tending them was the principal occupation of its men and boys. By them, also, the wool was sheared and carefully washed.

When the wool had been spun, often to extreme fineness, it was dyed. Preserving the attractive but sometimes dubious lore of Oriental rugs, many writers have stated that this last operation was carried on largely in secret by one man, a specialist whose standing in the tribe rose in proportion to the excellence of his colors. This worthy is said to have made a striking appearance as he went about clad in his Jacob's coat of many colors, samples of his dyes upon him, a walking testimonial. Until the 1860's or 1870's when aniline dyes were probably brought to Turkestan, natural dyes were used exclusively, and these produced colors of marvelous depth and constancy. They cannot have been easy to make, and it is no wonder that when Western traders appeared offering the easy-to-use synthetic dyes, they found a ready market for their wares. Unfortunately, such dyes usually produced harsh and fugitive colors, not all of whose evils came out in the wash.

The arduous job of weaving was given to the women. This skill was learned early, and many Turkoman rugs are the work of very young girls. It has been said that a Turkoman girl's marriageability was considerably influenced by her ability to produce fine rugs. Indeed, if the need arose to marry more than once, she may have found herself regarded a better and better catch as time went on.

The Turkoman woman was perhaps the most accomplished of Oriental weavers in the technical aspect of her art, capable of surpassing all but the finest craftsmen of Persia and Mogul India. This is all the more remarkable when one considers that her equipment was primitive and had also to be easily portable, for she was regularly interrupted in her work by the migrations of her tribe. Even under ideal circumstances, her achievement would have been prodigious. Some Turkoman rugs claim more than five hundred hand-tied knots per square inch, and a count of fewer than one hundred is uncommon. In a rug measuring six by eight feet, with three hundred knots to the inch, there are a total of 2,073,600 knots; and when one considers that an expert weaver could tie eight to ten thousand knots in a long day, one learns something of the Oriental mind.

Most Turkoman weaving was intended for home use, not for export. The nomad weaver made large rugs to cover the floor of her tentlike dwelling. She made small rugs on which to pray. Using the same pile technique, the Turkoman woman made pillows, saddlebags, tent bags, door hangings, tent bands, saddle blankets, gun cases, water-bottle covers, and many other small, useful items. She made them well, to endure, lavishing weeks on the smallest bags, months on the larger rugs. Worn out, they were discarded. Before we begin to understand Turkoman rugs, we must

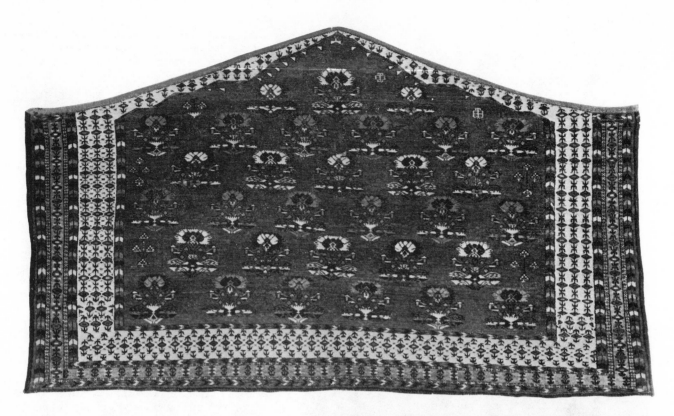

Yomud tent-bag face. Only the Yomuds wove penta-gonal tent bags. The elaborate floral forms of the field and the delicate borders make this an especially attrac-tive and rare rug. The field color is a soft red. Size, 4 feet, 4 inches by 2 feet, 6 inches. *Collection of Mr. and Mrs. Leslie Leifer.*

Turkoman door surround. The exception to the rule, this is a purely decorative piece intended to hang above the entrance to a tent. It is thought to be of Yomud origin. Size, 3 feet, 11 inches (including fringe) by 3 feet, 7 inches. *Collection of Arthur D. Jenkins.*

recognize a fundamental reason for their being: seldom were they purely decorative; almost in-variably they were intended for the hardest of use. Perhaps the proof of the utilitarian nature of Turkoman rugs is that none in existence can be proved to antedate the nineteenth century.

Despite their practical nature, many Turkoman rugs are works of art. Of the elements of their art, color is of primary importance. A glance will reveal that red was the favorite color, but red in many hues, from deep mahogany to brilliant crimson. Because of the appearance in some rugs of bright spots of light color in a mass of dark, creating strong contrasts, Turkoman rugs have been called the Rembrandts of the East. In color they seem the ultimate statement of virility.

Boldness and strength are given further ex-pression in Turkoman rug design. The basic de-sign element of the field is the gul, literally "rose," usually octagonal or of diamond shape. Various geometric forms are contained within the gul. The gul's design gives helpful clues to the tribal origin of the rug in which it appears, and we

speak of the Salor, Saryk, Tekke, Yomud, Ersari, and Afghan guls, named after major Turkoman tribes. The varieties of gul encountered in Turk-oman rugs are many; some of the more typical ones are shown in the illustrations.

The Turkoman was master of the straight line; there is hardly a curve to be found in any of his work. Rhythm, the illusion of movement, was achieved through repetition of forms, gradations of color, and slight variations in ornament. Mon-otony was skillfully avoided. The rude, untutored

190

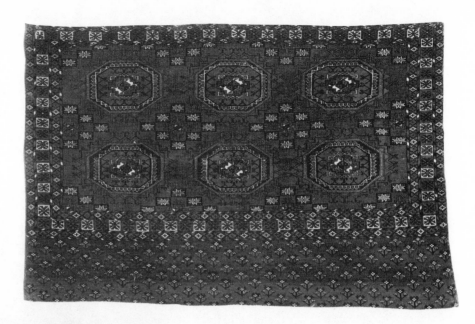

Salor tent-bag face. The ground color is a deep red, the weave is exceptionally fine, the pile is velvetlike. The typical Salor major gul has turretlike projections around its perimeter. Size, 4 feet, 2 inches by 2 feet, 9 inches. *Collection of Mr. and Mrs. Christopher Reed.*

Turkoman rug (detail). Of exceptionally bright color, this lovely and rare rug is of the kind often called Punjdeh after the district in which it probably was made. It contains design elements suggestive of both Saryk and Afghan work. Size, 11 feet, 9 inches by 9 feet. *Leifer collection.*

Turkoman showed remarkable sophistication in the creation of his designs.

Although no really ancient Turkoman rugs are available for study, we have ample evidence that the rugs of the nineteenth century are only the recent embodiments of a long tradition. Proof is yet to be found, but scholars are of the opinion that Turkoman design was most probably brought to Persia, the Caucasus, and Turkey by peoples of Turkish stock moving westward, beginning with the Seljuks in the eleventh or twelfth century. The considerable refinement of Turkoman design is the work of generations.

Turkoman weavings represent a marriage of art and utility, a union of equals to which they owe much of their charm. Unblushingly useful, they seldom fail to achieve a forceful handsomeness. The rug itself, a covering designed originally to combat the cold of the ground, might have remained long of nap and shaggy, warm but artless. But the other partner pressed her claim. Art demanded finely drawn designs, and utility conceded that if they were to be successfully rendered upon the surface of a rug, its texture must be as velvetlike as skill allowed. The tent bag, laboriously made in the same technique as the rug, was intended as a trunk or bureau to contain the diverse household paraphernalia of a nomadic people, either in camp or on the move—the most utilitarian of objects. Still, it was undeniably lovely, rich in color and striking in design. Rarely do the many forms of Turkoman weaving fail to display this happy blend of art and utility. In the dark tents of a notably unrefined race such an expression of beauty provides a startling illumination.

Mr. Reed is the author of *Turkoman Rugs*, a catalogue of the exhibition opening late this month at the Fogg Art Museum and an introduction to this class of Oriental rug. Containing over fifty illustrations, four in color, and with a foreword by the collector and expert Joseph V. McMullan, it is published by the Fogg Art Museum and distributed by Harvard University Press at a price of $8.50.

191

Some peasant and nomad Oriental rugs

BY MAURICE S. DIMAND, *Curator emeritus of Near Eastern Art, Metropolitan Museum of Art*

THANKS TO THREE or four generations of American collectors, we have in this country today, in museums and private ownership, some of the greatest Oriental rugs in the world. They may be roughly divided into three groups: court rugs, peasant or village rugs, and nomad rugs. The court rugs, made for Persian shahs and Turkish sultans, enjoyed their golden age in the sixteenth and seventeenth centuries. The peasant and nomad rugs —the subject of this article—have been made for hundreds of years throughout the Near and Middle East and Central Asia. While they may show the influence of classic design, they offer extreme variety and vitality. Some of the major types are illustrated here in examples of the eighteenth and nineteenth centuries.

TURKEY. Peasant rugs of the province of Anatolia in Asia Minor, a part of Turkey, were popular in Europe from the fourteenth century on, as we know from depictions of them in early Italian, Flemish, Dutch, German, and English paintings. Certain geometrical, floral, and angular arabesque types of prayer rugs (some of them known as Holbeins or Lottos because depicted by those artists) are attributed to the town of Ushak in Anatolia; often the border designs are interlaced straplike motifs which simulate Kufic, or archaic Arabic, lettering. Characteristic Ushak motifs are the star, four- or eight-pointed, and the "octagon," or medallion; these survived in many eighteenth- and nineteenth-century Anatolian rugs of the Bergama and Melas varieties (see color plate).

The most popular and best known of Anatolian peasant rugs of the eighteenth and nineteenth centuries are the prayer rugs of Ghiordes, Kulah, and Ladik. Prayer rugs usually have a central arched panel or niche, called a mihrab, to indicate the direction of Mecca, toward which the Moslem faces at the time of prayer. In the Ghiordes rugs (Fig. 1), which are vivid in color, with red and blue predominating, the arch of the niche takes various shapes and is often supported by two columns or pilasters. Sometimes a mosque lamp, which may be transformed into a floral device, is suspended from the apex of the arch. The border decoration of Ghiordes rugs and related Kulahs is usually floral, consisting of carnations, tulips, hyacinths, and roses, which the peasant

Color plate, facing page. Turkish rug, Anatolia (Asia Minor), Bergama; first half of the nineteenth century. Eight-pointed stars and "octagons," or medallions, are motifs derived from fifteenth-century Ushak rugs. Size, 6 feet, 8 inches by 5 feet, 4 inches. *Collection of Joseph V. McMullan.*

Fig. 1. Turkish prayer rug, Anatolia, Ghiordes; first half of the eighteenth century. A floral decoration takes the place of the mosque lamp in the mihrab, or niche; stylized flowers in border, derived from Turkish court rugs. Colors: niche, red; spandrels, light blue with yellow; border, dark blue, with pattern in white, tan, green, red, and black. *Metropolitan Museum of Art.*

Detail of lower border, with stylized flowers: pomegranate with leaves, rose (above), carnation (below), hyacinth, palmette.

1962

2

3

4

weavers adopted from Turkish court rugs of the sixteenth and seventeenth centuries. In the Kulah variety, the borders are usually divided into a number of narrow stripes, and the niche and spandrels sometimes have an all-over pattern of small floral motifs or star rosettes.

A fine and distinctive group of Anatolian prayer rugs was made in Ladik and its neighborhood. The early examples, of the first half or middle of the eighteenth century, have creamy-white, yellow, or red backgrounds, and are known as column Ladiks, because the high triple arch of the niche is supported by slender double columns. A characteristic feature is a panel above or below the niche decorated with pointed arches like arrowheads, from which issue stalks of stylized tulips. In Ladiks of the late eighteenth century, some of which are dated, the floral decoration has become highly stylized and the columns are reduced to ornamental bands (Fig. 2).

PERSIA. In Persia rugmaking had developed many types and a great variety of patterns by the late fifteenth century. The finest Persian carpets were made during the sixteenth and seventeenth centuries on the court looms established in Tabriz, Kashan, Herat, Isfahan, and other centers. The rug was elevated to a work of art produced by master craftsmen, often from cartoons designed by famous illuminators and court painters. Every Persian rug shows a well-balanced composition of arabesques and floral scrolls forming a background for

194

various other decorative elements, often including animal and figure subjects. Persian poets were inspired to compare the beautiful royal carpets to "a garden full of tulips and roses" or "a wild white rose."

After the gradual decline of royal patronage in the late seventeenth century, the court rugs were copied by nomad and peasant weavers in various regions of Persia. Some of the finest rugs were made in Kurdistan, in northwest Persia, where the rug industry organized in villages flourished until the nineteenth century. Here were woven imitations of the court rugs of Isfahan which had schematic representations of gardens divided into plots and separated by canals, as though seen from above, while trees and shrubs grow horizontally (Fig. 3). The highly decorative quality of Kurdish work is apparent also in landscape rugs with animals derived from earlier Persian carpets (Fig. 4). Another well-known rug center of the province of Kurdistan was Senna, famous for its fine kilims (rugs of tapestry weave, with no pile).

CAUCASUS. The best-known peasant and nomad rugs of the Near East are those of the Caucasus, situated between the Black Sea and the Caspian and populated by Armenians, Georgians, and many tribes of Iranian and Turanian origin, including the nomad Tartars. From earliest times the Caucasus was exposed to outside influences—Scythian, Arabian, Turkish, Persian, Russian—which affected its rug design.

The earliest Caucasian rugs, the so-called dragon rugs, which have been frequently called Armenian, can be assigned to the region of Kuba. They show a lozenge diaper pattern formed by serrated leaves, enclosing

5

6

Fig. 2. Turkish prayer rug (kilim), Anatolia, Ladik; figures near top of mihrab indicate the date 1188 A.H. (*Anno hegirae; i.e.,* 1774/5 A.D.). Columns are reduced to ornamental bands, and floral decoration is highly stylized. Colors: niche, green; spandrels, red; border, light tan; guard bands, light and dark blue; pattern, white, yellow, tan, orange, greens, blues, red, brown, purple, gold. Size, 5 feet, 2 inches by 3 feet, 6 inches. *Collection of Mr. and Mrs. Charles K. Wilkinson.*

Fig. 3. Persian garden rug, Kurdistan; c. 1800. Schematic representation of a garden as seen from above, derived from Isfahan court rugs. Colors: water channels and several garden plots, red; other garden plots, light blue, dark blue, creamy white; border, dark blue; guard bands, creamy white. Size, 18 feet, 3 inches by 7 feet, 8 inches. *Collection of Karekin Beshir.*

Fig. 4. Persian animal rug, Kurdistan; eighteenth century. Animals and birds against background design of trees and flowers, a type of composition derived from Persian court carpets of the classic period. Colors: field, red; animals, white, rose, light and dark blue; background pattern, white, cream, rose, reds, and blues; border, red and light blue on dark blue. Size, 13 feet, 3 inches by 6 feet, 7 inches. *Collection of Mr. and Mrs. Arthur M. Brilant.*

Fig. 5. Caucasian dragon rug (woven and embroidered), Kuba; early nineteenth century. Dragon forms almost unrecognizably stylized but still full of vitality; other small animal forms interspersed. Colors: field, red; dragons, white, dark blue; pattern, white, yellow, orange, brick red, light and dark blue, violet, black-brown. Size, 7 feet, 3½ inches by 8 feet, 8¾ inches. *Collection of Joseph V. McMullan.*

Fig. 6. Caucasian palmette rug, Shirvan; dated in upper left corner of field 1278 A.H. (1861/2 A.D.). Colors: field, white; border, dark blue; pattern, white, yellow, light and dark blue, red, violet, black. Size, 4 feet, 3 inches by 3 feet, 3 inches. *Author's collection.*

7

8

9

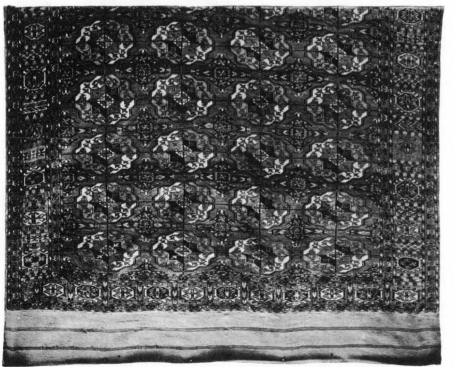

Fig. 7. Caucasian prayer rug, Baku; dated in border, upper left, 1223 A.H. (1808/9 A.D.). All-over decoration of cone-shape palmettes. Colors: field, dark blue; border, white; pattern, white, yellow, light and dark blue, red, black. Size, 4 feet, 8 inches by 3 feet, 2 inches. *Metropolitan Museum of Art.*

Fig. 8. Caucasian floral rug, Kazak; first half of the nineteenth century. Modified cross in lobed floral medallion. Colors: field, red; border and background of medallion, white; pattern, yellow, rose, light and dark blue, black. Size, 7 feet, 2 inches by 4 feet, 10 inches. *Wilkinson collection.*

Fig. 9. Turkoman geometrical rug, Tekke (called Bukhara); first half of the nineteenth century. All-over pattern of roughly octagonal guls, or medallions. Colors: field, red brown; pattern, white, orange, dark blue, red. Size, 9 feet by 6 feet. *Metropolitan Museum of Art.*

Fig. 10. Turkoman geometrical rug, Afghan; mid-nineteenth century. Pattern of octagonal guls with stars and clover leaves. Color: field, reddish brown; pattern, blue, green, reddish brown. Size, 8 feet, 2 inches by 6 feet. *Collection of Mrs. Amos Thatcher.*

stylized dragons—sometimes in combat with other creatures—and large palmettes. The pattern is bold and rendered in vivid contrasting colors mostly on a red or blue ground. These rugs, which in many ways are related to Persian vase carpets and floral rugs of the Shah Abbas period (1586-1628), were produced from the end of the sixteenth century for more than two hundred years. Eventually the dragon forms degenerated into virtually unrecognizable geometrical motifs (Fig. 5). Related to the dragon carpets are rugs with a similar palmette decoration in vivid colors but without animals. Rugmaking in the Kuba district continued into the nineteenth century, when the pattern is enhanced by a purely decorative color scheme often on a yellow background.

Many of the Caucasian rugs, known in the trade as Kabistans, were made in the southeast district of Shirvan. They come in various sizes and types, with stylized floral designs or purely geometrical patterns, and show affinities to carpets of northwest Persia and of Anatolia. Some of the floral Shirvans of the nineteenth century, closely related to the eighteenth-century Persian floral rugs of Kurdistan, have a pattern of large composite palmettes connected by stems, with short arabesque scrolls. In others the stems disappear entirely and the palmettes, rendered in bright vivid colors, are arranged in rows; small geometrically stylized animal and human figures are often interspersed (Fig. 6). To Baku is assigned a group of prayer rugs, some dated, which are decorated with a repeat pattern of cone-shape palmettes, derived from Persian rugs, mostly of the Senna variety (Fig. 7).

Among other popular Caucasian rugs are the Kazaks, made by Tartar tribes of the southern Caucasus. They usually have a high lustrous pile and a bold design in vivid colors. In general they are of two types: one with an abstract pattern of elaborated octagon and star shapes combined with hook motifs, the other with medallions and strongly stylized floral designs derived from Kuba rugs (Fig. 8).

CENTRAL ASIA. The wandering Turkoman tribes of Transcaspia and Western Turkestan have long been skilled weavers of rugs, which serve these tent-dwelling people not only as floor coverings but as rugs for the tent entrance, tent bags, and saddle bags. The Turkoman rugs, none of which are earlier than the nineteenth century, were made by various tribes, whose names usually designate the types of rugs. These tribes occupy the regions from the Caspian Sea eastward to Bukhara, northward to the Aral Sea, and southward to the boundary of Iran. Although all Turkoman rugs have characteristics in common, each tribe developed its own peculiar features of design with its own peculiar tribal device, or gul, an octagon or medallion often composed of stylized floral or animal forms. The pattern of the rugs is entirely geometrical and goes back to old Turkish and Central Asiatic traditions. The predominant color ranges from a reddish brown to a dark brown, with the addition of blues or greens, orange or yellow.

The best-known Turkoman rugs are the Tekkes, known in trade as Bukharas. They have an all-over pattern of oblong guls of angular outline ("octagons"), arranged in rows and separated by secondary cross-shape guls (Fig. 9). Octagonal guls of different designs occur in rugs made by the Saryk tribes, and likewise in those of the

10

Salor tribe which until 1856 occupied the Merv oasis. The tribe of Yomuds is also known for its fine, richly colorful rugs, in a great variety of patterns; it was particularly fond of the hook motif. An interesting group of Turkoman rugs is the so-called Afghans, whose large guls, consisting of three-leaf clovers and stars within octagons, are arranged in rows and are separated by clusters of stars and clovers (Fig. 10). These rugs were made by tribes which roamed both sides of the Turkestan-Afghanistan border.

These are but a few of the varieties of rugs made by nomads and peasants after the decline of the classic period—the sixteenth and seventeenth centuries—when the great court rugs were produced. They carry ancient traditions of technique and design into the eighteenth and nineteenth centuries, and examples even so recent as these are collector's items.

The rugs illustrated here were included in an exhibition, *Peasante and Nomad Rugs of Asia*, held last fall at Asia House Gallery, New York, and this article is condensed from the introduction to the exhibition catalogue.

197

Early influences in Turkish rugs

BY H. McCOY JONES

THE EXACT ORIGIN of Turkish rug weaving has never been established. The first influences undoubtedly came from the east and north, but specific information establishing this has not yet been found. The many conquests to which Anatolia (the part of Turkey which is in Asia Minor) was subjected led to an exchange of a great variety of cultures. The Turkish rugs discussed in this article date from the Seljuk dynasties (eleventh through thirteenth centuries) and the Ottoman empire which followed (thirteenth to twentieth centuries), and they reflect the tumultuous history of the Middle East. Most of the examples available today are of the late eighteenth and the nineteenth centuries.

Legend forms the rather questionable basis for some of our assumptions. Reliable information about Turkish carpets has been very limited in comparison with the amount of knowledge about Persian rug weaving gained from early illuminated manuscripts and books and beautiful miniatures. Written and pictorial records are virtually nonexistent, and until fairly recently the historic towns of Anatolia containing pertinent material could only be reached with great effort. As a result of discoveries made in the twentieth century, however, more has become known about the production of Turkish rugs of earlier periods. The government began to make information available; actual specimens were concentrated in museums at accessible places; research activities were established; publications on art were financed, and translations of them made into other languages. The exceptionally high quality of the early art of Turkey has now been recognized by foreign scholars.

Since so many influences from regions to the east are to be seen in Turkish rugs, any discussion of them must take into account the early work of these districts. The first evidence of a woven textile was found by the Russian archaeologist Rudenko in 1924 and 1925 at Pazyryk in Central Mongolia while excavating the tomb of a Scythian chieftain buried with his horses and chariot. The piece had been used in the tomb as a saddlecloth and is finely knotted (over two hundred Ghiordes knots to the square inch) with a design reminiscent of the carvings of horsemen and animals seen on stone slabs in the

Fig. 1. Ushak rug of the Lotto type, sixteenth century. Because Lorenzo Lotto (1480-1556) used rugs of this design in many of his paintings, they are known by his name. The cherry-red field, edged with a narrow border of light blue, has a pattern of gold and blue Turkish arabesques. In the main border are motifs in red, blue, green, white, gold, and light blue. This rug is in exceptionally fine condition considering its age. 26 feet by 8 feet, 6 inches. *Textile Museum.*

Fig. 2. Star Ushak, early seventeenth century. Rugs like this were made by Turkish commercial looms for the European as well as the Asiatic market. Some were made to order and bear European coats of arms. The medallions in this example are blue with predominantly yellow figures. The field is red with stylized green motifs, and it is lined by a narrow pale blue border. The main border is red with blue and green designs. 10 feet, 2 inches by 5 feet, 10 inches. *Textile Museum.*

Fig. 3. Anatolian rug with ivory ground, sixteenth or seventeenth century. This design is said to have been derived from the tiger and leopard skins worn by ancient rulers. The pattern is sometimes called the badge of Tamerlane (Timour Lenk), sometimes thunder and lightning, and was probably inspired by earlier textiles. The rust-red devices are repeated on an ivory field. The border is ivory with cloud-band patterns in red, blue, green, and yellow. Only three authentic examples are known to exist. 10 feet by 6 feet. *Dumbarton Oaks.*

Assyrian palaces of Nineveh. The date of this weaving has been placed at about 500 B.C.

The next earliest textiles, after those discovered at Pazyryk, had been found in burial sites excavated in Chinese Turkestan by Sir Aurel Stein between 1906 and 1908 and Le Coq in 1913. Fragments of rugs made between the third and sixth centuries A.D. were unearthed; but little information was obtained from these, beyond a few border designs, other than that the colors had remained fast.

Among the earliest known Turkish rugs are those found in the Ala-ud-din Mosque, built between 1220 and 1221 at the Seljuk capital, Konya, ancient Iconium. Three of the eight items discovered were very worn, nearly complete carpets, and there were five other rugs in fragments. All of these date from the end of the thirteenth century; most appear to be coarsely woven with a Ghiordes knot; and in two, red woolen threads had been used for the weft. Some of the carpets were originally fairly large and showed incredible richness of color. Although it is not certain that he went to Konya itself, Marco Polo traveled through Anatolia in 1271 and commented on the beauty and quality of the Turkish rugs he saw during his visit. The dating of the Konya discoveries is verified in the frescoes painted by Giotto in the Arena Chapel in Padua about 1304. According to a surviving document, the Turkish carpet used by the painter was lent to him by the local authorities of Venice and this would indicate that by this time the Seljuks had already gained a foothold for their products in Venice and elsewhere in Europe.

Fragments of three more Seljuk carpets of the end of the thirteenth century were found in the Esrefoglu

Fig. 4. Anatolian village rug strips, nineteenth century. These two pieces appear at first glance to be halves of the same rug. They were woven separately, however, and do not match; and each was used as a couch spread. The field in both is composed of shades of red-orange with elaborate geometric designs, and the spandrels at each end are in many different colors on a lighter ground. The borders are somewhat reminiscent of those seen in Transylvanian rugs. Both are 7 feet, 9 inches by 3 feet, 3 inches. *Author's collection.*

Fig. 5. Melas prayer rug, nineteenth century. The intense red field of the mihrab contrasts with a brown main border and a white outer border. Most of the brown sections have been eaten away, characteristically corroded by the dye. This example is outstanding for the careful harmonizing of its many lovely colors and its superior design. It is of a type considerably scarcer than the usual Melas prayer rug, which has a diamond-shape mihrab. 6 feet, 2 inches by 3 feet, 9 inches. *Collection of Ralph S. Yohe.*

Mosque at Beysehir by R. Riefstahl in 1930. Several modern scholars who have had the opportunity to study this last group of rugs have stated that while they appreciated the historical value of these pieces they were of the opinion that they were provincial in the quality of the weaving.

C. J. Lamm discovered approximately one hundred rugs while excavating grave mounds at Fostat (the first Moslem capital of Egypt, founded in 641 A.D., which later became Cairo). The knotting of these examples was finer and tighter, and their dimensions were somewhat smaller than those of the Konya group. A number of these rugs were identified as being of the Konya type and there was some opinion that they were a little earlier in date.

The carpets in the three discoveries mentioned above give some indication of the influence of earlier rugmaking traditions. One contains the famous octagon of Turkoman origin. Early products of the Turkoman nomads of Turkestan, northeast of Persia, were sold in only very scant volume. A culture so well developed must have taken many years to perfect, but examples made prior to the nineteenth century cannot be dated with any assurance. Two other carpets in these discoveries indicate the probability of nomadic or Persian origin. Several of them have the Kufic borders that later became so popular in both Turkish and Caucasian rugs. Also, the excavated rugs show the first use of continuous, strongly stylized arabesques.

At the end of the thirteenth century the Seljuk Sultan

Kaikobad faced certain defeat by a wandering Mongolian horde. However, a small body of unknown horsemen appeared, raced into the battle, turned the tide, and the Seljuks prevailed. The leader of the unknown ally was Ertoghrul, a chieftain of the Oghuz family of Turks, who had been dislodged by the Mongols from their camping grounds in the region of Khorassan Persia. He was rewarded with territory in Asia Minor immediately south of Constantinople. In 1258 a son—Osman, or Othman—had been born to Erthoghrul, and eventually became the first Sultan of the Othmanlis, or Ottoman Turks.

Early in the fifteenth century animal and bird designs were used in Turkish rugs, and such motifs appear on a rug seen in a fresco in the hospital of Santa Maria della Scala at Siena painted by Domenico di Bartolo between 1440 and 1444. This form of design lost favor in a relatively short time and disappeared. The origin of this pattern is still obscure, but there is a strong current of opinion that the designs were brought to Persia by the Mongolian conquest, and adapted by the Turks in the first half of the fifteenth century.

The oldest surviving rugs of the Ottoman Turks are fifteenth-century Ushaks; some variations of these rugs are known today by the names of two famous sixteenth-century European artists. Hans Holbein the younger and some of his contemporaries used so many of one type that it is now identified by his name. Lorenzo Lotto and other painters of his day used carpets of an entirely different pattern with so much frequency that rugs of this kind are called Lottos (Fig. 1). Ushaks chiefly feature the so-called star design (Fig. 2) and the medallion design, both of which were developed by the Turks under strong Persian influence. These two patterns were produced on commercial looms established to meet the demand, mostly from European markets, for these types. The best Ushaks were made in the seventeenth century, and at this period these carpets were large.

In the latter half of the fifteenth century Mohammed II (r. 1451-1481) was the Ottoman sultan and it was he who conquered Constantinople in 1453, a feat hitherto accounted impossible. At that time Bursa was the capital, and rug weaving flourished under court patronage. Apparently under this vigorous sultan new Ushak rug patterns emerged.

After a quiet period Selim I the Grim (r. 1512-1520) desired further conquest and captured the Persian capital of Tabriz in 1514. He sent back to Constantinople a

Fig. 6. Kula prayer rug, nineteenth century. The dark blue mihrab has typical Kula designs in gold, red, and light blue. The light blue section above the niche is filled with gold and red devices, and above that is a reddish-brown panel with S designs in gold, light and dark blues, and red. The numerous narrow borders in white, brown, gold, and a dull green are characteristic of Kulas. 5 feet, 10 inches by 3 feet, 11 inches. *Collection of Mr. and Mrs. Dave Chapman.*

Fig. 7. Makri prayer rug, nineteenth century. This single-panel example has a red field with dark blue tree designs; Makris are often divided into several elongated polygons. The field here is outlined by a brown and yellow band, and green spandrels. The outer borders have yellow and white backgrounds. The colors used in the designs are red, blue, yellow, green, and white. 5 feet, 6 inches by 3 feet, 6 inches. *Author's collection.*

thousand skilled workmen and massacred all the rest of his prisoners except women and children. Tabriz was famous for the work of these artisans, and had supplied Cairo, Damascus, and Venice with architects, carvers, skilled metalworkers, and rug weavers. This influx probably led to the introduction into Turkey of the style of Persian medallion carpets.

Selim I's next move was to make Egypt a Turkish province, bringing to an end the Mameluke dynasty. His penetration was so thorough that he assumed the title of caliph and head of the Mohammedan faith. This conquest caused a decline in the Egyptian art of rugmaking and the absorption of this art by the Ottoman Turks. Artisans from Cairo and Damascus were sent to Constantinople and Anatolia.

During the reign of Selim I two of the greatest innovations in rug design were introduced in the form of so-called white carpets. The ivory grounds of these rugs may have been suggested by similar backgrounds in Persian rugs, but it is much more likely that they were inspired by textiles other than rugs. The first group—given such names as cloud and globe, thunder and lightning, and others—consists of two strips in a cloud form with three balls above, a motif constantly found in other textiles of Asia Minor in the sixteenth century. The three balls are known to have been the mark of the great Mongol conqueror Tamerlane (1336?-1405), but some scholars claim that he took this from an earlier religious symbol. Authentic rugs of this pattern are extremely scarce: it has been said that there are only three in existence (Fig. 3). The second new group was the so-called bird rug, which gives the appearance of birds picking up honey from flowers, though in reality the design is a stylized leaf arrangement. The ivory rugs are dated between 1550 and 1650.

It was under the great Sultan Suleiman I the Magnificent (r. 1520-1566) that Persian influence in Turkish carpets reached its peak. He occupied Tabriz a second time in 1534 and imported more Persian weavers at a period when the art of rugmaking was at its height in that country.

Numerous carpets of Anatolian design have been found in the Christian churches of the Transylvanian region (much of which remained under Ottoman rule until the middle of the nineteenth century) between eastern Hungary and western Romania. These fine rugs were presented as thanksgiving offerings for successful ventures and safe journeys by merchants who plied their trade between Turkey and eastern Europe. It was originally believed that the carpets were all made in Anatolia, but recent research seems to indicate that the later rugs of this group were produced in the Transylvanian region by Anatolian weavers sent there for that purpose. Similar rugs have also turned up in churches in Poland, Italy, and South Germany.

The Turkish prayer rugs of the sixteenth century woven under court patronage in Constantinople were masterpieces of Islamic religious weaving and supreme works of art. Prayer rugs of Ushak origin made in the late sixteenth and early seventeenth centuries are considered archaic and show the influence of the work of earlier Turkoman weavers.

The variety of designs used in the village and nomad rugs of Turkey outnumbered those offered by other similarly primitive regions and are generally considered to

Fig. 8. Demirdji Kula, nineteenth century. Demirdji is a town near Ghiordes and Kula, and rugs from its looms characteristically have an oblong hexagon in the center. This one has a dark brown, almost black, field with red and blue figures. The wide border with stiff meander is another identifying mark of this group, and the best examples have gold as the field color in the main border, as does this one. The blue spandrels have predominantly red figures. 5 feet, 4 inches by 4 feet, 8 inches. *Collection of Herman O. Swanson.*

be superior to them (Fig. 4). The colors were brilliant, and beautiful effects were developed by harmonizing the various shades. Despite the early establishment of flourishing trade in the Near East, Europe, and Northern Africa by the Turks, Turkish rugs made before the nineteenth century are rare today. Anatolian rugs were often more sophisticated than those of the Caucasus (see ANTIQUES, March 1969, p. 370), because many of them were marketed in large native communities where great wealth and fine taste prevailed, and many were exported to distant countries.

An exhibition of Turkish rugs was held in Washington, D.C., during the summer of 1968, sponsored by the Washington Hajji Baba (the Rug Society of Washington, D.C.) in cooperation with the Textile Museum. This event was another step in the program of the two sponsors to encourage the current revival of interest in Oriental rugs. Illustrated catalogues of the exhibition may be obtained from Mrs. George Cox, 7404 Valley Crest Boulevard, Annandale, Virginia 22003. Hard-cover edition, $8.20; paper-bound edition, $4.00; prices include postage.

Rugs of the Caucasus

BY HAROLD M. KESHISHIAN

THE RUGS OF THE Caucasus are as varied as the peoples who have lived in and fought over the region through hundreds of years. Today these carpets enjoy a greater popularity in this country than ever before, though some of the best examples were imported here in the nineteenth and early twentieth centuries. Less research has been done on Caucasian rugs than on Persian—the favorite of both the collector and the public—or on Turkish, Indian, and Chinese, and few exhibitions exclusively of Caucasian rugs have been held. Two recent exhibitions

Kuba rug from the village of Chichi, nineteenth century. The center of the border—a band of rosettes and diagonals—and the field of stepped polygons are typical of the work of this locality. 4 feet, 1 inch by 6 feet, 2 inches. *Collection of H. McCoy Jones.*

Karabagh, nineteenth century. Because of its radial design this type of rug is called an eagle Kazak, though it was made in a Karabagh district bordering on the Kazak region. 4 feet, 1 inch by 10 feet 1 inch. *Collection of Mabel H. Grosvenor.*

Soumak saddlebag. The stylized animal pattern used here is rarely found outside the Caucasus. These bags were used for carrying everything from salt to clothing, and were also used for storing articles in the home. 2 feet square. *Collection of Mr. and Mrs. William R. Pickering.*

Dagestan, late nineteenth century. This is a classic Caucasian design, repeated by successive generations. The field of stylized blossoms of varied colors is placed on a ground of dull gold. 3 feet, 8 inches by 9 feet, 2 inches. *Jones collection.*

worthy of mention were that at the Museum für Kunsthandwerk in Frankfurt am Main in the fall of 1962, and one in the spring of 1963 at the Textile Museum, Washington, D.C. There are two books of note devoted to the subject, one in Russian by Z. Kerimov on Azerbaidzhan carpets (Baku, Azerbaidzhan S.S.R., 1961) and Ulrich Schurmann's *Caucasian Rugs* (London, 1966).

The Caucasus area extends from the Sea of Azov, just north of the Black Sea, eastward to the Caspian Sea, and the entire region is straddled by the high-peaked Caucasian mountain range. This range, broken by many valleys, is over nine hundred miles long, varies in width from thirty-five to one hundred and forty-five miles, and rises to over 18,000 feet. Today, three republics of the Soviet Union comprise most of the area: the Georgian, Armenian, and Azerbaidzhan. A small southern portion of this region is part of Persia. Some three hundred and fifty tribes live in the Caucasus and more than one hundred and fifty dialects are spoken there.

The history of the area is as varied as its tongues. The earliest settled communities were Greek maritime colonies established in the seventh century B.C. on the southeastern shores of the Black Sea. For the next two thousand years the most powerful state in the Caucasus was Georgia. The southern part of the Caucasus was taken over by the Armenians after the first century B.C., and was then under Roman rule. After that, the Caucasus was invaded and occupied or settled by many people, notably the Khazars, Huns, Mongols, Seljuks, Ottomans, and Persians. The Russians began their invasions early in the eighteenth century under Peter the Great (1672-1725), and all appreciable resistance ended by 1864.

In general the rugs of the Caucasus are identified by the names of the localities from which they came, but in some cases this is difficult if not impossible. Ornament which is characteristic of the rugs of one area is sometimes found also in the rugs of another; for instance, the field design typical of a Dagestan may be found in a Shirvan. This duplication resulted from intermarriage, travel, displacement of tribes, or outright copying. Then, too, certain features are common to the rugs of two or three localities. In these cases the rugs are dubbed simply Caucasian.

In identifying rugs of this region, much may be learned from the materials of which they are made and the ways in which these materials are used. One consistency found in all Caucasian rugs is the use of the Turkish knot, also known as the Ghiordes knot. The material of both warp and weft, with very few exceptions, is wool. In fine Shirvans and Dagestans, however, white cotton is occasionally used for the warp. On the whole, the wool of the Caucasus is of fine quality, and it is often used in its natural color. Wool in as many as three different natural colors may be found in one rug: black, brown, and white. The weft threads, however, are often dyed; in certain rugs, such as the Talish, they may be blue, and in Kazaks, red. In general the weft consists of two threads after each row of knots, though in the Gendje as many as eight rows are occasionally used. The warp threads running from end to end of the rug are often looped at the end, or sometimes braided. In other cases, the warp end is cut, so that there are fringes at both ends of the rug, and these may be knotted in an ornamental pattern. A lozenge pattern, characteristic of Dagestans, is one of the most beautiful ways of securing the ends of Caucasian rugs. Examples are hard to find today because the fringe is the part of the rug which shows the first signs of wear.

Design is the most important means of identification of Caucasian rugs. Many of the motifs are stylizations of certain symbols. In general, Caucasian rugs have a very strong geometrical, angular design. An exception is found in certain rugs from the Karabagh district, in which rose and other floral motifs reflect the influence of nearby Persia. The Chinese influence in Caucasian rugs seems to be strong, and some Caucasian symbols appear to be a corruption of Chinese characters. More interesting, usually, are the stylized depictions of horses, peacocks and other birds, carnations, tulips, roses, lotus, and other flowers, pomegranates, hands, shears, prayer houses, and Kufic writing. Rugs woven by Mohammedans do not usually depict the human form but are generally decorated with floral designs, or, in prayer rugs, a representation of the mihrab—the niche in a mosque indicating the direction of Mecca. Rugs with animal and human figures and with cruciform motifs were woven by the Christian Armenians and Georgians.

Kuba, late nineteenth century. Another traditional type of Caucasian design which is still frequently reproduced. 3 feet by 5 feet, 7 inches. *Collection of Dr. and Mrs. William Price.*

Soumak pillow cover, nineteenth century. A particularly finely woven piece, whose quality can best be appreciated by examining the back. 1 foot, 10 inches by 3 feet, 4 inches. *Collection of Mr. and Mrs. Mark Keshishian.*

A significant element of design is the border. Probably the most beautiful border found in Caucasian rugs is the one using the angular Kufic script (an archaic type of Arabic lettering often used in all the decorative arts in Moslem areas to the present day) which is found in Kuba or Chichi rugs. The distinctive feature of the borders of Chichi rugs produced in the Kuba area consists of diagonal bars alternated with rosettes. The so-called running-dog border, often seen in Sejshour rugs from the Kuba region, is also interesting.

During the reign of Catherine the Great (1762-1796), when the Caucasus was under the sway of the Russian Empire, the Russian court was influenced by the fashionable French court. The designs of rugs ordered by Russian officers stationed in the Caucasus, in turn, were inspired by the French styles of the period. Another very popular design of the Caucasus is the eagle Kazak, also called a sunburst Kazak. This radial design is sometimes considered an adaptation of the imperial Russian coat of arms.

Verné, mid-nineteenth century. This flat-woven piece is a combination of kilim, or tapestry-woven work, and embroidery in relief, with a white honeycomb, over-all pattern which includes cruciform motifs. 3 feet, 6 inches by 6 feet, 1 inch. *Textile Museum.*

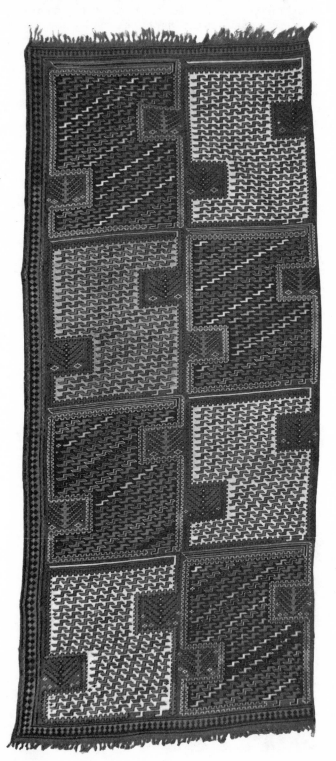

Silé, made in Dagestan, mid-nineteenth century. The S-shape elements of the design in this flat-woven piece are stylized dragons arranged in rows which are alternately blue and white. This piece is half of a rug; sections were often woven separately and later joined together. 3 feet, 6 inches by 7 feet, 6 inches. *Textile Museum.*

Moghan prayer rug, mid-nineteenth century. At each side of the mihrab, or prayer niche, is a crude configuration of a hand. Within the niche is a comb, which is often found in Caucasian rugs. An unusually small prayer rug, 3 feet, 3 inches by 4 feet, 10 inches. *Author's collection.*

Kazak prayer rug, late nineteenth century. The quality of the wool, dyeing, sophistication of design, and fineness of weave are particularly high in this piece. The date is worked into the ground at each side of the prayer niche. 3 feet, 7 inches by 4 feet, 10 inches. *Collection of Mr. and Mrs. Charles Meigh.*

Dates are woven into the colorful designs of Caucasian rugs more often than in any other type of rug. Most dates appear in Islamic figures and are based on Islamic chronology, though a few are based on Christian chronology; rugs thus dated were probably woven by Christian Armenians. Many different explanations are given for these dates; the most plausible seems to be that the rugs were woven for special occasions such as weddings, anniversaries, or birthdays. In later times it often happened that a date was copied from another rug used as a pattern; occasionally the date was copied backward, since it is easier to copy a rug from the back. In certain instances, too, rugs which appear to be relatively new have an early date, and this bears out the theory that they were copied from older rugs.

An important feature of Caucasian rugs is the coloring. Most of the rugs of the Caucasus were dyed with home-made vegetable, animal, and mineral dyes. Only with the coming of Russian influence did commercial dyes become available. Looking at a rug, one may notice, for instance, that a red field consists of several variegated shades. This change of tone adds to the beauty and desirability of the rug. The variation, which is called abrash, may have been caused by slight differences between one dye lot and another, or by the fact that one lot was spun a little tighter than another and thus did not take the dye in the same way.

Some rugs from the Caucasus can be recognized en-tirely by their colors. For example, the Karabagh (whose name means "black vineyard") has several wine shades used as field colors which are seen in no other rugs. Sejshours have an unmistakable blue in the running-dog borders and a green used as a field color which, though extremely rare, is also readily recognizable.

The colors are also an important factor in dating rugs. White natural wool, which was often used, tends to dull with time, and to the trained eye appropriate age is apparent from the degree of change. The acid dyes used for brown and black often lead to deterioration of the wool itself after a period of time. While color and design together can tell a good deal about the age of a rug, one should not forget that even with all available information it is possible to be wrong by fifty years or so.

While the older Kuba and dragon rugs were some-

Shirvan prayer rug, late nineteenth century.
The dark blue field is decorated
with stylized flowers and the date is included
on either side of the prayer niche.
4 feet, 3 inches by 5 feet. *Meigh collection.*

Shirvan prayer rug, mid-nineteenth century.
An exceptionally fine example of Caucasian workmanship.
The blue field is covered with palmettes,
and the border is made up of six ornamental bands.
3 feet, 7 inches by 4 feet, 2 inches. *Jones collection.*

times as large as ten by twenty feet, Caucasian rugs of the eighteenth and nineteenth centuries rarely exceeded six by nine feet. One reason for the generally small size is that the Caucasus was not wealthy and never had large courts and palaces such as existed in Turkey and Persia. Most rugs of the Caucasus were originally made on a small loom for individual use or local sale.

In addition to consideration of weave, design, size, color, and fineness of wool, one of the most important keys to rug identification comes only through the experience of actually handling thousands of rugs. No matter how much one has learned about rugs through study and observation, one needs the actual touch and feel of a rug. For instance, the Kazak and Karabagh have, comparatively speaking, a thicker, heavier weave than most of the other rugs of this area. The pile is generally higher and shaggier. The Dagestan and Shirvan are generally woven with finer wool and a lower pile, and there are more knots per square inch. The Gendje commonly has a medium-high pile. Derbend rugs are normally very loose in weave, the poorest weave of the Caucasus. Kubas usually have a low pile of fine wool and are of medium-heavy weight. Talish carpets have a medium weave, medium-high pile. Lesghi rugs have a tight weave and medium-high pile.

Kilims, or flat-weave rugs, as well as piled rugs, are made in the Caucasus, patricularly in the Shirvan, Karabagh, and Kazak districts. The colored threads used in the design of a kilim are drawn once over and once under a warp thread in such a manner that the rug may be used on either side. In many cases a slit occurs where one color ends and another begins.

The Soumak, also known as Shemakha, is another type of woven rug and is generally attributed to the Shirvan province. It is woven in such a way that only one side may be used, since the unfinished ends of the threads are left to hang free on the back. The English and French called them Kashmir rugs because they reminded them of the shawls made in the Valley of Kashmir in India.

Two other interesting woven rugs of the Caucasus are Silés and Vernés, which are woven in the manner of a tapestry but with ornamentation in relief. In the Silés the design is often composed of elements in the form of the letter S, thought to be a corruption of the old dragon design. Generally, these carpets are woven in two pieces and joined after completion. Vernés also have characteristic designs: squares or lozenges in an over-all pattern, or various animals and birds worked in relief.

Antique Caucasian rugs are very rare today, but those made in the nineteenth century are increasingly appreciated by collectors. Presenting as they do a world of color and bold, geometric design, they perpetuate the old traditions of the early nomadic weavers.

This article is based on the catalogue of an exhibition held in December 1967 at the Arts Club of Washington, D.C.

The Islamic tradition in Spanish rug weaving:

twelfth through seventeenth centuries

BY SARAH B. SHERRILL

THE MOORISH DOMINATION of much of Spain from the early eighth century until the late fifteenth left a strong mark on the arts and crafts of that country. To textiles as well as to ceramics the Moors brought not only new techniques but also patterns and designs from older cultures in the East. The Islamic armies conquered Egypt in 640 A.D. and during the seventh century gained more ground in North Africa, where they converted the native Berbers to Islam. The Arabs who settled in North Africa and intermarried with the Berbers became known as Moors. In the early eighth century the Moors invaded Andalusia, occupied Toledo, and easily defeated the crumbling Visigoth kingdom. Shortly thereafter, the Ommiad rulers of the Near East, defeated by the Abbassides, fled to Spain where they established the capital of the Western caliphate at Cordova. By the middle of the eighth century that city rivaled the capital of the Eastern caliphate, Baghdad, in prosperity, art, and scholarship. Under the Ommiads, whose power waned in the mid-eleventh century, and the Nasrid dynasty of Granada, which came to power in 1232, Moslem culture in general and the arts and crafts in particular reached their two highest points in Spain. Not long after their arrival in Spain in the early eighth century the Moors introduced the art of weaving fine silk fabrics, which were exported and were highly prized in foreign countries as well as in Spain. Silks from Spain are recorded among other treasured items in papal inventories of the ninth century. Surviving examples may be dated as early as the tenth century.

Rug weaving was another important Moorish contribution to the arts and crafts of the Iberian Peninsula, where it was a prosperous industry perhaps earlier than elsewhere in Europe. Stimulated by the caliphs, rug weaving became highly developed in Spain by at least the thirteenth century, to judge by the earliest preserved fragments. A contemporary account of the reception in 949 by the caliph of Cordova of Greek ambassadors admiringly reports that the court of the palace was strewn with luxurious carpets,[1] though whether these were made in Spain or imported is not known.

It has not been satisfactorily determined precisely when rug weaving originated in Spain nor how the single-warp knotting technique used there was first introduced. It is generally believed, however, that both the craft and the particular technique reached Spain from the Near East.

Some scholars believe that a similar technique was used in a Coptic fragment made in the seventh or eighth century in Egypt.[2] Coptic weavers were working in Spain in the tenth century. The knot that distinguishes rugs woven in Spain (until at least the mid-seventeenth century when the Ghiordes, or Turkish, knot—wrapped around two warps—was first used in Cuenca) is tied around every other warp and on alternate warps in succeeding rows. On the basis of research to date, no direct relationship may be established between the use of this particular knot in Spain and the very few isolated occurrences of this variety of single-warp knot: in fragments from two third-to-sixth-century excavation sites in Chinese Turkistan and in a late twelfth- or early thirteenth-century wall hanging with medieval figures woven in a convent in Quedlinburg, about one hundred miles southwest of Berlin.

The earliest known mention of rugs or tapestries specifically made in Spain is a Latin poem of the eleventh century, but the oldest surviving document that discusses rug weaving in Spain is one of the twelfth century. It indicates that by then the industry was well developed and rugs were exported, especially to Egypt and the Near East. Carpets from Andalusia were known at the court of the Fatimid caliphs in Cairo in 1124. In 1154 Al-Idrisi, an Arab geographer, scientist, and poet, wrote that there were eight hundred silk-weaving looms in Almería alone and that fine woolen rugs were being made in Chinchilla and Cuenca. Two other Arab authors, Ibn-Sa'ïd and the Cordovan poet Al-Saqundi, stated in the thirteenth century that the textile industries of Málaga, Almería, and Murcia were then prosperous. Al-Saqundi also said that rugs made in Chinchilla (al-Tantaliya) were exported to foreign countries including Egypt and parts of the Orient. According to a contemporary report, on the arrival in London in 1255 of Eleanor of Castile—the new bride of Prince Edward (later Edward I of England)—a great many Spanish silks and carpets (said to have come from Cordova and Granada) were displayed in the streets as well as at her lodgings in the Temple, following Spanish custom. From the thirteenth century onward, inventories of Spanish and other European royal and noble houses and religious institutions refer to rugs made in Spain. Alcaraz, in what was then the province of Murcia, emerges from these inventories as the major rug-producing center in Spain, at least until the late sixteenth or seventeenth century. Letur and Liétor (also in the province of Murcia) and Baeza (formerly spelled Baza, in what was then the province of Granada) are mentioned as well. Specific Spanish rugs cannot be attributed to definite production centers with absolute certainty; indications given in this article follow generally accepted attributions.

The best period of rug weaving in Spain coincided with the Moslem domination of the peninsula, particularly the southeastern part where the rug-weaving centers were located. Hispano-Moresque rugs (those produced in areas of Spain controlled by the Moslems) were as greatly appreciated in Spain and throughout Europe, England, and parts of the Near East as were the prized Hispano-Moresque silks. European inventories through the nineteenth century reveal that Spanish rugs were to be counted among treasured possessions for centuries. Rugs from Anatolia, particularly from the western part, were imported into Spain from at least the fifteenth century and probably earlier, and they provided inspiration to weavers there. Mudéjars (Moslems living in parts of Spain under Christian rule) continued to weave rugs under the new rulers in the single-warp technique. The Moors were slowly assimilated into the Christian population, however, and while they continued to work in the Islamic tradition, they adopted European decorative elements increasingly after the fifteenth century, frequently in combination with Near Eastern motifs, for which Christian nobles had developed a taste. The Islamic heritage thus survived the gradual extension of Catholic power in the peninsula and was allowed to co-exist with Christian art until the first decade of the seventeenth century when the remaining Moors were expelled from Spain.

Some of the earliest knotted carpets, complete examples as well as fragments, that still exist are Spanish. While they are of aesthetic and scholarly interest in themselves, they are particularly valuable not only because they probably represent the beginning of knotted carpet weaving in the Western world but also because they shed light on certain designs traceable to remote Central Asian origins and once used in other parts of the Islamic world from which examples no longer survive. Chance fragments of twelfth- to fourteenth-century Spanish rugs have allegedly been found in Fostat (Old Cairo) and Turkish fragments of the same period have been found in Konya, the Seljuk capital, in central Anatolia. (The Seljuks, Turkic people originally from Central Asia, had begun their conquest of Islamic territories in the early eleventh century and dominated much of Anatolia until well into the thirteenth century when the Ottomans, another Turkic people from Central Asia, slowly began to dominate Anatolia. The Ottomans established their supreme power after their conquest of Constantinople in the mid-fifteenth century.) A nearly complete Spanish rug of the fourteenth century (now in the Islamic Museum in East Berlin) and a number from the fifteenth survive. Rug weavers in Spain were conservative and apparently continued to use earlier Islamic, particularly Anatolian, designs long after these had been replaced elsewhere by later fashions; and in some cases Spanish weavers copied late versions of earlier Anatolian designs.

Thus certain Spanish weavings may provide clues to some apparently extinct Anatolian rug designs.

The earliest surviving Spanish rugs, mostly from the fifteenth century, indicate that rug weaving and design traditions on the peninsula had reached a high level and that these traditions were related to Near Eastern Islamic antecedents but, developing parallel to Anatolian weaving in the Seljuk period, remained to some degree independent of it. The Spanish rug attributed to the fourteenth century mentioned above is probably the oldest nearly complete Spanish rug in existence (Fig. 1). Originally it may perhaps have been as much as four times longer than it is wide. Acquired in the 1880's from a church in the Tyrol, it is the only one of its design known. Friedrich Sarre, writing in 1907,[3] suggests links with two Moorish tenth- or eleventh-century renderings at Cordova and Saragossa of analogous bud forms growing laterally from a vertical trunk—the tree of life symbol, this form of which is similar to a Sassanian symbol used about 600 A.D. in a relief at Tak i Bostan, in Iran. He also points out the architectonic character of this apparently floral motif and the closed door in the center topped by a gable. In 1930[4] he developed the theory, which has been generally accepted since, although Jewish liturgical scholars disagree among themselves on this point, that this motif represents the gabled

Fig. 1. Upper part of an incomplete rug with tree of life or Torah-shrine motif, Spain, fourteenth century. Spanish knot. Wool; 9 feet, 11¼ inches by 3 feet, 1 inch. *Islamic Museum, East Berlin.*

Fig. 2. Mosaic pavement with design of the Ark of the Law, or Torah shrine, in the Beth-Alpha Synagogue, Hefzibah, Israel; early sixth century. *Photograph by courtesy of the Hebrew University, Jerusalem.*

Fig. 3. Stucco relief wall decoration depicting the tree of life, in the synagogue built in 1366 in Toledo, now known as El Tránsito.

cupboard, the Ark of the Law, in which the Torah scrolls are kept in synagogues. He had also come to believe that the rug showed an elaborate candelabrum whose branches supported the Torah shrines. The use of a similar gabled motif, which represents the Ark of the Law, in an early sixth-century A.D. floor mosaic (Fig. 2) in the Beth-Alpha Synagogue in Hefzibah, Israel,[5] provides one interesting comparison. Another is a stucco relief, in Andalusian style, showing a tree of life (Fig. 3), in a synagogue built in 1366 in Toledo and later converted into a church, now known as El Tránsito. The debased Kufic (an angular form of writing used in the early centuries of Islam and succeeded by more cursive styles) has been used in the rug in Figure 1 merely as an ornamental device, separated by small rosettes. The decorative potential of Arabic calligraphy appealed strongly to Islamic taste, in Spain as in the rest of the Islamic world.

The so-called Synagogue carpet in Figure 1 is something of a mystery in the history of Spanish rug weaving, but the field motifs (stylized dark-blue flowers with hooks and stems on a mustard-yellow ground) of another early Spanish rug pattern, of which only one example is known,[6] show a relationship to a motif in a late thirteenth- or early fourteenth-century Seljuk fragment found at Konya (in which the design is worked in light red on a dark-purple field with a border of light medium blue on brown).[7] The Spanish rug was possibly made at Alcaraz in the early sixteenth century. The wide border with a geometric interlaced band is similar to the border of a rug with a field pattern like that shown in Plate II made in the second half of the fifteenth century at Alcaraz or Letur.[8] It also resembles the outer guard border of the rug in Plate III.

The first category of complete Spanish rugs that exist today in significant numbers (about eighteen are known) is a type called the armorial carpet, because many examples bear shields with coats of arms, particularly those of Alfonso Enríquez, Admiral of Castile (1354-1429), or those of members of his immediate family. Plate I is believed to carry the arms either of Alfonso[9] (who became Admiral of Castile in 1405) or of his eldest son, Fadrique[10] (who became admiral on his father's death and who died in 1473). Several similar carpets carry the arms of María of Castile (1401-1458, m. 1415), wife of Alfonso V of Aragon. Because of the heraldic bearings, both of these groups

Fig. 4. Rug with so-called large-pattern Holbein design, Anatolia, sixteenth century. Turkish, or Ghiordes, knot. Wool, 8 feet, 2 inches by 4 feet, 5½ inches. *Philadelphia Museum of Art, bequest of John D. McIlhenny.*

Fig. 5. Rug with so-called large-pattern Holbein design, Alcaraz, Spain, mid-fifteenth century. Spanish knot. Wool pile, ivory wool warp and weft; 11 feet, 5⅜ inches by 3 feet, 2³/₁₆ inches. *Textile Museum, Washington, D.C.*

of carpets, and similar ones without arms, can be dated to the first half of the fifteenth century. It is likely that this type of rug was made at least as early as the first part of the fourteenth century, as one without arms is depicted without a border in a mural painted between 1344 and 1346 by Matteo di Giovanetto of Viterbo in the Chapel of Saint Martial in the Palace of the Popes in Avignon.[11] There is documentary evidence that Pope John XXII (b. 1249, r. 1316-1334) bought for the palace in Avignon rugs woven by Moors in Spain with coats of arms. This category of rugs is attributed to workshops in what was then the province of Murcia (according to contemporary records the chief location of rug weaving in Spain, and an Arab emirate until annexed by Aragon in the late thirteenth century), perhaps in either or both of the towns of Letur and Liétor,[12] or in Alcaraz.[13] A number of Spanish and other European

Fig. 6. Rug with a variation of the so-called large-pattern Holbein design, Alcaraz, Spain, late fifteenth or early sixteenth century. Spanish knot. Wool pile, white wool warp and weft; 6 feet, 1¼ inches by 3 feet, 1 inch. *Textile Museum.*

paintings of the fifteenth and sixteenth centuries depict rugs of this type. Examples of such rugs are to be found in this country at the Philadelphia Museum of Art (Pl. I), the Metropolitan Museum of Art, the Hispanic Society of America in New York City, the Textile Museum, the Art Institute of Chicago, Dumbarton Oaks, Vizcaya (the Charles Deering estate in Miami), and the Detroit Institute of Arts.

The basic characteristics that distinguish the armorial carpets have their roots in Islamic artistic traditions, though a few motifs come from Spanish silk weaving and textile folk arts. These carpets, made by Mudéjars for Christian patrons, depart from orthodox Islamic canons to depict stylized animals and humans and, at each end of some of the rugs in this group, the cord worn by the Franciscan monks around their waists. A feature of some Anatolian rugs that appears in several of these and certain other Spanish rugs is the "apron" at each end, in which the Mudéjar weavers have included such non-Islamic motifs as wild men hunting lions, bears, and boars. Perhaps the most overtly Islamic feature of the armorial rugs is the very debased Kufic script in the main border. (Kufic and cursive script were also widely used as decorative motifs in Spanish silks.) The general Islamic character of these carpets, however, lies in part in the field pattern composed of a small-scale honeycomb of polygonal forms. The shape of these polygons and the motifs within them vary in different examples, and some motifs used in the field of one rug may sometimes be used in the guard border of another. The relationship of polygons of two different shapes in the field of the rug shown in Plate I resembles the design of certain Timurid carpets which we know today only through fourteenth- and fifteenth-century Persian miniature paintings.[14] Also, a similar arrangement in diagonal rows of octagons connected by small lozenges—all of which contain Spanish heraldic devices—appears in a thirteenth-century silk chasuble of the Infante Sancho of Aragon,[15] now in the Toledo cathedral. Similar endless patterns of polygonal figures are common in medieval Spanish textiles. Evident also in this group of Spanish rugs is an important Islamic artistic concept—related originally to the religious principle of infinity—represented by the potentially infinite repeat pattern of the field which is cut off by the borders which constitute a frame. The avoidance of absolute symmetry in this and other Islamic designs enhances their vitality and prevents the pattern from appearing monotonous. This seemingly accidental element of design was intentional.

During the late fifteenth century and early sixteenth, rugs with other field designs, of an apparently more Western character, were inspired by velvet and brocade patterns. Some had borders similar to the pseudo-Kufic borders of the armorial carpets. Examples of one such field design, in blue on a red ground, with palmettes enclosing pomegranates and framed by an ogival lattice, are in the Metropolitan Museum of Art (Pl. II),[16] the Textile Museum,[17] the National Museum of Decorative Arts in Madrid,[18] the Victoria and Albert Museum, and the Brooklyn Museum of Art. The latter example has an intriguing border derived from three different Anatolian interlaced-Kufic border designs in several of the so-called Holbein rugs. The ogival interlace framing smaller motifs, as used in the rug in Plate II, was fashionable in Spanish and Italian silks and velvets in the late Middle Ages and the Renaissance, as well as in Ottoman brocades. The designs of all of these ultimately

go back to Chinese silk and brocade patterns. Also clearly visible in this category of Spanish rugs is the Islamic infinite-repeat pattern cut off by the border.

In the fifteenth century, rug weavers in Spain were still using the rich colors and color-fast vegetable dyes that had been used for centuries both in the peninsula and in the Near and Middle East. The predominant dye colors were red and dark blue with green, yellow, and light blue; some natural off-white and brown wool was also employed. After the conquest of the New World, however, rug weavers in Spain began experimenting with different shades of red such as salmon and coral, apparently using cochineal, a red dye made from dried insects *(Dactylopius coccus)* indigenous to Mexico. The secrets, inherited from the eastern Islamic world, of setting dyes were lost or disregarded increasingly after the fifteenth century. Many Moorish craftsmen left the country when Ferdinand and Isabella conquered Granada in 1492. The parts of many

Fig. 7. *St. George with Banner,* by the Master of the Visitation, Catalan Aragonese school, Spain, fifteenth century. Tempera on wood panel, 70 by 33¼ inches. The rug on which the saint stands is a fairly accurate portrayal of an Anatolian rug with the so-called large-pattern Holbein design. *Art Institute of Chicago.*

Fig. 8. Rug with a variation of the so-called large-pattern Holbein design, Alcaraz, Spain, fifteenth century. Spanish knot. Wool pile, white wool warp and weft; 13 feet, 9 inches by 7 feet, 9 inches. *Cleveland Museum of Art.*

Pl. I. Armorial rug, with the coat of arms of Alfonso Enríquez, Admiral of Castile from 1405 to 1429 (or of his son Fadrique, Admiral of Castile from 1429 to 1473); Alcaraz, Letur, or Liétor, Spain; first half of the fifteenth century. Spanish knot. Wool pile, white wool warp, ivory wool weft; 19 feet, 1 inch by 8 feet, 9½ inches. *Philadelphia Museum of Art, Joseph Lees Williams Memorial collection; photograph by Otto E. Nelson.*

of the rugs in which the new dyes were used appear today considerably faded and in some cases have even turned a pale tan or ivory, giving no idea of the original vivid effect of the rugs. In other sixteenth- and seventeenth-century Spanish rugs, however, a two-color scheme was consciously sought (perhaps in imitation of velvets and brocades), using blue and yellow, green and yellow, red and green, or dark brown and off-white. In some sixteenth- and seventeenth-century Spanish rugs a monochrome scheme was even used, in shades of green, yellow, or blue.

Several other Spanish rug designs made during the second half of the fifteenth century, possibly in Alcaraz, that appear at first to be wholly inspired by Italian and Spanish brocades and velvets reveal an Islamic heritage. An example is a fragment with a lobed medallion in the Textile Museum.[19] At the center of the medallion is the familiar Islamic eight-pointed star, and the debased pseudo-Kufic border also continues the Islamic tradition. The eight-lobed medallion alternating with a cross-shape form has parallels in Timurid carpets[20] and in Near Eastern tile wall decoration as well as in thirteenth-century and later Italian and Spanish

Fig. 9. Rug with a variation of the so-called large-pattern Holbein design, Alcaraz, Spain, late fifteenth century. Spanish knot. Wool pile, white wool warp, white and brindled wool weft; 14 feet, 11½ inches by 6 feet, 10 inches. *Victoria and Albert Museum.*

Fig. 10. Rug with so-called small-pattern Holbein design, Anatolia, sixteenth century. Turkish knot. Wool pile, ivory wool warp, red wool weft; 9 feet, 2 inches by 4 feet, 11 inches. *Philadelphia Museum of Art, Joseph Lees Williams Memorial collection.*

216

Pl. II.   Detail of a rug with pomegranate pattern within an ogival interlace;
Alcaraz, Spain, late fifteenth century. Spanish knot. Wool pile, wool warp
and weft; entire rug 17 feet, 1 inch by 7 feet, 10 inches. *Metropolitan Museum
of Art, Cloisters Collection.*

silks. An alternating system of major and minor tribal emblems, or *guls,* is an important characteristic of later Central Asian weaving, and a similar alternating arrangement is to be seen in such Anatolian patterns as the so-called small-pattern Holbein and the so-called Lotto design, among others.

Anatolian rugs were imported in quantity into Spain from at least the early fifteenth century and perhaps earlier. In addition to providing inspiration to Moorish weavers, who combined Islamic traditions with elements from local artistic conventions, the Anatolian products also served as models that were copied more or less faithfully on the peninsula, although Moorish weavers used different borders. One fifteenth- and sixteenth-century Anatolian type that was popular in Europe, and in fact derives its name from its portrayal by European painters including Hans Holbein the younger (c. 1497-1543), is known as the large-pattern Holbein (Fig. 4). This design is composed of one or more rows of large octagons containing geometric elements and enclosed by squares. The large-octagon design was copied in Spain (where it was called the wheel pattern in contemporary inventories), chiefly at Alcaraz, during the second half of the fifteenth century. This class of fifteenth-century Spanish rugs may be subdivided into

Fig. 12.   Rug with Ottoman court design, Istanbul, Bursa, or Cairo, sixteenth or seventeenth century. Persian, or Sehna, knot. Wool, 11 feet, 6 inches by 7 feet, 5 inches. *Metropolitan Museum of Art, bequest of George Blumenthal.*

Fig. 11.   Rug with so-called Lotto design, Anatolia, seventeenth century. Turkish knot. Wool pile, natural wool warp, red wool weft; 6 feet, 8½ inches by 4 feet. *Philadelphia Museum of Art, Joseph Lees Williams Memorial collection.*

218

Pl. III. Rug with so-called small-pattern Holbein design; Alcaraz, Spain, fifteenth century. Spanish knot. Wool pile, ivory wool warp and weft; 14 feet, 9 inches by 6 feet, 9 inches. *Museum of Fine Arts, Boston.*

Fig. 13. Rug with Ottoman court design, Spain, late sixteenth or seventeenth century. Spanish knot. Wool pile, brown dyed wool warp and weft; 13 feet, 5¾ inches by 7 feet, 8¾ inches. *Victoria and Albert Museum.*

Pl. IV. Rug with so-called Lotto design, Cuenca, Spain, seventeenth century. Spanish knot. Wool pile, wool warp and weft; 11 feet by 5 feet, 7 inches. *Metropolitan Museum of Art, gift of James F. Ballard; photograph by Otto E. Nelson.*

groups according to the center devices in the octagon. One group has a small eight-pointed pinwheel star surrounded by eight palmettes (Fig. 5). Another variation has a large eight-pointed star composed of knotted interlacings (Fig. 6). A second example of this rare variant appeared in the 1933 Madrid exhibition of Spanish rugs.[21] No Anatolian examples of this particular interlaced-star design are known, though they may once have existed. Another group of Spanish rugs with the large-octagon design has a large, multicolor star with many points, which derives from an apparently extinct variety of Anatolian rug, late versions of which occasionally crop up in the Caucasus.[22] A Spanish example of this type with a large star with many points was included in the 1933 Madrid exhibition of Spanish rugs;[23] another is in the Textile Museum.[24] All of the Spanish versions of these large-octagon designs have a more or less close relationship with Islamic carpet design in general and with Anatolian models in particular, except for the borders, occasional minor field motifs, and the aprons. A fifteenth-century Spanish painting shows an Anatolian rug of this category (Fig. 7), an example of which is in the Textile Museum.[25]

The large-pattern Holbein rug made in Spain usually had more than one vertical row of octagons, as seen in an example in the Cleveland Museum (Fig. 8).[26] This type of Spanish rug suggests that there was once an Anatolian version with several vertical rows of large octagons, known to us today only through Spanish copies and European paintings. An example of another Spanish version of the large-pattern Holbein rug with more than one vertical row of octagons is at the Victoria and Albert Museum (Fig. 9). It was probably made in Alcaraz in the fifteenth century. A fifteenth-century fragment of a similar Turkish carpet, with a Turkish knot, is in the Archaeological Museum in Madrid.

A fifteenth- and sixteenth-century Anatolian type known as the small-pattern Holbein (Fig. 10) was also widely imported into Europe and copied in Spain. The Spanish version in Plate III was copied very closely from a contemporary example of the Anatolian prototype. This rug clearly shows the Islamic alternation of the octagon and a cross-shape-diamond motif in offset rows. The decorative Kufic in the border is modeled on Turkish examples in which the ends of the letter shafts are free and finished with a pointed curl[27] rather than on the interlaced rendition seen in Figure 10. A sixteenth-century example at the Textile Museum,[28] with a slightly looser drawing of the field pattern, is also attributed to Alcaraz. The knotting at the corners of the octagons relates to geometric Timurid rugs depicted in fourteenth- and fifteenth-century Persian miniatures,[29] which show rugs with a small-pattern, geometric field design and an interlaced-Kufic border. The interlaced Kufic in the border in the Anatolian and Spanish rugs is also similar to the Kufic lettering in the borders of the Timurid rugs.[30] Although the Spanish small-pattern Holbein rug in Plate III is meticulously copied from a good Anatolian example, the angular, braided interlace design of the outer guard border resembles border designs of a late fifteenth-century Spanish rug in the Textile Museum[31] and an early sixteenth-century Spanish rug (inventory No. 28) at Dumbarton Oaks.

Another Anatolian rug design, of the sixteenth and seventeenth centuries, was also copied in Spain (Pl. IV), at Cuenca and perhaps also at Alcaraz, during the sixteenth and seventeenth centuries. This Anatolian design is known as the Lotto pattern (Fig. 11) because Anatolian rugs (and

Fig. 14. Double-arch prayer rug, Anatolia, seventeenth century. Turkish knot. Wool pile, white wool warp, red wool weft; 5 feet, ½ inch by 3 feet, 6 inches. *Metropolitan Museum of Art, gift of Joseph V. McMullan; photograph by Otto E. Nelson.*

possibly close European copies) of this design appear in several paintings by Lorenzo Lotto (c. 1480-c. 1556). This pattern is related to the alternation in Timurid rugs of stars and gabled crosses,[32] which also occurs in Islamic tile wall decoration. In the Anatolian examples of the so-called Lotto design the angular shapes of the skeletal octagons and the gabled crosses are silhouetted in yellow on a red ground (except for several extremely rare examples known with a blue ground). There is great variation in the way the Spanish versions are drawn, but in general the Spanish examples are not as sharply drawn as the Anatolian originals, and are worked on a ground of pale yellow or buff (or occasionally what now appears as a very pale rose and may once have been red) with dark blue and some moss green, light blue, and off-white rather than the boldly contrasting red and yellow with some medium blue, dark green, off-white, and black of most Near Eastern prototypes. In both the Anatolian and Spanish Lottos the field design is not reduced in size for smaller carpets; rather, less of the repetitive design is used. When in a small rug only one row of octagons appears, it is sometimes difficult to recognize the design as an alternation of octagons and

Fig. 15. Double-arch prayer rug with coat of arms of Castile and Leon, Cuenca, Spain, late seventeenth or eighteenth century. Turkish knot. Wool pile, white bast warp and weft; 8 feet, 7 inches by 4 feet, 3 inches. *Glasgow Art Gallery and Museum, Burrell collection.*

lozenges or cross forms. The interlaced Kufic lettering (also used in the borders of Timurid rugs[33]), cloud bands, or Islamic scrolling vines and tendrils that appear variously in the borders of different Anatolian models are replaced in the Spanish versions by Renaissance scrolling motifs, winged dragons, or motifs related to plateresque decoration on sixteenth-century Spanish architecture, more or less carefully delineated in different rugs.

In the early sixteenth century, after most of the Moors had been expelled from Spain (some had been allowed to stay in Spain after 1492), a new pattern (Pl. V) of a much more Western character but still remotely related to Islamic design traditions, particularly to the large-pattern Holbein, emerged at Alcaraz and was woven throughout the century. Although at first glance the wreath of what appear to be oak leaves is reminiscent of Renaissance garland frames such as those of the sculpted, polychrome terra-cotta *tondi* of the Della Robbias, there are a number of links with Islamic rug traditions. The somewhat angular shape of the wreath (more pronounced in some examples than in others) and its arrangement in one or more vertical rows are derived from the octagons of the so-called large-pattern Holbein. In the very center of many of the wreaths is a small octagon with quartered coloring (resembling a reduction of the palmettes of one type of large-pattern Holbein) around an eight-pointed pinwheel star. The borders vary in different examples of the wreath carpet, but they generally show more or less clearly drawn Renaissance motifs, related to plateresque architectural decoration. Occasionally the Franciscan-cord motif is used in the guard borders. Some wreath carpets contain a variety of colors, predominantly salmon and shades of green. Others have faded and now appear to have a more limited color range. Many of the later wreath rugs were worked in a monochrome scheme, described in contemporary inventories as green and more green, yellow and more yellow, blue and more blue; or in a two-color scheme of black and white. The progressive reduction of the number of colors used and the instability of the dyes during the sixteenth century parallel a general simplification of Islamic design and a moving away from Islamic traditions at that period.

By the early sixteenth century Christian workmen may have almost entirely replaced Mudéjar weavers and certainly the patronage in Spain was entirely Christian from that time on, which would explain the increasingly Western character of Spanish rugs, the misunderstood renderings of certain earlier Anatolian patterns, and the unsure experimentation with newer, sometimes non-fast dyes. The wreath seems to represent a conscious desire to develop a new pattern, with almost subconscious remnants of an older design tradition.

A deliberate Spanish essay at reproducing a sixteenth-century Turkish design, the Ottoman court-rug pattern (Fig. 12), is represented by Figure 13. The Spanish version was even less precisely drawn than the late Turkish examples. This Turkish design was a new style of the Ottoman court, whose rise had been confirmed by the conquest of Constantinople in 1453 and who conquered Tabriz (temporarily) and Cairo in 1517. The design—worked in the Turkish examples in a Sehna, or Persian, knot—departed from the stylized geometric forms used earlier in Anatolia and Egypt and was in the new taste of the Ottoman court,

Fig. 16. Rug with medallion design, Ushak district, western Anatolia, eighteenth century. Turkish knot. Wool, 8 feet, 4 inches by 5 feet, 8¼ inches. *Metropolitan Museum of Art, gift of Joseph V. McMullan; photograph by Otto E. Nelson.*

with realistic renditions of favorite Turkish flowers (lilies, tulips, hyacinths, anemones, carnations, poppies) and large, curving, feathery lanceolate leaves around a circular or an oval center medallion. The colors of the Spanish versions are basically the same dark blue, red, green, light blue, and white of the Ottoman rugs but less vibrant. In the borders of the Ottoman carpets the sophisticated Persian corner solution with a full motif that turns the corner diagonally is employed, but the Spanish weavers used the simpler solution of a straight horizontal band across the top and bottom of the rug from edge to edge, with no attempt at a transitional turning at the corner.

Another Anatolian rug design that influenced Spanish rug weaving was the double-arch (one arch at each end) prayer rug made in western Anatolia (Fig. 14) beginning in the late sixteenth century. This design was copied in Spain in the seventeenth and eighteenth centuries with coats of arms in the center (Fig. 15). The example illustrated here is elongated and includes some curious lizardlike animals. A related type of Turkish prayer rug was also copied in Spain,[34] with (in place of the cloud-band border of Figs. 14 and 15) a border of palmettes bracketed by lanceolate leaves forming a wavy band. This border is derived from a provincial version of the border of the Ottoman court-style prayer rug.[35] Many details of some Spanish versions of

this second type seem to be based on the so-called Transylvanian rugs, which were in turn derived from Anatolian double-arch prayer rugs and Ottoman court prayer rugs.

Also popular in Spain was the Turkish carpet design known as the medallion Ushak, in use in or near Ushak in western Anatolia from the sixteenth century into the eighteenth (Fig. 16) and originally based in part on the Persian medallion design that reached Anatolia in the early sixteenth century. Rugs of this design appear in European paintings as early as about 1565 and are depicted by artists of the countries that traded actively with Turkey, especially Spain, the Netherlands, and England. These paintings may portray either Turkish or Spanish rugs. With rare exceptions, the Anatolian medallion Ushaks have a dark blue field pattern on a red ground or a yellow field pattern on blue. The Spanish example in Figure 17 is woven in orange, yellow, green, blue, and white. It was generally the later Turkish versions such as that in Figure 16—in which the center medallion has lost its ovoid shape and become hexagonal—that were crudely copied at Cuenca with the Turkish knot.

Rugs produced in Spain from the twelfth to the seventeenth century express traditional Islamic design elements in a manner peculiar to the peninsula. So little evidence of early weaving survives from either Anatolia or Spain before the fifteenth century that it is impossible to know whether certain earlier Spanish rug patterns were actually derived from Anatolian models or whether, as in the case of the different knotting techniques of the two regions, there was perhaps an independent, parallel development based on a common, remote Central Asian heritage brought westward to Persia, the Caucasus, and Anatolia by peoples of Turkic stock. The Islamic vocabulary in Spanish rug weaving was in any case enriched by characteristic Moorish adaptations of styles and individual motifs, especially in the borders, indicating an original treatment of a heritage shared by Moslems in Anatolia and in the Iberian Peninsula. In spite of the varying degrees of stylistic influence from Anatolia, however, rugs in Spain were made with the Spanish knot until the seventeenth century, when the Turkish knot was first used at Cuenca. Evidence of the Islamic tradition in Spanish rug weaving waned after the end of Moslem rule in the Iberian Peninsula in 1492. Throughout the sixteenth century, Renaissance motifs and a generally more Western flavor became dominant. During the seventeenth century the decrease in quality seems to reflect the departure of the Moslem craftsmen from the peninsula and a consequent lowering of rug-weaving standards in both technique and the rendition of design. After the mid-seventeenth century, carpet design in Spain largely followed current Western styles of interior decoration. In the eighteenth century, French carpets made at the Aubusson and Savonnerie factories as well as English styles were copied in Spain, with the Turkish knot and in tapestry weave. The taste of the Spanish Bourbons, influenced by the French Bourbons, dictated these imitations. The influence of the Islamic heritage on rug design in Spain ceased altogether, except for modern reproductions of traditional styles.

224

Pl. V. Rug with wreath design and, in the four corners, arms of the Dominican order, Alcaraz, Spain, sixteenth century. Spanish knot. Wool pile, ivory wool warp, dyed weft now faded to yellow; 15 feet, 10³/₁₆ inches by 8 feet, 3⅝ inches. *Hispanic Society of America, New York City.*

225

[1] Stanley Lane-Poole, *Moors in Spain*, London, 1911, p. 143.

[2] Maurice S. Dimand, "Two Fifteenth Century Hispano-Moresque Rugs," *Metropolitan Museum of Art Bulletin*, New York, June 1964, p. 342, Fig. 2; Dimand and Jean Mailey, *Oriental Rugs in the Metropolitan Museum of Art*, New York, 1973, p. 9, Fig. 14, p. 253.

[3] Friedrich Sarre, "Mittelalterliche Knüpfteppiche kleinasiatischer und spanischer Herkunft," *Kunst und Kunsthandwerk*, Vienna, 1907, pp. 503-525.

[4] Sarre, "A Fourteenth-century Spanish Synagogue Carpet," *Burlington Magazine*, London, February 1930, Vol. 56, pp. 89-95.

[5] Meyer Schapiro, *Israel: Ancient Mosaics*, Paris, 1960, Pl. VI and p. 18.

[6] Rug No. 28 at Dumbarton Oaks. The first detailed discussion of the design of this rug, by Louise W. Mackie, is to be published in a forthcoming issue of the *Textile Museum Journal*.

[7] Illustrated in color in Oktay Aslanapa, *Turkish Art and Architecture*, New York and Washington, 1971, Pl. XIV.

[8] Ernst Kühnel and Louisa Bellinger, *The Textile Museum Catalogue of Spanish Rugs, 12th to 19th Century*, Washington, D. C., 1953, Pl. IX.

[9] Florence Lewis May, "Hispano-Moresque Rugs," *Notes Hispanic*, New York, 1945, Vol. 5, p. 43.

[10] José Ferrandis Torres, *Exposición de Alfombras Antiguas Españolas*, Madrid, 1933, p. 37; n. 1.

[11] Kühnel and Bellinger, *Catalogue of Spanish Rugs*, p. 10; May, "Hispano-Moresque Rugs," p. 62, Fig. 32.

[12] Kühnel and Bellinger, *Catalogue of Spanish Rugs*, p. 10.

[13] Ferrandis Torres, *Alfombras Antiguas Españolas*, p. 105.

[14] Amy Briggs, "Timurid Carpets, I. Geometric Carpets," *Ars Islamica*, Ann Arbor, 1940, Vol. 7, Fig. 4.

[15] May, *Silk Textiles of Spain, 8th to 15th Century*, New York, 1957, Figs. 71, 72.

[16] Dimand, "Two Fifteenth Century Hispano-Moresque Rugs," pp. 341-353, Fig. 13 and color plate.

[17] Kühnel and Bellinger, *Catalogue of Spanish Rugs*, Pls. XVIII, XIX.

[18] Ferrandis Torres, *Alfombras Antiguas Españolas*, Pl. XI; Michele Campana, *European Carpets*, London, 1969, p. 30, No. 12.

[19] Kühnel and Bellinger, *Catalogue of Spanish Rugs*, Pl. XX.

[20] Briggs, "Timurid Carpets, I," Fig. 59.

[21] Ferrandis Torres, *Alfombras Antiguas Españolas*, p. 41 and Pl. IV.

[22] Joseph V. McMullan, *Islamic Carpets*, New York, 1965, No. 51.

[23] Ferrandis Torres, *Alfombras Antiguas Españolas*, p. 40, Fig. 7.

[24] Kühnel and Bellinger, *Catalogue of Spanish Rugs*, Pls. XIV, XV.

[25] Louise W. Mackie, *The Splendor of Turkish Weaving*, Washington, D.C., 1973, p. 70, No. 28.

[26] Dorothy G. Shepherd, "Fifteenth-century Spanish Carpet," *Cleveland Museum Bulletin*, October 1954, pp. 188-190.

[27] Kurt Erdmann, *Seven Hundred Years of Oriental Carpets*, Berkeley and Los Angeles, 1970, Fig. 184.

[28] Kühnel and Bellinger, *Catalogue of Spanish Rugs*, Pls. XXIV, XXV.

[29] Briggs, "Timurid Carpets, I," Figs. 29, 42, 43, 44, 53.

[30] Briggs, "Timurid Carpets, I."

[31] Kühnel and Bellinger, *Catalogue of Spanish Rugs*, Pl. IX.

[32] Briggs, "Timurid Carpets, I," Figs. 18, 25.

[33] Briggs, "Timurid Carpets, I."

[34] An example at the Archaeological Museum in Madrid is illustrated in Erdmann, *Seven Hundred Years of Oriental Carpets*, No. 276, and in color in Campana, *European Carpets*, p. 11, No. 1. Other examples exist at the Hearst Monument in San Simeon, California; at the Hispanic Society in New York City; and at the Victoria and Albert Museum.

[35] Erdmann, *Oriental Carpets*, New York, 1962, Pl. VII; Carel J. Du Ry, *Art of Islam*, New York, 1970, p. 183.

Fig. 17. Rug with design based on medallion Ushak, Cuenca, Spain, c. 1700. Turkish knot. Wool, 10 feet, $1/16$ inch by 4 feet, $8^5/16$ inches. Present whereabouts unknown. *Ex coll.* Count de Welczeck, Madrid; published in José Ferrandis Torres, *Exposición de Alfombras Antiguas Españolas* (Madrid, 1933, Pl. XLI).

V Doublecloths–The Complementary Set

There is unanimity regarding the nature of the workmanship and status of the American weaver who produced double-cloth, jacquard coverlets, and ingrain carpets. The term "double-cloth" is a specific weave structure which bridges the subtle differences between double weave, double-woven, and double-faced textiles. Double-cloth, as Irene Emery defines it, is a fabric in which "two complete and discrete weave structures are woven simultaneously. . . *interconnected* only where some elements of one pass briefly to and from the other. . . ." Although some jacquards, like the one seen in Figure 12 (p. 241) of Mildred Davison's article on hand-woven coverlets, were not double-cloth, they were part of the new nineteenth-century mechanical era of design. American ingrain carpets, which are covered in this survey only in passing, hold an important place nonetheless in the complementary structural weaves made in America. Portraits and advertisements for "ingrains . . . carpets and carpet coverlets" are clues to the existence of American double-cloth floor coverings and to the similarities between the carpet and the coverlet. An account of American ingrain carpets can be found in Rodris Roth's book, *Floor Coverings in 18th-Century America*, and some illustrations can be seen in *America Underfoot* by Anthony N. Landreau.

Design elements in double-cloth were as complex as those in Oriental carpets or Indian printed pompalores. The "Bird of Paradise" coverlet in Figure 11 (p. 232) of Catharine R. Miller's article "Some Hand-Woven Coverlets" is one example of the fanciful range of the loom with its new Jacquard equipment. Double-cloths did not necessarily have elaborate curving patterns, as one can observe in the angular knot in Figure 9 (p. 231) of the Miller article and in the geometry of Figure 2 (p. 233) of Irma Pilling Ander-

son's article on Ohio coverlets. Mildred Davison and Christa C. Mayer-Thurman's book, *Coverlets*, is a rich and current source for old jacquard designs.

The Jacquard mechanism opened up new, versatile, and profitable fields of weaving in the eastern United States as well as in the West. Jacquard double-cloths, however, were not prominent in the Southern states of Kentucky and Tennessee. (See the articles by Tate and Hulan in previous sections of this survey.) Double-cloth weavers were predominantly the Scotch in New York and the Germans in Pennsylvania, according to Mildred Davison. The correlation between nationality, state, and weave is reinforced and revised by the current research of John Heisey, who pins down double-cloth to the English, Scotch, and Dutch of New York, Indiana, and New Jersey; and jacquard single-cloths to the Germans of Pennsylvania, Maryland, and Ohio.

Etta Tyler Chapman's article, "The Tyler Coverlets," introduces us to the exciting work of the weaver Harry Tyler. Born in Connecticut, but settling in New York, Tyler was a beekeeper, a nurseryman, and a supporter of the Universalist church. A man of creativity and fine workmanship, of ideas as well as of machines, he built his own looms and designed his own drafts, threading one loom for ingrain carpets and another for double-cloth coverlets. He wove fabric in two strips and dyed his own yarns in the back of his house. Tyler's son Elman could weave two stips of a coverlet in two half-days. (Weavers know, of course, that such a timetable does not include warping or threading days.) Elman Tyler, a teacher of penmanship, designed his father's fruit and eagle patterns; Harry Tyler's emblem was a fanciful lion. Though spinning jennies were in use, local people still supplied their own yarns as late as 1856, and Tyler advertised directions for homespun yarns, recommending what he considered the proper number of knots, pounds, and twist. It was cheaper to buy two coverlets from the same web, because it eliminated the job of threading the loom twice. Ten shillings extra per coverlet was charged for dyeing in scarlet. This extra charge was hardly something new, since "scarlet," "ingrain," or "in the grain" were terms that, since the fourteenth century in England, had been practically synonymous with extra cost. Just as the European weaver-dyer-merchant imported from the Mediterranean dried grains of an insect called *Coccus Ilicis* for his scarlet, Americans imported a Mexican insect, *Dactylopius Coccus*, to produce a similar red known as "cochineal." Cloths dyed "without grain" connoted a less expensive material that was any color other than red or any red other than scarlet.

Jacquard double-cloth coverlets were ushered in with the progressive and materialistic age of the American "carpet factory," as New York weaver Archibald Davidson proudly called his shop. Weavers like Davidson took pride in "factory" work. To his community he offered variety, service, production, and quality, which he advertised in 1831 as "not inferior to any in Europe or America." Some small virtue was felt by the weaver in supplying people with material goods. Even the customer felt better owning "things," a new material frame of mind reflected in the inscription on a contemporary lustreware plate: "Now that I have a Sheep and a Cow, everybody bids me good morrow."

Materialism had its moral side. Men felt optimistic about the result of hard work, convinced it had saving grace. J. Hart of Ohio, for example, wove a reminder of man's moral and earthly responsibility into the corner of the coverlet pictured on p. 241: "If good we plant not, Vice will fill the place; And rankest weeds the richest soils deface."

Images of domesticity—houses, white picket fences, sailboats, birds nesting, farm animals, and fruit bowls—adorned coverlet borders. The nation as well as the family was commemorated and sentimentalized in fabric—Washingtons on horseback, Independence Halls, Masonic columns, classical state emblems, and *e pluribus unum* motifs among them. Taste for an elaboration of design and feeling pervaded nineteenth-century creations like the "Wood and Garden" coverlet by Ira Hadsell (p. 251). It resembled the floral profusion of an Axminster carpet or an Aubusson rug. Because the effects of jacquard design were more mechanically controlled than was true in eighteenth-century weaving, many critics have responded negatively to the later patterns. But in viewing the last of these textiles, we should enjoy them for their workmanship and appreciate the weavers who went about their business like artists "in the best possible manner."

Suggested Reading

Andrews, Gail C.; Heisey, John W.; and Walters, Donald R. *A Checklist of American Coverlet Weavers*. Williamsburg: Colonial Williamsburg for Abby Aldrich Rockefeller Folk Art Center, 1978.

Carus-Wilson, E. M. *Medieval Merchant Venturers*. London: Methuen & Co., Ltd., 1954.

———and Coleman, Olive. *England's Export Trade*. Oxford: The Clarendon Press, 1963.

Davison, Mildred and Mayer-Thurman, Christa C. *Coverlets*. Chicago: The Art Institute, 1973.

Emery, Irene, *The Primary Structures of Fabrics*. Washington, D.C.: The Textile Museum, 1966.

Landreau, Anthony N. *America Underfoot*. Washington, D.C.: Smithsonian Institution Press, 1976.

Pye, David. *The Nature and Art of Workmanship*. New York: Van Nostrand Reinhold Company, 1968.

Roth, Rodris. *Floor Coverings in 18th-Century America*. Washington, D.C.: Smithsonian Institution Press, 1967.

Some Hand Woven Coverlets

By Catharine R. Miller

SOME years ago I saw a picture, in a satiric magazine, entitled "The Mayflower as it Must Have Looked Coming into Harbor." Every inch of the gallant craft was covered with household gear; bureaus, spinning wheels and milking stools hanging from the crosstrees. I do not remember noting a loom, but surely one, at least, was there. Not much use spinning if they did not weave. In England, France and Holland for centuries the hand looms had been busy before the first weavers came to this country.

And looms were, in our own Colonial times, quite as familiar objects as spinning wheels. We do not often see them now as they are not considered so attractive for household ornaments as are the spinning wheels. However, if you go through certain parts of the country, stop at farm houses and ask for looms, you can find them. I saw four in one day last summer; one in a barn, another in a corn crib, and two partially set up in a house which had not been occupied in fifty years. All this was near Erie, Pennsylvania.

As a refreshment of memory, Figure I shows the Spinning Room at Mount Vernon. The old loom is set up with harness of two headle frames for making carpet. Above the mantel shelf hangs a reed; and on the shelf itself are combs for combing warp and a box of shuttles with a ball of rags. Beneath the shelf hang extra headle frames. All about stand spinning wheels, flax wheels, quill wheels, skein winders and bobbin winders, some of them looking like belligerent animals, ranged to protect the central mechanism. A swift hangs from the overstructure of the loom.

Now just a few words as to how the loom was strung. Two girls could do this and chatter at the same time, one holding the warp threads while the other turned the crank for winding the warp on the warp beam at the back of the loom. Young girls did much weaving looking towards their wedding day.

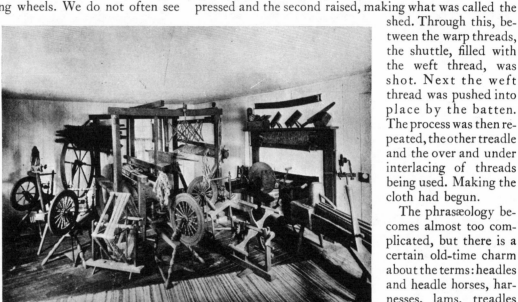

Fig. I — THE SPINNING ROOM AT MOUNT VERNON

For plain weaving of linen sheets, linsey-woolsey or cotton for new dresses, a harness of two headle frames hung from the overstructure was used. Threading through the headle eyes took a little more concentration on the part of the damsels, as no eye might be missed; and the alternation of threading, first in the front frame, next in the back frame, must be perfect. Now the batten, or beater, was threaded; and, after passing over the breast beam, the warp was secured to the cloth beam.

By pressing down with the foot on the treadle tied to the first headle frame, the first headle frame was depressed and the second raised, making what was called the shed. Through this, between the warp threads, the shuttle, filled with the weft thread, was shot. Next the weft thread was pushed into place by the batten. The process was then repeated, the other treadle and the over and under interlacing of threads being used. Making the cloth had begun.

The phraseology becomes almost too complicated, but there is a certain old-time charm about the terms: headles and headle horses, harnesses, lams, treadles and beams, shuttles, bobbins, quills, templets and stretchers.

For simple pattern work a loom with four headle frames tied to four treadles was used. Figure 2 shows the threading draft for a very simple pattern, the *Honeysuckle*. In this pattern work a tabby thread was shot through between each two pattern threads, making a background of plain weaving to hold the pattern threads in place.

Coverlets were the particular joy of the housewife. They were usually woven in two strips about thirty inches wide, with a white linen or cotton warp and a wool weft.

The women of the Appalachian Mountain region of Kentucky and Tennessee have always made "kivers," as they call them, using the old patterns for four headle looms, and making such treasures as Figures 3 and 4, called variously *Pine Cone* and *Snowball*.

Fig. 2 — THREADING PATTERN

For selvage and one repeat of *Honeysuckle*. The numerals refer to the 1st, 2nd, 3rd and 4th headle frames.

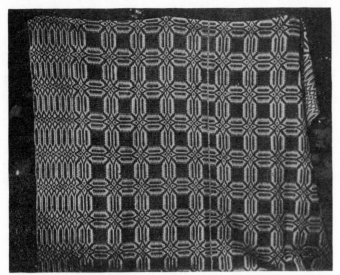

Fig. 3 — Pine Cone Pattern

White cotton warp with red and blue wool. This type of pattern appears to be as old as weaving. Its analogues can be traced into very dim periods of history. *Owned by Mrs. Edwin L. Mattern.*

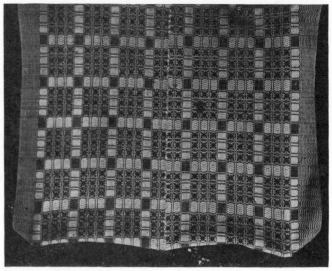

Fig. 4 — Snowball Pattern

White cotton warp with blue wool. *Owned by Mrs. Edwin L. Mattern.*

Figures 5, 6, 7 and 8, the floral patterns, are more complicated, with additional headle frames and tabby threads in the warp as well as in the weft. Such coverlets were often made by professional weavers who had, perhaps, four or five looms set up at their own homes, usually in a separate building called the loom house. Some of these professionals had full-width looms and, with an assistant, wove coverlets in one piece. Occasionally the fly shuttle was used. This was an invention whereby the weaver pulled a string, the shuttle was released from a box on one side of the loom, shot across, and very obligingly jumped into a box on the other side.

There were, too, itinerant weavers, who moved from place to place using the loom at hand to weave the coverlets for which the wool had been sheared, carded, dyed, spun into yarn and laid aside by the housewife until the weaver might make his round.

Some weavers would weave their names and the date in one or two corners of a coverlet. In Figure 5, we find "T. M. Alexander, Wayne County, S. C. T. Ohio," and in the diamonds of the border the date "1848." Figure 6 reveals "Varick, 1835;" Figure 8, "John Hartman, Lafayette, Ohio, 1851."

Peter and John Hartman were brothers, working at their craft together. I know of their coverlets in Pittsburgh and Chambersburg, Pennsylvania, and in Ashland, Ohio. They used the patriotic eagle emblem in their borders just before the Civil War.

In her book *The Harvester* Gene Stratton-Porter speaks of coverlets made by Peter and John Hartman, mentioning especially "the stiffly conventionalized birds facing each other in the border designs."

Early in the nineteenth century, Jacquard had perfected his system of patterns,—perforated card boards which brought certain threads into play and made the complicated patterns more simple of fabrication. Later, the English

Fig. 5 — Eight Feathers

White cotton warp with blue wool. *Owned by E. J. Knittle.*

Fig. 6 — The Four Roses

White cotton warp with blue wool. *Owned by Mrs. Edwin L. Mattern.*

weavers invented the Jack-in-the-box and drawboy machine, systems of pulleys and hooks in a complicated tie-up and connected to but two treadles.

In due course, weavers came from the old world offering to make wonderful patterns; and double weaving became the new fashion. Two warp beams, one for the wool warp and one for the cotton were required. For making the double coverlet illustrated in Figure 9 the set up required sixteen headle frames, twelve for the pattern and four for the tabby. Figures 10 and 11 also show double woven coverlets.

There are two distinct cloths in this type of coverlet, held together by the pattern where the color, the wool thread, goes through to the other side for a section. The pattern is the same on both sides, the difference being that what is wool on one side is linen or cotton on the other.

The cover illustrated in Figure 10 was loaned me by the great-granddaughter of the Langdons for whom it was woven. The weaver signed his work in both lower corners, one to be read on the right side, the other on the reverse. The inscription reads "G. S. E. M. Langdon, J. Gamble weaver, 1835." The work was done on the Langdon estate in Cecil County, Maryland, where, too, the wool had been prepared.

The cover shown in Figure 11 is not signed. The birds of

Fig. 7 — Penelope's Flower Pot
White cotton warp with bright blue wool. The name is my own and purely fanciful. *Owned by Miss Mabel L. Gillespie.*

paradise appear with worms in their mouths to feed the tiny birds in the nests. Eliza Calvert Hall in *A Book of Hand Woven Coverlets**, shows this same pattern, but with a different border, which is called *Boston Town*, quaint square houses alternating with pagodas and palm trees. She says, with her description, "Woven probably by Gabriel Miller, Bethlehem, Pa."

Many of these old coverlets have survived, but they are becoming scarcer. A friend has told me that she remembers a time when the coverlet she now fondly treasures was used as a blanket for the horse on winter nights. Others were found to make excellent pads for ironing boards and so disappeared. Last winter I saw, at different times, old scraps used as radiator coverings on parked automobiles.

Yet, to anyone who cares for them, these old weavings have much of the charm of oriental rugs or old tapestries and will well repay whatever treasure of time and thought is bestowed upon them. They occupy, too, an interesting position in the history of American handicrafts, for they mark the series of transitions from weaving as a housewifely task, until the time when it became a factory product.†

*Boston, 1914.

†For those who wish to make a study of weaving I recommend *A Book of Hand Woven Coverlets* by Eliza Calvert Hall; *Hand Loom Weaving* (Artistic Crafts Series of Technical Hand Books) by Luther Hooper; and *Foot Power Loom Weaving* by Edward F. Worst.

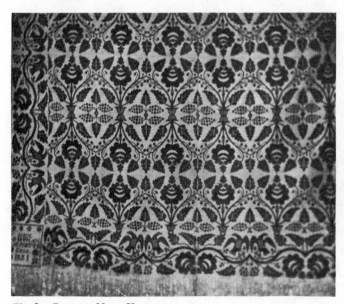

Fig. 8 — Pattern Name Unknown
White warp with bright red, blue and green wool. *Owned by E. J. Knittle.*

Fig. 9 — Double Woven Coverlet
In a variation of *Lover's Knot* with *Pine Tree* border. Owned by *Dr. Nancy B. Craighead.*

Fig. 10 (left) — NAME UNKNOWN
A very handsome piece of weaving, white cotton warp with brick red and green wool. *Owned by Mrs. D. L. Gillespie.*

Fig. 11 (right) — BIRD OF PARADISE
A pattern that the English weavers were very fond of, alternating with *Penelope's Flower Pot.* White cotton warp with madder red and blue wool. *Owned by the author.*

Fig. 12 — THE END OF AN ERA *(1856)*
It seems doubtful that this coverlet may strictly be classified as hand woven. The elaborate spread of the pattern suggests some use of automatic mechanism. But the piece is worth reproducing, on several counts. Its adoption of the Empire foliated scrolls gives richness to a pattern which is treated as an organized unit, with centre, borders and corners, instead of as a simple repeat to be indefinitely multiplied. Curiously enough the elements of design—other than the scrolls—are those familiar in early woven coverlets and in still earlier hand embroideries, but their treatment is naturalistic instead of stylistic. Such naturalism is a nineteenth century development. *Owned by Mrs. F. C. Yeomans.*

232

OHIO COVERLETS

By IRMA PILLING ANDERSON

A T THE TIME of the founding of the first permanent settlement in Ohio, at Marietta in 1788, the spinning of yarn and the weaving of cloth were foremost essentials of pioneer domestic economy. Necessarily at first, weaving equipment and also flax seed and sheep as sources of tow and wool were brought from the east and from New England. The fact that the textile arts developed early and rapidly in the Ohio country is evidenced by the census report of 1810 which listed a total of 10,586 looms at the time.

Since decorative bed coverings have always appealed to the homemaker, it is probable that coverlets were made in early times as well as household linens and cloth for garments. From advertisements in old newspapers, from legends woven into the coverlets, from county histories, and from information secured from descendants of pioneer weavers, the story of coverlets in Ohio is becoming increasingly clear. The quality of the work, as exemplified by coverlets still in existence, is high. All of the principal types of weaving used in coverlets have been found in this state.

The processes for preparing materials such as wool, flax, and cotton, are familiar to those interested in the subject and therefore need not be discussed here. Time, patience, and skill were required for this work and since the finished piece is dependent on the quality of the spinning, there is considerable evidence that many accomplished spinners resided in Ohio in the early 1800's. However, machines for the "making of cotton and wool rolls for the benefit of the home spinner" were operating in 1806, and two years later an advertisement of a spinning machine appeared in the Cincinnati *Liberty Hall* which guaranteed that the "yarn spun will be more even and in every way better than can be spun on a common wheel." How grateful the pioneer housewife must have been for this! Careful examination of the yarn in the coverlets will show whether it was hand-spun or produced by machine. The twist of the former is tight with some unevenness, while the latter is both regular and even. In hand-woven coverlets the materials employed were colored wool yarns with either linen or cotton in natural color.

Within a few years the work of the home weaver was further lightened by that of the professional weaver and by the establishment of numerous mills for the processing of materials and the weaving of fabrics. The professional weaver might reside in one community over a period of years or he might be an itinerant weaver, moving from place to place according to the demand for his services. The majority of the coverlets of the first decade of the nineteenth century in Ohio were, however, unquestionably produced in the home.

The home weaver also became a dyer, and with the exception of blue, much experimentation must have taken place before satisfactory colors were obtained. Indigo was easily secured, produced a beautiful blue, and combined harmoniously with other colors; hence, blue predominates in many of the early coverlets. This is particularly true of the double-cloth weaves of Ohio. In the overshot weave soft reds, bordering on rose, light blue, and light green are frequently seen, and brown, lavender, and orange occasionally appear. "The pioneer housewife commonly manufactured her own dyes from butternut, hickory, oak-galls, sumac and other materials which were near at hand, using alum as a mordant" (William T. Utter, *The Frontier State, 1803-1825*, Carl Wittke, ed., *History of the State of Ohio*, Columbus, 1924, II, 252).

As early as 1814, however, dyestuffs were an important item in Ohio's imports. Logwood, indigo, madder, arinetta, camwood, and redwood were offered to the public in general stores and the home dyer as well as the professional made use of them. Many advertisements by men appear in early newspapers but at least one enterprising woman, Ann Yaman of Cincinnati, conducted a dyeing establishment in 1809 and returned "her most grateful thanks to her friends for their custom."

Instructions for using dyes were available to early Ohioans. A handbook on dyeing published in London in 1800 is known to have been used in Ohio during the first quarter of the century. It is a compilation by James Haigh of Leeds and extracts from it were copied into an account book (*1814-1834*) which also contained drafts for weaving as well as diagrams of looms. Both the book on dyeing and the account book were owned by the MacFarland family of weavers who lived at Center Belpre, now Porterfield, Washington County. (They are now the property of Norris F. Schneider, great-grandson of Johann Schneider, a coverlet weaver of Lowell, Washington County.)

The types of weaves used in Ohio coverlets may easily be recognized, and to the owner of a handwoven piece this information is important. The four principal types in the chronological order of their appearance

Fig. 1 (*right*)—OVERSHOT WEAVE. Woven at the Zoar Separatist community, (*c. 1840*). Wool and cotton. Blue, green, a soft red and white. *At Zoar Museum, Division of State Memorials.*

Fig. 2 (*below*)—DOUBLE-CLOTH WEAVE (*c. 1840*). Wool and cotton. Blue and white. Geometric design. Woven by Sarah Whinery Coleman, Columbus. The design is single snowball with pinetree border.

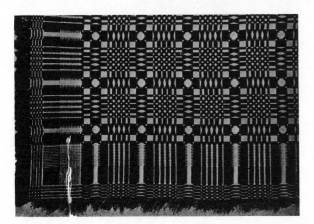

FIG. 3 (*above*)—DOUBLE-CLOTH WEAVE. Blue and white. Wool and cotton. Floral design. *Coverlets are property of Ohio State Archaeological and Historical Society, gifts of residents of the state.*

are overshot, double-cloth, summer and winter, and Jacquard.

The overshot weave is characterized by a plain tabby weave with the design in colored wools. Instead of the wool being closely interwoven with the linen or cotton background, it is floated or skipped over the background and so creates the design, which is always geometric (*Fig. 1*).

Double-cloth is the most easily recognized of all coverlet weaves but is more difficult in technique than the overshot. Briefly, it is two webs interwoven at the point of design. These webs can be separated easily, determining the double-cloth feature. Both geometric and floral types of designs are found in the double-cloth weave (*Figs. 2, 3*).

Summer and winter weave is the rarest of the weaves found in Ohio coverlets. It has been stated by Mary Meigs Atwater in her authoritative book that "it appears to be wholly of American invention" (*The Shuttle-craft Book of American Hand-weaving*, New York, 1928). The weave is difficult to describe and should be seen to be definitely recognized. The fabric is closely interwoven at every point. The distinguishing feature is the fine honeycomb-like appearance which is most easily seen on the light side of the coverlet (*Fig. 4*). All coverlets show the design in colors on a light background on the face or obverse side and in light on a colored background on the reverse side. I have seen only two coverlets and one fragment in this weave in the more than three hundred which I have examined in Ohio.

The Jacquard coverlet was made on a loom invented by a Frenchman of that name. The first loom of this type in America was set up in Philadelphia in 1826. The earliest weavers on this loom were professionals, for both the designs and the loom were complicated. Most Jacquard coverlets have the name of the weaver, the date, and other information in one or more corners (*Fig. 5*). The designs are never geometric in type and vary from floral to realistic representations of many subjects. Jacquards are hand-woven if they have a seam in the middle, which is true of other types of coverlets as well. In Ohio, there seem to be more Jacquards than any other kind, with the double-cloth weave second in number.

Very important to the early housewife were the drafts or designs for her

coverlets. Many of the designs here are common to other parts of the country though variations were worked out by skillful weavers. The drafts were written on paper and no doubt passed from weaver to weaver just as a treasured recipe was, but they seem to be rare in Ohio. They are fascinating documents with small crosses or tiny, black squares carefully arranged on parallel lines. The designs are generally placed in two classes: geometric and floral. The earliest were geometric and are to be seen in the overshot, double-cloth, and summer and winter weave. The floral designs are found in the double-cloth and Jacquard weaves.

The geometrics have a charm not surpassed although a few of the later Ohio geometrics are somewhat monotonous. In the hands of an artistic weaver, the floral patterns produced were lovely and they must have pleased the pioneer woman very much since we find so many examples. As the coverlet designs became more ornate and additional colors were employed, the results were less artistic and satisfying. When railroad trains, buildings, flags, scales of justice, lodge emblems, and the like appeared, skill in handweaving had reached the peak of excellence but design was at the lowest point. There are, at times, evidences of real artistic feeling in the composition of some of the earlier designs. The border, which usually severed the design of the body of the coverlet in an abrupt way, occasionally was planned to complement the overall design (*Fig. 4*).

The names of one hundred and seventy-four Ohio weavers of coverlets have

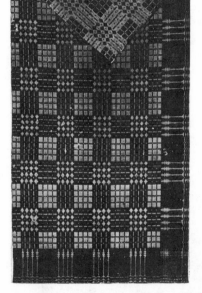

been recorded at the Ohio State Archaeological and Historical Society's Museum, with the coöperation of Mrs. Rhea Mansfield Knittle, Mrs. J. V. Cochran, and the Anne Simpson Davis Chapter, D. A. R. Additional names are constantly being found. Jacob and Michael Ardner, J. Heilbronn, L. Hesse, Benjamin Lichty, and G. Stich, prominent Ohio weavers of the double-cloth and Jacquard type, are names found most often on coverlets I have seen.

FIG. 4 (*left*)—RARE SUMMER AND WINTER WEAVE (*1800-1825*). Delaware County. Blue and white, geometric design, linen and wool. By a home weaver. Name of design is sixteen states with pinetree border.

FIG. 5 (*below*)—JACQUARD WEAVE. Wool and cotton. Red, white, and blue. The design is four roses and sixteen-pointed star.

Hand-woven coverlets
in the Art Institute of Chicago

BY MILDRED DAVISON

Fig. 1.   Coverlet, inscribed *A H 1800*.
Woven in Albany County, New York, by an itinerant weaver.
Blue wool and white linen; overshot weave.
All illustrations are from the Art Institute of Chicago.

The Art Institute collection of American hand-woven coverlets was founded by Dr. Frank W. Gunsaulus of Chicago, who became interested in them during his travels as a lecturer through the Middle West. In 1911 he acquired the collection of Florence S. Babbit of Ypsilanti, Michigan, including many fine and rare pieces, which he gave in part to the Art Institute. Since that time the collection has grown until today it is one of the largest and most important in the country. Until her recent retirement Miss Davison was curator of textiles at the Art Institute.

Fig. 2.   Coverlet, Vermont, c. 1820.
Blue wool and white cotton; summer-and-winter weave.
Gift of Lilian B. Carlisle.

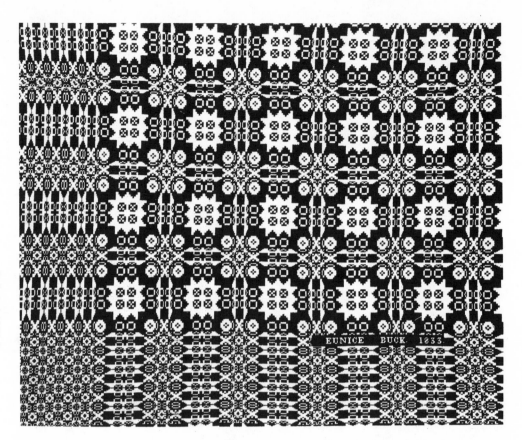

Fig. 3. Coverlet, inscribed *Eunice Buck 1833*. One of a pair (similar, but not identical) woven in Gorham, New York, for Zina J. Buck and his wife, Eunice, by an itinerant weaver. Blue wool and white cotton; double weave. *Gift of Dr. Frank W. Gunsaulus.*

HAND-WOVEN COVERLETS were the most universally produced and widely used of the early American bedspreads. They represented a blending of the traditional styles of the various nationalities that settled here, although they were distinctly American in their development. Handicapped by a lack of materials and faced with the responsibility for supplying the needs of their families, colonial women took great pride in their ability to produce practical and decorative fabrics for personal and household use, and coverlets were a proud achievement. The size of the coverlets was limited by the width of the loom, so they were woven in two or even three strips and fitted together harmoniously. Whether the work of housewives or professionals, they were made with love and pride and reflect the native background and individual creative ability of the people who produced them.

The early settlers brought with them a knowledge of and skill in the production of textiles from the raising and preparation of raw materials to the finished weaving. Linen and wool were commonly used. Flax was grown, prepared, and spun; sheep were reared and the wool was processed, spun, and dyed. Nearly every farmhouse had its own indigo pot and the universal color for wool was blue. As hand looms were an integral part of virtually every colonial household, each home became more or less self-sufficient in the production of the necessary fabrics, and the whole family was involved. This system of home manufacture, maintained early out of necessity, persisted in rural communities and on the frontier long after factories had taken over all phases of textile production in the older towns and cities.

Coverlets were products of the country rather than the city; thus they enjoyed their greatest vogue in territories farthest removed from the influence of factories and commercial goods. Their great popularity coincided with the early westward movement and led to widespread production throughout New York, Pennsylvania, Ohio, and Indiana.

Since they were purely utilitarian, few eighteenth-century examples have come down to us, and those that have are, for the most part, undated and fragmentary. When badly worn they were cut up and used for bench or chair cushions and, later, ironing-board covers and even dogs' beds.

The earliest coverlets woven on home looms were of hand-spun linen and wool, and generally in the overshot weave, which permits a wide variety of designs. This technique was used in practically every locality from the earliest days and was still standard on the frontier even after more sophisticated weaving replaced it in the thickly populated areas. An example of this weave is the earliest dated coverlet in the Art Institute's collection, produced in 1800 in Albany County, New York, by an itinerant craftsman (Fig. 1). Its beautiful even weaving is indicative of the skill and ability of its unknown maker. Another coverlet in overshot weave, made about 1840 in Stonington, Illinois, by Sarah Douglas Smith (Fig. 6), is in sharp contrast to the elaborate and complicated coverlets being woven in Eastern communities at that date. Stonington was settled in 1836 by a group from North Stonington, Connecticut, who made the long trek by way of the Ohio and Mississippi Rivers and ox team to Christian County.

Though the overshot weave was by far the most popular, summer-and-winter, twill, and other weaves were produced on hand looms. Summer and winter seems to have been a purely American invention, according to Mary Meigs Atwater (*The Shuttlecraft Book of American Hand-weaving,*

Fig. 4. Coverlet, inscribed *Matilda Terheun. 1834.*
Woven by an itinerant weaver.
Blue wool and ecru linen; double weave.
Gunsaulus gift.

Fig. 5. Coverlet, inscribed *Year 1839.*
The weaver's trade mark, a representation of a sailboat,
appears in one corner.
Woven by Joseph Gilmore, Dunlapville,
Union County, Indiana.
Blue wool and white cotton; double weave.
Gunsaulus gift.

New York, 1928, p. 205), and was apparently only made
on home looms. Due to the close weaving, patterns are
softened and lack the sharp contrast of the overshot. The
weave was reversible, durable, and practical, but never enjoyed wide popularity. A coverlet in this technique showing
the Lover's Knot pattern comes from Vermont and was
made about 1820 (Fig. 2).

Twill-woven coverlets were an elaboration of the commonly produced blankets and are comparatively rare. Figure 9 shows an interesting example, which dates about
1840-1850; its origin is unknown.

One of the major techniques used for coverlets was
double weave. This required a more complicated loom than
the ordinary household one, so pieces in this weave were
generally the work of professionals. Double-woven coverlets in geometric patterns are not uncommon, but few are
dated. Rare and unusual is the pair of coverlets, one of
which is illustrated in Figure 3, inscribed respectively *Zina
J. Buck 1833* and *Eunice Buck 1833*. Zina Buck was the
Methodist minister at Gorham, New York, and these coverlets made by an itinerant weaver were presented to him
and his wife by an admiring congregation. New York
weavers were predominantly Scottish, some trained in their
native land and others by Scottish-trained craftsmen in
America.

Another outstanding double-woven coverlet is the one
made for Matilda Terheun in 1834 (Fig. 4). The design
is strikingly unusual and reminiscent of Pennsylvania Dutch
ornament. Two other coverlets of similar pattern and general style are known in private collections, both woven by
itinerants. One was made for a member of the Haring family
of Bergen County, New Jersey, descendants of the Hudson River Dutch. All three have many points of similarity
and may have been made by the same weaver working in
New York State or Pennsylvania. Weavers from Germany
poured into Pennsylvania and produced coverlets in great
quantities. Their weavings reflect their native background

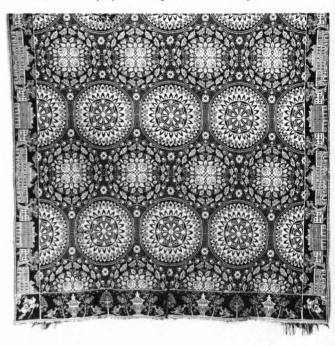

Fig. 6. Coverlet, c. 1840.
Woven by Sarah Douglas Smith, Stonington,
Christian County, Illinois.
Blue wool and white cotton; overshot weave.
Gift of Eunice and Agnes R. Chapman.

Fig. 7. Coverlet, attributed to Ohio, 1840-1845.
Red, blue, and green wool and cream-color cotton;
double weave. *Gift of the Chicago Historical Society.*

and are more colorful than the Scottish examples, with not only red and blue but green, yellow, and other shades as well.

In the early years of American independence, the Industrial Revolution, which brought many changes in the textile industry, greatly affected coverlet weaving and probably the most important innovation was the mechanical spinning of cotton yarn. The first cotton factory in New England was established at Beverly, Massachusetts, in 1787 and was followed a few years later by the highly successful one of Almy, Brown and Slater at Pawtucket, Rhode Island. The production of cotton yarn quickly and cheaply by the use of spinning jennies created a demand for raw material. This, augmented by the invention of the cotton gin by Eli Whitney and coupled with the use of slave labor, made cotton growing profitable, and large productive plantations developed in the South. Small mills sprang up everywhere and mechanically spun cotton yarn replaced linen in coverlet weaving.

The appearance of factory-produced cotton yarn and itinerant weavers relieved the housewife of many laborious chores. Itinerants made their rounds regularly and, in anticipation of their visits, housewives spun and dyed their wool during the long winter months. The weavers carried their own pattern books and generally used a loom owned in the community. As communities grew and the demand became greater, many itinerants established small shops and gave up traveling.

European pattern books were brought to this country by professionals, but the colonial housewife painstakingly recorded her patterns and sewed them together in book form. They were cherished possessions handed down from one generation to the next. Many patterns had their origin in European designs and the Americans gave them such picturesque names as Cat Tracks or Snail Trail, Wheel of Fortune, and Lover's Chain or Lover's Knot. This primitive kind of draft book continued in use until much later, particularly by apprentice weavers in rural communities. One such, owned by Daniel Stephenson, is in the Art Institute's collection. It is a small handwritten collection of drafts, executed in more than one hand, with the words of *Oh Susanna,* a recipe for yeast, various financial accounts, and other notes scattered throughout. Daniel Stephenson must have acquired it from another weaver, as on one page is the inscription *Wilmington, Clinton County, Ohio, 1839,* and Stephenson did not arrive in Ohio until 1845, when he was apprenticed to Isaac Balsaman of Springfield. Stephenson was born in Huddlesfield, England, in 1823, arrived in America in 1840, and in 1850, after learning his trade, moved to Fairfax, Iowa, where he wove coverlets.

The development of textile machinery and the introduction of the Jacquard loom to this country in the 1820's opened a profitable field of endeavor in the New World and created an attraction for trained European weavers. Professionals, well versed in the knowledge of their craft, arrived in numbers. Sometimes they worked a short time in Eastern factories before moving West; sometimes they traveled from place to place or, going directly to a definite destination, established themselves in small towns, setting up shops

Fig. 8. Coverlet, dated 1842. The weaver's trade mark, a representation of a house, appears in one corner. Woven by William Craig Sr., Decatur County, Indiana. Blue wool and white cotton; double weave. The wool was grown on a farm near Mt. Carmel and dyed and spun by Elizabeth Cunningham, grandmother of the donor. *Gift of Emma Stevens.*

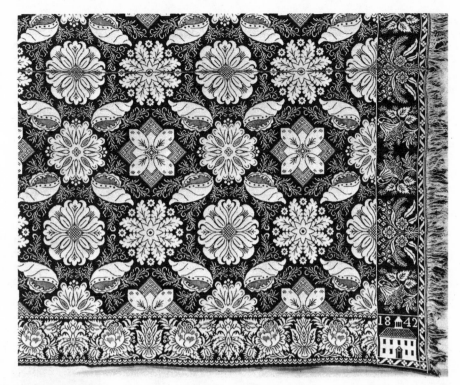

Fig. 9. Coverlet, 1840-1850. Red and blue wool and ecru cotton; fancy twill weave. *Gift of Clyde C. Rickes.*

and small factories for weaving not only coverlets but carpets and cloth as well. They were skilled in the intricacies of the draw loom and Jacquard attachment and kept pace as far as possible with improvements in the textile industry. They generally carried their own pattern books and a stock of cheap cotton yarn.

Among the many Pennsylvania weavers who moved west into Ohio was Dennis Cosley. Born in Virginia in 1816, he went to Fort Loudon, Franklin County, Pennsylvania, in 1831 where he learned spinning, weaving, and dyeing, and he remained in Pennsylvania for fifteen years. In 1837, he ran a mill in Bridgeport, which burned. To get the necessary funds to purchase his own mill, he conducted a school for four years and, in 1844, bought one at Fayetteville. Cosley also bought a loom for weaving coverlets, which fortunately he kept in his home, for in 1845 this mill also burned. A coverlet made by him in Fayetteville dated 1845 is in the collection of the United States National Museum in Washington, D.C. In 1846, Dennis and his brother George moved to Xenia, Ohio, where they built a log loom house at the rear of Dennis' residence and produced a great number of coverlets. Figure 11 shows a coverlet woven by Dennis Cosley during his early residence in Xenia, dated 1847 and similar to the one at the National Museum. Cosley did his own dyeing and, at the outbreak of the Civil War, dyed blankets for the Union soldiers. He left Xenia in 1864, ran a woolen mill in Miami County for three years, and later had a store in Troy, Ohio. He retired in 1890 and died in 1904.

Weavers' signatures generally appear in the corners, as on the Cosley coverlet in Figure 11, but occasionally they are woven into the borders. They include the weaver's name, locality, date, and sometimes the name of the owner, in full or in part. Figure 10 illustrates an example with an inscription that identifies the owner, weaver, locality, and date in one corner, as well as including *Michigan* in the borders. It is rare and important among the coverlets produced in the Middle West and was woven by Abram William Van Doren of Avon in Oakland County, Michigan. Van Doren was born in New Jersey in 1808 and went to Michigan in 1838, where he wove until 1864. He purchased his looms and other equipment from J. J. Davidson of New York. He was known as an excellent workman and produced many beautiful coverlets. After 1864 Van Doren moved to a farm and later to Supply Creek, Nebraska, where he died in 1884.

Another signed example is the child's coverlet (Fig. 12) made by Samuel Mundwiler who worked in Hopewell Township, Seneca County, Ohio, from 1847 to 1849. Small coverlets for children's cradles or cribs were often woven to match large ones. Weavers did not attempt to reduce the pattern to scale for these small coverlets, but used only the required lesser number of full-size motifs and signed the corners as in the large ones.

Sometimes moral sentiments were added to the signature, as in the coverlet (Fig. 13) by J. Hart of Wilmington, Ohio, in which he wove the following verse:

If good we plant
not, Vice will
fill the place;
And rankest
weeds the richest
soils deface.

The design of this coverlet was one of the most popular of the 1840's and came to be known as Birds of Paradise or Penelope's Flower Pot. The so-called Boston Town border is combined with another popular one of Birds and Cherry Trees.

Trade marks were often used by weavers, with or without dates and place names. Probably the best known were those of Harry Tyler of Jefferson County, New York (see ANTIQUES, March 1928, p. 215). Tyler's early pieces were signed with the figure of a lion, and his later ones with an eagle. Both trade marks are represented in the Art Institute collection; a coverlet with an eagle mark was the gift of Etta Tyler Chapman, granddaughter of Harry Tyler.

We are deeply indebted to the late Kate Milner Rabb for enlightening information concerning Indiana weavers and

Fig. 10.   Coverlet, inscribed in the corner *Sybil Duncan. A. W. [Abram William] Van-Doren, Weaver Avon* [Oakland County] *1845;* and along the borders, *Michigan.* Red wool and white cotton; double weave. *Gunsaulus gift.*

Fig. 11.   Coverlet, inscribed *Made by D. [Dennis] Cosley. Xenia Greene County Ohio. 1847.* Red and blue wool and tan cotton; double weave; seamless. *Gift of Frank Carpenter.*

Fig. 12. Child's cradle or crib coverlet, inscribed *Samuel Mundwiler Hopewell Township Seneca County Ohio 1848*. Red and blue wool and white cotton; single weave. 29½ by 25½ inches. *Gift of Mrs. Potter Palmer.*

Fig. 13. Coverlet, inscribed with a verse and *wove by J Hart Wilmington Clinton County Ohio 1851*. Blue wool and white cotton; double weave. *Gunsaulus gift.*

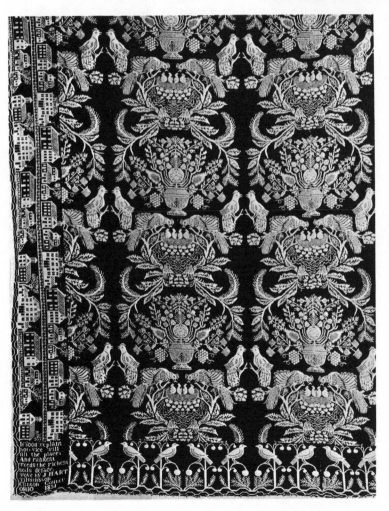

their trade marks (*Indiana Coverlets and Coverlet Weavers,* Indianapolis, 1928). One of the most common is the design of a house used with or without a date by William Craig Sr. of Decatur County (Fig. 8). Craig belonged to a large family of weavers, but seems to have been the only member to use a trade mark. He was born in Kilmarnock, Scotland, and came to the United States in 1820. After working for a time in an Eastern factory he settled in Mt. Carmel, Indiana, carrying on an extensive practice of coverlet weaving with members of his family.

Joseph Gilmore of Union County, Indiana, used a representation of a sailboat with the date as his trade mark (Fig. 5). He learned his trade in Scotland and came to America with his three brothers, who were also weavers. They set up their loom in a two-story, log loom house on a farm two miles west of Dunlapville and made coverlets. The border of two-story houses interspersed with trees and fences seems to have been a favorite of Gilmore's.

The cavalier in the corner of a particularly beautiful and unusual coverlet attributed to an unknown Ohio weaver of the 1840's (Fig. 7) may be a trade mark, but it seems more likely that it was woven to commemorate a military hero, a practice popular at this time. The close interweaving of red, blue, and green wool gives this example an iridescent quality. The intricate lacelike design is a variation of the popular Double Rose pattern; the side borders are composed of designs of buildings and trees; the lower one, of exotic birds and large urns.

The great era of the woven coverlet declined in the 1850's and came to an end with the Civil War. There was a revival of coverlet weaving at the time of the Philadelphia Centennial, but the style and method were different and hand-woven coverlets never attained their former status.

241

Five related coverlets

BY MILDRED DAVISON

SINCE MY ARTICLE about hand-woven coverlets at the Art Institute of Chicago appeared in ANTIQUES (May 1970, p. 734) five coverlets have been brought to my attention that strikingly resemble the one inscribed *Matilda Terheun. 1834* which was illustrated in that article.

In 1970 I speculated that the unsigned Terheun coverlet might have been woven by an itinerant working in Pennsylvania or New York State. But its great similarity to three coverlets signed by David D. Haring (Figs. 1, 2, 3) now leads me to believe that the Terheun coverlet was also woven by Haring.

David D. Haring has been identified by Margaret E. White[1] as having had his shop in West Norwood, Bergen County, New Jersey, where he installed and operated a Jacquard loom shortly after they were introduced into the United States in 1826. In view of this it is puzzling that the Demarest coverlet (Fig. 3,) should be inscribed *David D Haring/Tappan*. Tappan (New York) is about two miles north of Norwood.

Matilda Terheun (or Terhune) may have been the wife of Peter Berdan, whose oldest child was baptised in 1830 at the Greenwich Reformed Church in New York City.[2]

[1]*The Decorative Arts of Early New Jersey*, Princeton,1964, p. 63.
[2]H. S. Ackerman, *Descendants of A. A. Terhune*, Ridgewood, 1946.
[3]Ackerman, *Descendants of A. A. Terhune*.

A closely allied coverlet recently given to the Art Institute of Chicago could also be the work of David Haring (Fig. 4). The initials *H T H* in the corners stand for Hetty Haring Terhune (1805-1887), the wife of Albert J. Terhune, whom she married in 1823.[3] The coverlet remained in the family until 1950.

The Harings were among the early Dutch settlers who moved from New Amsterdam to Bergen County, New Jersey, in 1685. There the family grew in size and influence: Harrington Township, near Norwood, was named for them, and a Haring was one of the New Jersey representatives in the Continental Congress in Philadelphia.

The fifth related coverlet is inscribed *E. Haring* in the center above the border (Fig. 5, 5a). It is woven in one piece without a center seam, in blue wool and white cotton. Naturalistic floral ornament designed as a unit developed in the early 1840's, and its presence dates this coverlet about ten years later than the others. The original owner, E. Haring, may have been one of the two Elizabeth Harings listed in the index of wills and inventories of the state of New Jersey in 1912. While the piece could have been woven by David Haring, it seems more likely that it was the work of Nathaniel Young, an itinerant weaver who operated a Jacquard loom in Bergen and Hudson Counties in the early 1840's. At this time he was weaving seamless coverlets with the inscriptions in the center above the border rather than at the sides or corners.

Fig. 1. Coverlet, inscribed *David D Haring/Weaver* and *Margaret Ann Cole. Dec 14 1833*. Dark blue wool and white cotton; double weave. *Mrs. Alfred T. Gregory; photograph by Taylor and Dull.*

Fig. 2. Coverlet,
inscribed *David D Haring/Weaver*
and *Rachel Felter. July 4 1833.*
Blue wool and white cotton; double weave.
Ex coll. *Mabel Perry Smith.*

Fig. 3. Detail of coverlet,
inscribed *David D Haring/Tappan*
and *John. C. Demarest April 3. 1834.*
Dark blue wool and white cotton; double weave.
Bergen County Historical Society.

Fig. 4. Coverlet, inscribed *H T H March 8 1832*.
Made for Hetty Haring Terhune
and attributed to Haring.
Light and dark blue wool; double weave.
Art Institute of Chicago.

Fig. 5. Coverlet, inscribed *E. Haring*.
Possibly woven by Nathaniel Young
in the early 1840's.
Blue wool and white cotton;
double weave, seamless.
*Mr. and Mrs. Clifford Messaros Jr.;
photograph by Erik Nielson.*

Fig. 5a. Detail of coverlet
illustrated in Fig. 5.

Fig. 1 — TYLER COVERLET (*dated 1835*)
One of the earliest products of the weaver, who did not begin active operations until 1834.

The Tyler Coverlets

By ETTA TYLER CHAPMAN

Illustrations from Tyler coverlets supplied by the author

FOR a long time I have felt that my brother and I, as the only living grandchildren, owe it to our grandfather, his children, and their descendants to gather together the available facts about my grandfather, Harry Tyler, and his handiwork, that these might not be vanished by time and entirely lost; for when a man's work endures, his name should not be forgotten.

Harry Tyler was born in the year 1801, in the state of Connecticut. He was of English parentage. His father was a marine merchant, who was lost at sea with his ship and cargo while crossing the Atlantic.

Harry spent his early years in Millford, Otsego County, New York. He married Ann Cole, a beautiful and talented granddaughter of David French, who served as sergeant in Captain Luke Day's Company, Seventh Massachusetts Regiment, commanded by Ichabod Alden, in the war of the American Revolution. He served over four years, and was one of the few to receive a George Washington medal.

Four healthy, intelligent children were born to this union. Their names were Cynthia, Elman (who was my father), Leman and Leona.

In 1830 my grandfather moved to Boston, Erie County, New York, and, two years later, came to North Adams, a little hamlet east of Adams Center, Jefferson County, New York, where he purchased a farm and remained one year. But farming was not to his taste,

though he was a lover of nature and enjoyed the study of horticulture. He possessed a very scientific mind and rare mechanical ability. So he decided to settle in Butterville, a hamlet two miles south of Smithville, Jefferson County, New York; and to carry out his dream of weaving coverlets and carpets.

First he purchased seven acres of land next to the school and built a substantial wooden house. He set out a large orchard and nursery and established quite an extensive apiary. He was a man of high principles, very painstaking in all his work, and accurate to the last degree. A man of broad and liberal ideas, he helped to build the Universalist Church in Henderson County.

He not only invented his looms, but made every part of them himself. These he installed in the front room of the house, usually known as the parlor, with some of the machinery in the room above over the looms. These pieces of mechanism were complicated and intricate. One loom was for ingrain carpets and one for coverlets. He himself drew all of his designs (which were many and varied) except the fruit pattern and the eagle design, which were executed by Elman, his eldest son. These patterns were cut in heavy paper, which was perforated somewhat after the manner of music rolls for player pianos. The weaving was known as two-ply: that is, the finished work, wrought in two colors, was of double thickness;

Fig. 2 — TYLER COVERLET (dated 1840)
The border is like that shown in Figure 1.

Fig. 3 — TYLER COVERLET (dated 1841)
The border is like that shown in Figure 1.

and, though the pattern of each surface was the same, the dominant color of one surface became the secondary color of its reverse.*

---

*It is easy to overemphasize Tyler's personal inventiveness in building and equipping his looms. The methods which he pursued appear to have been those commonly employed by a small multitude of other weavers scattered through New York, Pennsylvania, Ohio, and Illinois, and, doubtless, other states of the young Republic. The punched pattern card, which so operated as mechanically to control the threading of the weft through the warp, was the invention of a Frenchman, Joseph Marie Jacquard of Lyons, who perfected his device about the time of Harry Tyler's birth, in 1801. Just when the Jacquard loom came into general use in the United States for the weaving of coverlets it would be difficult to determine. Coverlets made on this type of loom and bearing the date of 1825 are known. The great majority of such pieces, however, appear to have been turned out by professional weavers during the period from 1840 until the outbreak of the Civil War. The Jacquard loom with its punched cards made possible the elaboration of pictorial or semi-pictorial patterns, which, during the period noted, quite displaced the simple old-time geometrical designs to which the home weavers had been restricted by the limitations of their own skill and the mechanical inadequacies of their primitive looms. The admirer of those handicrafts which exhibit the minimum evidence of dependence upon mechanical aid will prize the old geometrical coverlets above their more brilliant Jacquard descendants. First cousin to the latter are the ingrain carpets, which are still manufactured, and which, since they show the same pattern — though with colors transposed — on both sides, may be reversed when the used surface shows distressing signs of wear. *The Editor.*

Fig. 4 — TYLER COVERLET (dated 1850)
Note that the heavy classic acanthus scrolls take the place of the more delicate trees of earlier borders.

Not until 1834 did my grandfather's dream crystallize and the shuttles begin to fly. Only four are living today who ever saw any of the work done, and, as they were mere children at the time, none of them can explain the process. All his coverlets were woven in two strips, however, which were subsequently pieced together.

All of the work he did by himself with the assistance of his three older children as they grew up. None was ever done by anyone outside of the family, and he never allowed even his children to warp a piece of work, lest the secret should escape. Elman felt sure that he could do this properly, but he was never allowed to try. The dyeing was done in a small building at the rear of the home, a large brass kettle serving as dye pot. To insure even coloring, this utensil had to be kept so brightly clean that "you could see your face in it." The task of polishing the kettle naturally fell to the two boys, who, every Saturday morning, had to climb, barefooted, into its depths. They never were allowed to wear anything on their feet for fear of making a scratch or dent in the

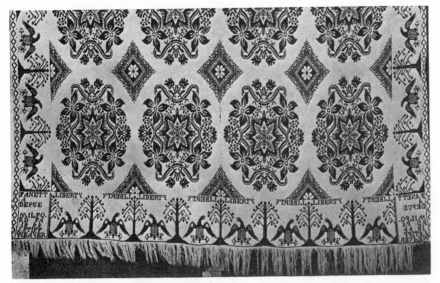

Fig. 5 — A Contemporary Coverlet (1844)
This coverlet, by J. Stiff, evidently a Pennsylvania-German weaver, is owned by Mrs. W. L. Bailey of Montrose, whose grandmother, for whom the coverlet was made, spun and dyed the wool a dark navy blue.
This coverlet is contemporary with the work of Harry Tyler, and is here published as one example of many similar pieces of the time. The white portions of the weft, as well as the entire warp, are of cotton. The side of the piece showing the dark pattern against a light ground has been reproduced.

borhood took great pride in making her thread smooth for the Tyler coverlets. Of these coverlets nearly every well-to-do household in the county possessed one or more; and no bride's "setting out" was considered complete without at least one, or more usually, a pair.

Grandfather, being of English descent, naturally loved the lion as an emblem, and he used it for several years. Then one day, Elman remarked, "Father, we should have the American eagle on our work in place of the lion."

"Well, son, if you want the eagle, draw the pattern," replied his father.

This was a simple task for Elman, as he was teacher of penmanship, and held evening writing classes in the different schoolhouses about the town. Thus the eagle and the motto *e pluribus unum* replaced the lion in all the work which followed.

A break in the family came in 1843. The loved and devoted wife and mother died. A few years later my grandfather married Harriette Ann Dye. Four children were born to this union: Beloit, Deloit, Harriette, and Ides. At the age of twenty, Elman left home to learn carriage making, and, a few years later, Leman also left the family fireside to engage in the same kind of work.

brass, which might result in discoloration of the goods in process of being dyed. So, with old house brooms, a liberal amount of salt and vinegar, and much elbow grease, they scrubbed and scrubbed until every vestige of stain was removed. No matter how well the fish were biting in the pond or how thick the ducks were on the marsh, the kettle must be polished each Saturday morning while the neighbor boys were enjoying their weekly recess.

My grandfather used indigo for all his blues. For his red he used cochineal — the bodies of a little insect gathered from cactus plants in Central America and Mexico. All of his dyes he purchased from Elisha Camp, father of Colonel Walter Camp of Sacket Harbor, for they could always be relied upon. Honor and integrity are always associated with the name of Camp in Jefferson County. As Elman was the eldest son, it fell to him to be his father's first assistant, and to make many horseback trips about the county, delivering finished work and returning with dyes and other wares.

Elman was the swiftest weaver of them all. He could weave the two strips of a coverlet in two half days, and was rewarded by freedom to go hunting on the remaining half days. He was a fine marksman, and was known as one who always brought home a bird from the turkey shoot. Spinning, as well as weaving, was an accomplishment in those days; and the best spinner in the neigh-

The proverbial shoemaker's children are never well shod. My grandfather made only two coverlets for his own family: one for the daughter Cynthia, and one for

Fig. 6 — Tyler Coverlet (dated 1853)
Here, as in an 1850 coverlet, the eagle supplants the lion as a corner decoration. The border design seems reminiscent of stencil designs on furniture.

my mother. The latter coverlet is all in white, and carries, in the corner, my mother's name and the date 1857. This coverlet, I remember, was always kept on the spare bed. It was not so attractive to my young eyes as the colored coverlets. The blue ones I admired especially. They had an air of dignity and elegance; and I shall never forget how thrilled I was when, some twenty years ago, my father gave me a blue and white one, for which he had paid ten dollars. I loved even the big mouse holes in it though they took me weeks to darn.

My grandfather's weaving continued until, one day, the youngest daughter, aged seven, was taken suddenly ill and died. The father's affection for this attractive child was more than usually keen, and so great was the shock of her death that he was stricken with apoplexy on his return from her burial. He survived but a single day. Only fifty-seven years old he was when his life's web was finished, but the product of his twenty-four years of labor offers impressive testimony to his skill, his industry, and his never-failing integrity. All who participated in my grandfather's enterprises have long been gone. Nothing remains but the old homestead and some examples of the work itself.

" 'Tis given to few to create, but to enjoy is the birth-right of us all."

Note.

The Tyler coverlets, like others of their type, were woven in wool over a cotton warp. It was not customary for the weaver to supply the materials. One of Tyler's advertising handbills, dated September 25, 1856, and still preserved by the author of this article, gives the following directions for the preparation of the yarn, which must be supplied by his patrons:

For Coverlets: Spin 60 knots to the pound in oil. When doubled and twisted, 7 runs for one Coverlet, or 13 runs for two Coverlets in the same web. 3½ lbs. Knitting Cotton, No. 12, three threaded, for one Coverlet, or 7 lbs. for two. N. B. The wool may be spun cross-band and not doubled, 30 knots to the pound.

For weaving, do not twist your yarn very hard if you wish good work. Yarn should be scoured with old soap, and not allowed to lie in the suds any time, and rinse perfectly clean in clear water, to color scarlet.

Tyler's prices for weaving were: for one coverlet, $2.75; for more than one in the same web, $2.50 each. An extra charge of ten shillings per coverlet was made for dyeing scarlet with the expensive and precious cochineal. At these prices, the weaver's profit must have been ridiculously small. The swift working son Elman could weave two strips of a coverlet in two half days. In addition, the yarn had to be dyed, the warp painstakingly set up, and the weft threads so arranged as to respond accurately to the urge of the pattern cards fulfilling the design. If Tyler had been aware of modern accounting methods and had loaded his books with charges against capital investment, overhead, and depreciation, he might perhaps have accounted himself into bankruptcy. As it was, he doubtless labored under the delusion that he was making a comfortable living. *The Editor.*

Fig. 7 — Tyler Coverlet (dated 1834)
Compare the design with that shown in Figure 1. Both pieces were made about the same time.

Fig. 1. — Horse and Eagle (*detail*)
The centre medallions are clever combinations of Scotch thistle and English rose. Woven in the corners, *Mary Van Dorn* (name of owner), *Liberty & Independance, Ithaca, 1837, A. Davidson, Fancy Weaver.* Color, indigo blue and white.
This and other coverlets illustrated are from the author's collection.

Weavers of New York's Historical Coverlets

By Jessie Farrall Peck

While American woven coverlets of the second quarter of the nineteenth century have received considerable attention, little has hitherto been done in the way of tracing their authorship or of estimating the relative quality of their designs. This phase of the subject is of primary interest to Mrs. Peck, whose investigations, now in progress, will form the basis for a book. The present article offers new material on certain of the New York State weavers. The coverlets of Harry Tyler were discussed in Antiques for March, 1928. — *The Editor.*

SEVENTY-FIVE or a hundred years turn most of humanity into mere names. That's what is happening to the old Jacquard loom weavers of America. If you are treasuring a blue and white coverlet with the name of its first owner and the date of its making tucked into a corner, aren't you curious sometimes about the artist who fashioned it; or interested in the thread of history woven into its fabric?

Archibald Davidson's shop offers a splendid illustration of the place of the professional weaver during that phase of our industrial history — the period of transition between home-craft and factory. He called his shop a "carpet factory," but it still had the home way of doing things. Picture the Ithaca Carpet Factory on a certain cold day in December of some such year as 1838:

On the site of the old Cornell farm east of Ithaca, snuggled close to the bridge over Cascadilla Creek, extends a long, shedlike structure, with cheerful wisps of smoke puffing from its chimney. Twenty-year-old Cordelia Wilsey canters up on horseback, blankets her horse, and bustles in — a trifle late, but three miles on a morning like this, with the wind blistering one's face! Red hands are limbered beside the comforting chunk stove. In a few moments, the idle spinning wheel is buzzing: Cordelia is the champion spinner of the countryside.

Three clanking looms, two wheels, and a steaming dye pot — these, with their six attendants, make up the Ithaca Carpet Factory. Archibald Davidson is the master weaver. He is the one who, in the borders of his coverlets, skilfully perpetuates his

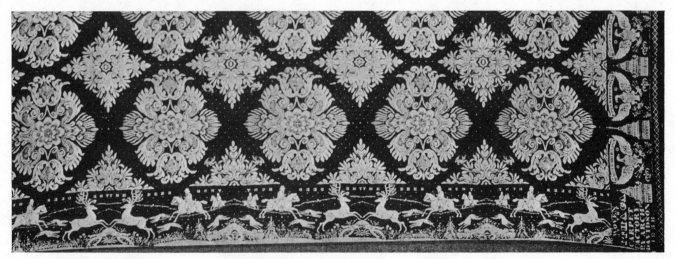

Fig. 2 — The Deer Hunt (*detail*)
Notice the delicate bit of weaving showing the tiny flowers and grass; the outlines of the hills; the perspective of the distant horsemen; the action depicted in the lithe bodies of the pursuing hounds. Woven inscription, *Woven at the Ithaca Carpet Factory by Arch^d Davidson, 1838.* Color, indigo blue and white.

memories of the horse and hound in old Scotland, and thoughts of the deer so plentiful in this newer country. John Davidson helps, sometimes, with the carpets. There is one on the loom now, with tiny meeting-houses scattered over it. The third weaver takes care of the clothmaking.

Cordelia's spinning wheel is slowing up. Twenty knots, two skeins — the "run" is finished. Now for the little dance that helps take the chill out of a winter's day. All join in with heartiness, and here is the song that guides their steps:

Hey, jin along, jin along Jessie,
Hey, jin along, jin along Joe.
The black-bird said, said he to the crow,
"If you ain't black then I don't know."
Hey, jin along, jin along Jessie,
Hey, jin along, jin along Joe.

Hey, etc.
First to the courthouse, then to the jail:
Hang your hat on a rusty nail.
Hey, etc.

The dance is similar to the Scotch sword dance, two sticks being used. There is much action, including patting of knees and stamping of feet. Ten minutes, and all are back at their tasks — till the spinners have finished one more "run" of twenty knots, two skeins.

Fig. 3 — ADVERTISEMENT OF THE ITHACA CARPET FACTORY
From the files of the *Ithaca Journal*, at Cornell University.

The location of the first Jacquard loom in America is open to question. The earliest I have been able to trace was in the Northrup Woolen Mill, at Roanoke, Genesee County, New York, which was built, in 1820, on a portion of the forty-eight acres purchased by the Northrups from the Holland Land Company. Its chief output was cloth and carpets; coverlets were made when ordered. In 1822, Isabella Norris of Morganville wanted the "latest thing in woven spreads" for her hope chest. It turned out to be quite an historic affair (*Fig. 4*). It shows, first, that Elijah Northrup was one of the pioneer Jacquard loom weavers in America; and, second, that he was the originator of the New York Masonic coverlet, with pillars, square, and compass in its border.

Northrup was a Mason, but the near-by trouble with Morgan and the consequent rise of the Anti-Masonic party cooled his ardor. Besides, after the stirring times of 1825, these emblems were unpopular. In a coverlet woven for Hulda Hudson, Pavilion, in 1829, we find thin pine trees taking the place of pillar, square, and compass. The Masonic border crops up again, however, in the Independence coverlet, done by J. A. Getty,

Fig. 4 — MASONIC COVERLET
One of the earliest of the double-woven type. The Masonic emblems and patriotic symbols harmonize, because patriotism is a cardinal principle of Masonry. Color, indigo blue and white.

Fig. 5 — INDEPENDENCE COVERLET
Most of the Independence Halls in coverlet borders lack the Liberty Bell. This pattern shows the influence of the earlier Masonic coverlet by Northrup. Color, indigo blue and white.

near Auburn, in 1839, and here illustrated in Figure 5.

In 1824, John Getty belonged to the same Masonic Lodge as Northrup — the Olive Branch Lodge at Bethany — and, once in a while, weavers passed along a few patterns. Both coverlets picture Independence Hall, but the later piece adds the Liberty Bell to the tower. Let me remind you of a bit of history; one needs it to appreciate this Independence pattern.

In 1752, Philadelphia ordered a two-thousand-pound bell from England. On its shining surface, the following words were engraved, like a prophecy: "Proclaim liberty throughout all the land, unto all the inhabitants thereof." On July 4, 1776, hundreds were gathered around Independence Hall. Within, something was whispered to a small boy. Breathlessly he rushed up the steps to the tower, shouting to the bellman, "They've signed it! Ring! Ring! Ring!" And the bell sent out its solemn message, while, from the steps below, the Declaration of Independence was read to the waiting crowds. When the British occupied Philadelphia, the Liberty Bell was hidden. But it completed the story of liberty, ringing out the signal that peace was declared. Ninety years ago, people were fairly close to our vital history; and they enjoyed having the things which they revered woven into an enduring fabric. Surely this memorial to American Independence ought to bring some credit to its author, John A. Getty.

Ira Hadsell was one of the later craftsmen. As a little twelve-year-old boy, in 1825, he came adventuring into Palmyra, and went to work on a farm. At fourteen, we find him traveling weary miles over the old Erie Canal towpath, urging along the "power" for a brand-new packet boat. Nine years more, and he is running his own boat, the *Eclipse*, loaded with wheat for Rochester. Having reached the height of his canal ambitions, he seemingly lost interest in waterways: it was time he was seeing more of the world. Soon he is making his way through Michigan, Ohio, Indiana — on foot. Finally, his wanderlust satisfied, he returns to Palmyra, and takes up weaving on Vienna Street with his friend Van Ness. In 1848, the old-fashioned loom is remodeled to weave seamless coverlets; and three years later it belongs to Hadsell.

There are no lovelier designs for coverlets than those given New

York State by Ira Hadsell. He was the naturalist among the weavers — spent hours tramping through the woods, learning the shape of leaf and flower and vine, and their ways of winding and clustering. His diaries still treasure some of his pressed models. The two examples of his work pictured here show his fondness for natural forms. One is a fascinating study in all kinds of leaves. The other has additional interest: first, in the fine drawing of the four heads of Liberty; and, second, in its historical meaning. The inspiration for the design as a whole came with the first signs of dissension between North and South: the two joined flags representing the union of the two sections; the eagle as the national emblem for both; the horn of plenty as a prophecy; and *E Pluribus Unum* as a motto. Truly a powerful plea against civil war! (*See Cover*.)

One old resident of Palmyra relates an incident in the life of the Hadsells that still amuses her greatly. "It was circus day," she says, "and almost the whole town turned out. The circus folk had begun unloading, when up over the hill poked Uncle Ira's old white horse, trailing the family market wagon. That horse didn't approve of a thing he saw, or heard, or smelled. Wheeling, he sent a double kick toward the whole business — a kick that upset the market wagon and sent the two passengers skyrocketing. Poor, proper Aunt Lydia. Her bonnet flew off; her switch, being pinned to it, followed. Both sailed over the fence and lit on a bramble bush, where they dangled disgracefully. No one was hurt, unless you count feelings."

Another aged settler told of living alone on the hill with a widowed mother. They bought milk and butter from the Hadsells — the richest milk and the sweetest butter in all the country. On butter day, "Uncle Ira" always pulled an "extra" out of the wagon. Sometimes it was a bag of mixed vegetables, sometimes a bushel of apples; but always something to make living easier.

In seeking information concerning weaver James Cunningham, I was almost discouraged. I had browsed around cemeteries, been through countless dusty newspaper files, written twenty or thirty letters to old inhabitants and to wardens of vital statistics. Then I found Miss Allie Davison of New Hartford, and she remembered. I am giving the account as nearly as possible in her words:

Fig. 6 — WOOD AND GARDEN
Hadsell is usually known by his E Pluribus Unum coverlet. This example shows simply his deep-rooted love of nature. It takes a magician so to control the threads of a loom that they weave themselves into a picture like this. Color, indigo blue and white.

"James Cunningham lived on Oxford Road — 'twas South Street then — the second house from the church. William Winship built that house more'n one hundred and forty years ago. Was one of the first frame houses west of Albany they say. Built when New Hartford was bigger'n Utica. Cellar kitchen, fireplaces all over, comfortable. And I remember *him*, a small old man with long white chin whiskers. He had four boys and two girls: Arthur was my age, born in 1847. George and William went to war and William was killed. Broke his father all up. Mr. Cunningham liked reading, mostly history things. Used to loan 'em around to the neighbors. My father would borrow his war books. We lived near by, just down the road a piece."

This weaver's coverlets are, as one would expect, historical. Washington on Horseback was first woven about 1835, when Cunningham was working his last year with his partner Butterfield. The early specimens of this pattern had four large circular medallions in the centre, and were nearly square. Later on, two elongated figures were added at the top, making the "bolster covering" for the pillows (*Fig. 7*).

Cunningham's New York State Emblem coverlet was designed about 1840. It is much rarer than the Washington on Horseback — the knightly figure of the latter seemed better to suit the hope chest fancies of young lady customers. The Emblem design, however, is historically more interesting. The arms of New York were adopted March 16, 1778. They have been called the happiest choice made by any state of the Union. The surmounting eagle belonged first to New York — the United States chose its eagle in 1782. Liberty and Justice as supporters of the shield could hardly be bettered; and the device on the shield, picturing the passage of the Hudson River through the mountains to the ocean, suggests the very foundations of the State's history. The whole rests on the motto *Excelsior* (*Fig. 8*).

Fig. 8 — THE NEW YORK STATE EMBLEM
A fine piece of weaving. The floral design of the border is worked out with the tulip as a basis, a tribute, perhaps, to the Dutch founders of the State. Color, copper red and white.

By 1798, the old seal needed repairing, and a new one was made. "Without authority some details were changed — such as removing the bandage and the scales from Justice; and, from this time on, many artists took all sorts of liberties." To Cunningham, with his English background, this loose conception of the State's coat of arms must have seemed a desecration.

Finally the Legislature was roused to action. The State had preserved no records of the original arms; but, luckily, an old military commission signed by Governor Clinton, June 25, 1778, was unearthed and the device upon it served as corrective material. Governor Cornell spoke the general feeling when he said, "The citizens of the State who are proud of her position and history should also delight in her insignia. The device of Arms of this State is so perfect in its conception that our aim is mainly how we can best restore the original." How Cunningham would have delighted in this awakening of the State's conscience! The correct design was restored in 1882.

During the Civil War, there was almost no coverlet weaving: the soldiers needed the wool. After the war, there was no call for it. The era of machinery was in full swing. In 1866, there crept into Ithaca a new railroad called the Shoefly. It was a queer little road, whose trains would stop for anyone, anywhere; but its chief business was to haul lumber from Cortland to the fast growing city. The workmen on this road discovered one day a dilapidated old building near Judd Bridge, on the bank of the Cascadilla. It would make a handy place for tools, and a fair shelter from the weather; so it was used that way. The old Ithaca Carpet Factory was rendering a last service to the commercial age which had rung its death knell. Yet changing fashion may have had something to do with the passing of elaborate coverlets. Commercialism is not to be blamed for everything.

Fig. 7 — WASHINGTON ON HORSEBACK
Artists have always considered the depiction of the horse a difficult feat. Cunningham, with his shuttle and loom, seems to have succeeded unusually well. Color, rose red (cochineal dye, softened by age) and white.

Index

Adam, Robert, 121, 178
Afghans, 190, 191, 196, 197
Aikens, James, 20
Alcaraz, 209, 211–219, 222, 223, 225
Alentours, 110, 116
Alexander, James 17–20, 63
Allerton, Robert, 99
Anatolia, 158, 168, 171, 174, 179, 192–194, 195, 198, 199, 200, 202, 210, 211, 213, 214, 218, 222, 224
Anergs, 106, 107
Appliqué, 42, 78
Archer, T. C., 97
Armorial carpets, 213, 215
Arras, 106, 107
Art Institute of Chicago, textiles in the, 99–104, 235–241
Atwater, Mary Meigs, 234, 236
Aubusson, 110, 152, 153, 154, 224
Axminster, 156, 165, 168, 169, 172–178, 180
Ayer, Edward E., 99

Babbit, Florence S., 235
Baeza, 210
Baise, 33–34, 166
Baku, 196–197
Baluchi (Beluchi), 127, 188
Barn-frame loom, 77
Basin, 91, 92, 95
Bast, 173
Bataille, Nicolas, 106
Batten, "beating" the weft with the, 27
"Beaming on," method of, 26
"Beating" the weft, 27
Beauvais manufactory, 46, 108, 109–120, 152
Bed hangings, 49, 78, 95, 105, 121, 122, 161
Bed rugs, 58, 60, 140–144, 161
Berain, Jean, 110
Berclé (points rentres), 147
Bergama (Bergamo), 186, 192
Bethnal Green, 148
Bird, Richard, 40
Bladon, Thomas, 59
Bobbins, 76
Bokhara (Bukhara), 184, 187, 196, 197
Bombasine, 32, 93
Bony, Jean François, 42
Boucher, François, 109, 110, 111–120
Bouclé, 42
Bourrette, 41, 57, 59
Brisson, Charles, 151
Broadcloth, 96
Brocade and brocading, 36, 41, 42, 43, 127, 147–149
Brocart, 43

Brocatelle, 35, 41, 42, 43
Brussels, 107–108, 166, 174, 180
Buckram, 39

Calamanco, 34, 48, 49, 50–51, 52, 57, 60, 61, 96–98
Calendering, 46, 50
Calico, 33, 37, 48, 52, 53, 56, 57, 58
Cambric, 34
Camlet, 32, 35, 48, 49–50, 57
Cannelé, 43
Carding, method of, 25
Carpet and rug, distinction between, 158
Carpet loom, 19
Carpets, 18, 19, 57, 58, 123–129, 153–226
Cartoons, 107, 108, 116, 194
Cashmere goats, 88
Catch-card, 44
Caucasus, weaving in, 124, 126, 128, 186, 195–197, 202, 203–209
Cavallo, Adolph S., 105
Chair backs, 116, 120
Chair-frame spinning wheel, 22
Charron, André Charlemagne, 113
Cheesecloth, 19
Chenille, 44, 45
Cheyney, 48, 49, 50
Chichi, 206
China, weaving in, 158
Chiné, 44
Chintz, 33, 37, 40, 53, 55, 57, 58, 60, 62, 73, 121
Chippendale, Haig and Company, 39
Chippendale, Thomas, 36, 39–40, 69
Chodor, 188
Church decorations, 43, 100, 102
Ciselé velvet, 46
Clouzot, Henri, 147
Cockrill, Mark R., 88
Colbert, Jean-Baptiste, 147
Coleman, Sarah Whinery, 233
Colonies, mercantilist theory of, 32
Colors, preferred 18th-century, 36
Connecticut, weaving in, 79–82
Copley, John Singleton, 28–29, 170 ff., 174 ff., 184
Copperplate printing, 37–38, 54, 58, 62, 63, 73, 103
Corduroy, 33
Cosley, Dennis and George, 139, 239
Côtelé, 43
Cotton, 19, 37, 39, 40, 57, 58, 76, 78, 238
Counterpanes, 56, 58, 60, 87
Coverlets, 18, 19, 56, 60, 61, 76, 78, 86, 87, 89, 132–133, 135–139, 229–252
Craig, William, 239, 241

Crumb cloth, 165
Cuenca, 221, 222, 223, 224, 226
Cummin, Hazel, 49, 50–51
Cummings, Abbott Lowell, 49, 50
Cunningham, James, 251–252
Curtains, 44, 48–56, 57, 64–73, 92, 121

Dagestan, 204, 206, 208
Damask, 18, 35, 36, 37, 39, 40, 41, 44, 45, 48, 51, 52, 54, 55, 56, 57, 61, 66, 78, 96
Damask diaper, 18, 19
Dangon, Claude, 42, 147
Davidson, Archibald, 249–250
Davison, Mildred, 99, 102
de Behagle, Philippe, 109
de Bruges, Jean, 106
de Comans, Marc, 108
Denim, 34
Derbend, 208
Diaper, 18, 19, 52, 57, 95
Dimity, 19, 33, 53, 56, 57, 91–95
Doppioni, 41
Double weave, 138, 231, 233, 237, 242–244
Dowlas, 34
Drafts (weaving plans), 19, 88, 89, 94, 95, 135, 229, 238
Dragon rugs, 195, 207
Draw-boy, 45, 231
Draw loom, 19, 147, 239
Drugget, 33, 44
Duffel (duffle), 33
Dyes, 44, 45, 76, 80–81, 82, 87, 136, 189, 207, 214, 216, 223, 233, 246–247, 248

Earle, Alice Morse, 28
Elbeuf, 151, 152
England, weaving in, 32, 103, 108, 110, 147–149, 153, 157 ff., 231, 232
Ersari, 188, 190
Evans, Elizabeth, 40
Exeter, 173, 174, 176

Faille, 44
Fancy weaves, 18
Farmers' Museum, The, textiles in, 76–78
Faults, 44, 45
Fearnoughts, 33
Feke, Robert, 164, 170, 183, 184
Figure-weaving, 44, 94–95
Fisher, Samuel Rowland, 175
"Flamestitch" fabric, pattern-woven, 150–152
Flat-woven rugs, 123–129
Flax, 76
Flax wheel, 21, 76, 77

Flemish weaving, 101, 106, 107–109, 152, 159
Float, 43
Floorcloths, 57, 58, 165
Fly shuttle, 230
Four-harness loom, 18, 136
Framing tapestries, 116
France, weaving in, 42–47, 91, 103–110, 147–152, 153, 154
Fringe, woven, 28–29
Frome factory, 174
Fulham, 174
Fustian, 34, 57, 91

Gendje, 205, 208
Genoese velvets, 44
Germany, weaving in, 100, 106, 237
Getty, John, 250, 251
Ghiordes, 179, 180, 192, 198, 205, 209
Gibbs, John, 20
Gilmore, Joseph, 241
Gingham, 19
Gobelins manufactory, 108–109, 110, 111, 116, 120, 152
Gold thread, 44, 45, 102, 103, 107
Gourgouran, 44
Grégoire, Gaspard, 44–45
Gromaire, Marcel, 110
Gros de Tours, 45
Guilds, weavers', 18, 32
Guls, 190, 191, 197, 218
Gunsaulus, Frank W., 235

Hadsell, Ira, 251
Haircloth, 36, 38
Harding, William G., 88
Haring, David D., 242–244
Harrateen, 48, 49, 50, 57
Hart, J., 240, 241
Hartford Woolen Manufactory, 82
Hartman, John and Peter, 230
Hearth rug, 158
Heckling, 76
Heddles, threading, 26
Hepplewhite, George, 36, 40, 92, 93, 121
Herat, 194
High-warp looms, 106–107
Holbein design, 192, 201, 212, 213, 214, 216, 218, 219, 223
Holland (cloth), 34, 52, 57
Horstmann, William H., 19
Howland, Thomas, 24
Huguenot weavers, 35, 148, 173, 174
Humhum, 33, 57
Hunter, George Leland, 111

Identification of old fabrics, 48
Illinois, weaving in, 236, 238
India, weaving in, 44, 45
Indiana, weaving in, 237, 239, 241
Industrial revolution, 32, 233, 238
Ingrain carpets, 174, 176, 180
Ireland, weaving in, 104

Irregularities. See Faults.
Isfahan, 194, 195
Italy, weaving in, 41, 42, 101, 102, 106 147
Ithaca Carpet Factory, 249–250, 252

Jacquard, Joseph Marie, 19, 42, 45, 246
Jacquard weaving, 19, 41, 45, 88, 138, 139, 174, 229, 234, 238, 239, 242, 246, 249, 250
Jacques, Maurice, 116
Jardinière, 45
Jarry, Madeleine, 106
Jefferson, Thomas, 54–56

Kabinstans, 197
Karabagh, 203, 207, 208
Kashan, 194
Kazak, 186, 196, 197, 203, 206, 207, 208
Kean, C. L. and F. A., 138, 139
Kenting, 33, 52
Kentucky, weaving in, 135–139, 229
Kersey, 33
Kidderminster, 176, 180
Kilims, 123, 126, 195, 208
Kuba, 195, 203, 204, 206, 207, 208
Kula, 192, 193, 201, 202
Kurdistan, 195, 197

Ladik, 178, 192, 193, 195
Lamé, 45
Lampas, 43, 45
La Planche, François de, 108
La Salle, Phillippe de, 42, 45, 47
Lasting, 98
Lawn, 59
Le Brun, Charles, 109
Lee, Jeremiah, 170 ff., 174 ff., 184–185
Letur, 209, 211, 212, 215
Liétor, 209, 212, 215
Linen, 19, 34, 37, 38, 39, 40, 43, 48, 52, 57, 58, 76, 78, 86, 102, 236
Linsey-woolsey, 76, 78
Little, Frances, 79
Lo Nano, Ernest, 56
Loom, operation of, 26, 229
Looms. See individual types.
Loop pile technique, 174
Lotto design, 160, 169, 192, 198, 201, 218, 221, 222
Low-warp looms, 107
Lurçat, Jean, 110
Lyons, 45, 147, 148

McCormick, Elizabeth Day, Collection, 147–149
Maguire, Adam, 87
Makri, 201
Mantua, 55
Maryland, weaving in, 231
Mason, John, 40
Massachusetts, weaving in, 48–53, 84
Melas, 192, 200
Merino sheep, 83

Michigan, weaving in, 240
Mifflin, Sarah Morris, 28–29
Mihrabs, 192, 201, 205
Miller, James, 88
Minor, Manasseh, 79
Mohair, 35, 121
Moiré, 46, 57, 59, 121
Monnoyer, J. B., 110
Montgomery, Florence M., 50
Moore, Thomas, 174
Moorfields, 172, 173, 174, 176, 178
Moreen, 37, 49, 50, 57, 121–122
Morris, William, 110
Mortlake factory, 108
Mudéjar style, 100, 213, 223
Mundwiler, Samuel, 240, 241
Murphy, John, 19
Musée Historique des Tissus, 45–46
Muslin, 57

Nankeen, 34, 57
Neilson, Jacques, 111, 116
Newell: Amos, 79–82; Josiah, 79–82; Olive, 82
New Hampshire, weaving in, 84, 86, 145–146
New Jersey, weaving in, 242, 244
New York, weaving in, 17–20, 132–134, 235, 236, 237, 240, 245–252
Non-pile rugs, 123–129
Northrup, Elijah, 250
Norton, John, & Sons, 58

Oberkampf, Christophe Philippe, 54
Ohio, weaving in, 230, 233–234, 239, 241
Old Sturbridge Village, textiles in, 83–86
Organzine, 41
Osnaburg, 32
Oudry, Jean-Baptiste, 109, 110, 113, 116
Overshot weave, 136, 234, 236

Painted silks, 46
Paris, 106, 107
Parisot, Peter, 173–174
Passavant, Claude, 174
Pennsylvania, weaving in, 104, 155–156, 230, 231, 237, 239
Perpetuana, 35
Persia, weaving in, 123, 129, 194–195, 198
Persian (Sehna) knot, 218, 223
Philadelphia Carpet Manufactory, 155–156, 177
Picart-Le Doux, Jean, 110
Pierre, Jean Baptiste, 116
Pillement, Jean Baptiste, 46
Plain weave, 124, 126, 128
Planta, John, 22
Platilla, 34
Point de Hongrie, 150–152
"Polonaise" carpets, 181 n
Prayer rugs, 162, 179, 180, 195, 196, 200, 201, 202, 205, 207, 208, 222, 223

Printing, textile, 37–38, 54, 55, 56
Pullicate, 33

Quilts, 78, 90, 132–134

Rabb, Kate Milner, 240–241
Reath, Nancy Andrews, 42
Reed, threading the, 27
Revel, Jean, 147
Robinson, James, 20
Rodier, Paul, 98
Roland de la Platière, Jean Marie, 57, 97, 121
Ross, Betsy and John, 28–29
Rouen, 151
Rowland, Walter, 40
Rugs. See Carpets.
Russel, 32–33, 57, 98
Ryerson, Martin A., 99

Sabin, A. K., 148
Sajjada, 162, 178
Salembier, Henri, 46
Salor, 190, 191, 197
Saryk, 190, 191, 197
Satin, 38, 42, 43, 45, 46, 96, 98
Savory des Bruslons, Jacques, 95, 121, 147, 151
Say, 35, 141
Scalamandré, Franco, 56
Schurmann, Ulrich, 204
Scotch carpets, 58
Seersucker, 57
Sejshour, 206, 207
Seljuk, 199–200, 210
Selvages, 44, 45, 46, 149
Senna, 124, 126, 195, 197
Serge, 34, 35, 39, 40, 96
Sericulture, 104
Shalloon, 33
Sheraton, Thomas, 36, 66, 70, 73, 93, 180
Shiraz, 126
Shirvan, 197, 204, 205, 208
Shuttle, throwing the, 27
Sicily, weaving in, 42
Silé, 123, 127, 206, 208
Silk, 36, 41, 42–47, 57, 66, 86, 102, 147–149, 209
Silver thread, 45, 46, 102, 103
Skeins, 76
Slipcovers, 39–40, 43, 44, 64–73
Slit tapestry weave, 123, 129

Smibert, John, 163, 169–170, 183, 184
Smith, Sarah Douglas, 236, 238
Smyrna carpets, 168, 174
Soumak (sumakh), 123, 124, 126–127, 129, 204, 205, 208
Souquette, 156
Spain, weaving in, 42, 100, 102, 106, 209–226
Spanish knot, 212–217, 219–221, 224, 225
Spinning, 25–27, 77, 136
Spinning wheels, 21–24
Spitalfields, 148, 149
Spolinato, 41
Sprague, William Peter, 155, 156, 177
Stamping, 46
Summer and winter weave, 138, 234, 236
Swanskin, 34
Swingling, 77
Synagogue carpet, 210, 211

Tabby weave, 35, 89, 100, 103, 104
Table carpets, 159 ff.
Tabriz, 194
Taffeta, 36, 39, 41, 46, 96, 121, 122
Talish, 205, 208
Tammies, 57
Tapestry, 46, 101, 105–120
Tattersall, C. E. C., 173
Tekke, 187, 190, 196, 197
Tennessee, weaving in, 87–90, 229
Textile printing, 37–38, 54, 55, 56
Thicksett, 33
Thornton, Peter, 151
Throwing the shuttle, 27
Thrum, 141
Ticklenburg, 32
Timurids, 213, 216, 222, 223
Toiles de Jouy, 37, 54, 55, 56
Tournai, 106, 107, 151, 159
Tours, 45, 46, 107, 147, 148
Tow, 76, 135, 136
Trademarks, 240–241
Transylvanian church carpets, 163, 164, 169, 170, 172, 176, 177, 178, 180, 183, 184, 200, 202, 224
Tufted rugs, 145–146
Turkestan, weaving in, 126, 187–191, 196, 197, 200
Turkey, weaving in, 157–182 passim, 183–186, 192–194, 198–202
Turkey work, 35, 39, 157
Turkish knot, 157, 173, 174, 175, 180 n, 205,

209, 212, 216, 218, 222, 223, 224, 226
Tuttle, Ann, 145–146
Twill, 46, 236, 237
Tyler, Elman and Harry, 240, 245–248

Upholstery fabrics, 35–38, 64–73, 110, 121
Upright looms, 106–107, 174
Ushak: medallion, 159, 169, 171, 177, 192, 201, 224, 226; star, 175, 178, 184, 192, 199, 210

Van Doren, Abram William, 240
Van Loo, Carle, 116
Velours épinglé, 46
Velours Grégoire, 45
Velverett, 33
Velvet, 35, 36, 39, 42, 44, 45, 46, 102
Velveteen, 33
Vermont, weaving in, 85, 235
Verné, 123, 127–129, 206, 208
Vien, Joseph Marie, 116
Vinci, Leonardo da, 21
"Virginia cloth," 57
Virginia, textiles in, 57–63
Vouet, Simon, 109

Wall hangings, 43
Warp, defined, 46
Washington: George, 40, 155–156, 177, 185; Martha, 28
Watteau, Jean Antoine, 112, 147–148
Weave, defined, 46–47
Weavers: itinerant, 138, 230, 233, 238; professional (public), 79, 88, 138, 230, 233, 238
Weaving, methods of, 25, 27
Weft, defined, 47
Weft-floats, 128
Weyman, Rebecca, 40
White, Margaret E., 242
Whitty, Thomas, 173, 174, 175, 177, 178
Width, defined, 47
Williamsburg, Colonial, 57–63
Wilson, H., 189
Wilton carpets, 57, 58, 165, 173, 174, 176, 177, 180
Wool, 19, 48–53, 57, 66, 236
Wool wheels, 23–24, 77

Yarn, method of winding, 25
Yamud, 189, 190, 197
Young, Nathaniel, 242–244